Understanding
Ourselves

Understanding Ourselves

Readings for Developing Writers

Ellen Andrews Knodt

PENN STATE UNIVERSITY, OGONTZ CAMPUS

 HarperCollins*CollegePublishers*

Acquisitions Editor: Ellen Schatz
Developmental Editor: Tom Maeglin
Cover Illustration: *E Pluribus Unum* by Mark Tobey. Courtesy Seattle Art Museum.
Project Coordination and Text Design: Ruttle, Shaw & Wetherill, Inc.
Cover Design: Joyce C. Weston
Photo Researcher: Leslie Coopersmith
Electronic Production Manager: Angel Gonzalez Jr.
Manufacturing Manager: Willie Lane
Electronic Page Makeup: Ruttle, Shaw & Wetherill, Inc.
Printer and Binder: RR Donnelley & Sons Company
Cover Printer: The Lehigh Press, Inc.

For permission to use copyrighted material, grateful acknowledgment is made to the copyright holders on pages 338–340, which are hereby made part of this copyright page.

Library of Congress Cataloging-in-Publication Data

    Understanding Ourselves: Readings for Developing Writers / Ellen Andrews Knodt.
        p. cm.
    Includes Index
    ISBN 0-673-99235-7 (student edition)
    ISBN 0-673-99236-5 (instructor's edition)
    1. Readers—Social sciences.   2. United States—Social conditions—Problems, exercises, etc.   3. group identity—Problems, exercises, etc.   4. English language—Rhetoric.   5. Readers—Group identity.   6. Readers—United States.   7. College readers.   I. Knodt, Ellen Andrews.
    PE1127.S6U53 1996
    808'.0427—dc20

                                          94-49197
                                           CIP

95 96 97 98   9 8 7 6 5 4 3 2 1

For K.S.K. and A.S.K.

Contents

TWO
On the Outside Looking In: Achieving Identity as a Member of a Minority Group   79

*Editor's Title

THREE
The Meaning of Male and Female: Establishing Identity in the Face of Gender Conflicts   129

FOUR
A Changing Sense of Self: Redefining Identity in Mid-Life
181

FIVE
What Do I Believe? Defining a National Identity   221

APPENDIX
Understanding Grammar and Usage   271

Rhetorical Contents

*Editor's Title

FICTION

POETRY

Preface

Understanding Ourselves: Readings for Developing Writers is a multicultural reader for composition students with two important goals. First, the text encourages active reading through high-interest, accessible essays, short stories, and poems on the theme of identity. Minority and women authors are well represented in all sections of the text and on a wide variety of subjects, not only on minority or feminist concerns. Broken into five main chapters, the thematic contents illuminate several ways people perceive themselves.

The text is designed to meet the needs of the unusually diverse writing classroom. At any one time, a writing class may have traditional 18–20–year-old students from many backgrounds and differing levels of preparation, nontraditional-age returning adult students, senior citizens, international students, and students whose first language is not English. I have found the topic of establishing or reassessing one's identity in the face of pressures of modern American society relevant to all students. This topic provides a unifying theme for the course, allowing students from many different backgrounds to talk with each other and avoiding the "theme-of-the-week" fragmentation of other composition readers. While each chapter may have particular appeal to one group in a typical writing class, selections should stimulate discussion among all class members.

Chapter One: Making Choices: Establishing an Adult Identity appeals most to traditional-age freshmen just beginning to assert an adult identity. Selections address moments of personal crisis, relationships with parents, and the young adult's place in society. These selections, which are also multicultural, should have wide appeal to the diverse students in writing classrooms.

Chapter Two: On the Outside Looking In: Achieving Identity as a Member of a Minority Group focuses specifically on the dimensions of race, ethnicity, or disability as they affect Americans' personal identities. Included are selections by African American, Asian American, Hispanic American, and Native American writers, as well as by a father of a Down syndrome child.

Chapter Three: The Meaning of Male and Female: Establishing Identity in the Face of Gender Conflicts provides insights into many issues that affect the way people see themselves and the way they enter into relationships with others including abortion, men's and women's education, language, image, divorce, and sexual roles.

Chapter Four: A Changing Sense of Self: Redefining Identity in Mid-Life acknowledges the presence and importance of the many nontraditional-age students in our community college and four-year college composition classrooms. While many of these students have been contributing their life experience to their younger classmates, little attention has been paid to their need to discuss concerns at their stage in life. Selections in this chapter address meeting new challenges at mid-life, the problems of parenting, adjusting to aging, and the knowledge that comes with experience. Since traditional-age students presumably have parents nearing mid-life, the readings may help them get in touch with their parents' concerns as well and provide a way for differing generations in the classroom to talk to each other.

Chapter Five: What Do I Believe? Defining a National Identity appeals to all students, native or foreign born, to reach a deeper understanding of American philosophy and contemporary issues. Thomas Jefferson and Martin Luther King, Jr., illuminate democratic philosophy in their classic arguments while contemporary writers like William A. Henry, Anna Quindlen, and Alice Walker focus on current issues of immigration, the homeless, and the care of our environment.

A second and equally important goal of *Understanding Ourselves* is its linking the complementary functions of reading and writing. As many writing researchers, including Rose, Bartholomae, Petrosky, and Lunsford argue, reading and writing are synergistic, and improving skills in both produces even bigger gains than just improving skills in one. Many writing instructors have felt the need for some time to use a reader to provide a stimulus for class discussion and writing topics and to acquaint students with "real world" writing. *Understanding Ourselves* serves as such a reader but also offers explicit links to the writing program.

The introduction focuses on how students can use writing to become more active readers, presenting them with concrete strategies for highlighting the text, responding to a selection, and using a reading journal. Writing is a tool to help students read and understand.

Each selection is linked to the writing program through the apparatus. Preview: Thinking Ahead provides context for each selection and asks students to think about some particular point. Respond: Thinking Independently prompts a writing journal reader response to the selection before class discussion. Reconsider: Thinking Collaboratively focuses questions for small group or large class discussion. Review: Thinking Critically asks students to write analytical answers to questions of content or rhetoric. The final section, Reading to Write, discusses a rhetorical feature of the selection just read and provides writing assignment prompts. So, for example, following N. Scott Momaday's narrative "The End of My Childhood," students receive instruction in Understanding Narration that ties the rhetorical principle directly to what they have just read. The writing prompts frequently ask students to write an essay based on the rhetorical structure of the essay just read.

Understanding Ourselves is designed to be as flexible as possible. A Rhetorical Table of Contents and a brief but comprehensive Appendix: Understanding Grammar and Usage, along with the Reading to Write feature, should enable writing instructors to use it as the sole text in a course. The appendix includes a Quick Reference Chart for each subject should students need a brief reminder of a grammatical principle, and it also presents easily understood explanations, some exercises, and Working Collaboratively sections which use that powerful technique to help students apply grammatical principles. However, instructors may wish to couple *Understanding Ourselves* with a rhetorical text.

Community and two-year colleges, four-year colleges, and universities teach a variety of composition courses on many levels. In some institutions this text may be appropriate for developmental students, in others for a general composition course. The reading difficulty of the selections varies so that instructors may adapt assignments to the needs of their students.

Understanding Ourselves should contribute to the students' sense of themselves, lead them to an appreciation of others' lives, improve their ability to comprehend what they read, and enhance their writing skills.

For their many ideas and reactions to the readings, I would like to thank the students and faculty at Penn State University's Ogontz Campus. Their diversity helped me improve the scope and variety of the selections in *Understanding Ourselves*. I'd also like to thank colleagues from other institutions with whom I discussed this text as it evolved as we met at National Council of Teachers of English or College Composition and Communication conferences. At HarperCollins, I would like to thank Jane Kinney, Patricia Rossi, and Mark Paluch for their early interest and help shaping the idea for the text. I thank Tom Maeglin and Ellen Schatz for their final guidance through the publishing process. I appreciate my many colleagues who reviewed the manuscript and helped me make it more useful to their students: Mary Boyles, Penbroke State University; Patricia Bridges, Mt. Union College; Mark Connelly, Milwaukee Area Technical College; Linda Daigle, Houston Community College; Teddie McFerrin, Collin County Community College; Betty Jo Peters, Moorhead State University; and Diane Scott, Mesa College.

As ever, I thank my husband, Ken, and son, Andrew, for sharing the computer, eating pizza, listening to my ideas, and generally being patient with me.

Ellen Andrews Knodt

INTRODUCTION

Strategies for Active Reading in the Writing Class

Many people think of themselves as either "good" readers or "poor" readers, but probably most have not stopped to consider whether they are "active" readers. What does being an active reader mean? Contrary to what many people may think, active reading does not depend on how fast one can read or even on how much one remembers after reading. Instead, active reading means that readers think about what they are reading as they read. They do not just let the words wash over them like waves at the beach (as nice as that is at times). Nor do they feel they have read the material just because their eyes have looked at each line of text in a reading selection. Active readers ask themselves questions as they read, quarrel with the author, and connect what they are reading to other experiences they have had or to other reading they have done. Even when people read for their own pleasure, they can be active readers, but active reading is especially important when the text must be learned for a class or on the job. Any reader—slow or fast, good memory or poor memory—can become a better reader by practicing some strategies for active reading.

Having said that, let me add that improving speed and comprehension skills may also bring great rewards. Increasing the number of words your eyes can take in each time they stop on a line of prose (called "fixations") will cut the time it takes you to read. As your reading speed increases, your comprehension or understanding of what you read may increase because the faster you read, the easier it is for your short-term memory to hold on to details. (It just doesn't take as long, so there is not as much time to forget.) This connection between speed and comprehension is particularly true for reading material with familiar vocabulary and sentence structure. New and difficult material can't be read at the same speed. Although some people can help themselves read faster by consciously trying to take in more words with each glance at a line of text, others benefit from reading instruction. Many colleges provide such instruction in learning centers, so if you feel you could improve your reading skills, seek the help that may be available in such centers.

Understanding Ourselves hopes to help all readers get more out of reading fiction, nonfiction, and poetry through several easily practiced strategies for active reading. And because reading and writing are complementary activities, the text should help you improve your writing as well. The last section of each selection called "Reading to Write" makes the connection between reading and writing quite clear. Now let's begin looking at some reading strategies.

Strategy 1: Marking Your Books (What Others Never Told You)

Marking books, a powerful aid to active reading, is routinely denied to most school students and library users for good reasons. If many people have to use the same books, marking them would be discourteous and distracting. After all, someone else might not agree with what you consider to be important to highlight or with your opinions of the author's ideas. But as many college students have discovered (much to the joy of highlighting pen manufacturers), marking books they own helps them pick out important points as they read and helps them review later for tests. While marking books may affect their resale value at the bookstore, most students find that they are paid so little for used books and they get so much more information out of what they read by marking their books, that they go ahead and mark. Highlighting, then, is the first strategy to look at, and later, other powerful techniques that go beyond highlighting will be explored.

Highlighting to Understand Main Ideas

You have certainly seen someone reading, pen or highlighting marker in hand, and you may have tried this strategy yourself. Marking a text as you read can focus your attention on important points and draw your attention back to those points when you review later. After years of reading with marker or pen in hand, I feel lost if I can't highlight (say with a borrowed book). However, if you haven't marked your books, now is the time to give this strategy a try. Use a pen, pencil, marker, or whatever you would like to try. Each has its own characteristics, and you will find out what you like. Getting over the prohibition against marking drummed into you by teachers and librarians is easy. Harder is deciding what to mark—too much may be just as bad as too little. You want to mark those ideas that will give you the gist of the selection—the main ideas, the key words—but how do you do that? The answer may vary depending on what you are reading—fiction, nonfiction, or poetry—so we will take a look at each in turn.

Reading and Highlighting Fiction

When we read fiction as part of a course, we want to notice and remember certain elements. First, the title may suggest to us what the story is about, or connect the story with another idea, or perhaps puzzle us so that we want to read the story to find out what it means. Since people often decide what to read by responding to a title, authors usually put considerable thought into what their story is called. Active readers highlight the title and think about its meaning.

Second, the characters deserve a reader's focus. Marking their names and perhaps highlighting some brief description of them as they appear in the story or novel helps readers keep track of the characters and their role in the work. It may be helpful to note if one of the characters is telling the story (that is, is the narrator), or if the narrator is the author or someone else. Since who tells the story may influence the way we read a story, it is an important piece of information. (Think, for example, of the difference if the story is told by a murderer, such as in Poe's "The Tell Tale Heart," or a victim, such as in his classic "The Pit and the Pendulum.") You may want to note in the margin next to a highlighted name: Narrator.

Whether a character is the narrator or not, an active reader marks what the main characters think or say that might be important to recall later. Such highlighting helps a reader remember the characters and review their actions later for a test or writing assignment.

As the story unfolds, focus on the series of events or plot in the story and mark words and phrases that show these events and how they turn out.

Other elements of a story may be noted: the setting (place and time) of the story, the mood or atmosphere of the story, the theme (a main idea or message the story carries), and the author's style (the way he or she writes including length of sentences, word choices, and use of images and symbols). Many readers do not consider matters such as theme and style while reading but only afterward when thinking about a story and therefore might not mark or highlight them the first time through. Follow your own reading preference—highlighting can be done as one reads the first time or in separate "sweeps" through a text.

Unfamiliar words or puzzling references to history or other literature may be marked if they are not already footnoted by the author. The reader can then more easily look up the unfamiliar words later or ask about them in class discussion.

To see how the strategy works, read the following excerpt from "The Lottery" to see how one reader highlighted the passage (in **bold**). Readers may vary in what they decide is important to highlight because we all bring different backgrounds and experiences to what we read. However, active readers, thinking with pen in hand as they read, will understand and retain more of what they read.

The Lottery
Shirley Jackson

The **morning of June 27th** was clear and sunny, with the fresh warmth of a full-summer day; the flowers were blossoming **profusely** and the grass was richly green. The **people of the village began** to **gather in the square,** between the post office and the bank, around ten o'clock; **in some towns there were so many people that the lottery took two days and had to be started on June 26th,** but **in this village,** where there were only about three hundred people, the whole **lottery took less than two hours,** so it could begin at ten o'clock in the morning and still be through in time to allow the villagers to get home for noon dinner.

The children assembled first, of course. School was recently over for the summer, and the feeling of liberty sat uneasily on most of them; they tended to gather together quietly for awhile before they broke into **boisterous** play, and their talk was still of the classroom and the teacher, of books and reprimands. **Bobby Martin had already stuffed his pockets full of stones,** and the other boys soon followed his example, selecting the smoothest and roundest stones; . . .

Comment: The title makes us think of what a lottery is—most of us think of winning a prize in a lottery. Next, the highlighting shows when and where the story takes place, and the fact that the lottery is held in other towns besides this one. The children of the village are introduced first, with the boys gathering stones. An active reader might begin wondering what stones have to do with a lottery, but early in the story that question remains unanswered. The narration is in the third person ("he or they did this") and does not seem to be from one character's perspective or point of view. The words "profusely" and "boisterous" are highlighted as being unfamiliar. Practice highlighting the following passage that continues the story:

> . . . Bobby and Harry Jones and Dickie Delacroix—the villagers pronounced this name "Delacroy"—eventually made a great pile of stones in one corner of the square and guarded it against the raids of the other boys. The girls stood aside, talking among themselves, look over their shoulders at the boys, and the very small children rolled in the dust or clung to the hands of their older brothers and sisters.
>
> Soon the men began to gather, surveying their own children, speaking of planting and rain, tractors and taxes. They stood together, away from the pile of stones in the corner, and their jokes were quiet and they smiled rather than laughed. . . .

Compare your highlighting with that of other students and your instructor.

To continue our discussion of highlighting for main ideas, we now turn to nonfiction.

Reading and Highlighting Nonfiction

Most of your academic reading is nonfiction, that is textbook information, encyclopedia articles, opinion essays, and the like. You may have had more experience picking out main ideas in nonfiction reading, and the strategies that follow may serve as a review.

As in fiction, titles are important and should be highlighted and thought about. Sometimes titles clearly declare the content of an essay (Gloria Steinem's "Why Young Women Are More Conservative," for example). Sometimes, however, an essay does not announce itself in a title (such as Claire Safran's "Hidden Lessons"). In either case, the title is something the active reader notes and considers.

Nonfiction essays sometimes have a "thesis sentence" near the beginning of the essay which tells the reader the essay's main idea and perhaps suggests the author's opinion or attitude toward the subject. If you find such a "capsule statement," highlight it in order to keep it in your mind as you read and to review later. For example, in the following excerpt from an opinion editorial, Roger Hernandez indicates in his title and in a sentence early in the essay the main point he want to make:

Hispanics Come with Many Voices
ROGER E. HERNANDEZ

When I arrived in this country, in the mid-1960's, America didn't worry about Hispanics. The big issues were the black civil rights movement, Vietnam, and those crazy college kids. The Hispanic population was relatively small and did not compete for attention.

Today, with that population at well over 20 million, Hispanics have become central in the great debate about ethnicity.

Trouble is, the term "Hispanic" is often misused. Advertisers, government, political activists, and the media throw the word around as if it described a homogeneous, unified community. **But a recent nationwide survey among Mexicans, Puerto Ricans, Cubans, and Anglos showed a more complex reality.**

The survey, organized by four Hispanic scholars from universities across the country, found substantial differences among the three Hispanic groups, especially when it comes to political beliefs. Politicians who dream of rounding up "the Hispanic vote" will not find the survey encouraging. The differences were sometimes traceable to country of origin, sometimes to social class. Among the findings: . . .

The highlighted sentences are the subject of the rest of the essay—the differences among Hispanic groups—and thus form the writer's thesis. Active readers help themselves remember and review by marking such sentences when they read.

Not all essay writers use a thesis sentence. They expect their readers to infer (or conclude) from the reading what the main idea is. In that case, an active reader could write down the main idea of an essay following his or her reading of the text.

Another thing to highlight in an essay is a fact or two that proves the author's main point. Readers don't want to highlight everything, or they will be back where they started with a complete text. Instead they want to mark a few things to review so that they can recall enough of the facts to explain the author's ideas and how he or she supported them. As you read the essays in this text, you will be discussing with your instructor and other classmates what facts to highlight and what to leave unmarked. After some experience, you will feel confident in your ability to decide what to highlight.

As is true with fiction, highlighting unfamiliar words is a good idea. Later, you can look them up and put the definitions in the margin. Some textbooks put terms and definitions in bold type—a kind of highlighting done for you. Active readers pay particular attention to items set off in some way—bold type, underlines, italics—because they know the author wants them to notice these ideas. Highlighting is also useful for locating problems in a text that you want to come back to—perhaps a sentence or idea you don't understand or an idea you don't agree with. As we will discuss later, you may want to go beyond highlighting these areas and write a question or comment in the margin, but highlighting at least points out the area to consider.

Because the ending of an essay is the writer's last chance to make sure the reader understands the writer's ideas, active readers pay attention to the final part of an essay and highlight conclusions. Conclusions may repeat the thesis, summarize evidence, explore the importance of a topic, indicate what other study needs to be done, or leave the reader with a striking image or thought. Note that the ending of Roger Hernandez's essay (begun earlier) restates the main idea and indicates a further complication:

> One lesson out of all this is that there are more differences among Hispanics than a lot of people think. Another is that, despite these differences, there is indeed such a thing as a Hispanic. The trick is finding out just what that means.

Reading and Highlighting Poetry

Readers probably have less experience reading poetry than fiction or nonfiction. Poetry is taught less in schools; it is not found extensively in magazines, newspapers, or other general reading material; and it is demanding on the reader. What do I mean, demanding? Poetry expresses its ideas in a very compressed language. In just a few lines, complicated ideas about nature, people's characters, historical events, and emotions like love, grief, or jealousy are expressed, often in a particular rhythm or rhyme. Each word counts in a poem. In fact, one definition of a poem is "The best words in the best order."

So how do you read and highlight a poem? First, it is probably wise to try to read the poem all the way through to try to get the "gist" or basic idea of what it's about. Read it by following the punctuation rather than the individual lines—that is, pause at commas and stop at periods, as you would if you were reading prose. And, as before, note the title. For example, note in the two columns that follow the way the poem was written on the left and the way it could be read in conventional sentences on the right. (Note that this technique is an aid to reading a poem, but that the original arrangement of lines serves the poet's purpose of rhyme, rhythm, emphasis, or other element of style which must be considered after discovering the gist of the poem.)

Fire and Ice
ROBERT FROST

Original	Conventional
Some say the world will end in fire	Some say the world will end in
Some say in ice.	fire. Some say in ice. From what
From what I've tasted of desire	I've tasted of desire, I hold with
I hold with those who favor fire.	those who favor fire. But if it
But if it had to perish twice,	had to perish twice, I
I think I know enough of hate	think I know enough of
To say that for destruction ice	hate to say that for destruction
Is also great	ice is also great
And would suffice.	and would suffice.

After reading the poem through, the reader probably understands that this poem discussing the end of the world is debating just how it will end. So now the reader's attention is drawn to the key words of the poem. Because "fire" and "ice" appear in the title and in the poem itself, these are two key words. The active reader begins to think about the word "fire" in connection with the end of the world and explores the possible meanings of that word. "Fire" could mean war, nuclear explosions, volcanic eruptions, a biblical apocalypse, global warming, burning of the rain forests, etc. "Ice" could mean a new ice age, a nuclear winter following a nuclear war, the death of agriculture and mass starvation, etc.

Next the active reader notices that "desire" is linked with "fire," and "hate" is linked with "ice." These connections require more thought. "Desire" could mean greed, the taking of someone's territory, sexual lust, or several other things. The poet says that because of his experience with desire, he thinks the world will end as a result of it—and will be a fiery end. However, "hate," a cold emotion, is also a powerful force leading to "destruction." Note also that the words "would suffice," which mean "would be enough," ending the poem point out that hate can destroy the world just as surely (but less dramatically) as the fiery causes of war or other explosions.

Now, every reader does not develop all these ideas upon reading the poem, but highlighting and thinking about key words in a poem, and perhaps asking about them in a class discussion, may help active readers develop a greater understanding of a poem. Read the following poem in its original form and highlight the title and the words you find important to its meaning. Then discuss the poem with your classmates.

My Life Closed Twice Before Its Close
EMILY DICKINSON

My life closed twice before its close;
It yet remains to see
If Immortality unveil
A third event to me,

So huge, so hopeless to conceive,
As these that twice befell
Parting is all we know of heaven,
And all we need of hell.

Beyond Highlighting: Asking Questions in the Margins

Active readers carry on a conversation with the text they are reading. Many times this conversation consists of questions written in the margins about things in the text they do not understand or about what point an author is trying to establish or about connections the reader is beginning to see between ideas. These questions can become the focus of class discussion or the basis for a writing assignment about a work. It is certainly not necessary for a reader to know the answers to the questions as he or she is reading. However, the active reader searches for the answers by rereading or by discussing the work with others.

What kinds of margin questions do active readers ask? According to Karen Rodis, an instructor at Dartmouth, active readers ask in seeking to make something clear, "what does this mean"; in probing for the truth of something, "why is this being said?" or "why is this the case"; and in challenging the writer to come up with proof, "what makes you so sure?" As an example, look at the sections of "The Lottery" you have already read and note the marginal questions a student wrote (see page 9).

Readers benefit from asking such questions about nonfiction and poetry as well as fiction. Try your hand at asking questions in the margin of Roger Hernandez's essay on pages 4–5 or the poem by Emily Dickins which you highlighted previously. The poem is reproduced for your convenience here:

My Life Closed Twice Before Its Close
EMILY DICKINSON

My Life closed twice before its close;
It yet remains to see
If Immortality unveil
A third event to me,

So huge, so hopeless to conceive,
As these that twice befell.
Parting is all we know of heaven,
And all we need of hell.

Evaluating the Writer: Opinions in the Margins

A final strategy to help you become more active in your reading is to jot down opinions of what you have read in the margins. You could write "good" or "yes" if you read something you admire, or "bad" or "no" if you don't like the way a writer has expressed an idea. Put down "I agree" where the ideas fit your opinions, and "I disagree" where your experience or philosophy differs from that of the writer. Of course, you may wish to make your marginal conversation longer than just a word or two—some readers have explained quite fully in margin notes why they agree or disagree with an author. Such full notes are a great start for a paper on a text. However long your notes, these opinions should be seen as just your first reactions to a piece of writing. You should be willing to test your reactions with others in the class and with your instructor's ideas. You may want to reevaluate your opinions after hearing others' interpretations, but your comments in the margins give you specific places in a text to focus. Both in class and in writing assignments, citing specific places in a text as evidence for an opinion shows that you are actively thinking about what you read. Citing such evi-

THE LOTTERY
by Shirley Jackson

The morning of June 27th was clear and
sunny, with the fresh warmth of a full-summer
day; the flowers were blooming profusely and
the grass was richly green. The people of the
village began to gather in the square,
between the post office and the bank, around
ten o'clock; in some towns there were so many
people that the lottery took two days and had
to be started on June 26th, but in this
village, where there were only about three
hundred people, the whole lottery took less
than two hours, so it could begin at ten
o'clock in the morning and still be through
in time to allow the villagers to get home
for noon dinner.

The children assembled first, of course.
School was recently over for the summer, and
the feeling of liberty sat uneasily on most
of them; they tended to gather together
quietly for awhile before they broke into
boisterous play, and their talk was still of
the classroom and the teacher, of books and
reprimands. Bobby Martin had already stuffed
his pockets full of stones, and the other
boys soon followed his example, selecting the
smoothest and roundest stones; Bobby and
Harry Jones and Dickie Delacroix—the
villagers pronounced this name "Delacroy"—
eventually made a great pile of stones in one
square and guarded it against the raids of
the other boys. The girls stood aside,
talking among themselves, looking over their
shoulders at the boys, and the very small
children rolled in the dust or clung to the
hands of their older brothers and sisters.

Soon the men began to gather, surveying
their own children, speaking of planting and
rain, tractors and taxes. They stood
together, away from the pile of stones in the
corner, and their jokes were quiet and they
smiled rather than laughed . . . .

meaning?

Lotteries are held in other towns?

What could take so long?

What do stones have to do with a lottery?

Why did they stand there?

Were they always quiet?

dence also allows for meaningful dialogue among people discussing a work because they can compare reactions to specific sentences instead of trying to discuss vague, overall opinions. Think of it this way: If you and your friends are discussing a movie you have seen, and one says, "I liked it," while another says, "It stunk," what do the people in the group say to try to understand this difference of opinion? Usually they ask questions about the film to try to get specific answers—what was good? "The action scenes, the special effects, the surprise ending." Why did another person say that it stunk? "The plot was dumb, I'd seen the special effects before in other movies, and the ending was too fake to be believed." People certainly do not agree on films, short stories, poems, or anything else, but we usually want to know why we disagree.

These strategies—highlighting, asking questions, and evaluating—will involve you in the act of reading and prepare you for an active role in class discussion. You will be more likely to remember what you have read because you have thought about it more. Two more strategies for becoming a more active reader follow.

Strategy 2: Writing a Response Statement

A colleague of mine at Penn State, Dr. Lois Rubin, has created exercises for her classes to encourage them to be active readers. I have adapted her ideas in what follows to encourage you to read as actively as you can. These response statements are based on the idea that authors surprise us sometimes with what they write. Perhaps a character does not behave the way we think he or she should, or the plot doesn't seem realistic to us, or an idea in an essay presents a point of view that we have a hard time accepting. As we have already discussed, readers may have divergent opinions on readings or parts of readings, and part of your classroom experience is to compare the way you read a text with the way others read it in order to fully understand its possibilities. If you can identify characters, incidents, ideas, or other places in the text that surprised you (or disappointed you), you will be prepared for an active class discussion of the reading.

How does this work? Some examples follow illustrating how you might write a response statement. Then in the text following each reading will be some "prompts" that may help you formulate such a statement. Each example that follows is based on an element of the reading that changed the way you had thought about something or that struck you as different in another way.

SAMPLE RESPONSE STATEMENTS

I would have expected _____ from a character or incident but instead I learned _____.

I had always assumed that _____ but in this reading I saw that _____.

I was surprised when the author _____ because _____.

Let's apply this idea to the poem you saw above "Fire and Ice." It is reproduced again here.

Fire and Ice
ROBERT FROST

Some say the world will end in fire,
Some say in ice.
From what I've tasted of desire
I hold with those who favor fire.
But if it had to perish twice,
I think I know enough of hate
To say that for destruction ice
Is also great
And would suffice.

Some example response statements:

I was surprised when Robert Frost linked desire and fire because I had not thought of desire as being destructive like fire. I was surprised when Frost used the word "favor" because I don't think anyone should prefer one way for the world to end, but maybe he is saying that fire is the more likely way for the world to end.

I was interested that Frost thought that hate and desire were both destructive forces. I had always thought that hate was more destructive than desire.

I was surprised when Frost used ice as an image of hate because I always saw hate as hot like fire.

Some of your response statements may lead you to ask questions: What is destructive about desire? Why does Frost use the word "favor"? Which force is more destructive: desire or hate? Is ice an appropriate image for hate?

Practicing this technique may help you become more prepared for class discussion of a work and become an active participant in the discussion.

Strategy 3: Recording Thoughts in a Reading Journal

Why Write About What You Read?

Another way for you to be actively engaged in what you are reading is to keep a reading journal. This small notebook is a place for you to freewrite your thoughts about the ideas you have been reading. You may use it to record reactions to what you like and dislike, your agreements or objections to what others in your class think, or a comparative evaluation of two or more works. Putting your thoughts in writing will help you crystallize what you think and will prepare you for a possible formal writing assignment later. Your instructor may engage in a written dialogue with you about the reading by writing comments in your journal and asking you questions about your reactions. Or he or she may treat the journal as if it is a private diary that only you need see.

Recyling Ideas: Exchanging Old Thoughts for New Ones

Another function of a reading journal is to record new ideas that you acquire during class discussion and reading. One purpose of education is to expose you to new ideas. And although you are not expected to accept all new ideas, writing about those you do accept and those you reject will help you think through these new thoughts. Again, the journal may become a dialogue between you and your instructor or may be your private diary of these changes in thinking.

Moving beyond first impressions is a key to critical thinking because a first impression may be based on superficial things, perhaps an idea you've heard discussed casually or a reaction based on emotion or prejudice rather than on a detailed look at the facts of a situation. Two parts of this text ask you to "Reconsider" a reading selection by entering into a dialogue with your peers and then to "Review" it in more depth by a process of inquiry. Finally, a "Reading to Write" section ties the reading selection to what you are learning in your writing class by focusing on a feature of the writing in the selection you have just finished and by providing you with the opportunity to write an essay yourself. By writing about what you have read or on a related topic, you will have truly become an active reader and writer.

ONE

Making Choices: Establishing an Adult Identity

One of the most difficult parts of becoming an adult is finding out who we really are. Young people may absorb their family's identity, and, as they grow, friends, enemies, classmates, teachers, and many others influence their ideas of themselves (sometimes for better, sometimes for worse). But at some point in our lives, we make choices for ourselves to decide who we are. Sometimes these choices hinge on a main event as happens to N. Scott Momaday in "The End of My Childhood." Other times the choices are gradual as Jade Snow Wong describes in "Fifth Chinese Daughter." Sometimes forces over which we have little control shape our lives as Randall Williams illustrates in "Daddy Tucked the Blanket," or we may not be fully aware of the forces influencing us as Gail Sheehy explains in "Predictable Crises of Adulthood." In these cases, choices are still made, but they are not full independent choices, and we must strive to understand them. Reading the accounts in this chapter may offer a different perspective on the struggle to establish identity. Even those well into adulthood may reflect on some of their choices, the forces influencing those choices, and the consequences that have resulted. Writing about these struggles may bring us more in touch with who we really are and what we believe. If we understand ourselves better, we may understand others better as well.

The End of My Childhood
N. Scott Momaday

Preview: Thinking Ahead

For most of us becoming an adult is a gradual process. We can't think of a specific moment when we knew we had passed from childhood to adulthood. But Native American writer N. Scott Momaday recalls such an experience in his autobiography The Names: A Memoir, *published in 1976. Momaday, who was born in 1934, is exploring a mesa (a high flat-topped hill with steep sides) when he realizes he's in danger. Put yourself in his place. What would you have done? If you have had a similar experience, think about what it taught you.*

At Jemez I came to the end of my childhood. There were no schools within easy reach. I had to go nearly thirty miles to school at Bernalillo, and one year I lived away in Albuquerque. My mother and father wanted me to have the benefit of a sound preparation for college, and so we read through many high school catalogues. After long deliberation we decided that I should spend my last year of high school at a military academy in Virginia.

The day before I was to leave I went walking across the river to the red mesa, where many times before I had gone to be alone with my thoughts. And I had climbed several times to the top of the mesa and looked among the old ruins there for pottery. This time I chose to climb the north end, perhaps because I had not gone that way before and wanted to see what it was. It was a difficult climb, and when I got to the top I was spent. I lingered among the ruins for more than an hour, I judge, waiting for my strength to return. From there I could see the whole valley below, the fields, the river, and the village. It was all very beautiful, and the sight of it filled me with longing.

I looked for an easier way to come down, and at length I found a broad, smooth runway of rock, a shallow groove winding out like a stream. It appeared to be safe enough, and I started to follow it. There were steps along the way, a stairway, in effect. But the steps became deeper and deeper, and at last I had to drop down the length of my body and more. Still it seemed convenient to follow in the groove of rock. I was more than halfway down when I came upon a deep, funnel-shaped formation in my path. And there I had to make a decision. The slope on either side was extremely steep and forbidding, and yet I thought that I could work my way down on either side. The formation at my feet was something else. It was perhaps ten or twelve feet deep, wide at the top and narrow at the bottom, where there appeared to be a level ledge. If I could get down through the funnel to the ledge, I should be all right; surely the rest of the way down was negotiable. But I realized that there could be no turning back. Once I was down in that rocky chute I could not get up again, for the round wall which nearly encircled the space there was too high and sheer. I elected to go down into it, to try for the ledge directly below. I eased myself down the smooth, nearly vertical wall on my back, pressing my arms and legs outward against the sides. After what seemed a long time I was trapped in the rock. The ledge was no longer there below me; it had been an optical illusion. Now, in this angle of vision, there was nothing but the ground, far, far below, and jagged boulders set there like teeth. I remember that my arms were scraped and bleeding, stretched out against the walls with all the pressure that I could exert. When once I looked down I saw that my legs, also spread out and pressed hard against the walls, were shaking violently. I was in an impossible situation: I could not move in any direction, save downward in a fall, and I could not stay beyond another minute where I was. I believed then that I would die there, and I saw with a terrible clarity the things of the valley below. They were not the less beautiful to me. It seemed to me that I grew suddenly very calm in view of that beloved world. And I remember nothing else of that moment. I passed out of my mind, and the next thing I knew I was sitting down on the ground, very cold in the shadows, and looking up at the rock where I had been within an eyelash of eternity. That was a strange thing in my life, and I think of it as the end of an age. I should never again see the world as I saw it on the other side of that moment, in the bright reflection of time lost. There are such reflections, and for some of them I have the names.

Respond: Thinking Independently

1. Respond in your journal to Momaday's statement "I came to the end of my childhood." What do you think he means? Could the statement mean more than one thing? At the end of the essay he says, "That was a strange thing in my life, and I think of it as an end of an age." How do you interpret this remark?
2. Choose something that you highlighted in Momaday's story of an incident and comment on why you chose it to highlight. Write a response statement (as explained in the introduction). Use this one as a guide or write your own: I (expected, was surprised at, or found interesting) _____ because _____

_____

3. Did Momaday's story connect with any incident in your life? Can you think of a time when you knew childhood was over? Have you ever been in physical danger? Briefly record any of these incidents in your journal and your feelings at the time.

Reconsider: Thinking Collaboratively

1. Discuss your response statements with a group or with your class. How much variation in opinions is there?
2. Discuss what parts of the essay class members chose to highlight. What reasons did people have for their choices?
3. What do you and class members think happened to Momaday to enable him to get down from the mesa? Why doesn't he tell the reader?

Review: Thinking Critically

1. What did Momaday's leaving for school in Virginia have to do with his decision to climb the mesa? Why do you think he took a different path than he had before?
2. On his climb down, Momaday faced a dilemma, that is, a situation which has no really good alternatives. What was his dilemma?
3. At the end of the essay, Momaday says what the incident meant to him: "I should never again see the world as I saw it on the other side of that moment, in the bright reflection of time lost." What had changed for him? How do you think he saw the world after this moment?

READING TO WRITE

Understanding Narration: Writing a Narrative Essay

Narration means telling a story, but narratives can be nonfiction (as this one is) or fiction. The essay writer usually uses the story, or narrative, that he or she is telling to explain an idea. Writers of narratives have some important decisions to make:

1. Who should tell the story? Who tells the story obviously influences what information the reader is going to get. For example, in this narrative the young Momaday tells the story as it happened to him. What information would you have had if his mother had told the story of his leaving the house to climb the mesa? In a famous Agatha Christie mystery, *The Murder of Roger Ackroyd,* the story teller or narrator turns out to be the murderer. How does that affect the reader's understanding of what went on?

2. When should the story begin and end? We all know people who tell "shaggy dog" stories that never seem to have any real beginning or ending. But readers lose their patience if it takes too long to get into the story or to finish the story to make the point the writer seems to be making. Let's say, for example, that Momaday had told you for several pages of all the schools that he and his family had considered for him, the visits they made to the schools, and how he finally decided to go to the military school in Virginia. You might have gotten impatient, feeling that all that information was not necessary for you to know. However, readers need some background so that they know what the situation or context is as the story begins.

   Endings also take good judgment. You want the reader to know that the story has ended and to know something of the importance of the event. But you don't want to weaken the story itself with too long-winded an ending.

3. How should I organize the story? Stories, whether true or fictional, are often told as they happened, that is, chronologically. They have a beginning, middle, and end. Sometimes a writer of either true or fictional narratives will use a "flashback," a mention of an earlier event. Or the writer may depart from the actual narrative of events and discuss a side issue, called a digression. Momaday has a brief digression at the end of the second paragraph when he describes the view and the way it made him feel. Why do you suppose that he pauses to discuss the view?

   Frequently, the nonfiction storyteller will give the reader a reason for reading the story toward the beginning of the essay. Momaday begins his story with "At Jemez I came to the end of my childhood." He probably wants the reader to ask what that means, how that happened, to get the reader involved in what will follow. A sentence that states a point such as this is sometimes called a thesis, topic, or focus sentence.

4. How should I tell the story? Writers have many choices—to be formal or casual in their word choices, have long or short sentences, use dialogue or not, etc. But most narratives are strengthened by very specific details—words that describe what the writer sees, hears, feels, even tastes. Notice how Momaday describes the rocks as a "smooth runway" at one end and then later as "jagged boulders set there like teeth." His legs were "shaking violently." You can find many other good details in this short narrative.

Writing Applications: Narration

1. Write about an incident that you could say marked the end of your childhood. It might have been a time when you had to take an adult responsibility or an event that changed your outlook from trusting to cynical, from innocent to worldly, from careless to careful, or some other change.
2. Tell a story about a time that you faced a dangerous physical challenge. Be sure to explore the meaning of the incident to you.
3. Write about a time when you discovered something—in nature or about a person.

Salvation
LANGSTON HUGHES

Preview: Thinking Ahead

One part of many people's identities is religious faith. Frequently, young people in the process of establishing an adult identity question the faith of their childhood. Sometimes they cannot reconcile their own feelings about religion with the expectations of those around them. In this selection from his autobiography The Big Sea *(1940), Langston Hughes, one of America's most prominent writers and a spokesman for the African American community, recalls his own struggle between these two forces. As you read, think about the choice Hughes makes. Did he have another alternative? Think also about the consequences of his choice. Think about some important choices you have made.*

I was saved from sin when I was going on thirteen. But not really saved. It happened like this. There was a big revival at my Auntie Reed's church. Every night for weeks there had been much preaching, singing, praying, and shouting, and some very hardened sinners had been brought to Christ, and the membership of the church had grown by leaps and bounds. Then just before the revival ended, they held a special meeting for children, "to bring the young lambs to the fold." My aunt spoke of it for days ahead. That night I was escorted to the front row and placed on the mourners' bench with all the other young sinners, who had not yet been brought to Jesus.

My aunt told me that when you were saved you saw a light, and something happened to you inside! And Jesus came into your life! And God was with you from then on! She said you could see and hear and feel Jesus in your soul. I believed her. I had heard a great many old people say the same thing and it seemed to me they ought to know. So I sat there calmly in the hot, crowded church, waiting for Jesus to come to me.

The preacher preached a wonderful rhythmical sermon, all moans and shouts and lonely cries and dire pictures of hell, and then he sang a song about the ninety and nine safe in the fold, but one little lamb was left out in the cold. Then he said: "Won't you come? Won't you come to Jesus? Young lambs, won't you come?" And he held out his arms to all us young sinners there on the mourners' bench. And the little girls cried. And some of them jumped up and went to Jesus right away. But most of us just sat there.

A great many old people came and knelt around us and prayed, old women with jet-black faces and braided hair, old men with work-gnarled hands. And the church sang a song about the lower lights are burning, some poor sinners to be saved. And the whole building rocked with prayer and song.

Still I kept waiting to *see* Jesus.

Finally all the young people had gone to the altar and were saved, but one boy and me. He was a rounder's son named Westley. Westley and I were surrounded by sisters and deacons praying. It was very hot in the church, and getting late now. Finally Westley said to me in a whisper: "God damn! I'm tired o' sitting here. Let's get up and be saved." So he got up and was saved.

Then I was left all alone on the mourners' bench. My aunt came and knelt at my knees and cried, while prayers and songs swirled all around me in the little church. The whole congregation prayed for me alone, in a mighty wail of moans and voices. And I kept waiting serenely for Jesus, waiting, waiting—but he didn't come. I wanted to see him, but nothing happened to me. Nothing! I wanted something to happen to me, but nothing happened.

I heard the songs and the minister saying: "Why don't you come? My dear child, why don't you come to Jesus? Jesus is waiting for you. He wants you. Why don't you come? Sister Reed, what is this child's name?"

"Langston," my aunt sobbed.

"Langston, why don't you come? Why don't you come and be saved? Oh, Lamb of God! Why don't you come?"

Now it was really getting late. I began to be ashamed of myself, holding everything up so long. I began to wonder what God thought about Westley, who certainly hadn't seen Jesus either, but who was now sitting proudly on the platform, swinging his knickerbockered legs and grinning down at me, surrounded by deacons and old women on their knees praying. God had not struck Westley dead for taking his name in vain or for lying in the temple. So I decided that maybe to save further trouble, I'd better lie, too, and say that Jesus had come, and get up and be saved.

So I got up.

Suddenly the whole room broke into a sea of shouting, as they saw me rise. Waves of rejoicing swept the place. Women leaped in the air. My aunt threw her arms around me. The minister took me by the hand and led me to the platform.

When things quieted down, in a hushed silence, punctuated by a few ec- static "Amens," all the new young lambs were blessed in the name of God. Then joyous singing filled the room.

That night, for the last time in my life but one—for I was a big boy twelve years old—I cried. I cried, in bed alone, and couldn't stop. I buried my head under the quilts, but my aunt heard me. She woke up and told my uncle I was crying because the Holy Ghost had come into my life, and be- cause I had seen Jesus. But I was really crying because I couldn't bear to tell her that I had lied, that I had deceived everybody in the church, that I hadn't seen Jesus, and that now I didn't believe there was a Jesus any more, since he didn't come to help me.

Respond: Thinking Independently

1. Write in your journal why you think young Langston waited to be saved and why he stood up at last.
2. Choose a sentence that you highlighted as you read and discuss why you chose it. Was it because of its writing style, its emotional impact, or some other reason?
3. Write a response statement: I expected_____ in a story called "Salvation," and it did/did not fulfill my expectations be- cause _____.
4. Have you ever felt a similar pressure to do what parents, neighbors, or friends expected you to do? Discuss in the journal what pressure there was and what choice you made.

Reconsider: Thinking Collaboratively

1. Discuss your response statements in class and/or in groups. Did every- one expect the same things from this autobiographical essay? What dif- ferences in expectation and/or fulfillment were there?
2. What do other class members think about Hughes's decision to stand up and be saved despite his misgivings?
3. What does Westley have to do with Langston's decision?
4. Why does Langston Hughes cry in bed that night? What do you and your classmates feel are the most important reasons?

Review: Thinking Critically

1. "Irony" is a term applied to a situation in which something appears to mean one thing but in reality it means another. What is "ironic" about Langston's aunt's comments about why Langston is crying? What is ironic about Langston's religious faith after this incident?
2. Sometimes when we are young we build up expectations about some- thing to impossible levels—a birthday celebration, a vacation, Christmas

or Chanukah presents. Was Langston expecting too much during the church revival? Who gave him his information? Were they to blame for building the event up too high? Did he take what they said too literally?

3. Sometimes expectations that are not realized lead to disillusionment, a condition many people experience as they reach adulthood. Was Langston Hughes disillusioned? About what? What has disillusioned you?

4. Does the fact that Momaday's essay centers on a physical challenge while Hughes's presents more of a psychological concern affect your reaction to the essays? Explain.

READING TO WRITE

Understanding Narration: Two Ways to Organize Narratives

A narrative essay may begin with an incident and then conclude with the writer's point (for example, a choice made and its results). This is called an inductive approach. Or a writer may wish to begin with the point (or thesis) and then tell the incident that led to it (a deductive approach). The first way of organizing involves a reader or audience in the story without their knowing where it will lead or why a writer is telling them the story. In that way, it creates suspense. The second method tells the reader upfront (as both Momaday and Hughes do) that the incident he or she is about to read had some importance for the writer. This method gives the audience some context for the incident, but doesn't involve them as quickly in the story. In the applications that follow, you may wish to experiment with these approaches to see which works best for your essay.

Writing Applications: Narration

1. Write an essay building on your journal entry about a time you felt pressure to "go along" with family or friends' expectations and the choice you made.

2. Tell about an incident in your life that led to your becoming disillusioned about something.

Growing Up
RUSSELL BAKER

Preview: Thinking Ahead

In the opening paragraph of this essay, do you notice a different tone, or attitude, between this selection and the two before it? What is the difference? Try to decide what the writer does to cause this change in tone. Russell Baker continues to, as he puts it, "work in journalism," having been a correspondent and columnist for The New York Times *since 1954. He has won two*

Pulitzer Prizes, one for the 1982 autobiography Growing Up *from which this selection was taken.*

I began working in journalism when I was eight years old. It was my mother's idea. She wanted me to "make something" of myself and, after a levelheaded appraisal of my strengths, decided I had better start young if I was to have any chance of keeping up with the competition.

The flaw in my character which she had already spotted was lack of "gumption." My idea of a perfect afternoon was lying in front of the radio rereading my favorite Big Little Book, *Dick Tracy Meets Stooge Viller*. My mother despised inactivity. Seeing me having a good time in repose, she was powerless to hide her disgust. "You've got no more gumption than a bump on a log," she said. "Get out in the kitchen and help Doris do those dirty dishes."

My sister Doris, though two years younger than I, had enough gumption for a dozen people. She positively enjoyed washing dishes, making beds, and cleaning the house. When she was only seven she could carry a piece of short-weighted cheese back to the A&P, threaten the manager with legal action, and come back triumphantly with the full quarter-pound we'd paid for and a few ounces extra thrown in for forgiveness. Doris could have made something of herself if she hadn't been a girl. Because of this defect, however, the best she could hope for was a career as a nurse or schoolteacher, the only work that capable females were considered up to in those days.

This must have saddened my mother, this twist of fate that had allocated all the gumption to the daughter and left her with a son who was content with Dick Tracy and Stooge Viller. If disappointed, though, she wasted no energy on self-pity. She would make me make something of myself whether I wanted to or not. "The Lord helps those who help themselves," she said. That was the way her mind worked.

She was realistic about the difficulty. Having sized up the material the Lord had given her to mold, she didn't overestimate what she could do with it. She didn't insist that I grow up to be President of the United States.

Fifty years ago parents still asked boys if they wanted to grow up to be President, and asked it not jokingly but seriously. Many parents who were hardly more than paupers still believed their sons could do it. Abraham Lincoln had done it. We were only sixty-five years from Lincoln. Many a grandfather who walked among us could remember Lincoln's time. Men of grandfatherly age were the worst for asking if you wanted to grow up to be President. A surprising number of little boys said yes and meant it.

I was asked many times myself. No, I would say, I didn't want to grow up to be President. My mother was present during one of these interrogations. An elderly uncle, having posed the usual question and exposed my lack of interest in the Presidency, asked, "Well, what *do* you want to be when you grow up?"

I loved to pick through trash piles and collect empty bottles, tin cans with pretty labels, and discarded magazines. The most desirable job on earth sprang instantly to mind. "I want to be a garbage man," I said.

My uncle smiled, but my mother had seen the first distressing evidence of a bump budding on a log. "Have a little gumption, Russell," she said. Her calling me Russell was a signal of unhappiness. When she approved of me I was always "Buddy."

When I turned eight years old she decided that the job of starting me on the road toward making something of myself could no longer be safely delayed. "Buddy," she said one day, "I want you to come home right after school this afternoon. Somebody's coming and I want you to meet him."

When I burst in that afternoon she was in conference in the parlor with an executive of the Curtis Publishing Company. She introduced me. He bent low from the waist and shook my hand. Was it true as my mother had told him, he asked, that I longed for the opportunity to conquer the world of business?

My mother replied that I was blessed with a rare determination to make something of myself.

"That's right," I whispered.

"But have you got the grit, the character, the never-say-quit spirit it takes to succeed in business?"

My mother said I certainly did.

"That's right," I said.

He eyed me silently for a long pause, as though weighing whether I could be trusted to keep his confidence, then spoke man-to-man. Before taking a crucial step, he said, he wanted to advise me that working for the Curtis Publishing Company placed enormous responsibility on a young man. It was one of the great companies of America. Perhaps the greatest publishing house in the world. I had heard, no doubt, of the *Saturday Evening Post*?

Heard of it? My mother said that everyone in our house had heard of the *Saturday Post* and that I, in fact, read it with religious devotion.

Then doubtless, he said, we were also familiar with those two monthly pillars of the magazine world, the *Ladies Home Journal* and the *Country Gentleman.*

Indeed we were familiar with them, said my mother.

Representing the *Saturday Evening Post* was one of the weightiest honors that could be bestowed in the world of business, he said. He was personally proud of being a part of that great corporation.

My mother said he had every right to be.

Again he studied me as though debating whether I was worthy of a knighthood. Finally: "Are you trustworthy?"

My mother said I was the soul of honesty.

"That's right," I said.

The caller smiled for the first time. He told me I was a lucky young man. He admired my spunk. Too many young men thought life was all play. Those young men would not go far in this world. Only a young man willing to work and save and keep his face washed and his hair neatly combed could hope to come out on top in a world such as ours. Did I truly and sincerely believe that I was such a young man?

"He certainly does," said my mother.

"That's right," I said.

He said he had been so impressed by what he had seen of me that he was going to make me a representative of the Curtis Publishing Company. On the following Tuesday, he said, thirty freshly printed copies of the *Saturday Evening Post* would be delivered at our door. I would place these magazines, still damp with the ink of the presses, in a handsome canvas bag, sling it over my shoulder, and set forth through the streets to bring the best in journalism, fiction, and cartoons to the American public.

He had brought the canvas bag with him. He presented it with reverence fit for a chasuble. He showed me how to drape the sling over my left shoulder and across the chest so that the pouch lay easily accessible to my right hand, allowing the best in journalism, fiction, and cartoons to be swiftly extracted and sold to a citizenry whose happiness and security depended upon us soldiers of the free press.

The following Tuesday I raced home from school, put the canvas bag over my shoulder, dumped the magazines in, and, tilting to the left to balance their weight on my right hip, embarked on the highway of journalism.

We lived in Belleville, New Jersey, a commuter town at the northern fringe of Newark. It was 1932, the bleakest year of the Depression. My father had died two years before, leaving us with a few pieces of Sears, Roebuck furniture and not much else, and my mother had taken Doris and me to live with one of her younger brothers. This was my Uncle Allen. Uncle Allen had made something of himself by 1932. As salesman for a soft-drink bottler in Newark, he had an income of $30 a week; wore pearl-gray spats, detachable collars, and a three-piece suit; was happily married; and took in threadbare relatives.

With my load of magazines I headed toward Belleville Avenue. That's where the people were. There were two filling stations at the intersection with Union Avenue, as well as an A&P, a fruit stand, a bakery, a barber shop, Zuccarelli's drugstore, and a diner shaped like a railroad car. For several hours I made myself highly visible, shifting position now and then from corner to corner, from shop window to shop window, to make sure everyone could see the heavy black lettering on the canvas bag that said THE SATURDAY EVENING POST. When the angle of the light indicated it was suppertime, I walked back to the house.

"How many did you sell, Buddy?" my mother asked.

"None."

"Where did you go?"

"The corner of Belleville and Union Avenues."

"What did you do?"

"Stood on the corner waiting for somebody to buy a *Saturday Evening Post*."

"You just stood there?"

"Didn't sell a single one."

"For God's sake, Russell!"

Uncle Allen intervened. "I've been thinking about it for some time," he said, "and I've about decided to take the *Post* regularly. Put me down as a regular customer." I handed him a magazine and he paid me a nickel. It was the first nickel I earned.

Afterwards my mother instructed me in salesmanship. I would have to ring doorbells, address adults with charming self-confidence, and break down resistance with a sales talk pointing out that no one, no matter how poor, could afford to be without the *Saturday Evening Post* in the home.

I told my mother I'd changed my mind about wanting to succeed in the magazine business.

"If you think I'm going to raise a good-for-nothing," she replied, "you've got another thing coming." She told me to hit the streets with the canvas bag and start ringing doorbells the instant school was out next day. When I objected that I didn't feel any aptitude for salesmanship, she asked how I'd like to lend her my leather belt so she could whack some sense into me, I bowed to superior will and entered journalism with a heavy heart.

My mother and I had fought this battle almost as long as I could remember. It probably started even before memory began, when I was a country child in northern Virginia and my mother, dissatisfied with my father's plain workman's life, determined that I would not grow up like him and his people, with calluses on their hands, overalls on their backs, and fourth-grade educations in their heads. She had fancier ideas of life's possibilities. Introducing me to the *Saturday Evening Post,* she was trying to wean me as early as possible from my father's world where men left with their lunch pails at sunup, worked with their hands until the grime ate into the pores, and died with a few sticks of mail-order furniture as their legacy. In my mother's vision of the better life there were desks and white collars, well-pressed suits, evenings of reading and lively talk, and perhaps—if a man were very, very lucky and hit the jackpot, really made something important of himself—perhaps there might be a fantastic salary of $5,000 a year to support a big house and a Buick with a rumble seat and a vacation in Atlantic City.

And so I set forth with my sack of magazines. I was afraid of the dogs that snarled behind the doors of potential buyers. I was timid about ringing the doorbells of strangers, relieved when no one came to the door, and scared when someone did. Despite my mother's instructions, I could not deliver an engaging sales pitch. When a door opened I simply asked, "Want to buy a *Saturday Evening Post?*" In Belleville few persons did. It was a town of 30,000 people, and most weeks I rang a fair majority of its doorbells. But I rarely sold my thirty copies. Some weeks I canvassed the entire town for six days and still had four or five unsold magazines on Monday evening; then I dreaded the coming of Tuesday morning, when a batch of thirty fresh *Saturday Evening Posts* were due at the front door.

"Better get out there and sell the rest of those magazines tonight," my mother would say.

I usually posted myself then at a busy intersection where a traffic light controlled commuter flow from Newark. When the light turned red I stood on the curb and shouted my sales pitch at the motorists.

"Want to buy a *Saturday Evening Post?*"

One rainy night when car windows were sealed against me I came back soaked and with not a single sale to report. My mother beckoned to Doris.

"Go back down there with Buddy and show him how to sell these magazines," she said.

Brimming with zest, Doris, who was then seven years old, returned with me to the corner. She took a magazine from the bag, and when the light turned red she strode to the nearest car and banged her small fist against the closed window. The driver, probably startled at what he took to be a midget assaulting his car, lowered the window to stare, and Doris thrust a *Saturday Evening Post* at him.

"You need this magazine," she piped, "and it only costs a nickel."

Her salesmanship was irresistible. Before the light changed half a dozen times she disposed of the entire batch. I didn't feel humiliated. To the contrary, I was so happy I decided to give her a treat. Leading her to the vegetable store on Belleville Avenue, I bought three apples, which cost a nickel, and gave her one.

"You shouldn't waste money," she said.

"Eat your apple." I bit into mine.

"You shouldn't eat before supper," she said. "It'll spoil your appetite."

Back at the house that evening, she dutifully reported me for wasting a nickel. Instead of a scolding, I was rewarded with a pat on the back for having the good sense to buy fruit instead of candy. My mother reached into her bottomless supply of maxims and told Doris, "An apple a day, keeps the doctor away."

By the time I was ten I had learned all my mother's maxims by heart. Asking to stay up past normal bedtime, I knew that a refusal would be explained with, "Early to bed and early to rise, makes a man healthy, wealthy, and wise." If I whimpered about having to get up early in the morning, I could depend on her to say, "The early bird gets the worm."

The one I most despised was, "If at first you don't succeed, try, try again." This was the battle cry with which she constantly sent me back into the hopeless struggle whenever I moaned that I had rung every doorbell in town and knew there wasn't a single potential buyer left in Belleville that week. After listening to my explanation, she handed me the canvas bag and said, "If at first you don't succeed . . ."

Three years in that job, which I would gladly have quit after the first day except for her insistence, produced at least one valuable result. My mother finally concluded that I would never make something of myself by pursuing a life in business and started considering careers that demanded less competitive zeal.

One evening when I was eleven I brought home a short "composition" on my summer vacation which the teacher had graded with an A. Reading it with her own schoolteacher's eye, my mother agreed that it was top-drawer seventh grade prose and complimented me. Nothing more was said about it immediately, but a new idea had taken life in her mind. Halfway through supper she suddenly interrupted the conversation.

"Buddy," she said, "maybe you could be a writer."

I clasped the idea to my heart. I had never met a writer, had shown no previous urge to write, and hadn't a notion how to become a writer, but I loved stories and thought that making up stories must surely be almost as much fun as reading them. Best of all, though, and what really gladdened my heart, was the ease of the writer's life. Writers did not have to trudge through the town peddling from canvas bags, defending themselves against angry dogs, being rejected by surly strangers. Writers did not have to ring doorbells. So far as I could make out, what writers did couldn't even be classified as work.

I was enchanted. Writers didn't have to have any gumption at all. I did not dare tell anybody for fear of being laughed at in the schoolyard, but secretly I decided that what I'd like to be when I grew up was a writer.

Respond: Thinking Independently

1. Write in your journal what you thought about Baker's mother (her advice, her ambition for her son, her attitude toward her daughter, her life circumstances). How did Baker seem to feel toward his mother when he was young? How does he seem to feel now as an adult?

2. What did you decide about the tone of this essay (the author's attitude toward his subject)? How does it differ from either Hughes's or Momaday's essays?

3. Write a response statement: "Growing Up" made me feel (sad, angry, impatient, amused) or _____ because _____
_____.

4. Write in your journal anything you remember about what parents, teachers, or others expected of you. How did you react to their expectations? Were expectations based in part on whether you are male or female? Explain.

Reconsider: Thinking Collaboratively

1. Compare views of class members toward Russell and his mother (also sister Doris and Uncle Allen). Do class members agree in their opinions? Why or why not? Does a person's life situation affect the way he or she reads an autobiography?

2. Do you and your classmates feel that Baker is telling the truth in the last paragraph when he explains why he decided to become a writer?

Review: Thinking Critically

1. What were the family circumstances when Baker was growing up? In which paragraph does Baker tell us these details? Why does he choose to put the information there? What would have been the difference to the reader if he had started the essay with the family's situation?

2. In another paragraph late in the essay, Baker guesses that his mother pushed him to "make something" of himself because she was "dissatisfied with my father's plain workman's life." Could he have known this when he was 8 years old? What effect does it have on us as readers to have the adult Baker (rather than the child) tell us his mother's motives?

READING TO WRITE

Understanding Examples/Illustration: Using Examples to Support a Point

Writers frequently use examples to "prove" their points to readers. It would not have been enough for Baker to TELL us that his mother was ambitious for her son—he had to SHOW us by giving us an example of her behavior. How does Baker illustrate his mother's ambition for him? How does he show Doris's "gumption"? Note how specific Baker is in his illustration. For example, he recounts conversations that he and his mother had with each other, the route sales manager for the *Saturday Evening Post,* and Uncle Allen. The reader can put him or herself in the scene, as if watching a video.

Writers may use one longer incident, as Baker does, or may choose several shorter examples to "back up" their ideas. A longer incident such as this one is organized chronologically like a narrative. Shorter examples are often arranged in an essay from those of least importance to those of most importance.

Writing Applications: Examples/Illustration

1. Cite an example of a "lesson" you learned in childhood, either through your own experience or from parents or other adults. You may wish to use one long example to illustrate this lesson; however, if the lesson was the result of a number of instances, organize them in time order, or from least significant to most significant. For example, you may have learned that fire was dangerous through one dramatic incident (setting the field near your home on fire) or in a series of smaller encounters with fire.
2. Did your parents have pet phrases like "If at first you don't succeed, try, try again"? If so, choose one, and explain how it was used as you were growing up.
3. If you know your career goal, give examples of the influences on your life that led to your choice of career. If there have been several influences, you may wish to limit your explanation to one or two.

Fifth Chinese Daughter
JADE SNOW WONG

Preview: Thinking Ahead

Whatever your cultural background or ethnic group, did you ever wonder what growing up in another culture would be like? Perhaps you know someone whose family background is quite different from yours, but you are not really sure how those differences affect his or her life. In this essay, Jade Snow Wong describes for us what her life was like in San Francisco, growing up in a traditional Chinese family. As you read, note differences between her life as she describes it and yours. In what respects are her parents to be admired? What does she criticize? How much of their confrontation is typical parent-teen disagreement, and how much is a clash between Chinese and American cultures? What differences in treatment did she receive because she was female? Compare her circumstances with those of Russell Baker who also grew up during the Depression.

Wong eventually graduated from Mills College and became a writer. This account of her life published in 1971 became a PBS special in 1976. Maxine Hong Kingston and Amy Tan, two contemporary female Chinese-American writers, have cited her as their role model.

From infancy to my sixteenth year, I was reared according to nineteenth-century ideals of Chinese womanhood. I was never left alone, though it was not unusual for me to feel lonely, while surrounded by a family of seven others, and often by ten (including bachelor cousins) at meals.

My father (who enjoyed our calling him Daddy in English) was the unquestioned head of our household. He was not talkative, being preoccupied with his business affairs and with reading constantly otherwise. My mother was mistress of domestic affairs. Seldom did these two converse before their children, but we knew them to be a united front, and suspected that privately she both informed and influenced him about each child.

In order to support the family in America, Daddy tried various occupations—candy making, the ministry to which he was later ordained—but finally settled on manufacturing men's and children's denim garments. He leased sewing equipment, installed machines in a basement where rent was cheapest, and there he and his family lived and worked. There was no thought that dim, airless quarters were terrible conditions for living and working, or that child labor was unhealthful. The only goal was for all in the family to work, to save, and to become educated. It was possible, so it would be done.

My father, a meticulous bookkeeper, used only an abacus, a brush, ink, and Chinese ledgers. Because of his newly learned ideals, he pioneered for the right of women to work. Concerned that they have economic independence, but not with the long hours of industrial home work, he went to shy housewives' apartments and taught them sewing.

My earliest memories of companionship with my father were as his passenger in his red wheelbarrow, sharing space with the piles of blue-jean materials he was delivering to a worker's home. He must have been forty. He was lean, tall, inevitably wearing blue overalls, rolled shirt sleeves, and high black kid shoes. In his pockets were numerous keys, tools, and pens. On such deliveries, I noticed that he always managed time to show a mother how to sew a difficult seam, or to help her repair a machine, or just to chat.

I observed from birth that living and working were inseparable. My mother was short, sturdy, young looking, and took pride in her appearance. She was at her machine the minute housework was done, and she was the hardest-working seamstress, seldom pausing, working after I went to bed.

The hum of sewing machines continued day and night, seven days a week. She knew that to have more than the four necessities, she must work and save. We knew that to overcome poverty, there were only two methods: working and education.

Having provided the setup for family industry, my father turned his attention to our education. Ninety-five percent of the population in his native China had been illiterate. He knew that American public schools would take care of our English, but he had to nurture our Chinese knowledge. Only the Cantonese tongue was ever spoken by him or my mother. When the two oldest girls arrived from China, the schools of Chinatown received only boys. My father tutored his daughters each morning before breakfast. In the midst of a foreign environment, he clung to a combination of the familiar old standards and what was permissible in the newly learned Christian ideals.

My eldest brother was born in America, the only boy for fourteen years, and after him three daughters—another older sister, myself, and my younger sister. Then my younger brother, Paul, was born. That older brother, Lincoln, was cherished in the best Chinese tradition. He had his own room; he kept a German shepherd as his pet; he was tutored by a Chinese scholar; he was sent to private school for American classes. As a male Wong, he would be responsible some day for the preservation of and pilgrimages to ancestral graves—his privileges were his birthright. We girls were content with the unusual opportunities of working and attending two schools. By day, I attended American public school near our home. From 5:00 P.M. to 8:00 P.M. on five weekdays and from 9:00 A.M. to 12 noon on Saturdays, I attended the Chinese school. Classes numbered twenty to thirty students, and were taught by educated Chinese from China. We studied poetry, calligraphy, philosophy, literature, history, correspondence, religion, all by exacting memorization.

Daddy emphasized memory development; he could still recite fluently many lengthy lessons of his youth. Every evening after both schools, I'd sit by my father, often as he worked at his sewing machine, sing-songing my lessons above its hum. Sometimes I would stop to hold a light for him as he threaded the difficult holes of a specialty machine, such as one for bias bindings. After my Chinese lessons passed his approval, I was allowed to attend to American homework. I was made to feel luckier than other Chinese girls who didn't study Chinese, and also luckier than Western girls without a dual heritage.

There was little time for play, and toys were unknown to me. In any spare time, I was supplied with embroidery and sewing for my mother. The Chinese New Year, which by the old lunar calendar would fall sometime in late January or early February of the Western Christian calendar, was the most special time of the year, for then the machines stopped for three days. Mother would clean our living quarters very thoroughly, decorate the sitting room with flowering branches and fresh oranges, and arrange candied fruits or salty melon seeds for callers. All of us would be dressed in bright new clothes, and relatives or close friends, who came to call, would give each of us a red paper packet containing a good luck coin—usually a quarter. I remember how my classmates would gleefully talk of *their* receipts. But my mother made us give our money to her, for she said that she needed it to reciprocate to others.

Yet there was little reason for unhappiness. I was never hungry. Though we had no milk, there was all the rice we wanted. We had hot and cold running water—a rarity in Chinatown—as well as our own bathtub. Our sheets were pieced from dishtowels, but we had sheets. I was never neglected, for my mother and father were always at home. During school vacation periods, I was taught to operate many types of machines—tacking (for pockets), overlocking (for the raw edges of seams), buttonhole, double seaming; and I learned all the stages in producing a pair of jeans to its final inspection, folding, and tying in bundles of a dozen pairs by size, ready for pickup. Denim jeans are heavy—my shoulders ached often. My father set up a modest nickel-and-dime piecework reward for me, which he recorded in my own notebook, and paid me regularly.

My mother dutifully followed my father's leadership. She was extremely thrifty, but the thrifty need pennies to manage, and the old world had denied her those. Upon arrival in the new world of San Francisco, she accepted the elements her mate had selected to shape her new life: domestic duties, seamstress work in the factory-home, mothering each child in turn, church once a week, and occasional movies. Daddy frowned upon the community Chinese operas because of their very late hours (they did not finish till past midnight) and their mixed audiences.

Very early in my life, the manners of a traditional Chinese lady were taught to me. How to hold a pair of chopsticks (palm up, not down); how to hold a bowl of rice (one thumb on top, not resting in an open palm); how to pass something to elders (with both hands, never one); how to pour tea into the tiny, handleless porcelain cups (seven-eighths full so that the top edge would be cool enough to hold); how to eat from a center serving dish (only the piece in front of your place; never pick around); not to talk at table; not to show up outside of one's room without being fully dressed; not to be late, ever; not to be too playful—in a hundred and one ways, we were molded to be trouble-free, unobtrusive, cooperative.

We were disciplined by first being told, and then by punishment if we didn't remember. Punishment was instant and unceremonious. At the table, it came as a sudden whack from Daddy's chopsticks. Away from the table, punishment could be the elimination of a privilege or the blow on our legs from a bundle of cane switches.

Only Daddy and Oldest Brother were allowed individual idiosyncrasies. Daughters were all expected to be of one standard. To allow each one of many daughters to be different would have posed enormous problems of cost, energy, and attention. No one was shown physical affection. Such familiarity would have weakened my parents and endangered the one-answer authoritative system. One standard from past to present, whether in China or in San Francisco, was simpler to enforce. My parents never said "please" and "thank you" for any service or gift. In Chinese, both "please" and "thank you" can be literally translated as "I am not worthy" and naturally, no parent is going to say that about a service which should be their just due.

Traditional Chinese parents pit their children against a standard of perfection without regard to personality, individual ambitions, tolerance for human error, or exposure to the changing social scene. It never occurred to that kind of parent to be friends with their children on common ground.

During the Depression, my mother and father needed even more hours to work. Daddy had been shopping daily for groceries (we had no icebox) and my mother cooked. Now I was told to assume both those duties. My mother would give me fifty cents to buy enough fresh food for dinner and breakfast. In those years, twenty-five cents could buy a small chicken or three sanddabs, ten cents bought three bunches of green vegetables, and fifteen cents bought some meat to cook with these. After American school I rushed to the stores only a block or so away, returned and cleaned the foods, and cooked in a hurry in order to eat an early dinner and get to Chinese school on time. When I came home at 8:00 P.M., I took care of the dinner dishes before starting to do my homework. Saturdays and Sundays were for housecleaning and the family laundry, which I scrubbed on a board, using big galvanized buckets in our bathtub.

I had no sympathetic guidance as an eleven-year-old in my own reign in the kitchen, which lasted for four years. I finished junior high school, started high school, and continued studying Chinese. With the small earnings from summer work in my father's basement factory (we moved back to the basement during the Depression), I bought materials to sew my own clothes. But the routine of keeping house only to be dutiful, to avoid tongue or physical lashings, became exasperating. The tiny space which was the room for three sisters was confining. After I graduated from Chinese evening school, I began to look for part-time paying jobs as a mother's helper. Those jobs varied from cleaning house to baking a cake, amusing a naughty child to ironing shirts, but wearying, exhausting as they were, they meant money earned for myself.

As I advanced in American high school and worked at those jobs, I was gradually introduced to customs not of the Chinese world. American teachers were mostly kind. I remember my third-grade teacher's skipping me half a year. I remember my fourth-grade teacher—with whom I am still friendly. She was the first person to hold me to her physically and affectionately—because a baseball bat had been accidentally flung against my hand. I also remember that I was confused by being held, since physical comfort had not been offered by my parents. I remember my junior high school principal, who skipped me half a grade and commended me before the school assembly, to my great embarrassment.

In contrast, Chinese schoolteachers acted as extensions of Chinese parental discipline. There was a formal "disciplinarian dean" to apply the cane to wayward boys, and girls were not exempt either. A whisper during chapel was sufficient provocation to be called to the dean's office. No humor was exchanged; no praise or affection expressed by the teachers. They presented the lessons, and we had to learn to memorize all the words, orally, before the class. Then followed the written test, word for word. Without an alphabet, the Chinese language requires exact memorization. No originality or deviation was permitted and grading was severe. One word wrong during an examination could reduce a grade by 10 percent. It was the principle of learning by punishment.

Interest and praise, physical or oral, were rewards peculiar to the American world. Even employers who were paying me thanked me for a service or complimented me on a meal well cooked, and sometimes helped me with extra dishes. Chinese often said that "foreigners" talked too much about too many personal things. My father used to tell me to think three times before saying anything, and if I said nothing, no one would say I was stupid. I perceived a difference between two worlds.

By the time I was graduating from high school, my parents had done their best to produce an intelligent, obedient daughter, who would know more than the average Chinatown girl and should do better than average at a conventional job, her earnings brought home to them in repayment for their years of child support. Then, they hoped, she would marry a nice Chinese boy and make him a good wife, as well as an above-average mother for his children. Chinese custom used to decree that families should "introduce" chosen partners to each other's children. The groom's family should pay handsomely to the bride's family for rearing a well-bred daughter. They should also pay all bills for a glorious wedding banquet for several hundred guests. Then the bride's family could consider their job done. Their daughter belonged to the groom's family and must henceforth seek permission from all persons in his home before returning to her parents for a visit.

But having been set upon a new path, I did not oblige my parents with the expected conventional ending. At fifteen, I had moved away from home to work for room and board and a salary of twenty dollars per month. Having found that I could subsist independently, I thought it regrettable to terminate my education. Upon graduating from high school at the age of sixteen, I asked my parents to assist me in college expenses. I pleaded with my father, for his years of encouraging me to be above mediocrity in both Chinese and American studies had made me wish for some undefined but brighter future.

My father was briefly adamant. He must conserve his resources for my oldest brother's medical training. Though I desired to continue on an above-average course, his material means were insufficient to support that ambition. He added that if I had the talent, I could provide for my own college education. When he had spoken, no discussion was expected. After his edict, no daughter questioned.

But this matter involved my whole future—it was not simply asking for permission to go to a night church meeting (forbidden also). Though for years I had accepted the authority of the one I honored most, his decision that night embittered me as nothing ever had. My oldest brother had so many privileges, had incurred unusual expenses for luxuries which were taken for granted as his birthright, yet these were part of a system I had accepted. Now I suddenly wondered at my father's interpretation of the Christian code: was it intended to discriminate against a girl after all, or was it simply convenient for my father's economics and cultural prejudice? Did a daughter have any right to expect more than a fate of obedience, according to the old Chinese standard? As long as I could remember, I had been told that a female followed three men during her lifetime: as a girl, her father; as a wife, her husband; as an old woman, her son.

My indignation mounted against that tradition and I decided then that my past could not determine my future. I knew that more education would prepare me for a different expectation than my other female schoolmates, few of whom were to complete a college degree. I, too, had my father's unshakable faith in the justice of God, and I shared his unconcern with popular opinion.

So I decided to enter junior college, now San Francisco's City College, because the fees were lowest. I lived at home and supported myself with an after-school job which required long hours of housework and cooking but paid me twenty dollars per month, of which I saved as much as possible. The thrills derived from reading and learning, in ways ranging from chemistry experiments to English compositions, from considering new ideas of sociology to the logic of Latin, convinced me that I had made a correct choice. I was kept in a state of perpetual mental excitement by new Western subjects and concepts and did not mind long hours of work and study. I also made new friends, which led to another painful incident with my parents, who had heretofore discouraged even girlhood friendships.

The college subject which had most jolted me was sociology. The instructor fired my mind with his interpretation of family relationships. As he explained to our class, it used to be an economic asset for American farming families to be large, since children were useful to perform agricultural chores. But this situation no longer applied and children should be regarded as individuals with their own rights. Unquestioning obedience should be replaced with parental understanding. So at sixteen, discontented as I was with my parents' apparent indifference to me, those words of my sociology professor gave voice to my sentiments. How old-fashioned was the dead-end attitude of my parents! How ignorant they were of modern thought and progress! The family unit had been China's strength for centuries, but it had also been her weakness, for corruption, nepotism, and greed were all justified in the name of the family's welfare. My new ideas festered; I longed to release them.

One afternoon on a Saturday, which was normally occupied with my housework job, I was unexpectedly released by my employer, who was departing for a country weekend. It was a rare joy to have free time and I wanted to enjoy myself for a change. There had been a Chinese-American boy who shared some classes with me. Sometimes we had found each other walking to the same 8:00 A.M. class. He was not a special boyfriend, but I had enjoyed talking to him and had confided in him some of my problems. Impulsively, I telephoned him. I knew I must be breaking rules, and I felt shy and scared. At the same time, I was excited at this newly found forwardness, with nothing more purposeful than to suggest another walk together.

He understood my awkwardness and shared my anticipation. He asked me to "dress up" for my first movie date. My clothes were limited but I changed to look more graceful in silk stockings and found a bright ribbon for my long black hair. Daddy watched, catching my mood, observing the dashing preparations. He asked me where I was going without his permission and with whom.

I refused to answer him. I thought of my rights! I thought he surely would not try to understand. Thereupon Daddy thundered his displeasure and forbade my departure.

I found a new courage as I heard my voice announce calmly that I was no longer a child, and if I could work my way through college, I would choose my own friends. It was my right as a person.

My mother heard the commotion and joined my father to face me; both appeared shocked and incredulous. Daddy at once demanded the source of this unfilial, non-Chinese theory. And when I quoted my college professor, reminding him that he had always felt teachers should be revered, my father denounced that professor as a foreigner who was disregarding the superiority of our Chinese culture, with its sound family strength. My father did not spare me; I was condemned as an ingrate for echoing dishonorable opinions which should only be temporary whims, yet nonetheless inexcusable.

The scene was not yet over. I completed my proclamation to my father, who had never allowed me to learn how to dance, by adding that I was attending a movie, unchaperoned, with a boy I met at college.

My startled father was sure that my reputation would be subject to whispered innuendos. I must be bent on disgracing the family name; I was ruining my future, for surely I would yield to temptation. My mother underscored him by saying that I hadn't any notion of the problems endured by parents of a young girl.

I would not give in. I reminded them that they and I were not in China, that I wasn't going out with just anybody but someone I trusted! Daddy gave a roar that no man could be trusted, but I devastated them in declaring that I wished the freedom to find my own answers.

Both parents were thoroughly angered, scolded me for being shameless, and predicted that I would some day tell them I was wrong. But I dimly perceived that they were conceding defeat and were perplexed at this breakdown of their training. I was too old to beat and too bold to intimidate.

Respond: Thinking Independently

1. Write your reactions to Wong's essay in your journal. What details of her life struck you as particularly harsh or unfair? In what ways was she fortunate?

2. Write a response statement mentioning one thing you learned about Chinese culture._____

_____

3. In your opinion, is it more difficult for someone growing up in two cultures to establish his or her identity?

Reconsider: Thinking Collaboratively

1. In discussions with your classmates, compare what they thought were the hardships of Wong's life with your responses above. Did they choose different things on which to focus? Why?
2. To what extent does the background that the reader brings to this essay affect the way he or she reacts to it? Does the gender of the reader affect the reaction to the essay?

Review: Thinking Critically

1. What was the role of education in the Wong family? The role of work? The role of the oldest son? What accounts for their importance?
2. How was education personally important to Jade Snow Wong? How did it change her?
3. What is the author's tone or attitude in this essay? That is, is she describing her life objectively, or is she angry, upset, confused, or defiant?
4. Describe the differences between the traditional Chinese way and the American way of education, child raising, social life, etc.

READING TO WRITE

Understanding Description: Using Descriptive Details to Support a Point

Some people think that description means merely using strings of colorful adjectives like the "rainbow-hued craggy cliffs of the Grand Canyon." While such words may be helpful in "painting a picture" in words for the reader to appreciate, description really means more than that. Descriptive details, like examples, SHOW a reader rather than TELL him or her what the author is writing about. When Jade Snow Wong says in her opening sentence that she "was reared according to nineteenth-century ideals of Chinese womanhood," we as readers really need to see what those ideals were and how they were acted upon. So Wong shows us by describing just how a proper lady holds her chopsticks, or pours tea, or speaks. We need details to understand just how long her average day of education was (until 8 on weekdays and 9–12 on Saturdays).

Details help a reader to comprehend fully the author's point. How else can we understand that the oldest brother was privileged than by the details that he alone had his own room and got to keep a German shepherd as his pet?

Most essays, whether classified as narration, examples, or some other category, use descriptive details. For example, notice the description of the cliff walls Momaday uses in his story about the day he climbed the mesa. Such details can be the focus of an essay or remain as an important part of the background. What is important for the writer is to be as specific and clear about what one is writing, so that the reader will understand it clearly also. It may help a writer to pretend that he or she is filming a scene and to put in writing just how the actors and the scene appear in the camera's lens.

Sometimes when we read a writer's description it goes beyond being a good, specific detail or image. It freezes a picture in our minds, as if preserved in ice or crystal. I think of Mark Twain's description in *Huckleberry Finn* of Huck's father's unhealthy pale skin, as "fishbelly white." In Snow Wong's essay, her description of her father and his red wheelbarrow is such a detail. What others do you find?

Writing Applications: Description

1. Describe your relationship with a member of your family as you were growing up. Try to choose details that will show a reader your rivalry with a brother or sister, your conflict with a parent, or some other relationship.
2. Choose a person you know well and try to describe his or her personal qualities (including personal appearance if you wish, but not just that).
3. Describe attitudes toward women in your family, in the schools you attended, or in the workplace. If you are a woman, how do (or did) these attitudes affect your identity? If you are a man, how do (or did) these attitudes affect your identity and your attitudes toward women?

Other Writing Applications

1. If you have firsthand knowledge of someone changing cultures, explain what giving up one culture for another meant to that person.
2. What advantages are there to being "multicultural"?

Daddy Tucked the Blanket

RANDALL WILLIAMS

Preview: Thinking Ahead

Our environment affects our identity because frequently we become what other people think we are. It takes a strong, confident person to hold an opinion of him- or herself different from those around us. Similarly, one's economic position is harder to bear if it is poorer than everyone else's. When older people who lived during the Great Depression are interviewed, they frequently say that while they were poor, they never felt poor because everybody was in the same boat. Randall Williams explains in this 1975 essay what being poor meant to him as he was growing up. Furthermore, he tries to explain poverty's effect on others in his family. As you read, think about how your environment has affected your identity.

About the time I turned 16, my folks began to wonder why I didn't stay home any more. I always had an excuse for them, but what I didn't say was that I had found my freedom and I was getting out.

I went through four years of high school in semirural Alabama and became active in clubs and sports; I made a lot of friends and became a regular guy, if you know what I mean. But one thing was irregular about me: I managed those four years without ever having a friend visit at my house.

I was ashamed of where I lived. I had been ashamed for as long as I had been conscious of class.

We had a big family. There were several of us sleeping in one room, but that's not so bad if you get along, and we always did. As you get older, though, it gets worse.

Being poor is a humiliating experience for a young person trying hard to be accepted. Even now—several years removed—it is hard to talk about. And I resent the weakness of these words to make you feel what it was really like.

We lived in a lot of old houses. We moved a lot because we were always looking for something just a little better than what we had. You have to understand that my folks worked harder than most people. My mother was always at home, but for her that was a full-time job—and no fun, either. But my father worked his head off from the time I can remember in construction and shops. It was hard, physical work.

I tell you this to show that we weren't shiftless. No matter how much money Daddy made, we never made much progress up the social ladder. I got out thanks to a college scholarship and because I was a little more articulate than the average.

I have seen my Daddy wrap copper wire through the soles of his boots to keep them together in the wintertime. He couldn't buy new boots because he had used the money for food and shoes for us. We lived like hell, but we went to school well-clothed and with a full stomach.

It really is hell to live in a house that was in bad shape 10 years before you moved in. And a big family puts a lot of wear and tear on a new house, too, so you can imagine how one goes downhill if it is teetering when you move in. But we lived in houses that were sweltering in summer and freezing in winter. I woke up every morning for a year and a half with plaster on my face where it had fallen out of the ceiling during the night.

This wasn't during the Depression; this was in the late 60's and early 70's.

When we boys got old enough to learn trades in school, we would try to fix up the old houses we lived in. But have you ever tried to paint a wall that crumbled when the roller went across it? And bright paint emphasized the holes in the wall. You end up more frustrated than when you began, especially when you know that at best you might come up with only enough money to improve one of the six rooms in the house. And we might move out soon after, anyway.

The same goes for keeping a house like that clean. If you have a house full of kids and the house is deteriorating, you'll never keep it clean. Daddy used to yell at Mama about that, but she couldn't do anything. I think Daddy knew it inside, but he had to have an outlet for his rage somewhere, and at least yelling isn't as bad as hitting, which they never did to each other.

But you have a kitchen which has no counter space and no hot water, and you will have dirty dishes stacked up. That sounds like an excuse, but try it. You'll go mad from the sheer sense of futility. It's the same thing in a house with no closets. You can't keep clothes clean and rooms in order if they have to be stacked up with things.

Living in a bad house is generally worse on girls. For one thing, they traditionally help their mother with the housework. We boys could get outside and work in the field or cut wood or even play ball and forget about living conditions. The sky was still pretty.

But the girls got the pressure, and as they got older it became worse. Would they accept dates knowing they had to "receive" the young man in a dirty hallway with broken windows, peeling wallpaper and a cracked ceiling? You have to live it to understand it, but it creates a shame which drives the soul of a young person inward.

I'm thankful none of us ever blamed our parents for this, because it would have crippled our relationships. As it worked out, only the relationship between our parents was damaged. And I think the harshness which they expressed to each other was just an outlet to get rid of their anger at the trap their lives were in. It ruined their marriage because they had no one to yell at but each other. I knew other families where the kids got the abuse, but we were too much loved for that.

Once I was about 16 and Mama and Daddy had had a particularly violent argument about the washing machine, which had broken down. Daddy was on the back porch—that's where the only water faucet was—trying to fix it and Mamma had a washtub out there washing school clothes for the next day and they were screaming at each other.

Later that night everyone was in bed and I heard Daddy get up from the couch where he was reading. I looked out from my bed across the hall into their room. He was standing right over Mama and she was already asleep. He pulled the blanket up and tucked it around her shoulders and just stood there and tears were dropping off his cheeks and I thought I could faintly hear them splashing against the linoleum rug.

Now they're divorced.

I had courses in college where housing was discussed, but the sociologists never put enough emphasis on the impact living in substandard housing has on a person's psyche. Especially children's.

Small children have a hard time understanding poverty. They want the same things children from more affluent families have. They want the same things they see advertised on television, and they don't understand why they can't have them.

Other children can be incredibly cruel. I was in elementary school in Georgia—and this is interesting because it is the only thing I remember about that particular school—when I was about eight or nine.

After Christmas vacation had ended, my teacher made each student describe all his or her Christmas presents. I became more and more uncomfortable as the privilege passed around the room toward me. Other children were reciting the names of the dolls they had been given, the kinds of bicycles and the grandeur of their games and toys. Some had lists which seemed to go on and on for hours.

It took me only a few seconds to tell the class that I had gotten for Christmas a belt and a pair of gloves. And then I was laughed at—because I cried—by a roomful of children and a teacher. I never forgave them, and that night I made my mother cry when I told her about it.

In retrospect, I am grateful for that moment, but I remember wanting to die at the time.

Respond: Thinking Independently

1. In your journal write your reaction to Williams's feelings of shame at his family's living conditions.
2. Write a response statement: The part of this essay that affected me most was_____ because _____
   _____.
3. How did you react to the relationship between Williams's parents?
4. What effect do you think that environment has had on your identity?

Reconsider: Thinking Collaboratively

1. Compare the response statements of the class or group. What incidents affected readers most? Why?
2. Besides giving readers an account of his own life, what purpose does Williams seem to have in writing this essay? Why do you think so? That is, what ideas does he mention that go beyond his own life?
3. Do class members agree that "living in a bad house is generally worse on girls"? Why or why not?

Review: Thinking Critically

1. Why does Williams mention his parents' divorce immediately after the incident of tucking the blanket? Why does he use that incident for his title?
2. Why does Williams say at the end of the essay that he is now grateful for the moment in his school when the children and the teacher laughed at his Christmas presents?
3. How different would this essay have been if Williams had written it when he was 16? What advantages are there to writing about events later? What disadvantages are there?

READING TO WRITE

Understanding Examples: Using Inference

Williams uses examples to "show" the audience the poverty of his family. As Russell Baker does, he tries to get the reader to experience what he experienced by picturing the details like the plaster falling in his face each night.

Sometimes when Williams gives us an example of the poverty he lived in he makes an explicit point. For example, he says after explaining that his father worked in construction, "I tell you this to show that we weren't shiftless." Other times, however, Williams chooses not to explain his meaning. He wants readers to draw their own conclusions, to "infer" the meaning from the example. For instance, when his father cried as he tucked the blanket tenderly around his mother, readers may infer that his father cared more for his mother than the frequent fights would indicate, or that he was sorry for yelling at her earlier, or that he was sorry about the broken-down condition of the house, or a number of other things. Inference is powerful because it stimulates a reader's thought and imagination.

Writing Applications: Examples

1. Williams says "I had found my freedom and I was getting out." Many other young people may have done the same thing for quite different reasons. If you separated yourself from your family, write an essay in which you illustrate the conditions that caused you to leave.
2. Write about the relationship between two persons: friends, brother or sister, parents, grandparents, etc. Give examples of incidents or behavior that "show" the relationship instead of just telling the reader that it was loving, argumentative, jealous, etc.

Other Writing Applications

1. Compare the tone of Williams's essay with that of Russell Baker or Jade Snow Wong, who also grew up poor. What attitudes toward their subject matter do the two authors you chose take? Why? How do they convey their different attitudes?

My Papa's Waltz
THEODORE ROETHKE

Preview: Thinking Ahead

The way we view our parents can be mixed, as Randall Williams illustrates in the previous essay. In this 1942 poem by modern American poet Theodore

Roethke, the reader is challenged to interpret the child's view of the father. Since poetry is compressed and the poet does not explain himself or herself at length, readers need to look for "clues" to meaning in the words the poet chooses so carefully. As you read, think about the words describing the father, the mother's reaction, and the dance.

The whiskey on your breath
Could make a small boy dizzy;
But I hung on like death:
Such waltzing was not easy.

We romped until the pans
Slid from the kitchen shelf;
My mother's countenance
Could not unfrown itself.

The hand that held my wrist
Was battered on one knuckle;
At every step you missed
My right ear scraped a buckle.

You beat time on my head
With a palm caked hard by dirt,
Then waltzed me off to bed
Still clinging to your shirt.

Respond: Thinking Independently

1. Record in your journal your first reaction to the relationship between father and child in this poem.
2. What words in the poem created your reaction?
3. Write a response statement: This poem about a child and father shows
   _____.

Reconsider: Thinking Collaboratively

1. Compare views of your classmates. In the past, people have held widely varying views of the relationship shown in this poem. Is that the case in your class? What are the views?
2. What does the class think "I hung on like death" means?
3. What interpretation does the word "romped" prompt?
4. How do class members view "My right ear scraped a buckle" and "You beat time on my head"?

Review: Thinking Critically

1. How does the mother's reaction ("My mother's countenance / Could not unfrown itself") affect your interpretation of the father-child relationship?
2. How do you interpret the last two lines?

READING TO WRITE

Understanding Poetry: Paraphrasing to Appreciate Meaning

One way to appreciate how condensed poetry is is to try to write a prose version of the poem, that is to paraphrase the poet's words in your own sentences. Usually (but not always) the prose version will be much longer than the poem. Try it with this poem. You may wish to work in groups on this task.

What lines or words of the poem took longer for you to express in prose? What words or lines were hard for you to express in your own sentences? Why? What advantage does poetry have in being condensed? What disadvantages does this compression of words have?

Many people express frustration when reading poetry, yet they really like the lyrics of songs (which often are poems set to music). What do you think accounts for this difference in attitude? Bring to class the lyrics of a song you like and attempt to paraphrase it. What does putting the song into sentences do to the song as you think of it?

Writing Applications: Paraphrasing

1. Choose a popular song about some aspect of becoming an adult. Write out the lyrics and then write a prose version of the song.

Other Writing Applications

1. Write an essay about the relationship between the father and child in this poem. Use the lines of the poem to support your interpretation of their relationship.

My Father's Song

SIMON J. ORTIZ

Preview: Thinking Ahead

As you read this poem published in 1988 by Native American writer Simon Ortiz, compare the relationship between father and child with that in the previous poem. Think about the first and last lines of the poem: what connection is there between the speaker's "Wanting to say things" and "my father saying things"?

Wanting to say things,
I miss my father tonight.
His voice, the slight catch,
the depth from his thin chest,

the tremble of emotion
in something he has just said
to his son, his song:

We planted corn one spring at Acu—
we planted several times
but this one particular time
I remember the soft damp sand
in my hand.

My father had stopped at one point
to show me an overturned furrow;
the plowshare had unearthed
the burrow nest of a mouse
in the soft moist sand.

Very gently, he scooped tiny pink animals
into the palm of his hand
and told me to touch them.
We took them to the edge
of the field and put them in the shade
of a sand moist clod.

I remember the very softness
of cool and warm sand and tiny alive mice
and my father saying things.

Respond: Thinking Independently

1. Record in your journal your first reaction to the relationship shown in this poem.
2. What words created your reaction?
3. Write a response statement: This poem about a child and father shows
   _____.
4. Which poem do you think is better? Why?

Reconsider: Thinking Collaboratively

1. Compare reactions with your classmates. Is there more agreement than there was on "My Papa's Waltz"? Why or why not?
2. What does the class think the first and last lines mean?

Review: Thinking Critically

1. What is the importance of the land to the relationship between father and child?
2. What "lesson" has the father taught the child in this incident?
3. Note the words in the poem that seem connected with life or growing things. Make a list of these. What connection do these words have with the overall idea the poet is conveying to the reader?

READING TO WRITE

Understanding Poetry: A Writer's Word Choice

One of the ways poets use language is to choose words that suggest more meanings than just the words themselves. For example, Simon Ortiz uses the word "moist" twice and "damp" once in his poem, both of which mean holding a certain quantity of water. But "moist" and "damp" also relate to the experience of planting corn, or growing things, or the renewal of life. In Theodore Roethke's poem "My Papa's Waltz," we are told that the father's hand "was battered on one knuckle" and had "a palm caked hard by dirt." While these are literal descriptions of the hand, what else do these details possibly show about the father's job or economic status?

Prose writers have more space to explain their thoughts than poets do, but good prose writers strive to make their words count too. There are some memorable phrases in literature as when Mark Twain describes an undertaker as having "no more smile to him than there is to a ham." Trying for the right word is hard work but may bring more clarity or meaning to your writing.

Writing Application: Word Choice

1. We learn much by observing what people do—how they behave. Choose an incident to share that told you a great deal about the person or about life just by indirect observation. Try to choose just the right words to convey behavior through the person's actions.

The Terrible Twenties

DANIEL SMITH-ROWSEY

Preview: Thinking Ahead

Much has been written about the "baby boomers," the generation born just after World War II who were teenagers and college students in the 1960s. Now attention is passing to the boomers' children, whom the media have named "Generation X." In this 1991 essay from Newsweek's *"My Turn" column, Daniel Smith-Rowsey, a 20-year-old college student, criticizes both his and his parents' generations for their concern with "style over substance." Do you agree with his complaints and concerns? What do adults owe the next generation? If you are close to Smith-Rowsey's age, what problems of your generation does he not address? If you are in his parents' generation or older, do you think his criticism is valid?*

Sometimes I wonder what it would be like to have been 20, my age, in the '60s. Back when you could grow up, count on a career and maybe think about buying a house. When one person could expect to be the wage earner for a household.

In the space of one generation those dreams have died. The cost of living has skyrocketed, unemployment has gone up, going to college doesn't guarantee you can get a good job. And no one seems to care. Maybe it's because the only people my age you older people have heard from are those who *do* make a lot of money: investment bankers, athletes, musicians, actors. But more and more of us twentysomethings are underachievers who loaf around the house until well past our college years.

This is an open letter to the baby boomers from the *next* generation. I think it's time we did a little hitting back. Aside from the wealthy, none of you ever told your children, "Someday this will all be yours," and you're the first middle class to fail that way. Did you think we wouldn't care? Thanks a lot. But the real danger lies in the way we've been taught to deal with failure: gloss over and pretend the problem doesn't exist. It's evidence you never taught us to be smart—you only taught us to be young.

We are the stupidist generation in American history, we 20-year-olds. You already know that. We really do get lower SAT scores than our parents. Our knowledge of geography is pathetic, as is our ability with foreign languages and even basic math. We don't read books like you did. We care only about image. We love fads. Talk to college professors, and they'll tell you they don't get intelligent responses like they used to, when you were in school. We're perfectly mush-headed.

You did this to us. You prized your youth so much you made sure ours would be carefree. It's not that you didn't love us; you loved us so much you pushed us to follow your idea of what you were—or would like to have been—instead of teaching us to be responsible. After legitimizing youthful rebellion you never let us have our own innocence—perhaps because Vietnam and Watergate shattered yours. That's why we're already mature enough to understand and worry about racism, the environment, abortion, the homeless, nuclear policy. But we also were fed on the video culture you created to idealize your own irresponsible days of youth. Your slim-and-trim MTV bimbos, fleshy beer commercials and racy TV shows presented adolescence as a time only for fun and sex. Why should we be expected to work at learning anything?

Not that we're not smart—in some ways. We're street smart, David Letterman clever, whizzes at Nintendo. We can name more beers than presidents. Pop culture is, to us, more attractive than education.

I really don't think we can do this dance much longer. Not a single industrialized country has survived since 1945 without a major re-evaluation of its identity except ours. That's what you thought you were doing in the '60s, but soon you gave way to chasing the dreams of the Donald Trump–Michael Milken get-rich-quick ethos—and all you had left for us was a bankrupt economy. The latchkey lifestyle you gave us in the name of your own "freedom" has made us a generation with missing parents and broken homes. And what about the gays and blacks and Hispanics and Asians and women who you pretended to care so much about, and then forgot? It's not that I'm angry at you for selling out to the system. It's that there won't be a system for *me* to sell out to, if I want to. The money isn't there anymore because you spent it all.

To be honest, I can't blame you for all that's happened. The pre-eminence of new technologies and the turn toward cutthroat capitalism over the past two decades would have happened with or without the peculiarities of your generation. If I had been born in the '50s, I too would have been angry at racism and the war in Vietnam. But that's not the same thing as allowing the system to unravel out of my own greed. Don't say you didn't start the fire of selfishness and indulgence, building it up until every need or desire was immediately appeased. Cable TV, BMWs, cellular phones, the whole mall culture has reduced us all to 12-year-olds who want everything *now*. I'm not in love with everything your parents did, but at least they gave you a chance. As Billy Joel said, "Every child has a pretty good shot to get at least as far as their old man got." For most of us, all we've been left with are the erotic fantasies, aggressive tendencies and evanescent funds of youth. Pretty soon we won't have youth *or* money, and that's when we may get a little angry.

Or maybe we won't. Perhaps you really have created a nation of mushheads who will always prefer style over substance, conservative politics and reading lessons. If that's so, the culture can survive, as it seems to be doing with the bright smile of optimism breaking through the clouds of decaying American institutions. And then you really will be the last modern smart generation because our kids will be even dumber, poorer and more violent than us. You guys will be like the old mule at the end of Orwell's "Animal Farm," thinking about how great things used to be when you were kids. You will differ from your own parents in that you will have missed your chance to change the world and robbed us of the skills and money to do it ourselves. If there's any part of you left that still loves us enough to help us, we could really use it. And it's not just your last chance. It's our only one.

Respond: Thinking Independently

1. Daniel Smith-Rowsey makes a number of strong statements. Choose one or more of these to respond to in your journal:
   a. "But the real danger lies in the way we've been taught to deal with failure: gloss over and pretend the problem doesn't exist."
   b. "Your slim-and-trim MTV bimbos, fleshy beer commercials and racy TV shows presented adolescence as a time only for fun and sex. Why should we be expected to work at learning anything?"
   c. "The latchkey lifestyle you gave us in the name of your own 'freedom' has made us a generation with missing parents and broken homes."

    d. ". . . our kids will be even dumber, poorer and more violent than us."

2. Write a response statement: The most interesting/most outrageous remark made by the author was _____ because
_____.

3. Did you recognize yourself or your friends in the writer's remarks, or
does he seem to be talking about another set of people? If so, who?

Reconsider: Thinking Collaboratively

1. Compare journal responses of your classmates to the quotes above.
Does this essay generate sharp disagreement? If so, how do people disagree? If not, on what issues does the class generally agree?

2. If class members could give their parents advice on what they should or
should not have done, what would that advice be? Write down class responses.

Review: Thinking Critically

1. What is the purpose of Smith-Rowsey's essay?

2. If you could ask him to explain one of his statements in more detail
which would it be?

3. For the purposes of his argument, Smith-Rowsey generalizes: "We love
fads." "We're perfectly mush-headed." What dangers are there in making such statements? Why does he do it?

READING TO WRITE

Understanding Argument/Persuasion: The Editorial

Essays that argue a point or attempt to persuade a reader take many
forms. This essay by Daniel Smith-Rowsey is an editorial, a brief opinion essay that makes provocative statements but offers only minimal evidence to
support the statements. The editorial author's aim is to provide a point of
view that will stimulate the reader's thinking, so the statements tend to be
bold and aren't qualified by saying "some," or "30 percent of survey respon-
dents," or "these ideas may be limited to me and my friends." These over-
generalizations would not be appropriate in a research paper or scholarly
article, but they serve Smith-Rowsey's purpose and his audience of
Newsweek "My Turn" readers.

    When you read an editorial in a newspaper or magazine, be particularly
critical of the ideas and recognize that the writer's purpose is to "shake you
up," to get you to think about a situation in a new way.

    Let's examine Smith-Rowsey's organization. He begins with an intro-
duction that contrasts what a 20-year-old in the 1960s could expect (good
job, economic security) with what his generation finds (poor job prospects
for college grads, little security). (Note that he ignores the problem that

loomed for many males in the 1960s—fighting in the Vietnam War. Can you think of a reason he omits that?)

Next, he states his thesis: he's writing a letter to his parents' generation that blames them for their self-centeredness and failure to raise their children (his generation) responsibly. The rest of his editorial shows these failures. Make a list of the faults Smith-Rowsey sees in his parents' generation. Then make a list of what effects these failures have had on him and his friends. Under each item of the list, note what examples or details he uses to convince you that this really is a failure or really has had a bad effect. His last paragraph concludes with the consequences of continuing to ignore his generation. What are they?

Writing Applications: Argument/Persuasion

1. Choose any one of Smith-Rowsey's statements, perhaps one that you wrote about in your journal or one you discussed in class. Decide whether you agree or disagree and present your reasons supported by examples from your own experience. If your instructor agrees, this assignment could be written in teams or small groups.
2. Write an essay discussing the problems your generation has had growing into adulthood.
3. Write an open letter to your parents, praising or criticizing their efforts to raise you.

Teen-agers in Dreamland
Robert J. Samuelson

Preview: Thinking Ahead

You may wish to consider this essay a companion to the previous one by Daniel Smith-Rowsey. Both appeared in Newsweek, *this one in 1989, and both voice concerns with the attitudes and values of young people. Robert Samuelson writes an economics column for* Newsweek *that also appears in many newspapers. Born in 1945, Samuelson received a degree in government from Harvard and began his career as a reporter for* The Washington Post. *As you read, compare his concerns with those of Smith-Rowsey. Does the fact that they are from two generations make a difference? Do the authors seem to agree with each other or do they point to different factors when analyzing the younger generation? Do you think one essay is better than the other?*

Meet Carlos. He's a senior at American High School in Fremont, California. He's also a central character in a recent public television documentary on U.S. education. Carlos is a big fellow with a crew cut and a friendly manner. We see him driving his pickup truck, strolling with a girlfriend and playing in a football game. "I don't want to graduate," he says at one point. "It's fun. I like it."

If you want to worry about our economic future, worry about Carlos and all those like him. It is the problem of adolescence in America. Our teen-agers live in a dreamland. It's a curious and disorienting mixture of adult freedoms and childlike expectations. Hey, why work? Average high school students do less than an hour of daily homework. Naturally, they're not ac-quiring the skills they will need for their well-being and the nation's.

Don't mistake me: I'm not blaming today's teen-agers. They are simply the latest heirs of an adolescent subculture—we have all been part of it—that's been evolving for decades. American children are becoming more and more independent at an earlier and earlier age. By 17, two-fifths of Ameri-cans have their own car or truck. About 60 percent have their own tele-phones and televisions. Adult authority wanes, and teen-age power rises. It's precisely this development that has crippled our schools.

Consider the research of sociologist James Coleman of the University of Chicago. He found that students from similar economic and social back-grounds consistently do better at Catholic high schools than at public high schools. The immediate explanation is simple: students at Catholic schools take more rigorous courses in math, English and history, and they do nearly 50 percent more homework. But why do Catholic schools make these de-mands when public schools don't?

The difference, Coleman concluded, lies with parents. "Parents [of pub-lic school students] do not exercise as much authority over their high-school-aged students as they once did," he recently told a conference at the Manhattan Institute. Since the 1960s, public schools have become less de-manding—in discipline, required course work and homework—because they can't enforce stiffer demands. By contrast, parents of parochial school students impose more control. "The schools therefore [are] able to operate under a different set of ground rules," Coleman said.

There are obviously many good public schools and hard-working stu-dents. But the basic trends are well-established and have been altered only slightly by recent "reforms." Change comes slowly, because stricter acade-mic standards collide with adolescent reality. In the TV documentary, Tony—a pal of Carlos—is asked why he doesn't take tougher math courses to prepare him as a computer technician, which is what he wants to be. "It's my senior year," he says, "and I think I'm going to relax."

Adolescent autonomy continues to increase. "Teens have changed so dramatically in the past decade that more advertisers . . . are targeting 'adults' as 15-plus or 13-plus rather than the typical 18-plus," notes Teenage Research Unlimited, a market research firm. It estimates that the average 16-to-17-year-old has nearly $60 a week in spending money from jobs and allowances. By junior year, more than 40 percent of high school students have jobs.

These demanding school-time jobs are held predominantly by middle-class students. Popular wisdom asserts that early work promotes responsi-bility, but the actual effect may be harmful. In a powerful book ("When

Teenagers Work"), psychologists Ellen Greenberger of the University of California (Irvine) and Laurence Steinberg of Temple University show that jobs hurt academic performance and do not provide needed family income. Rather, they simply establish teen-agers as independent consumers better able to satisfy their own wants. Jobs often encourage drug use.

Our style of adolescence reflects prosperity and our values. We can afford it. In the 19th century, children worked to ensure family survival; the same is true today in many developing countries. Our culture stresses freedom, individuality and choice. Everyone has "rights." Authority is to be questioned. Self-expression is encouraged. These attitudes take root early. My 4-year-old daughter recently announced her philosophy of life: "I should be able to do anything I want to do."

Parental guilt also plays a role. The American premise is that the young ought to be able to enjoy their youth. Schools shouldn't spoil it, as if an hour and a half of daily homework (well above the average) would mean misery for teen-agers. Finally, more divorce and more families with two wage-earners mean that teen-agers are increasingly left to themselves. They often assume some family responsibilities—shopping or caring for younger children. Many teen-agers feel harried and confused, because the conflicts among all these roles (student, worker, child and adult) are overwhelming.

Americans, young and old, delude themselves about the results of these changes. A recent study of 13-year-olds in six countries placed Americans last in mathematics and Koreans first. But when students were asked whether they were "good at mathematics," 68 percent of the Americans said yes (the highest) compared with only 23 percent of the Koreans (the lowest).

This was no quirk. Psychologist Harold Stevenson of the University of Michigan, who has studied American and Asian students for years, finds the same relationship. Americans score lower in achievement but, along with their parents, are more satisfied with their performance. "If children believe they are already doing well—and their parents agree with them— what is the purpose of studying harder?" he writes.

Good question. No one should be surprised that U.S. businesses complain about workers with poor skills, or that a high school diploma no longer guarantees a well-paying job. More school spending or new educational "theories" won't magically give students knowledge or skills. It takes work. Our style of adolescence is something of a national curse. Americans are growing up faster, but they may not be growing up better.

Respond: Thinking Independently

1. Write in your journal what you think of Samuelson's definition of "dreamland" as a "mixture of adult freedoms and childlike expectations."
2. Write a response statement: I agreed/disagreed with Samuelson when he said_____ because _____
   _____.
3. What is your experience with schoolwork, part-time jobs, attitudes toward studying?

Reconsider: Thinking Collaboratively

1. Discuss with your classmates their response statements. Was there general agreement among the students or divergent opinions? Why?
2. What experiences do your classmates have with schoolwork and jobs. Discuss Samuelson's contrast between public and parochial schools—is the difference noted true for the students in your class? If so, do they agree that parents' involvement made the difference or were there other factors?

Review: Thinking Critically

1. Make a list of the studies that Samuelson cites to support his points. Did his use of studies help persuade you to agree with him?
2. Compare your reaction to this essay and the previous one "The Terrible Twenties." Which essay was more convincing?
3. What are the causes Samuelson cites for teenagers living in "dreamland?" What are the effects?

READING TO WRITE

Understanding Causal Analysis: Principles of Cause and Effect

Although we use cause and effect every day to think about our lives, we may not be aware that we are doing so. Take, for example, something simple like being late for class. An instructor may ask, "Why are you late?" You answer, "Because my car wouldn't start this morning, and I had to take a bus."' Your answer, a cause of your lateness, will probably satisfy the instructor. However, you may be thinking, "Why didn't my car start?" That question may set in motion a long investigation of your car's engine, ignition, battery and electrical system, or fuel line to try to determine the cause of that event. If you or your mechanic are successful, you may be able to fix your car so that it will start reliably, and you won't be late to class again. Causes and effects frequently exist in chains—one cause leading to an effect, which in turn causes another effect:

Because your battery was dead, your car did not start. — Because your car would not start, you were late to class. — Because you were late to class, you missed an important explanation and so forth.

The challenge for a writer is to know where in the chain of cause and effect to begin and to be careful to judge causes and effects. Certainly, if you had begun your answer to your instructor about your lateness with a history of your car's problems from the day you purchased it, your answer would have been inappropriately lengthy. However, the mechanic needs that history, but he or she is not interested in the trouble you got into at school because of your lateness. The writer begins the discussion based on his or her purpose (is the cause or effect more important here?) and his or her reader (how far back in the chain of events does the reader need to go to understand your discussion?).

In addition to your decision on where to begin, you need to base your judgment of causes or effects on sound reasoning. Just because your black cat crossed your path that morning would not be sufficient cause for your car not to start. (Superstitions arise from such coincidental events—just because two things follow each other in time, does not necessarily mean that one has caused the other.) Also, discussions of causes and effects may become simple assertions without evidence to back them up. "Because I say so" may be all right for parents to say to their children, but it is not enough for writers trying to convince an audience of readers.

If a reader looks carefully at Robert Samuelson's discussion of American teenagers, he or she will ask if Carlos and Tony are typical, if the studies of working adolescents are well researched, if the culture of teen independence and adult complacency is described accurately. Note how frequently Samuelson refers to expert opinion backed by studies to bolster his assertions. If you took away all of Samuelson's evidence, what would you be left with? You can see that most of an essay's content is in the support or evidence needed to "prove" one's points.

Writing Applications: Causal Analysis

1. Choose one of the following topics and examine the causes or effects (or both) by giving examples from your own experience:
   a. Effects of holding jobs on teenagers
   b. Effects of parochial or private schools versus public schools and reasons (causes) of those effects
   c. Attitudes of teenagers toward selecting courses or studying and why they hold these attitudes
2. a. Look at any major decision in your life and try to determine what caused you to make that decision. Be sure to examine both the immediate causes and the more remote causes for making the decision. For example, suppose you decided to quit a job. The immediate cause may have been a disagreement with the boss, but other factors may have entered in (too much work for too little pay, work interfering with school, dissatisfaction with the type of work, etc.). Try to be as specific as possible in examining the causes for your decision.
   b. Analyze the short- and long-term effects of a decision you have made. For example, if you quit a job, you could briefly mention why (the causes), but then explain the effects (more time for school and friends but less money to fix your car or buy books, resulting in the need to get a loan or eventually find another job).
3. Write a collaborative paper in teams or small groups, comparing classmates' responses to Samuelson's definition of "dreamland" as a "mixture of adult freedoms and childlike expectations." Draw on your journal entries as you write the paper.

Predictable Crises of Adulthood
GAIL SHEEHY

Preview: Thinking Ahead

People struggling to find out who they are may think that they are the only ones struggling with the problem. They may not want to talk about this issue because it is too painful, or because they think it will make them seem weak or not "cool." In her best-selling book Passages *(1976), Gail Sheehy examines what researchers and ordinary people find are the stages of life that most of us experience. Sheehy, a journalist who has written for* New York *Magazine among other publications, increasingly has turned to social and psychological issues. As you read this essay, ask yourself what stage of adult development you are in and how true to your own experience is Sheehy's description of that stage.*

We are not unlike a particularly hardy crustacean. The lobster grows by developing and shedding a series of hard, protective shells. Each time it expands from within, the confining shell must be sloughed off. It is left exposed and vulnerable until, in time, a new covering grows to replace the old.

With each passage from one stage of human growth to the next we, too, must shed a protective structure. We are left exposed and vulnerable—but also yeasty and embryonic again, capable of stretching in ways we hadn't known before. These sheddings may take several years or more. Coming out of each passage, though, we enter a longer and more stable period in which we can expect relative tranquility and a sense of equilibrium regained. . . .

As we shall see, each person engages the steps of development in his or her own characteristic *step-style.* Some people never complete the whole sequence. And none of us "solves" with one step—by jumping out of the parental home into a job or marriage, for example—the problems in separating from the caregivers of childhood. Nor do we "achieve" autonomy once and for all by converting our dreams into concrete goals, even when we attain those goals. The central issues or tasks of one period are never fully completed, tied up, and cast aside. But when they lose their primacy and the current life structure has served its purpose, we are ready to move on to the next period.

Can one catch up? What might look to others like listlessness, contrariness, a maddening refusal to face up to an obvious task may be a person's own unique detour that will bring him out later on the other side. Developmental gains won can later be lost—and rewon. It's plausible, though it can't be proven, that the mastery of one set of tasks fortifies us for the next period and the next set of challenges. But it's important not to think too mechanistically. Machines work by units. The bureaucracy (supposedly) works step by step. Human beings, thank God, have an individual inner dynamic that can never be precisely coded.

Although I have indicated the ages when Americans are likely to go through each stage, and the differences between men and women where they are striking, do not take the ages too seriously. The stages are the thing, and most particularly the sequence.

Here is the briefest outline of the developmental ladder.

Pulling Up Roots

Before 18, the motto is loud and clear: "I have to get away from my parents." But the words are seldom connected to action. Generally still safely part of our families, even if away at school, we feel our autonomy to be subject to erosion from moment to moment.

After 18, we begin Pulling Up Roots in earnest. College, military service, and short-term travels are all customary vehicles our society provides for the first round trips between family and a base of one's own. In the attempt to separate our view of the world from our family's view, despite vigorous protestations to the contrary—"I know exactly what I want!"—we cast about for any beliefs we can call our own. And in the process of testing those beliefs we are often drawn to fads, preferably those most mysterious and inaccessible to our parents.

Whatever tentative memberships we try out in the world, the fear haunts us that we are really kids who cannot take care of ourselves. We cover that fear with acts of defiance and mimicked confidence. For allies to replace our parents, we turn to our contemporaries. They become conspirators. So long as their perspective meshes with our own, they are able to substitute for the sanctuary of the family. But that doesn't last very long. And the instant they diverge from the shaky ideals of "our group," they are seen as betrayers. Rebounds to the family are common between the ages of 18 and 22.

The tasks of this passage are to locate ourselves in a peer group role, a sex role, an anticipated occupation, an ideology or world view. As a result, we gather the impetus to leave home physically and the identity to *begin* leaving home emotionally.

Even as one part of us seeks to be an individual, another part longs to restore the safety and comfort of merging with another. Thus one of the most popular myths of this passage is: We can piggyback our development by attaching to a Stronger One. But people who marry during this time often prolong financial and emotional ties to the family and relatives that impede them from becoming self-sufficient.

A stormy passage through the Pulling Up Roots years will probably facilitate the normal progression of the adult life cycle. If one doesn't have an identity crisis at this point, it will erupt during a later transition, when the penalties may be harder to bear.

The Trying Twenties

The Trying Twenties confront us with the question of how to take hold in the adult world. Our focus shifts from the interior turmoils of late adolescence—"Who am I?" "What is truth?"—and we become almost totally preoccupied with working out the externals. "How do I put my aspirations into effect?" "What is the best way to start?" "Where do I go?" "Who can help me?" "How did *you* do it?"

In this period, which is longer and more stable compared with the passage that leads to it, the tasks are as enormous as they are exhilarating: To shape a Dream, that vision of ourselves which will generate energy, aliveness, and hope. To prepare for a lifework. To find a mentor if possible. And to form the capacity for intimacy, without losing in the process whatever consistency of self we have thus far mustered. The first test structure must be erected around the life we choose to try.

Doing what we "should" is the most pervasive theme of the twenties. The "shoulds" are largely defined by family models, the press of the culture, or the prejudices of our peers. If the prevailing cultural instructions are that one should get married and settle down behind one's own door, a nuclear family is born. If instead the peers insist that one should do one's own thing, the 25-year-old is likely to harness himself onto a Harley-Davidson and burn up Route 66 in the commitment to have no commitments.

One of the terrifying aspects of the twenties is the inner conviction that the choices we make are irrevocable. It is largely a false fear. Change is quite possible, and some alteration of our original choices is probably inevitable.

Two impulses, as always, are at work. One is to build a firm, safe structure for the future by making strong commitments, to "be set." Yet people who slip into a ready-made form without much self-examination are likely to find themselves *locked* in.

The other urge is to explore and experiment, keeping any structure tentative and therefore easily reversible. Taken to the extreme, these are people who skip from one trial job and one limited personal encounter to another, spending their twenties in the *transient* state.

Although the choices of our twenties are not irrevocable, they do set in motion a Life Pattern. Some of us follow the lock-in pattern, others the transient pattern, the wunderkind pattern, the caregiver pattern, and there are a number of others. Such patterns strongly influence the particular questions raised for each person during each passage. . . .

Buoyed by powerful illusions and belief in the power of the will, we commonly insist in our twenties that what we have chosen to do is the one true course in life. Our backs go up at the merest hint that we are like our parents, that two decades of parental training might be reflected in our current actions and attitudes.

"Not me," is the motto, "I'm different."

Catch-30

Impatient with devoting ourselves to the "shoulds," a new vitality springs from within as we approach 30. Men and women alike speak of feeling too narrow and restricted. They blame all sorts of things, but what the restrictions boil down to are the outgrowth of career and personal choices of the twenties. They may have been choices perfectly suited to that stage. But now the fit feels different. Some inner aspect that was left out is striving to be taken into account. Important new choices must be made, and commitments altered or deepened. The work involves great change, turmoil, and often crisis—a simultaneous feeling of rock bottom and the urge to bust out.

One common response is the tearing up of the life we spent most of our twenties putting together. It may mean striking out on a secondary road toward a new vision or converting a dream of "running for president" into a more realistic goal. The single person feels a push to find a partner. The woman who was previously content at home with children chafes to venture into the world. The childless couple reconsiders children. And almost everyone who is married, especially those married for seven years, feels a discontent.

If the discontent doesn't lead to a divorce, it will, or should, call for a serious review of the marriage and of each partner's aspirations in their Catch-30 condition. The gist of that condition was expressed by a 29-year-old associate with a Wall Street law firm:

"I'm considering leaving the firm. I've been there four years now; I'm getting good feedback, but I have no clients of my own. I feel weak. If I wait much longer, it will be too late, too close to that fateful time of decision on whether or not to become a partner. I'm success-oriented. But the concept of being 55 years old and stuck in a monotonous job drives me wild. It drives me crazy now, just a little bit. I'd say that 85 percent of the time I thoroughly enjoy my work. But when I get a screwball case, I come away from court saying, 'What am I doing here?' It's a *visceral* reaction that I'm wasting my time. I'm trying to find some way to make a social contribution or a slot in city government. I keep saying, 'There's something more.'"

Besides the push to broaden himself professionally, there is a wish to expand his personal life. He wants two or three more children. "The concept of a home has become very meaningful to me, a place to get away from troubles and relax. I love my son in a way I could not have anticipated. I never could live alone."

Consumed with the work of making his own critical life-steering decisions, he demonstrates the essential shift at this age: an absolute requirement to be more self-concerned. The self has new value now that his competency has been proved.

His wife is struggling with her own age-30 priorities. She wants to go to law school, but he wants more children. If she is going to stay home, she wants him to make more time for the family instead of taking on even wider professional commitments. His view of the bind, of what he would most like from his wife, is this:

"I'd like not to be bothered. It sounds cruel, but I'd like not to have to worry about what she's going to do next week. Which is why I've told her several times that I think she should do something. Go back to school and get a degree in social work or geography or whatever. Hopefully that would fulfill her, and then I wouldn't have to worry about her line of problems. I want her to be decisive about herself."

The trouble with his advice to his wife is that it comes out of concern with *his* convenience, rather than with *her* development. She quickly picks up on this lack of goodwill: He is trying to dispose of her. At the same time, he refuses her the same latitude to be "selfish" in making an independent decision to broaden her horizons. Both perceive a lack of mutuality. And that is what Catch-30 is all about for the couple.

Rooting and Extending

Life becomes less provisional, more rational and orderly in the early thirties. We begin to settle down in the full sense. Most of us begin putting down roots and sending out new shoots. People buy houses and become very earnest about climbing career ladders. Men in particular concern themselves with "making it." Satisfaction with marriage generally goes downhill in the thirties (for those who have remained together) compared with the highly valued, vision-supporting marriage of the twenties. This coincides with the couple's reduced social life outside the family and the inturned focus on raising their children.

The Deadline Decade

In the middle of the thirties we come upon a crossroads. We have reached the halfway mark. Yet even as we are reaching our prime, we begin to see there is a place where it finishes. Time starts to squeeze.

The loss of youth, the faltering of physical powers we have always taken for granted, the fading purpose of stereotyped roles by which we have thus far identified ourselves, the spiritual dilemma of having no absolute answers—any or all of these shocks can give this passage the character of crisis. Such thoughts usher in a decade between 35 and 45 that can be called the Deadline Decade. It is a time of both danger and opportunity. All of us have the chance to rework the narrow identity by which we defined ourselves in the first half of life. And those of us who make the most of the opportunity will have a full-out authenticity crisis.

To come through this authenticity crisis, we must reexamine our purposes and reevaluate how to spend our resources from now on. "Why am I doing all this? What do I really believe in?" No matter what we have been doing, there will be parts of ourselves that have been suppressed and now need to find expression. "Bad" feelings will demand acknowledgement along with the good.

It is frightening to step off onto the treacherous footbridge leading to the second half of life. We can't take everything with us on this journey through uncertainty. Along the way, we discover that we are alone. We no longer have to ask permission because we are the providers of our own safety. We must learn to give ourselves permission. We stumble upon feminine or masculine aspects of our natures that up to this time have usually been masked. There is grieving to be done because an old self is dying. By taking in our suppressed and even our unwanted parts, we prepare at the gut level for the reintegration of an identity that is ours and ours alone—not some artificial form put together to please the culture of our mates. It is a dark passage at the beginning. But by disassembling ourselves, we can glimpse the light and gather our parts into a renewal.

Women sense this inner crossroads earlier than men do. The time pinch often prompts a woman to stop and take an all-points survey at age 35. Whatever options she has already played out, she feels a "my last chance" urgency to review those options she has set aside and those that aging and biology will close off in the *now foreseeable* future. For all her qualms and confusion about where to start looking for a new future, she usually enjoys an exhilaration of release. Assertiveness begins rising. There are so many firsts ahead.

Men, too, feel the time push in the mid-thirties. Most men respond by pressing down harder on the career accelerator. It's "my last chance" to pull away from the pack. It is no longer enough to be the loyal junior executive, the promising young novelist, the lawyer who does a little *pro bono* work on the side. He wants now to become part of top management, to be recognized as an established writer, or an active politician with his own legislative program. With some chagrin, he discovers that he has been too anxious to please and too vulnerable to criticism. He wants to put together his own ship.

During this period of intense concentration on external advancement, it is common for men to be unaware of the more difficult, gut issues that are propelling them forward. The survey that was neglected at 35 becomes a crucible at 40. Whatever rung of achievement he has reached, the man of 40 usually feels stale, restless, burdened, and unappreciated. He worries about his health. He wonders, "Is this all there is?" He may make a series of departures from well-established lifelong base lines, including marriage. More and more men are seeking second careers in midlife. Some become self-destructive. And many men in their forties experience a major shift of emphasis way from pouring all their energies into their own advancement. A more tender, feeling side comes into play. They become interested in developing an ethical self.

Renewal or Resignation

Somewhere in the mid-forties, equilibrium is regained. A new stability is achieved, which may be more or less satisfying.

If one has refused to budge through the midlife transition, the sense of staleness will calcify into resignation. One by one, the safety and supports will be withdrawn from the person who is standing still. Parents will become children; children will become strangers; a mate will grow away or go away; the career will become just a job—and each of these events will be felt as an abandonment. The crisis will probably emerge again around 50. And although its wallop will be greater, the jolt may be just what is needed to prod the resigned middle-ager toward seeking revitalization.

On the other hand . . .

If we have confronted ourselves in the middle passage and found a renewal of purpose around which we are eager to build a more authentic life structure, these may well be the best years. Personal happiness takes a sharp turn upward for partners who can now accept the fact: "I cannot expect *anyone* to fully understand me." Parents can be forgiven for the burdens of our childhood. Children can be let go without leaving us in collapsed silence. At 50, there is a new warmth and mellowing. Friends become more important than ever, but so does privacy. Since it is so often proclaimed by people past midlife, the motto of this stage might be "No more bullshit."

Respond: Thinking Independently

1. Respond in your journal to Sheehy's statement "With each passage from one stage of human growth to the next we, too, must shed a protective structure. We are left exposed and vulnerable—but also yeasty and embryonic again, capable of stretching in ways we hadn't known before."
2. Write a response statement. One thing I learned from this essay was

   _____.
3. Who among your friends or family can you understand better after reading Sheehy's essay?

Reconsider: Thinking Collaboratively

1. In your class, examine one stage of development per group. Have class members write down all the examples of their experience that confirms what Sheehy is saying about that stage and all those that go against what she is saying. Then compare your finding with the other groups in a class discussion.

Review: Thinking Critically

1. Sheehy explains in the third and fourth paragraphs that these stages are typical but not absolute for all humans. Why does she mention that? If she had not included these paragraphs, what effect would it have had on her essay?
2. This chapter in *Passages* is followed by chapters devoted to each stage. What would you expect each of those later chapters to include? Why do you think Sheehy decided to give an overview in an early chapter if she has later chapters on each stage?

READING TO WRITE

Understanding Classification: Principles of Classifying Objects or Groups

We are overwhelmed with information and things. Each day as we shop for necessities such as groceries or clothing, or consider big-ticket items like a television set or car, or even read a newspaper, if we couldn't organize everything into sets or groups, we might never finish our tasks. For example, suppose the supermarket where you buy food had no way of organizing the canned goods? The soup could be next to the applesauce and next to that could be a can of soda and then perhaps a can of corn. Worse, the bread could be next to the lettuce, the meat in the dairy case, etc. There could be no signs over the aisles telling you what was on those shelves. In the newspaper, the comics could be next to the front page headlines and the weather next to the baseball scores.

Fortunately, we have ways to prevent such confusion. We classify items into groups so that we can find them and understand their relationship to each other. In the newspaper, sports are on the sports pages, and all the classified ads are in one place. In the grocery store, the canned goods are grouped into fruits, vegetables, prepared foods, etc., and the other items have their own places.

Classification works for ideas too. We group data into related sets, helping us to see relationships. For example, methods of governing can be classified according to who holds the power (democracy, monarchy, autocracy). In this essay Gail Sheehy classified developmental patterns of adults into several more easily explained stages. It is important for writers to classify according to the same principle and to make reasonably sure that all members of a group belong to one of the classifications. It would not be good to classify college students into freshmen, sophomores, and math majors, for instance, since those categories are based on different principles (year in school and the chosen major) and would not include all students. But colleges can (and do) classify students into liberal arts, education, science, and engineering, with subclassifications under each of these major areas.

Once the classification categories are established, writers use examples to explain the feature of each category or compare and contrast categories or use some other rhetorical technique to write about each one.

Writing Applications: Classification

1. Take any one of Gail Sheehy's crises, such as "Pulling up Roots" or "The Deadline Decade," and classify responses to this crisis among people you know. In other words, examine a group of people from this age group and explain their responses to the challenge of this age in categories that a reader will easily understand.
2. Thinking about the students at your college, can you classify them into any groups based on their attitudes or activities that would help an outsider to understand them better?
   a. Horror movies—are there different kinds?
   b. Customers you see at your job.
   c. Bosses you have had.

Where Are You Going, Where Have You Been?
JOYCE CAROL OATES

Preview: Thinking Ahead

This 1967 short story got its start, according to the contemporary American writer Joyce Carol Oates, from a true incident. In her hands, the story takes on symbolic overtones of innocence and evil. Connie, a typical teenager, part of America's mall culture, suddenly is faced with some terrifying choices. As you read, notice how Oates creates the characters of Connie and Arnold Friend.

For Bob Dylan

Her name was Connie. She was fifteen and she had a quick, nervous giggling habit of craning her neck to glance into mirrors or checking other people's faces to make sure her own was all right. Her mother, who noticed everything and knew everything and who hadn't much reason any longer to look at her own face, always scolded Connie about it. "Stop gawking at yourself. Who are you? You think you're so pretty?" she would say. Connie would raise her eyebrows at these familiar old complaints and look right through her mother, into a shadowy vision of herself as she was right at that moment: she knew she was pretty and that was everything. Her mother had been pretty once, too, if you could believe those old snapshots in the album, but now her looks were gone and that was why she was always after Connie.

"Why don't you keep your room clean like your sister? How've you got your hair fixed—what the hell stinks? Hair spray? You don't see your sister using that junk."

Her sister June was twenty-four and still lived at home. She was a secretary in the high school Connie attended, and if that wasn't bad enough—with her in the same building—she was so plain and chunky and steady that Connie had to hear her praised all the time by her mother and her mother's sisters. June did this, June did that, she saved money and helped clean the house and cooked and Connie couldn't do a thing, her mind was all filled with trashy daydreams. Their father was away at work most of the time and when he came home he wanted supper and he read the newspaper at supper and after supper he went to bed. He didn't bother talking much to them, but around his bent head Connie's mother kept picking at her until Connie wished her mother was dead and she herself was dead and it was all over. "She makes me want to throw up sometimes," she complained to her friends. She had a high, breathless, amused voice that made everything she said sound a little forced, whether it was sincere or not.

There was one good thing: June went places with girl friends of hers, girls who were just as plain and steady as she, and so when Connie wanted to do that her mother had no objections. The father of Connie's best girl friend drove the girls the three miles to town and left them at a shopping plaza so they could walk through the stores or go to a movie, and when he came to pick them up again at eleven he never bothered to ask what they had done.

They must have been familiar sights, walking around the shopping plaza in their shorts and flat ballerina slippers that always scuffed the sidewalk, with charm bracelets jingling on their thin wrists; they would lean together to whisper and laugh secretly if someone passed who amused or interested them. Connie had long dark blond hair that drew anyone's eye to it, and she wore part of it pulled up on her head and puffed out and the rest of it she let fall down her back. She wore a pull-over jersey blouse that looked one way when she was at home and another way when she was away from home. Everything about her had two sides to it, one for home and one for anywhere that was not home: her walk, which could be childlike and bobbing, or languid enough to make anyone think she was hearing music in her head; her mouth, which was pale and smirking most of the time, but bright and pink on these evenings out; her laugh, which was cynical and drawling at home—"Ha, ha, very funny,"—but high-pitched and nervous anywhere else, like the jingling of the charms on her bracelet.

Sometimes they did go shopping or to a movie, but sometimes they went across the highway, ducking fast across the busy road, to a drive-in restaurant where older kids hung out. The restaurant was shaped like a big bottle, though squatter than a real bottle, and on its cap was a revolving figure of a grinning boy holding a hamburger aloft. One night in midsummer they ran across, breathless with daring, and right away someone leaned out a car window and invited them over, but it was just a boy from high school they didn't like. It made them feel good to be able to ignore him. They went up through the maze of parked and cruising cars to the bright-lit, fly-infested restaurant, their faces pleased and expectant as if they were entering a sacred building that loomed up out of the night to give them what haven and blessing they yearned for. They sat at the corner and crossed their legs at the ankles, their thin shoulders rigid with excitement, and listened to the music that made everything so good: the music was always in the background, like music at a church service; it was something to depend upon.

A boy named Eddie came in to talk with them. He sat backwards on his stool, turning himself jerkily around in semi-circles and then stopping and turning back again, and after a while he asked Connie if she would like something to eat. She said she would and so she tapped her friend's arm on her way out—her friend pulled her face up into a brave, droll look—and Connie said she would meet her at eleven, across the way. "I just hate to leave her like that," Connie said earnestly, but the boy said that she wouldn't be alone for long. So they went out to his car, and on the way Connie couldn't help but let her eyes wander over the windshields and faces all around her, her face gleaming with a joy that had nothing to do with Eddie or even this place; it might have been the music. She drew her shoulders up and sucked in her breath with the pure pleasure of being alive, and just at that moment she happened to glance at a face just a few feet from hers. It was a boy with shaggy black hair, in a convertible jalopy painted gold. He stared at her and then his lips widened into a grin. Connie slit her eyes at him and turned away, but she couldn't help glancing back and there he was, still watching her. He wagged a finger and laughed and said, "Gonna get you, baby," and Connie turned away again without Eddie noticing anything.

She spent three hours with him, at the restaurant where they ate hamburgers and drank Cokes in wax cups that were always sweating, and then down an alley a mile or so away, and when he left her off at five to eleven only the movie house was still open at the plaza. Her girl friend was there, talking with a boy. When Connie came up, the two girls smiled at each other and Connie said, "How was the movie?" and the girl said, "*You* should know." They rode off with the girl's father, sleepy and pleased, and Connie couldn't help but look back at the darkened shopping plaza with its big empty parking lot and its signs that were faded and ghostly now, and over at the drive-in restaurant where cars were still circling tirelessly. She couldn't hear the music at this distance.

Next morning June asked her how the movie was and Connie said, "So-so."

She and that girl and occasionally another girl went out several times a week, and the rest of the time Connie spent around the house—it was summer vacation—getting in her mother's way and thinking, dreaming about the boys she met. But all the boys fell back and dissolved into a single face that was not even a face but an idea, a feeling, mixed up with the urgent insistent pounding of the music and the humid night air of July. Connie's mother kept dragging her back to the daylight by finding things for her to do or saying suddenly, "What's this about the Pettinger girl?"

And Connie would say nervously, "Oh, her. That dope." She always drew thick clear lines between herself and such girls, and her mother was simple and kind enough to believe it. Her mother was so simple, Connie thought, that it was maybe cruel to fool her so much. Her mother went scuffling around the house in old bedroom slippers and complained over the telephone to one sister about the other, then the other called up and the two of them complained about the third one. If June's name was mentioned her mother's tone was approving, and if Connie's name was mentioned it was disapproving. This did not really mean she disliked Connie, and actually Connie thought that her mother preferred her to June just because she was prettier, but the two of them kept up a pretense of exasperation, a sense that they were tugging and struggling over something of little value to either of them. Sometimes, over coffee, they were almost friends, but something would come up—some vexation that was like a fly buzzing suddenly around their heads—and their faces went hard with contempt.

One Sunday Connie got up at eleven—none of them bothered with church—and washed her hair so that it could dry all day long in the sun. Her parents and sister were going to a barbecue at an aunt's house and Connie said no, she wasn't interested, rolling her eyes to let her mother know just what she thought of it. "Stay home alone then," her mother said sharply. Connie sat out back in a lawn chair and watched them drive away, her father quiet and bald, hunched around so that he could back the car out, her mother with a look that was still angry and not at all softened through the windshield, and in the back seat poor old June, all dressed up as if she didn't know what a barbecue was, with all the running yelling kids and the flies. Connie sat with her eyes closed in the sun, dreaming and dazed with the warmth about her as if this were a kind of love, the caresses of love, and her mind slipped over onto thoughts of the boy she had been with the night before and how nice he had been, how sweet it always was, not the way someone like June would suppose but sweet, gentle, the way it was in movies and promised in songs; and when she opened her eyes she hardly knew where she was, the back yard ran off into weeds and a fence-like line of trees and behind it the sky was perfectly blue and still. The asbestos "ranch house" that was now three years old startled her—it looked small. She shook her head as if to get awake.

It was too hot. She went inside the house and turned on the radio to drown out the quiet. She sat on the edge of the bed, barefoot, and listened for an hour and a half to a program called XYZ Sunday Jamboree, record after record of hard, fast, shrieking songs she sang along with, interspersed by exclamations from "Bobby King": "An' look here, you girls at Napoleon's—Son and Charley want you to pay real close attention to this song coming up!"

And Connie paid close attention herself, bathed in a glow of slow-pulsed joy that seemed to rise mysteriously out of the music itself and lay languidly about the airless little room, breathed in and breathed out with each gentle rise and fall of her chest.

After a while she heard a car coming up the drive. She sat up at once, startled, because it couldn't be her father so soon. The gravel kept crunching all the way in from the road—the driveway was long—and Connie ran to the window. It was a car she didn't know. It was an open jalopy, painted a bright gold that caught the sunlight opaquely. Her heart began to pound and her fingers snatched at her hair, checking it, and she whispered, "Christ. Christ," wondering how bad she looked. The car came to a stop at the side door and the horn sounded four short taps, as if this were a signal Connie knew.

She went into the kitchen and approached the door slowly, then hung out the screen door, her bare toes curling down off the step. There were two boys in the car and now she recognized the driver: he had shaggy, shabby black hair that looked crazy as a wig and he was grinning at her.

'I ain't late, am I?" he said.

"Who the hell do you think you are?" Connie said.

"Toldja I'd be out, didn't I?"

"I don't even know who you are."

She spoke sullenly, careful to show no interest or pleasure, and he spoke in a fast, bright monotone. Connie looked past him to the other boy, taking her time. He had fair brown hair, with a lock that fell onto his forehead. His sideburns gave him a fierce, embarrassed look, but so far he hadn't even bothered to glance at her. Both boys wore sunglasses. The driver's glasses were metallic and mirrored everything in miniature.

"You wanta come for a ride?" he asked.

Connie smirked and let her hair fall loose over one shoulder.

"Don'tcha like my car? New paint job," he said. "Hey."

"What?"

"You're cute."

She pretended to fidget, chasing flies away from the door.

"Don'tcha believe me, or what?" he said.

"Look, I don't even know who you are," Connie said in disgust.

"Hey, Ellie's got a radio, see. Mine broke down." He lifted his friend's arm and showed her the little transistor radio the boy was holding, and now Connie began to hear the music. It was the same program that was playing inside the house.

"Bobby King?" she said.

"I listen to him all the time. I think he's great."

"He's kind of great," Connie said reluctantly.

"Listen, that guy's *great*. He knows where the action is."

Connie blushed a little, because the glasses made it impossible for her to see just what this boy was looking at. She couldn't decide if she liked him or if he was just a jerk, and so she dawdled in the doorway and wouldn't come down or go back inside. She said, "What's all that stuff painted on your car?"

"Can'tcha read it?" He opened the door very carefully, as if he were afraid it might fall off. He slid out just as carefully, planting his feet firmly on the ground, the tiny metallic world in his glasses slowing down like gelatin hardening, and in the midst of it Connie's bright green blouse. "This here is my name, to begin with," he said. ARNOLD FRIEND was written in tarlike black letters on the side, with a drawing of a round, grinning face that reminded Connie of a pumpkin, except it wore sunglasses. "I wanta introduce myself, I'm Arnold Friend and that's my real name and I'm gonna be your friend, honey, and inside the car's Ellie Oscar, he's kinda shy." Ellie brought his transistor radio up to his shoulder and balanced it there. "Now, these numbers are a secret code, honey." Arnold Friend explained. He read off the numbers 33, 19, 17 and raised his eyebrows at her to see what she thought of that, but she didn't think much of it. The left rear fender had been smashed and around it was written, on the gleaming gold background: DONE BY CRAZY WOMAN DRIVER. Connie had to laugh at that. Arnold Friend was pleased at her laughter and looked up at her. "Around the other side's a lot more—you wanta come and see them?"

"No."

"Why not?"

"Why should I?"

"Don'tcha wanta see what's on the car? Don'tcha wanta go for a ride?"

"I don't know."

"Why not?"

"I got things to do."

"Like what?"

"Things."

He laughed as if she had said something funny. He slapped his thighs. He was standing in a strange way, leaning back against the car as if he were balancing himself. He wasn't tall, only an inch or so taller than she would be if she came down to him. Connie liked the way he was dressed, which was the way all of them dressed: tight faded jeans stuffed into black, scuffed boots, a belt that pulled his waist in and showed how lean he was, and a white pull-over shirt that was a little soiled and showed the hard small muscles of his arms and shoulders. He looked as if he probably did hard work, lifting and carrying things. Even his neck looked muscular. And his face was a familiar face, somehow: the jaw and chin and cheeks slightly darkened because he hadn't shaved for a day or two, and the nose long and hawklike, sniffing as if she were a treat he was going to gobble up and it was all a joke.

"Connie, you ain't telling the truth. This is your day set aside for a ride with me and you know it," he said, still laughing. The way he straightened and recovered from his fit of laughing showed that it had been all fake.

"How do you know what my name is?" she said suspiciously.

"It's Connie."

"Maybe and maybe not."

"I know my Connie," he said, wagging his finger. Now she remembered him even better, back at the restaurant, and her cheeks warmed at the thought of how she had sucked in her breath just at the moment she passed him—how she must have looked to him. And he had remembered her. "Ellie and I come out here especially for you," he said. "Ellie can sit in back. How about it?"

"Where?"

"Where what?"

"Where're we going?"

He looked at her. He took off the sunglasses and she saw how pale the skin around his eyes was, like holes that were not in shadow but instead in light. His eyes were like chips of broken glass that catch the light in an amiable way. He smiled. It was as if the idea of going for a ride somewhere, to someplace, was a new idea to him.

"Just for a ride, Connie sweetheart."

"I never said my name was Connie," she said.

"But I know what it is. I know your name and all about you, lots of things," Arnold Friend said. He had not moved yet but stood still leaning back against the side of his jalopy. "I took a special interest in you, such a pretty girl, and found out all about you—like I know your parents and sister are gone somewheres and I know where and how long they're going to be gone, and I know who you were with last night, and your best girl friend's name is Betty. Right?"

He spoke in a simple lilting voice, exactly as if he were reciting the words to a song. His smile assured her that everything was fine. In the car Ellie turned up the volume of his radio and did not bother to look around at them.

"Ellie can sit in the back seat," Arnold Friend said. He indicated his friend with with a casual jerk of his chin, as if Ellie did not count and she should not bother with him.

"How'd you find out all that stuff?" Connie said.

"Listen: Betty Schultz and Tony Fitch and Jimmy Pettinger and Nancy Pettinger," he said in a chant. "Raymond Stanley and Bob Hutter—"

"Do you know all those kids?"

"I know everybody."

"Look, you're kidding. You're not from around here."

"Sure."

"But—how come we never saw you before?"

"Sure you saw me before," he said. He looked down at his boots, as if he were a little offended. "You just don't remember."

"I guess I'd remember you," Connie said.

"Yeah?" He looked up at this, beaming. He was pleased. He began to mark time with the music from Ellie's radio, tapping his fists lightly together. Connie looked away from his smile to the car, which was painted so bright it almost hurt her eyes to look at it. She looked at that name, ARNOLD FRIEND. And up at the front fender was an expression that was familiar—MAN THE FLYING SAUCERS. It was an expression kids had used the year before but didn't use this year. She looked at it for a while as if the words meant something to her that she did not yet know.

"What're you thinking about? Huh?" Arnold Friend demanded. "Not worried bout your hair blowing around in the car, are you?"

"No."

"Think I maybe can't drive good?"

"How do I know?"

"You're a hard girl to handle. How come?" he said. "Don't you know I'm your friend? Didn't you see me put my sign in the air when you walked by?"

"What sign?"

"My sign." And he drew an X in the air, leaning out toward her. They were maybe ten feet apart. After his hand fell back to his side the X was still in the air, almost visible. Connie let the screen door close and stood perfectly still inside it, listening to the music from her radio and the boy's blend together. She stared at Arnold Friend. He stood there so stiffly relaxed, pretending to be relaxed, with one hand idly on the door handle as if he were keeping himself up that way and had no intention of ever moving again. She recognized most things about him, the tight jeans that showed his thighs and buttocks and the greasy leather boots and the tight shirt, and even that slippery friendly smile of his, that sleepy dreamy smile that all the boys used to get across ideas they didn't want to put into words. She recognized all this and also the sing-song way he talked, slightly mocking, kidding, but serious and a little melancholy, and she recognized the way he tapped one fist against the other in homage to the perpetual music behind him. But all these things did not come together.

She said suddenly, "Hey, how old are you?"

His smile faded. She could see then that he wasn't a kid, he was much older—thirty, maybe more. At this knowledge her heart began to pound faster.

"That's a crazy thing to ask. Can'tcha see I'm your own age?"

"Like hell you are."

"Or maybe a coupla years older. I'm eighteen."

"Eighteen?" she said doubtfully.

He grinned to reassure her and lines appeared at the corners of his mouth. His teeth were big and white. He grinned so broadly his eyes became slits and she saw how thick the lashes were, thick and black as if painted with a black tarlike material. Then, abruptly, he seemed to become embarrassed and looked over his shoulder at Ellie. "*Him*, he's crazy," he said. "Ain't he a riot? He's a nut, a real character." Ellie was still listening to the music. His sunglasses told nothing about what he was thinking. He wore a bright orange shirt unbuttoned halfway to show his chest, which was a pale, bluish chest and not muscular like Arnold Friend's. His shirt collar was turned up all around and the very tips of the collar pointed out past his chin as if they were protecting him. He was pressing the transistor radio up against his ear and sat there in a kind of daze, right in the sun.

"He's kinda strange," Connie said.

"Hey, she says you're kinda strange! Kinda strange!" Arnold Friend cried. He pounded on the car to get Ellie's attention. Ellie turned for the first time and Connie saw with shock that he wasn't a kid either—he had a fair, hairless face, cheeks reddened slightly as if the veins grew too close to the surface of his skin, the face of a forty-year-old baby. Connie felt a wave of dizziness rise in her at this sight and she stared at him as if waiting for something to change the shock at the moment, make it all right again. Ellie's lips kept shaping words, mumbling along with the words blasting in his ear.

"Maybe you two better go away," Connie said faintly.

"What? How come?" Arnold Friend cried. "We come out here to take you for a ride. It's Sunday." He had the voice of the man on the radio now. It was the same voice, Connie thought. "Don'tcha know it's Sunday all day? And honey, no matter who you were with last night, today you're with Arnold Friend and don't you forget it! Maybe you better step out here," he said, and this last was in a different voice. It was a little flatter, as if the heat was finally getting to him.

"No. I got things to do."

"Hey."

"You two better leave."

"We ain't leaving until you come with us."

"Like hell I am—"

"Connie, don't fool around with me. I mean—I mean, don't fool *around*," he said, shaking his head. He laughed incredulously. He placed his sunglasses on top of his head, carefully, as if he were indeed wearing a wig, and brought the stems down behind his ears. Connie stared at him, another wave of dizziness and fear rising in her so that for a moment he wasn't even in focus but was just a blur standing there against his gold car, and she had the idea that he had driven up the driveway all right but had come from nowhere before that and belonged nowhere and that everything about him and even about the music that was so familiar to her was only half real.

"If my father comes and sees you—"

"He ain't coming. He's at a barbecu."

"How do you know that?"

"Aunt Tillie's. Right now they're—uh—they're drinking. Sitting around," he said vaguely, squinting as if he were staring all the way to town and over to Aunt Tillie's back yard. Then the vision seemed to get clear and he nodded energetically. "Yeah. Sitting around. There's your sister in a blue dress, huh? And high heels, the poor sad bitch—nothing like you, sweetheart! And your mother's helping some fat woman with the corn, they're cleaning the corn—husking the corn—"

"What fat woman?" Connie cried.

"How do I know what fat woman, I don't know every goddamn fat woman in the world!" Arnold Friend laughed.

"Oh, that's Mrs. Hornsby. . . . Who invited her?" Connie said. She felt a little lighthearted. Her breath was coming quickly.

"She's too fat. I don't like them fat. I like them the way you are, honey," he said, smiling sleepily at her. They stared at each other for a while through the screen door. He said softly, "Now, what you're going to do is this: you're going to come out that door. You're going to sit up front with me and Ellie's going to sit in the back, the hell with Ellie, right? This isn't Ellie's date. You're my date. I'm your lover, honey."

"What? You're crazy—"

"Yes, I'm your lover. You don't know what that is but you will," he said. "I know that too. I know all about you. But look: it's real nice and you couldn't ask for nobody better than me, or more polite. I always keep my word. I'll tell you how it is, I'm always nice at first, the first time. I'll hold you so tight you won't think you have to try to get away or pretend anything because you'll know you can't. And I'll come inside you where it's all secret and you'll give in to me and you'll love me—"

"Shut up! You're crazy!" Connie said. She backed away from the door. She put her hands up against her ears as if she'd heard something terrible, something not meant for her. "People don't talk like that, you're crazy," she muttered. Her heart was almost too big for her chest and its pumping made sweat break out all over her. She looked out to see Arnold Friend pause and then take a step toward the porch, lurching. He almost fell. But, like a clever drunken man, he managed to catch his balance. He wobbled in his high boots and grabbed hold of one of the porch posts.

"Honey?" he said. "You still listening?"

"Get the hell out of here!"

"Be nice, honey. Listen."

"I'm going to call the police—"

He wobbled again and out of the side of his mouth came a fast spat curse, an aside not meant for her to hear. But even this "Christ!" sounded forced. Then he began to smile again. She watched this smile come, awkward as if he were smiling from inside a mask. His whole face was a mask, she thought wildly, tanned down to his throat but then running out as if he had plastered make-up on his face but had forgotten about his throat.

"Honey—? Listen, here's how it is. I always tell the truth and I promise you this: I ain't coming in that house after you."

"You better not! I'm going to call the police if you—if you don't—"

"Honey," he said, talking right through her voice, "honey, I'm not coming in there but you are coming out here. You know why?"

She was panting. The kitchen looked like a place she had never seen before, some room she had run inside but that wasn't good enough, wasn't going to help her. The kitchen window had never had a curtain, after three years, and there were dishes in the sink for her to do—probably—and if you ran your hand across the table you'd probably feel something sticky there.

"You listening honey? Hey?"

"—going to call the police—"

"Soon as you touch the phone I don't need to keep my promise and can come inside. You won't want that."

She rushed forward and tried to lock the door. Her fingers were shaking. "But why lock it," Arnold Friend said gently, talking right into her face. "It's just a screen door. It's just nothing." One of his boots was at a strange angle, as if his foot wasn't in it. It pointed out to the left, bent at the ankle. "I mean, anybody can break through a screen door and glass and wood and iron or anything else if he needs to, anybody at all, and especially Arnold Friend. If the place got lit up with a fire, honey, you'd come runnin' out into my arms, right into my arms an' safe at home—like you knew I was your lover and'd stopped fooling around. I don't mind a nice shy girl but I don't like no fooling around." Part of those words were spoken with a slight rhythmic lilt, and Connie somehow recognized them—the echo of a song from last year, about a girl rushing into her boy friend's arms and coming home again—

Connie stood barefoot on the linoleum floor, staring at him. "What do you want?" she whispered.

"I want you," he said.

"What?"

"Seen you that night and thought, that's the one, yes sir. I never needed to look anymore."

"But my father's coming back. He's coming to get me. I had to wash my hair first—" She spoke in a dry, rapid voice, hardly raising it for him to hear.

"No, your daddy is not coming and yes, you had to wash your hair and you washed it for me. It's nice and shining and all for me. I thank you sweetheart," he said with a mock bow, but again he almost lost his balance. He had to bend and adjust his boots. Evidently his feet did not go all the way down; the boots must have been stuffed with something so that he would seem taller. Connie stared out at him and behind him at Ellie in the car, who seemed to be looking off toward Connie's right, into nothing. This Ellie said, pulling the words out of the air one after another as if he were just discovering them, "You want me to pull out the phone?"

"Shut your mouth and keep it shut," Arnold Friend said, his face red from bending over or maybe from embarrassment because Connie had seen his boots. "This ain't none of your business."

"What—what are you doing? What do you want?" Connie said. "If I call the police they'll get you, they'll arrest you—"

"Promise was not to come in unless you touch that phone, and I'll keep that promise," he said. He resumed his erect position and tried to force his shoulders back. He sounded like a hero in a movie, declaring something important. But he spoke too loudly and it was as if he were speaking to someone behind Connie. "I ain't made plans for coming in that house where I don't belong but just for you to come out to me, the way you should. Don't you know who I am?"

"You're crazy," she whispered. She backed away from the door but did not want to go into another part of the house, as if this would give him permission to come through the door. "What do you . . . you're crazy, you. . . ."

"Huh? What're you saying, honey?"

Her eyes darted everywhere in the kitchen. She could not remember what it was, this room.

"This is how it is, honey: you come out and we'll drive away, have a nice ride. But if you don't come out we're gonna wait till your people come home and then they're all going to get it."

"You want that telephone pulled out?" Ellie said. He held the radio away from his ear and grimaced, as if without the radio the air was too much for him.

"I toldja shut up, Ellie," Arnold Friend said, "you're deaf, get a hearing aid, right? Fix yourself up. This little girl's no trouble and she's gonna be nice to me, so Ellie keep to yourself, this ain't your date—right? Don't hem in on me, don't hog, don't crush, don't bird dog, don't trail me," he said in a rapid, meaningless voice, as if he were running through all the expressions he'd learned but was no longer sure which of them was in style, then rushing on to new ones, making them up with his eyes closed. "Don't crawl under my fence, don't squeeze in my chipmunk hole, don't sniff my glue, suck my popsicle, keep your own greasy fingers on yourself!" He shaded his eyes and peered in at Connie, who was backed against the kitchen table. "Don't mind him, honey, he's just a creep. He's a dope. Right? I'm the boy for you and like I said, you come out here nice like a lady and give me your hand, and nobody else gets hurt, I mean, your nice old bald-headed daddy and your mummy and your sister in her high heels. Because listen: why bring them in this?"

"Leave me alone," Connie whispered.

"Hey, you know that old woman down the road, the one with the chickens and stuff—you know her?"

"She's dead!"

"Dead? What? You know her?" Arnold Friend said.

"She's dead—"

"Don't you like her?"

"She's dead—she's—she isn't here any more—"

"But don't you like her, I mean, you got something against her? Some grudge or something?" Then his voice dipped as if he were conscious of a rudeness. He touched the sunglasses perched up on top of his head as if to make sure they were still. "Now, you be a good girl."

"What are you going to do?"

"Just two things, or maybe three," Arnold Friend said. "But I promise it won't last long and you'll like me the way you get to like people you're close to. You will. It's all over for you here, so come on out. You don't want your people in any trouble, do you?"

She turned and bumped against a chair or something, hurting her leg, but she ran into the back room and picked up the telephone. Something roared in her ear, a tiny roaring, and she was so sick with fear that she could do nothing but listen to it—the telephone was clammy and very heavy and her fingers groped down the dial but were too weak to touch it. She began to scream into the phone, into the roaring. She cried out, she cried for her mother, she felt her breath start jerking back and forth in her lungs as if it were something Arnold Friend was stabbing her with again and again with no tenderness. A noisy sorrowful wailing rose all about her and she was locked inside it the way she was locked inside this house.

After a while she could hear again. She was sitting on the floor with her wet back against the wall.

Arnold Friend was saying from the door, "That's a good girl. Put the phone back."

She kicked the phone away from her.

"No, honey. Pick it up. Put it back right."

She picked it up and put it back. The dial tone stopped.

"That's a good girl. Now, you come outside."

She was hollow with what had been fear but what was now just an emptiness. All that screaming had blasted it out of her. She sat, one leg cramped under her, and deep inside her brain was something like a pinpoint of light that kept going and would not let her relax. She thought, I'm not going to see my mother again. She thought, I'm not going to sleep in my bed again. Her bright green blouse was all wet.

Arnold Friend said, in a gentle-loud voice that was like a stage voice, "The place where you came from ain't there any more, and where you had in mind to go is cancelled out. This place you are now—inside your daddy's house—is nothing but a cardboard box I can knock down any time. You know that and always did know it. You hear me?"

She thought, I have got to think. I have got to know what to do.

"We'll go out to a nice field, out in the country here where it smells so nice and it's sunny," Arnold Friend said. "I'll have my arms tight around you so you won't need to try to get away and I'll show you what love is like, what it does. The hell with this house! It looks solid all right," he said. He ran a fingernail down the screen and the noise did not make Connie shiver, as it would have the day before. "Now, put your hand on your heart, honey. Feel that? That feels solid too but we know better. Be nice to me, be sweet like you can because what else is there for a girl like you but to be sweet and pretty and give in?—and get away before her people come back?"

She felt her pounding heart. Her hand seemed to enclose it. She thought for the first time in her left that it was nothing that was hers, that belonged to her, but just a pounding, living thing inside this body that wasn't really hers either.

"You don't want them to get hurt," Arnold Friend went on. "Now, get up, honey. Get up all by yourself."

She stood.

"Now, turn this way. That's right. Come over here to me.—Ellie, put that away, didn't I tell you? You dope. You miserable creepy dope," Arnold Friend said. His words were not angry but only part of an incantation. The incantation was kindly. "Now, come out through the kitchen to me, honey, and let's see a smile, try it, you're a brave, sweet little girl and now they're eating corn and hot dogs cooked to bursting over an outdoor fire, and they don't know one thing about you and never did and honey, you're better than them because not a one of them would have done this for you."

Connie felt the linoleum under her feet; it was cool. She brushed her hair back out of her eyes. Arnold Friend let go of the post tentatively and opened his arms for her, his elbows pointing in toward each other and his wrists limp, to show that this was an embarrassed embrace and a little mocking, he didn't want to make her self-conscious.

She put out her hand against the screen. She watched herself push the door slowly open as if she were back safe somewhere in the other doorway, watching this body and this head of long hair moving out into the sunlight where Arnold Friend waited.

"My sweet little blue-eyed girl," he said in a half-sung sigh that had nothing to do with her brown eyes but was taken up just the same by the vast sunlit reaches of the land behind him and on all sides of him—so much land that Connie had never seen before and did not recognize except to know that she was going to it.

Respond: Thinking Independently

1. Record in your journal what you thought of Connie at first? Did your opinion change by the end of the story?
2. How did you react to Arnold Friend at first? Did your opinion change by the end of the story?
3. Ask a question about the story to be answered in group discussion:

   _____

4. How does popular music or other aspects of "teen" culture figure in the story?

Reconsider: Thinking Collaboratively

1. Pool your questions from above and work on answers to them in groups or as a class.
2. After thinking about the story, who or what do you and your classmates think Arnold Friend is? List all his qualities and talents.
3. Arnold tells Connie at the end that "you're better than them because not one of them [her family] would have done this for you." What is she doing and why?

Review: Thinking Critically

1. Writers frequently give hints of what is to follow, called foreshadowing. What foreshadowing does Oates do in this story?
2. What does the title mean?
3. Do you think the story is realistic? Symbolic? Both?
4. Could the story have ended another way? How?

READING TO WRITE

Understanding Fiction: Introducing Point of View

When we read a short story or novel, as the Introduction indicates, we pay attention to who is telling the story, the narrator. This is called the point of view. We can tell from the first words in Oates's story that the story is in third person (she) rather than being told in first person by Connie herself (I). With this point of view, Oates is free to comment on what the characters do and why: "Everything about her had two sides to it, one for home and one for anywhere that was not home. . . ." However, Oates only follows Connie in this way. The reader does not get the mother's or father's or June's thoughts. An active reader might consider what the story would have been like if another point of view had been used. What would be the effect, for example, if Arnold Friend had told the story in first person or if he were the central focus instead of Connie? As disturbing as the story is, would Arnold's point of view have made it more so?

Writing Applications

1. How do you think teen culture—music, malls, fast food restaurants—affects teens' maturing and achieving identity?
2. All of us make choices—of friends, jobs, schools. Write about a good or bad choice you have made and why.

TWO

On the Outside Looking In: Achieving Identity as a Member of a Minority Group

As hard as it is to establish one's identity as a adult, being a member of a minority group may make it even harder. As many people know from experience, American society creates special burdens for members of ethnic minorities such as African Americans, Asian Americans, Hispanics, and Native Americans and for people who are physically or mentally handicapped in some way.

People often define other people as if they were cast in a mold—a stereotype. So we hear "blond" jokes, assuming that everyone with blond hair is stupid. We also stereotype ethnic and racial groups. Think of the labels we put on Irish, Italian, Polish, Jewish, Puerto Rican, Mexican, African, or Asian Americans. Why we do this is complex. Perhaps we fear a group different from our own, so we label it in some negative way to control our fear. Maybe we don't understand another group, so we seize on one instance of someone's behavior and make it stand for the whole group. At the turn of the century, for example, when many Irish immigrants crowded into American cities, living in poor, unclean tenements, the stereotype of "dirty Irishmen" sprang up. The stereotype, which ignored poverty as the cause of some people's uncleanliness, generalized that characteristic and applied it to the whole group, the majority of whom were quite clean. Finally, stereotyping may be a way to make ourselves feel superior by downgrading someone else.

There also are the burdens of outright discrimination or discrimination from members of one's own minority group, who impose their own ideas of group identity on individuals striving to achieve their unique place in the society.

The authors in this chapter reflect these problems from Roger Hernadez's reminder that all people with Spanish surnames do not hold the same values or beliefs to William Raspberry's warning that African Americans should not accept the definition of what constitutes "white" or "black" abilities.

As you read these selections, try to enter the experience of the authors, which may enlarge your perceptions of the challenges faced by many different minority group members to achieve identity.

Theme for English B
LANGSTON HUGHES

Preview: Thinking Ahead

Langston Hughes, whom we last met in the selection "Salvation," was a highly influential African American poet. This poem may have been written at Columbia University in New York, during the year Hughes attended that school (1920). In 1929 he graduated from Lincoln University after spending some time at sea on a ship's crew and in Europe working at odd jobs, but always writing poetry. He was actually "discovered" as a poet twice, but the time that he, as a waiter in a Washington, D.C. hotel, served some poems along with dinner to famous poet Vachel Lindsay is the most well-known incident. Lindsay read the poems at his own poetry reading, praising Hughes, and newspapers picked up the story.

As you read the poem, think about the conflict of a student writing for a teacher, a black person writing of his or her experience to a white person, and also about how one person's life can become part of another person's life.

The instructor said,

> *Go home and write*
> *a page tonight.*
> *And let that page come out of you—*
> *Then, it will be true.*

I wonder if it's that simple?
I am twenty-two, colored, born in Winston-Salem.
I went to school there, then Durham, then here
to this college on the hill above Harlem.
I am the only colored student in my class.
The steps from the hill lead down into Harlem,
through a park, then I cross St. Nicholas,
Eighth Avenue, Seventh, and I come to the Y,
the Harlem Branch Y, where I take the elevator
up to my room, sit down, and write this page:

It's not easy to know what is true for you or me
at twenty-two, my age. But I guess I'm what
I feel and see and hear. Harlem, I hear you:
hear you, hear me—we two—you, me, talk on this page.
(I hear New York, too.) Me—who?

Well, I like to eat, sleep, drink, and be in love.
I like to work, read, learn, and understand life.
I like a pipe for a Christmas present,
or records—Bessie, bop, or Bach.
I guess being colored doesn't make me *not* like
the same things other folks like who are other races.
So will my page be colored that I write?
Being me, it will not be white.
But it will be
a part of you, instructor.
You are white—
yet a part of me, as I am a part of you.
That's American.
Sometimes perhaps you don't want to be a part of me.
Nor do I often want to be a part of you.
But we are, that's true!
As I learn from you,
I guess you learn from me—
although you're older—and white—
and somewhat more free.

This is my page for English B.

Respond: Thinking Independently

1. In your journal, write a brief prose summary of the poem as you read it.
2. Write a response statement: I agree/disagree with Hughes when he says
   _____.
3. What do you think the instructor in the poem can learn from the student and the student from the instructor?

Reconsider: Thinking Collaboratively

1. In groups, read your summaries to each other. Are the summaries similar or do they vary considerably? If they vary, how are they different? Why? When writers summarize, they pick out the most important features, as they see it. Therefore, a summary, though supposedly objective, is also interpretive.
2. Discuss Hughes's lines "Sometimes perhaps you don't want to be a part of me./Nor do I often want to be a part of you./But we are, that's true!" Is he just talking about the student and the teacher or larger elements of society? Do you agree with him?

Review: Thinking Critically

1. Lines 16–20 in stanza 2 are likely to puzzle many readers. What do you think the speaker is saying here?
   Note that before this is some personal background of the speaker (not Hughes himself since he was born in Missouri and went to high school

in Cleveland, Ohio). This first section ends with the speaker sitting down to "write this page." Perhaps, put yourself in the student-speaker's position. You have been given a theme assignment for English class and go home and begin to write. What does your first effort look like?

2. Note that the lines giving the assignment at the beginning of the poem rhyme and the lines at the end of the poem rhyme, while much of the rest of the poem has an irregular rhyme scheme. Why does the poet write it that way?

3. In line 33 the speaker says "That's American." What does he mean?

READING TO WRITE

Understanding Poetry: Figurative Language

Because poets must compress their language to express their thoughts, they frequently use words to suggest more than the literal meaning of the word. For example, when Langston Hughes says that for English B, "So will my page be colored that I write," he doesn't necessarily mean that it will be green, or yellow, or pink, but that it will represent his African American heritage and culture. ("Colored" was an accepted term for African American at the time Hughes was writing.) Similarly, when Hughes uses the expression "I am a part of you," he does not mean literally or physically a part of the other person, but that figuratively the lives of all Americans impact on each other, no matter to what race or ethnic group they belong. Figurative language can be hard to understand, but it contributes to the poem's ability to express much in just a few words.

Writing Applications

1. Write about how an older person, whether a teacher, neighbor, or family member, became "a part of you."

2. Discuss a unique part of your cultural heritage, whether music, religion, food, holidays, or some other feature, and how it is tied to your identity.

3. Write about a time when you felt discouraged or about a time when you "beat the odds" and triumphed over difficult circumstances. Be sure to tell what the situation was and account for your feelings of discouragement or triumph.

The Lesson

TONI CADE BAMBARA

Preview: Thinking Ahead

Fiction can allow us to get inside the head of someone who is as far from our own identity as possible, or allow us to find a kindred spirit, that is, a person just like us with the same beliefs and experiences. So a deskbound accountant can temporarily become a master spy like James Bond, or a high school student can find a person just as confused as he is in the character of Holden Caulfield. In this 1972 story, Toni Cade Bambara creates a young female narrator who tells the story of her trip to F.A.O. Schwartz, a famous toy store in New York, in colorful street language. Whether you know many characters like this one or this is your first meeting, try to appreciate what the character tells you about herself and also what she doesn't tell you but that you figure out by her actions and reactions. In this way, determine who or what the narrator thinks she is.

Back in the days when everyone was old and stupid or young and foolish and me and Sugar were the only ones just right, this lady moved on our block with nappy hair and proper speech and no makeup. And quite naturally we laughed at her, laughed the way we did at the junk man who went about his business like he was some big-time president and his sorry-ass horse his secretary. And we kinda hated her too, hated the way we did the winos who cluttered up our parks and pissed on our handball walls and stank up our hallways and stairs so you couldn't halfway play hide-and-seek without a goddamn gas mask. Miss Moore was her name. The only woman on the block with no first name. And she was black as hell, cept for her feet, which were fish-white and spooky. And she was always planning these boring-ass things for us to do, us being my cousin, mostly, who lived on the block cause we all moved North the same time and to the same apartment then spread out gradual to breathe. And our parents would yank our heads into some kinda shape and crisp up our clothes so we'd be presentable for travel with Miss Moore, who always looked like she was going to church, though she never did. Which is just one of things the grownups talked about when they talked behind her back like a dog. But when she came calling with some sachet she'd sewed up or some gingerbread she'd made or some book, why then they'd all be too embarrassed to turn her down and we'd get handed over all spruced up. She'd been to college and said it was only right that she should take responsibility for the young ones' education, and she not even related by marriage or blood. So they'd go for it. Specially Aunt Gretchen. She was the main gofer in the family. You got some ole dumb shit foolishness you want somebody to go for, you send for Aunt Gretchen. She been screwed into the go-along for so long, it's a blood-deep natural thing with her. Which is how she got saddled with me and Sugar and Junior in the first place while our mothers were in a la-de-da apartment up the block having a good ole time.

So this one day Miss Moore rounds us all up at the mailbox and it's puredee hot and she's knockin herself out about arithmetic. And school suppose to let up in summer I heard, but she don't never let up. And the starch in my pinafore scratching the shit outta me and I'm really hating this nappy-head bitch and her goddamn college degree. I'd much rather go to the pool or to the show where it's cool. So me and Sugar leaning on the mailbox being surly, which is a Miss Moore word. And Flyboy checking out what everybody brought for lunch. And Fat Butt already wasting his peanut-butter-and-jelly sandwich like the pig he is. And Junebug punchin on Q.T.'s arm for potato chips. And Rosie Giraffe shifting from one hip to the other waiting for somebody to step on her foot or ask her if she from Georgia so she can kick ass, preferably Mercedes'. And Miss Moore asking us do we know what money is, like we a bunch of retards. I mean real money, she say, like it's only poker chips or monopoly papers we lay on the grocer. So right away I'm tired of this and say so. And would much rather snatch Sugar and go to the Sunset and terrorize the West Indian kids and take their hair ribbons and their money too. And Miss Moore files that remark away for next week's lesson on brotherhood, I can tell. And finally I say we oughta get to the subway cause it's cooler and besides we might meet some cute boys. Sugar done swiped her mama's lipstick, so we ready.

So we heading down the street and she's boring us silly about what things cost and what our parents make and how much goes for rent and how money ain't divided up right in this country. And then she gets to the part about we all poor and live in the slums, which I don't feature. And I'm ready to speak on that, but she steps out in the street and hails two cabs just like that. Then she hustles half the crew in with her and hands me a five-dollar bill and tells me to calculate 10 percent tip for the driver. And we're off. Me and Sugar and Junebug and Flyboy hangin out the window and hollering to everybody, putting lipstick on each other cause Flyboy a faggot anyway, and making farts with our sweaty armpits. But I'm mostly trying to figure how to spend this money. But they all fascinated with the meter ticking and Junebug starts laying bets as to how much it'll read when Flyboy can't hold his breath no more. Then Sugar lays bets as to how much it'll be when we get there. So I'm stuck. Don't nobody want to go for my plan, which is to jump out at the next light and run off to the first bar-b-que we can find. Then the driver tells us to get the hell out cause we there already. And the meter reads eight-five cents. And I'm stalling to figure out the tip and Sugar say give him a dime. And I decide he don't need it bad as I do, so later for him. But then he tries to take off with Junebug foot still in the door so we talk about his mama something ferocious. Then we check out that we on Fifth Avenue and everybody dressed up in stockings. One lady in a fur coat, hot as it is. White folks crazy.

"This is the place," Miss Moore say, presenting it to us in the voice she uses at the museum. "Let's look in the windows before we go in."

"Can we steal?" Sugar asks very serious like she's getting the ground rules squared away before she plays. "I beg your pardon," say Miss Moore, and we fall out. So she leads us around the windows of the toy store and me and Sugar screamin, "This is mine, that's mine, I gotta have that, that was made for me, I was born for that," till Big Butt drowns us out.

'Hey, I'm goin to buy that there."

"That there? You don't even know what it is, stupid."

"I do so," he say punchin on Rosie Giraffe. "It's a microscope."

"Whatcha gonna do with a microscope, fool?"

"Look at things."

"Like what, Ronald?" ask Miss Moore. And Big Butt ain't got the first notion. So here go Miss Moore gabbing about the thousands of bacteria in a drop of water and the somethinorother in a speck of blood and the million and one living things in the air around us is invisible to the naked eye. And what she say that for? Junebug go to town on that "naked" and we rolling. Then Miss Moore ask what it cost. So we all jam into the window smudgin it up and the price tag say $300. So then she ask how long'd take for Big Butt and Junebug to save up their allowances. "Too long," I say. "Yeh," adds Sugar, "outgrown it by that time." And Miss Moore say no, you never outgrow learning instruments. "Why, even medical students and interns and," blah, blah, blah. And we ready to choke Big Butt for bringing it up in the first damn place.

"This here costs four hundred eighty dollars," say Rosie Giraffe. So we pile up all over her to see what she pointin out. My eyes tell me it's a chunk of glass cracked with something heavy, and different-color inks dripped into the splits, then the whole thing put into a oven or something. But for $480 it don't make sense.

"That's a paperweight made of semi-precious stones fused together under tremendous pressure," she explains slowly, with her hands doing the mining and all the factory work.

"So what's a paperweight?" ask Rosie Giraffe.

"To weigh paper with, dumbell," say Flyboy, the wise man from the East.

"Not exactly," say Miss Moore, which is what she say when you warm or way off too. "It's to weigh paper down so it won't scatter and make your desk untidy." So right away me and Sugar curtsy to each other and then to Mercedes who is more the tidy type.

"We don't keep paper on top of the desk in my class," say Junebug, figuring Miss Moore crazy or lyin one.

"At home, then," she say. "Don't you have a calendar and a pencil case and a blotter and a letter-opener on your desk at home where you do your homework?" And she know damn well what our homes look like cause she nosys around in them every chance she gets.

"I don't even have a desk," say Junebug. "Do we?"

"No. And I don't get no homework neither," say Big Butt.

"And I don't even have a home," say Flyboy like he do at school to keep the white folks off his back and sorry for him. Send this poor kid to camp posters, is his specialty.

"I do," says Mercedes. "I have a box of stationery on my desk and a picture of my cat. My godmother bought the stationery and the desk. There's a big rose on each sheet and the envelopes smell like roses."

"Who wants to know about your smelly-ass stationery," say Rosie Giraffe fore I can get my two cents in.

"It's important to have a work area all your own so that . . ."

"Will you look at this sailboat, please," say Flyboy, cuttin her off and pointin to the thing like it was his. So once again we tumble all over each other to gaze at this magnificent thing in the toy store which is just big enough to maybe sail two kittens across the pond if you strap them to the post tight. We all start reciting the price tag like we in assembly. "Hand-crafted sailboat of fiberglass at one thousand one hundred ninety-five dollars."

"Unbelievable," I hear myself say and am really stunned. I read it again for myself just in case the group recitation put me in a trance. Same thing. For some reason this pisses me off. We look at Miss Moore and she lookin at us, waiting for I dunno what.

"Who'd pay all that when you can buy a sailboat set for a quarter at Pop's, a tube of glue for a dime, and a ball of string for eight cents? It must have a motor and a whole lot else besides," I say. "My sailboat cost me about fifty cents."

"But will it take water?" say Mercedes with her smart ass.

"Took mine to Alley Pond Park once," say Flyboy. "String broke, Lost it. Pity."

"Sailed mine in Central Park and it keeled over and sank. Had to ask my father for another dollar."

"And you got the strap," laugh Big Butt. "The jerk didn't even have a string on it. My old man wailed on his behind."

Little Q.T. was staring hard at the sailboat and you could see he wanted it bad. But he too little and somebody's just take it from him. So what the hell. "This boat for kids, Miss Moore?"

"Parents silly to buy something like that just to get all broke up," say Rosie Giraffe.

"That much money it should last forever," I figure.

"My father'd buy it for me if I wanted it."

"Your father, my ass," say Rosie Giraffe getting a chance to finally push Mercedes.

"Must be rich people shop here," say Q.T.

"You are a very bright boy," say Flyboy. "What was your first clue?" And he rap him on the head with the back of his knuckles, since Q.T. the only one he could get away with. Though Q.T. liable to come up behind you years later and get his licks in when you half expect it.

"What I want to know is," I says to Miss Moore though I never talk to her, I wouldn't give the bitch that satisfaction, "is how much a real boat costs? I figure a thousand'd get you a yacht any day."

"Why don't you check that out," she says, "and report back to the group?" Which really pains my ass. If you gonna mess up a perfectly good swim day least you could do is have some answers. "Let's go in," she say like she got something up her sleeve. Only she don't lead the way. So me and Sugar turn the corner to where the entrance is, but when we get there I kinda hang back. Not that I'm scared, what's there to be afraid of, just a toy store. But I feel funny, shame. But what I got to be shamed about? Got as much right to go in as anybody. But somehow I can't seem to get hold of the door, so I step away for Sugar to lead. But she hangs back too. And I look at her and she looks at me and this is ridiculous. I mean, damn, I have never ever been shy about doing nothing or going nowhere. But then Mercedes steps up and then Rosie Giraffe and Big Butt crowd in behind and shove, and next thing we all stuffed intot he doorway with only Mercedes squeezing past us, smoothing out her jumper and walking right down the aisle. Then the rest of us tumble in like a glued-together jigsaw done all wrong. And people lookin at us. And it's like the time me and Sugar crashed into the Catholic church on a dare. But once we got in there and everything so hushed and holy and the candles and the bowin and the handkerchiefs on all the drooping heads, I just couldn't go though with the plan. Which was for me to run up to the alter and do a tap dance while Sugar played the nose flute and messed around in the holy water. And Sugar kept givin me the elbow. Then later teased me so bad I tied her up in the shower and turned it on and locked her in. And she'd be there till this day if Aunt Gretchen hadn't finally figured I was lyin about the boarder taking a shower.

Same thing in the store. We all walkin on tiptoe and hardly touchin the games and puzzles and things. And I watched Miss Moore who is steady watchin us like she waitin for a sign. Like Mama Drewery watches the sky and sniffs the air and takes note of just how much slant is in the bird formation. Then me and Sugar bump smack into each other, so busy gazing at the toys, 'specially the sailboat. But we don't laugh and go into our fat-lady bump-stomach routine. We just stare at that price tag. Then Sugar run a finger over the whole boat. And I'm jealous and want to hit her. Maybe not her, but I sure want to punch somebody in the mouth.

"Watcha bring us here for, Miss Moore?"

"You sound angry, Sylvia. Are you mad about something?" Givin me one of them grins like she tellin a grown-up joke that never turns out to be funny. And she's lookin very closely at me like maybe she plannin to do my portrait from memory. I'm mad, but I won't give her that satisfaction. So I slouch around the store bein very bored and say, "Let's go."

Me and Sugar at the back of the train watchin the tracks whizzin by large then small then gettin gobbled up in the dark. I'm thinkin about this tricky toy I saw in the store. A clown that somersaults on a bar then does chin-ups just cause you yank lightly at his leg. Cost $35. I could see me askin my mother for a $35 birthday clown. "You wanna who that costs what?"she'd say, cocking her head to the side to get a better view of the hole in my head. Thirty-five dollars could buy new bunk beds for Junior and Gretchen's boy. Thirty-five dollars and the whole household could go visit Granddaddy Nelson in the country. Thirty-five dollars would pay for the rent and the piano bill too. Who are these people that spend that much for performing clowns and $1,000 for toy sailboats? What kinda work they do and how they live and how come we ain't in on it? Where we are is who we are, Miss Moore always pointin out. But it don't necessarily have to be that way, she always adds then waits for somebody to say that poor people have to wake up and demand their share of the pie and don't none of us know what kind of pie she talkin about in the first damn place. But she ain't so smart cause I still got her four dollars from the taxi and she sure ain't gettin it. Messin up my day with this shit. Sugar nudges me in my pocket and winks.

Miss Moore lines us up in front of the mailbox where we started from, seem like years ago, and I got a headache for thinkin so hard. And we lean all over each other so we can hold up under the draggy-ass lecture she always finishes us off with at the end before we thank her for borin us to tears. But she just looks at us like she readin tea leaves. Finally she say, "Well, what did you think of F.A.O. Schwartz?"

Rosie Giraffe mumbles, "White folks crazy."

"I'd like to go there again when I get my birthday money," says Mercedes, and we shove her out the pack so she has to lean on the mailbox by herself.

"I'd like a shower. Tiring day," say Flyboy.

The Sugar surprises me by sayin, "You know, Miss Moore, I don't think all of us here put together eat in a year what that sailboat costs." And Miss Moore lights up like somebody goosed her. "And?" she say, urging Sugar on. Only I'm standin on her foot so she don't continue.

"Imagine for a minute what kind of society it is in which some people can spend on a toy what it would cost to feed a family of six or seven. What do you think?"

"I think," say Sugar pushing me off her feet like she never done before, cause I whip her ass in a minute, "that this is not much of a democracy if you ask me. Equal chance to pursue happiness means an equal crack at the dough, don't it?" Miss Moore is besides herself and I am disgusted with Sugar's treachery. So I stand on her foot one more time to see if she'll shove me. She shuts up, and Miss Moore looks at me, sorrowfully I'm thinkin. And somethin weird is goin on, I can feel it in my chest.

"Anybody else learn anything today?" lookin dead at me. I walk away and Sugar has to run to catch up and don't even seem to notice when I shrug her arm off my shoulder.

"Well, we got four dollars anyway," she says.

"Uh hunh."

"We could go to Hascombs and get half a chocolate layer and then go to the Sunset and still have plenty money for potato chips and ice-cream sodas."

"Uh hunh."

"Race you to Hascombs," she say.

We start down the block and she gets ahead which is O.K. by me cause I'm goin to the West End and then over to the Drive to think this day through. She can run if she want to and even run faster. But ain't nobody gonna beat me at nuthin.

Respond: Thinking Independently

1. Write your reactions to Sylvia, the narrator, in your journal.
2. Write a response statement: I laughed when I read _____
   _____. I was puzzled by _____
   _____.

3. How did you view Miss Moore?

Reconsider: Thinking Collaboratively

1. Discuss opinions of the narrator in your class. How much did they vary? Why? What did some class members value? Was Sylvia only the way she appeared to be from her tough talk? How do you know?
2. How did class members see Miss Moore? Why was she taking the children on these excursions?
3. Why does the narrator let Sugar run ahead of her at the end of the story?
4. Why is the story entitled "The Lesson"?

Review: Thinking Critically

1. What does Sylvia resent about Miss Moore?
2. How do Sugar and the other children react to Miss Moore?
3. What is Sylvia's reaction to F.A.O. Schwartz? What does it mean when she says, "And somethin weird is goin on, I can feel it in my chest."
4. What do think of Miss Moore's taking the children to the toy store when they can't afford to buy any of the toys?
5. How do you react to the narrator's statement, "But ain't nobody gonna beat me at nuthin"?

READING TO WRITE

Understanding Fiction: Using the First Person Point of View

In Joyce Carol Oates's story "Where Are You Going? Where Have You Been?" the narration was in third person (she), although it followed only Connie's actions and thoughts. In "The Lesson," the reader is treated to a first person story (I), told from the point of view of a young African American girl in her own language. This point of view offers the advantage of putting the reader directly in the action of the story ("Then we check out that we on Fifth Avenue and everybody dressed up in stockings."). The reader also learns what Sylvia thinks, but only what she is willing to say to herself. So we learn at the end of the story what the narrator feels when she says "I am disgusted with Sugar's treachery," but we don't know what Sylvia means exactly when she says, "And something weird is goin on, I can feel it in my chest," because the narrator herself doesn't know why she feels that way. We as readers have to interpret her remarks.

Writing Applications: First Person

1. Describe an incident that happened to you as a child in the first person as the child sees it.

Other Writing Applications

1. Compare the way you experienced an incident as a child with the way you see that event now. Does it have greater or lesser importance now? Why?

2. Explain what lesson Miss Moore was trying to teach the children. Was her method effective, cruel, necessary? Consider in your essay the reactions of several of the children, not just Sylvia.

Knoxville, Tennessee
NIKKI GIOVANNI

Preview: Thinking Ahead

Our cultures are composed of many elements. Some issues like religion or political beliefs are so important to us that we may fight over them. But some aspects of culture are small, warm, comforting things like a homemade peach pie sitting on a grandmother's windowsill. In this 1968 poem by African American poet, essayist, and recording artist Nikki Giovanni, the joys of a summer at home are part of the speaker's culture. Giovanni, author of Grand Mothers: Poems, Reminiscences, and Short Stores About the Keeping of Our Traditions, *wishes for us to celebrate our diverse cultures.*

I always like summer
best
you can eat fresh corn
from daddy's garden
and okra
and greens
and cabbage
and lots of
barbecue
and buttermilk
and homemade ice-cream
at the church picnic
and listen to
gospel music
outside
at the church
homecoming
and go to the mountains with
your grandmother
and go barefooted
and be warm
all the time
not only when you go to bed
and sleep

Respond: Thinking Independently

1. Record your reactions to the things the speaker likes in this poem and make a list of your own "summer bests."
2. Write a response statement to the poem: _____
_____.

Reconsider: Thinking Collaboratively

1. Share your list of summer bests with your classmates. What foods are on the list? Are they tied to your culture?

Review: Thinking Critically

1. Look at the arrangement of the poem. Why do you think so many lines start with "and"?
2. As you read the poem aloud, does it sound like a person of any particular age? Why or why not?

READING TO WRITE

Understanding Poetry: Free Verse

As you read Nikki Giovanni's poem, you notice that the poem is strung out on the page like a list, not clustered in groups of two or four lines or some other pattern of lines that rhyme. Poets call this "free verse," a flexible form that doesn't conform to any particular pattern of line length, rhyme, or rhythm. An advantage of free verse is the ability to put words exactly where one wishes to without worry about fitting them in to a rhyme scheme or line length. As a result, we should look carefully at Giovanni's placement of words. What words does she put all alone on a line? Do the words "best," "barbecue," and "outside" have important meaning in her poem? Also notice how she ends each line before she breaks and goes to the next line. What is the effect that accumulates from each of the summer things she mentions?

Not all poets like free verse, in part because it is unconventional. Poet Robert Frost said, "Writing free verse is like playing tennis without a net." He preferred the challenge of writing within certain patterns. After reading several different poetic forms, form your own opinion of free verse.

Writing Applications

1. Describe a cultural event or celebration or simply a family gathering.
2. What universal feelings does Giovanni evoke in this poem? That is, though the details may be about a specific place, what feeling does a reader respond to that could trigger a memory of quite another place?

Back Again, Home
DON L. LEE

Preview: Thinking Ahead

The stress of being a minority member in a majority culture may take several forms. As you read the following poem published in 1969 by African American poet Don Lee, try to identify the stress the speaker is under and what his reaction is to that stress. Think about how the speaker is viewed by those in the majority culture.

(confessions of an ex-executive)

Pains of insecurity surround me;
    shined shoes,
    conservative suits,
    button down shirts with silk ties.
    bi-weekly payroll.

Ostracized, but not knowing why;
    executive haircut,
    clean shaved,
    "yes" instead of "yeah" and "no" instead of "naw",
    hours, nine to five. (after five he's alone)

"Doing an excellent job, keep it up;"
    promotion made—semi-monthly payroll,
    very quiet—never talks,
    budget balanced—saved the company money,
    quality work—production tops.
    He looks sick. (but there is a smile in his eyes)

He resigned, we wonder why;
    let his hair grow—a mustache too,
    out of a job—broke and hungry,
    friends are coming back—bring food,
    not quiet now—trying to speak,
    what did he say?

    "Back Again,

        BLACK AGAIN,

            Home."

Respond: Thinking Independently

1. What surprised you about this poem? Record your reaction in your journal.

2. Write a response statement: Home for the speaker of the poem meant
_____.

3. Have you ever been an outsider (for any reason)? Record your thoughts on why you were an outsider and how it made you feel.

Reconsider: Thinking Collaboratively

1. Discuss why the speaker resigned his job. Compare classmates' reactions to his resignation.
2. Is there anything people at his workplace could have done? Why didn't they do it?
3. What are the effects of being an outsider?

Review: Thinking Critically

1. The poet uses dashes frequently in this poem. Why? Do dashes create a certain mood or attitude?
2. What does the speaker mean by "pains of insecurity surround me"?
3. What does "ostracized" mean? The speaker says that he doesn't know why, do you?

READING TO WRITE

Understanding Poetry: Punctuation and Capitalization

Poets use many means to make their meanings clear. As you have seen, arranging words in certain line lengths is one way. In Lee's free verse poem, a reader also notes the punctuation, particularly the dashes in the third and fourth stanza. The dash in prose is said to show a break in thought. What does it do here? How is it related to the corporation for which the speaker in the poem works?

Note too the impact of the capitalized words inserted at the end of the poem in the phrase "Back Again, Home." The fact that "back" and "black" rhyme also increases the impact, but would lower case type have made Lee's point as well?

Writing Applications

1. Using your journal entry, explain how your experience as an outsider affected your sense of self or identity.
2. Are there aspects of the business culture pictured in this poem that would cause people who were *not* racial or ethnic minorities some problems? If you think so, write a description of the way corporations operate and explain what problems you see.

The Handicap of Definition

WILLIAM RASPBERRY

Preview: Thinking Ahead

William Raspberry, a widely syndicated columnist, discusses not only how black people are defined, or stereotyped, by white society, but also how black people accept or believe the stereotypes. He argues that a much broader definition of "white" or "black" abilities is necessary in order for everyone to reach his or her potential.

As you read this 1982 essay, think about how stereotypes limit our ability to create an individual identity. How can we say who we are in the face of others who say who we must be?

I know all about bad schools, mean politicians, economic deprivation and racism. Still, it occurs to me that one of the heaviest burdens black Americans—and black children in particular—have to bear is the handicap of definition: the question of what it means to be black.

Let me explain quickly what I mean. If a basketball fan says that the Boston Celtics' Larry Bird plays "black," the fan intends it—and Bird probably accepts it—as a compliment. Tell pop singer Tom Jones he moves "black" and he might grin in appreciation. Say to Teena Marie or The Average White Band that they sound "black" and they'll thank you.

But name one pursuit, aside from athletics, entertainment or sexual performance in which a white practitioner will feel complimented to be told he does it "black." Tell a white broadcaster he talks "black" and he'll sign up for diction lessons. Tell a white reporter he writes "black" and he'll take a writing course. Tell a white lawyer he reasons "black" and he might sue you for slander.

What we have here is a tragically limited definition of blackness, and it isn't only white people who buy it.

Think of all the ways black children can put one another down with charges of "whiteness." For many of these children, hard study and hard work are "white." Trying to please a teacher might be criticized as acting "white." Speaking correct English is "white." Scrimping today in the interest of tomorrow's goals is "white." Educational toys and games are "white."

An incredible array of habits and attitudes that are conducive to success in business, in academia, in the non-entertainment professions are likely to be thought of as somehow "white." Even economic success, unless it involves such "black" undertakings as numbers banking, is defined as "white."

And the results are devastating. I wouldn't deny that blacks often are better entertainers and athletes. My point is the harm that comes from too narrow a definition of what is black.

One reason black youngsters tend to do better at basketball, for instance, is that they assume they can learn to do it well, and so they practice constantly to prove themselves right.

Wouldn't it be wonderful if we could infect black children with the notion that excellence in math is "black" rather than white, or possibly Chinese? Wouldn't it be of enormous value if we could create the myth that morality, strong families, determination, courage and love of learning are traits brought by slaves from Mother Africa and therefore quintessentially black?

There is no doubt in my mind that most black youngsters could develop their mathematical reasoning, their elocution and their attitudes the way they develop their jump shots and their dance steps: by the combination of sustained, enthusiastic practice and the unquestioned belief that they can do it.

In one sense, what I am talking about is the importance of developing positive ethnic traditions. Maybe Jews have an innate talent for communication; maybe the Chinese are born with a gift for mathematical reasoning; maybe blacks are naturally blessed with athletic grace. I doubt it. What is at work, I suspect, is assumption, inculcated early in their lives, that this is a thing our people do well.

Unfortunately, many of the things about which blacks make this assumption are things that do not contribute to their career success—except for that handful of the truly gifted who can make it as entertainers and athletes. And many of the things we concede to whites are the things that are essential to economic security. So it is with a number of assumptions black youngsters make about what it is to be a "man": physical aggressiveness, sexual prowess, the refusal to submit to authority. The prisons are full of people who, by this perverted definition, are unmistakably men.

But the real problem is not so much that the things defined as "black" are negative. The problem is that the definition is much too narrow.

Somehow, we have to make our children understand that they are intelligent, competent people, capable of doing whatever they put their minds to and making it in the American mainstream, not just in a black subculture.

What we seem to be doing, instead, is raising up yet another generation of young blacks who will be failures—by definition.

Respond: Thinking Independently

1. In your journal, record all the stereotypes of others you have heard. As you have gotten older and met more people, which of the stereotypes have you changed or discarded? What made you change your view?
2. Write a response statement: I agree/disagree with William Raspberry when he says _____ because _____
_____.
3. Respond to Raspberry's idea of the "importance of developing positive ethnic traditions." Are they a factor in your life?

Reconsider: Thinking Collaboratively

1. Compare in groups or as a class the statements of agreement and disagreement.
2. Discuss the danger of accepting society's stereotype as your identity.
3. Explain what Raspberry means by the "handicap of definition."

Review: Thinking Critically

1. What does Raspberry say are stereotyped "black" skills? Why does he say these are a "tragically limited definition of blackness"? What would he like to see added to the list? Why?
2. What does Raspberry say accounts for black skill at basketball? What assumption does he say is a key ingredient to anyone's success at anything? Do you agree?
3. Reread Raspberry's opening sentence. Do you agree that the "handicap of definition" is one of the "heaviest burdens" to bear? If that burden were lifted, would the other items mentioned (bad schools, mean politicians, economic deprivation, and racism) be as important?

READING TO WRITE

Understanding Definition: Principles of Definition

Learning what words mean starts when we first learn language. We are full of questions, asking constantly, "What's that." As our vocabularies of everyday words grow, we also become exposed to more specialized words in history (monarchy), biology (photosynthesis), English (verb), geography (latitude), art (mosaic), music (chord), and so forth. In fact, much of our schooling is learning the specialized words of our school subjects.

As we learn new words, we also learn the shades of meaning that words have. That is, we learn the connotation or full implication of what a word means, as well as its denotation or explicit definition. For example, the words policeman, detective, cop, or flatfoot may mean law enforcement person, but they all have different shades of meaning.

When we write, we need to make clear the meanings of words we use, so we may define terms in a sentence or two. Sometimes, as in the case of William Raspberry's piece, exploring the meaning of a word is the subject matter for the whole essay. We develop such an essay in one of several ways. Raspberry, you will note, uses many examples of black and white stereotypes as well as examples of assumptions about Jewish and Chinese people to make his point about the way society expects certain behaviors from certain people. Make a list of his examples and you will see that much of the evidence in the essay comes from them. The more specific the examples, the better a reader can understand. For example, Raspberry doesn't just say doing well in school is "white." He says, "Speaking correct English is 'white.'"

Writing Applications: Definition

1. Explain what being black, Polish, Jewish, etc., means to you. Use examples to make sure that your reader understands.
2. Define what was "cool" or socially acceptable behavior in your high school or neighborhood group as you were growing up. Was the definition of socially acceptable behavior different for males than for females? Did the definition have any consequences for people's self-image, or for educational or occupational choices?
3. Understanding what it takes to be a college student may mean defining the role of being a student. What behavior defines the successful college student?

Hispanics Come with Many Voices
ROGER E. HERNANDEZ

Preview: Thinking Ahead

Sometimes, as Roger Hernandez explains, people think of an ethnic group such as Hispanics as one unified group, all believing the same thing. As he reports, this is not the case. A survey shows that the three component groups of Hispanics in the United States can have quite different beliefs. As you read, note what differences exist among the groups and with their Anglo neighbors. Anglo usually refers to non-Hispanics, who are also not African, Asian, or Native American.

When I arrived in this country, in the mid-1960s, America didn't worry about Hispanics. The big issues were the black civil rights movement, Vietnam and those crazy college kids. The Hispanic population was relatively small and did not compete for attention.

Today, with that population at well over 20 million, Hispanics have become central in the great debate about ethnicity.

Trouble is, the term *Hispanic* is often misused. Advertisers, government, political activists and the media throw the word around as if it described a homogeneous, united community. But a recent nationwide survey among Mexicans, Puerto Ricans, Cubans and Anglos showed a more complex reality.

The survey, organized by four Hispanic scholars from universities across the country, found substantial differences among the three Hispanic groups, especially when it comes to political beliefs. Politicians who dream of rounding up "the Hispanic vote" will not find the survey encouraging. The differences were sometimes traceable to country of origin, sometimes to social class. Among the findings:

Overall, Puerto Ricans were the most supportive of a strong government role in providing a minimum income, jobs and housing. Mexicans were next, followed by Cubans and Anglos. Ironically, at the other end of the scale, the percentage of Mexicans and Cubans who believed it is up to individuals to provide for themselves was larger than the percentage of Anglos who believed the same thing. And when education and income were factored in, Mexicans and Cubans tended to agree with Anglos of the same social class. This suggest that at least when it comes to opinions about government services, social class counts for more than ethnicity.

Cubans were the least likely of the three Hispanic groups to believe they face discrimination. For instance, 52.1 percent of Cubans thought they encountered "a lot" or "some" bigotry, compared to 65 percent of Puerto Ricans and 75.7 percent of Mexicans.

The relative lack of Cuban concern about discrimination (just 20.5 percent agreed there was "a lot" of bigotry) is probably due to the fact the community focuses more on Cuba and communism than on U.S. domestic issues: An overwhelming 62.5 percent of Cubans chose communists as the most disliked group. No others were as universally disliked by anyone else. The KKK, the most disliked group among Mexicans, Puerto Ricans and Anglos, received about a third of the vote from each community.

Among Anglos, second place went to Nazis. Among Puerto Ricans and Mexicans, it was gays. Interestingly, USEnglish—the organization that wants to make English the official language—was cited by tiny percentages. Just 3.2 percent of Puerto Ricans, 2.4 percent of Mexicans and 1 percent of Cubans saw it as their biggest enemy.

One finding contradicts the popular belief that Hispanics perceive the government as an agent of discrimination. For instance, 10.6 percent of Puerto Ricans, 15.3 percent of Mexicans and 27.9 percent of Cubans said their trust in government was "high," compared to just 1.1 percent of Anglos.

The survey also pointed out the lack of communication among the different Hispanic communities. Few people in each group reported "a lot of contact" with Hispanics in the other two groups. It's a reminder that most Mexicans live in California and the Southwest, most Puerto Ricans in the Northeast, and most Cubans in South Florida.

Hispanics overwhelmingly prefer to identify themselves by their national origin rather than by a panethnic label like *Hispanic* or *Latino.* Mexicans were the most likely to choose the broader tag. But it was the first choice of just 306 out of 1,546 Mexicans surveyed.

Still, the survey showed there indeed exists a consciousness about being "Hispanic." By and large, each of the three groups acknowledged significant political differences among them. But all three agreed there also exists a shared culture. And 73.5 percent of Cubans, 72.4 percent of Mexicans and 67.3 percent of Puerto Ricans said Hispanics were "very similar" or "somewhat similar."

One lesson out of all this is that there are more differences among Hispanics than a lot of people think. Another is that, despite these differences, there is indeed such a thing as a Hispanic. The trick is finding out just what that means.

Respond: Thining Independently

1. In your journal make four columns: Mexicans, Puerto Ricans, Cubans, Anglos. Under each column put the facts from the survey.
2. Write a response statement: I expected _____ from the survey, but I didn't expect _____.
3. Write about your perceptions of ethnic groups: Do you see more similarities than differences among them or the reverse? How well do you know these ethnic groups? Does your knowledge make a difference in the ways you perceive the groups?

Reconsider: Thinking Collaboratively

1. Compare your response statements with classmates. To what extent did you expect or not expect the same things?
2. What does Hernandez mean that "when education and income were factored in, Mexicans and Cubans tended to agree with Anglos of the same social class"? How does this fact affect your predictions for future agreement among ethnic groups?
3. How can groups differ on specific beliefs and still see themselves as "a shared culture"? How would you define that culture, perhaps?

Review: Thinking Critically

1. If you were a politician running for political office, how would this survey help you to communicate with these ethnic groups?
2. What popular beliefs about Hispanics seem to be contradicted in the survey report?

READING TO WRITE

Understanding Comparison and Contrast: Principles of Comparing and Contrasting

When a writer wants to show differences between two things, he or she can organize the contrast by explaining differences in the two subjects separately (all about one subject first and then all about the second subject), or by alternating the contrast between the two subjects in each category. For example, if a person is contrasting two colleges, he or she could write all about Rural University first and then about City University, or could write about the location of the schools (first Rural and then City), the size (first Rural, then City), the students (first Rural, then City), finally the academic programs (first Rural, then City). Whichever method is chosen, the writer has to be sure to compare or contrast subjects on the same issues.

In this essay Roger Hernandez compares the responses of Mexicans, Puerto Ricans, Cubans, and Anglos to survey questions. That is, he is looking at four different groups, not just two. How does he organize his information? Notice that he uses the alternating method, which sets up categories such as the groups' attitudes toward a strong government role and their views on discrimination, and then looks at the groups' responses to each of these issues.

How does Hernandez keep his essay from being just a list of survey responses? He carefully sets up his essay in the first three paragraphs to summarize the importance of the survey in pointing out differences among various Hispanic groups. Furthermore, he uses a conclusion to point out the need for further study of Hispanic groups and their ideas.

Writing Applications: Comparison and Contrast

1. Make up a survey to give to fellow students (not just those in your English class). The topic may be any issue you think people might have opinions on: tuition, parking, attendance policy, registration procedures, safety on campus, the cafeteria, grading standards, or any topic of national interest. Then write a brief essay explaining how various groups within the student population responded.
2. Compare or contrast a place you lived once with where you live now. Try to capture the different feeling of the place as well as its physical differences.
3. Have you ever visited a place that has a different culture from your own? If so, try to contrast the differences in life-style, food, clothing, or other things that you noticed.
4. Even the same place can change through different seasons of the year or through the passage of time. Write about a place in different times.
5. Sometimes a place or person seen through the eyes of a child is quite different when viewed as an adult. Write about a place or person you remember from memory and the way you see it or him/her today.

Like Mexicans
GARY SOTO

Preview: Thinking Ahead

In this 1986 essay, Gary Soto begins by comparing two groups, Mexicans and Okies, defined by his grandmother and his friend. Although his grandmother calls anyone who is not Mexican an "Okie," the term comes from a group of people from Oklahoma who moved to California during the horrible dust bowl years of the 1930s because their farms ceased to be fertile and were often sold due to bankruptcy. The term was originally derogatory, but Soto's friend Scott seems to say it as a matter of course.

Later, as Soto thinks about marrying his Japanese girlfriend, he tries to quiet his fears about marrying someone non-Mexican. The conclusion he comes to might surprise you and get you to rethink how we group people. Soto, an author and teacher at the University of California at Berkeley, included this essay in the collection entitled Small Faces.

My grandmother gave me bad advice and good advice when I was in my early teens. For the bad advice, she said that I should become a barber because they made good money and listened to the radio all day. "Honey, they don't work como burros," she would say every time I visited her. She made the sound of donkeys braying. "Like that, honey!" For the good advice, she said that I should marry a Mexican girl. "No Okies hijo"—she would say—"Look, my son. He marry one and they fight every day about I don't know what and I don't know what." For her, everyone who wasn't Mexican, black, or Asian were Okies. The French were Okies, the Italians in suits were Okies. When I asked about Jews, whom I had read about, she asked for a picture. I rode home on my bicycle and return with a calendar depicting the important races of the world. "Pues si, son Okies tambien!"* she said, nodding her head. She waved the calendar away and we went to the living room where she lectured me on the virtues of the Mexican girl: first, she could cook and, second, she acted like a woman, not a man, in her husband's home. She said she would tell me about a third when I got a little older.

I asked my mother about it—becoming a barber and marrying Mexican. She was in the kitchen. Steam curled from a pot of boiling beans, the radio was on, looking as squat as a loaf of bread. "Well, if you want to be a barber—they say they make good money." She slapped a round steak with a knife, her glasses slipping down with each strike. She stopped and looked up. "If you find a good Mexican girl, marry her of course." She returned to slapping the meat and I went to the backyard where my brother and David King were sitting on the lawn feeling the inside of their cheeks.

"This is what girls feel like," my brother said, rubbing the inside of his cheek. David put three fingers inside his mouth and scratched. I ignored them and climbed the back fence to see my best friend, Scott, a second-generation Okie. I called him and his mother pointed to the side of the house where his bedroom was a small aluminum trailer, the kind you gawk at when they're flipped over on the freeway, wheels spinning in the air. I went around to find Scott pitching horseshoes.

I picked up a set of rusty ones and joined him. While we played, we talked about school and friends and record albums. The horseshoes scuffed up dirt, sometimes ringing the iron that threw out a meager shadow like a sundial. After three argued-over games, we pulled two oranges apiece from his tree and started down the alley still talking school and friends and record albums. We pulled more oranges from the alley and talked about who we would marry. "No offense, Scott," I said with an orange slice in my mouth, "but I would never marry an Okie." We walked in step, almost touching, with a sled of shadows dragging behind us. "No offense, Gary,"

* Well yes, they're Okies too.

Scott said, "but I would *never* marry a Mexican," I looked at him: a fang of orange slice showed from his munching mouth. I didn't think anything of it. He had his girl and I had mine. But our seventh-grade vision was the same: to marry, get jobs, buy cars and maybe a house if we had money left over.

We talked about our future lives until, to our surprise, we were on the downtown mall, two miles from home. We bought a bag of popcorn at Penneys and sat on a bench near the fountain watching Mexican and Okie girls pass. "That one's mine," I pointed with my chin when a girl with eyebrows arched into black rainbows ambled by. "She's cute," Scott said about a girl with yellow hair and a mouthful of gum. We dreamed aloud, our chins busy pointing out girls. We agreed that we couldn't wait to become men and lift them onto our laps.

But the woman I married was not Mexican but Japanese. It was a surprise to me. For years, I went about wide-eyed in my search for the brown girl in a white dress at a dance. I searched the playground at the baseball diamond. When the girls raced for grounders, their hair bounced like something that couldn't be caught. When they sat together in the lunchroom, heads pressed together, I knew they were talking about us Mexican guys. I saw them and dreamed them. I threw my face into my pillow, making up sentences that were good as in the movies.

But when I was twenty, I fell in love with this other girl who worried my mother, who had my grandmother asking once again to see the calendar of the Important Races of the World. I told her I had thrown it away years before. I took a much-glanced-at snapshot from my wallet. We looked at it together, in silence. Then grandma reclined in her chair, lit a cigarette, and said, "Es pretty." She blew and asked with all her worry pushed up to her forehead: "Chinese?"

I was in love and there was no looking back. She was the one. I told my mother who was slapping hamburger into patties. "Well, sure if you want to marry her," she said. But the more I talked, the more concerned she became. Later I began to worry. Was it all a mistake? "Marry a Mexican girl," I heard my mother say in my mind. I heard it at breakfast. I heard it over math problems, between Western Civilization and cultural geography. But then one afternoon while I was hitchhiking home from school, it struck me like a baseball in the back: my mother wanted me to marry someone of my own social class—a poor girl. I considered my financee, Carolyn, and she didn't look poor, though I knew she came from a family of farm workers and pull-yourself-up-by-your-bootstraps ranchers. I asked my brother, who was marrying Mexican poor that fall, if I should marry a poor girl. He screamed "Yeah" above his terrible guitar playing in his bedroom. I considered my sister who had married Mexican. Cousins were dating Mexican. Uncles were remarrying poor women. I asked Scott, who was still my best friend, and he said, "She's too good for you, so you better not."

I was worried about it until Carolyn took me home to meet her parents. We drove in her Plymouth until the houses gave way to farms and ranches and finally her house fifty feet from the highway. When we pulled into the drive, I panicked and begged Carolyn to make a U-turn and go back so we could talk about it over a soda. She pinched my cheek, calling me a "silly boy." I felt better, though, when I got out of the car and saw the house: the chipped paint, a cracked window, boards for a walk to the back door. There were rusting cars near the barn. A tractor with a net of spiderwebs under a mulberry. A field. A bale of barbed wire like children's scribbling leaning against an empty chicken coop. Carolyn took my hand and pulled me to my future mother-in-law who was coming out to greet us.

We had lunch: sandwiches, potato chips, and iced tea. Carolyn and her mother talked mostly about neighbors and the congregation at the Japanese Methodist Church in West Fresno. Her father, who was in khaki work clothes, excused himself with a wave that was almost a salute and went outside. I heard a truck start, a dog bark, and then the truck rattle away.

Carolyn's mother offered another sandwich, but I declined with a shake of my head and a smile. I looked around when I could, when I was not saying over and over that I was a college student, hinting that I could take care of her daughter. I shifted my chair. I saw newspapers piled in corners, dusty cereal boxes and vinegar bottles in corners. The wallpaper was bubbled from rain that had come in from a bad roof. Dust. Dust lay on lamp shades and window sills. These people are just like Mexicans, I thought. Poor people.

Carolyn's mother asked me through Carolyn if I would like a *sushi*. A plate of black and white things were held in front of me. I took one, wideeyed, and turned it over like a foreign coin. I was biting into one when I saw a kitten crawl up the window screen over the sink. I chewed and the kitten opened its mouth of terror as she crawled higher, wanting in to paw the leftovers from our plates. I looked at Carolyn who said that the cat was just showing off. I looked up in time to see it fall. It crawled up, then fell again.

We talked for an hour and had apple pie and coffee, slowly. Finally, we got up with Carolyn taking my hand. Slightly embarrassed, I tried to pull away but her grip held me. I let her have her way as she led me down the hallway with her mother right behind me. When I opened the door, I was startled by a kitten clinging to the screen door, its mouth screaming "cat food, dog biscuits, *sushi*. . . ." I opened the door and the kitten, still holding on, whined in the language of hungry animals. When I got into Carolyn's car, I looked back: the cat was still clinging. I asked Carolyn if it were possibly hungry, but she said the cat was being silly. She started the car, waved to her mother, and bounced us over the rain-poked drive, patting my thigh for being her lover baby. Carolyn waved again. I looked back, waving, then gawking at a window screen where there were now three kittens clawing and screaming to get in. Like Mexicans, I thought. I remembered the Molinas and how the cats clung to their screens—cats they shot down with squirt guns. On the highway, I felt happy, pleased by it all. I patted Carolyn's thigh. Her people were like Mexicans, only different.

Respond: Thinking Independently

1. Write your own interpretation of Soto's grandmother's definition of Okies. What do you think she meant about her son fighting with his Okie wife? Have you heard the term Okie before? Where?

2. Write a response statement. One thing that confused me in Soto's essay was _____.

3. Did you ever receive advice to marry a person from a certain group or not to marry a person from another group? Why? What were the reasons? How did you react? How do you react today?

Reconsider: Thinking Collaboratively

1. In small groups consider each other's response statements, trying to explain what confused each of you. Save the parts you couldn't clear up for the whole class discussion.
2. Why did Soto decide that Carolyn's family were "like Mexicans"? Why did that make him more comfortable?
3. What parts do mothers play in the essay? Why?
4. What do the kittens have to do with anything?

Review: Thinking Critically

1. Why does Soto say that his mother wants him to marry a poor girl? Discuss ethnic status and social class. Do you think one is more important than the other in a marriage partner? Why or why not?
2. How do you see Soto's relationship with Scott, his best friend? Why does Scott say that Carolyn is "too good for you"?
3. Why does Soto continue to say that his grandmother's advice to marry a Mexican girl was "good advice," even though he married a Japanese girl?

READING TO WRITE

Understanding Comparison and Contrast: Indirect Comparison and Contrast

Soto presents both a contrast (Mexicans are unlike Okies) and a comparison (Carolyn's Japanese family are like Mexicans) in his essay. Both are handled somewhat indirectly. For example, Soto describes looking at girls at the mall with his friend Scott, and only the color of eyebrows and hair distinguishes Mexicans from Okies. The details that establish Carolyn's family being "like Mexicans" are the physical details of her cluttered and somewhat run-down house. Make a list of the details that Soto uses to establish these differences and similarities.

Writing Applications: Comparison and Contrast

1. Much of the time writers search for differences between two subjects, in order to draw distinctions or to judge the subjects. This time you should think of similarities between groups that might otherwise be different. For example, how is a family of a different race or ethnic background the same as your family? How are you the same as a classmate who is of

a different background? How are men and women the same (though obviously different in many ways)?

2. F. Scott Fitzgerald, an American writer, is supposed to have said, "The rich are very different from you and me." To which, Ernest Hemingway, another writer, replied, "Yes, they have more money." Based on your observations, do you see great differences in people who are wealthy or at least have more money than you do? If so, write about the differences. If not, how are they similar to you?

The Culture of Silence*
MAXINE HONG KINGSTON

Preview: Thinking Ahead

In this selection from her autobiography, The Woman Warrior *(1976), Maxine Hong Kingston tries to recreate her experiences of being a Chinese-American girl, speaking English in a public school. Kingston, born in 1940 to Chinese immigrant parents, lived in Stockton, California, graduated from the University of California at Berkeley, and now teaches writing at the University of Hawaii.*

When I went to kindergarten and had to speak English for the first time, I became silent. A dumbness—a shame—still cracks my voice in two, even when I want to say "hello" casually, or ask an easy question in front of the check-out counter, or ask directions of a bus driver. I stand frozen, or I hold up the line with the complete, grammatical sentence that comes squeaking out at impossible length. "What did you say?" says the cab driver, or "Speak up," so I have to perform again, only weaker the second time. A telephone call makes my throat bleed and takes up that day's courage. It spoils my day with self-disgust when I hear my broken voice come skittering out into the open. It makes people wince to hear it. I'm getting better, though. Recently I asked the postman for special-issue stamps; I've waited since childhood for postmen to give me some of their own accord. I am making progress, a little every day.

My silence was thickest—total—during the three years that I covered my school paintings with black paint. I painted layers of black over houses and flowers and suns, and when I drew on the blackboard, I put a layer of chalk on top. I was making a stage curtain, and it was the moment before the curtain parted or rose. The teachers called my parents to school, and I saw they had been saving my pictures, curling and cracking, all alike and black. The teachers pointed to the pictures and looked serious, talked seriously too, but my parents did not understand English. ("The parents and teachers of criminals were executed," said my father.) My parents took the pictures

* Editor's title

home. I spread them out (so black and full of possibilities) and pretended the curtains were swinging open, flying up, one after another, sunlight underneath, mighty operas.

During the first silent year I spoke to no one at school, did not ask before going to the lavatory, and flunked kindergarten. My sister also said nothing for three years, silent in the playground and silent at lunch. There were other quiet Chinese girls not of our family, but most of them got over it sooner than we did. I enjoyed the silence. At first it did not occur to me I was supposed to talk or to pass kindergarten. I talked at home and to one or two of the Chinese kids in class. I made motions and even made some jokes. I drank out of a toy saucer when the water spilled out of the cup, and everybody laughed, pointing at me, so I did it some more. I didn't know that Americans don't drink out of saucers.

I liked the Negro students (Black Ghosts) best because they laughed the loudest and talked to me as if I were a daring talker too. One of the Negro girls had her mother coil braids over her ears Shanghai-style like mine; we were Shanghai twins except that she was covered with black like my paintings. Two Negro kids enrolled in Chinese school, and the teachers gave them Chinese names. Some Negro kids walked me to school and home, protecting me from the Japanese kids, who hit me and chased me and stuck gum in my ears. The Japanese kids were noisy and tough. They appeared one day in kindergarten, released from concentration camp, which was a tic-tac-toe mark, like barbed wire, on the map.

It was when I found out I had to talk that school become a misery, that the silence became a misery. I did not speak and felt bad each time that I did not speak. I read aloud in first grade, though, and heard the barest whisper with little squeaks come out of my throat. "Louder," said the teacher, who scared the voice away again. The other Chinese girls did not talk either, so I knew the silence had to do with being a Chinese girl.

Reading out loud was easier than speaking because we did not have to make up what to say, but I stopped often, and the teacher would think I'd gone quiet again. I could not understand "I." The Chinese "I" has seven strokes, intricacies. How could the American "I," assuredly wearing a hat like the Chinese, have only three strokes, the middle so straight? Was it out of politeness that this writer left off the strokes the way a Chinese has to write her own name small and crooked? No, it was not politeness; "I" is a capital and "you" is lower-case. I started at that middle line and waited so long for its black center to resolve into tight strokes and dots that I forgot to pronounce it. The other troublesome word was "here," no strong consonant to hang on to, and so flat, when "here" is two mountainous ideographs. The teacher, who had already told me every day how to read "I" and "here," put me in the low corner under the stairs again, where the noisy boys usually sat.

When my second grade class did a play, the whole class went to the auditorium except the Chinese girls. The teacher, lovely and Hawaiian, should have understood about us, but instead left us behind in the classroom. Our voices were too soft or nonexistent, and our parents never signed the permission slips anyway. They never signed anything unnecessary. We opened the door a crack and peeked out, but closed it again quickly. One of us (not me) won every spelling bee, though.

I remember telling the Hawaiian teacher, "We Chinese can't sing 'land where our fathers died.' " She argued with me about politics, while I meant because of curses. But how can I have that memory when I couldn't talk? My mother says that we, like the ghosts, have no memories.

After American school, we picked up our cigar boxes, in which we had arranged books, brushes, and an inkbox neatly, and went to Chinese school, from 5:00 to 7:30 P.M. There we chanted together, voices rising and falling, loud and soft, some boys shouting, everybody reading together, reciting together and not alone with one voice. When we had a memorization test, the teacher let each of us come to his desk and say the lesson to him privately, while the rest of the class practiced copying or tracing. Most of the teachers were men. The boys who were so well behaved in the American school played tricks on them and talked back to them. The girls were not mute. They screamed and yelled during recess, when there were no rules; they had fistfights. Nobody was afraid of children hurting themselves or of children hurting school property. The glass doors to the red and green balconies with the gold joy symbols were left wide open so that we could run out and climb the fire escapes. We played capture-the-flag in the auditorium, where Sun Yat-sen and Chiang Kai-shek's pictures hung at the back of the stage, the Chinese flag on their left and the American flag on their right. We climbed the teak ceremonial chairs and made flying leaps off the stage. One flag headquarters was behind the glass door and the other on stage right. Our feet drummed on the hollow stage. During recess the teachers locked themselves up in their office with the shelves of books, copybooks, inks from China. They drank tea and warmed their hands at a stove. There was no play supervision. At recess we had the school to ourselves, and also we could roam as far as we could go—downtown, Chinatown stores, home—as long as we returned before the bell rang.

At exactly 7:30 the teacher again picked up the brass bell that sat on his desk and swung it over our heads, while we charged down the stairs, our cheering magnified in the stairwell. Nobody had to line up.

Not all of the children who were silent at American school found voice at Chinese school. One new teacher said each of us had to get up and recite in front of the class, who was to listen. My sister and I had memorized the lesson perfectly. We said it to each other at home, one chanting, one listening. The teacher called on my sister to recite first. It was the first time a teacher had called on the second-born to go first. My sister was scared. She glanced at me and looked away; I looked down at my desk. I hoped that she could do it because if she could, then I would have to. She opened her mouth and a voice came out that wasn't a whisper, but it wasn't a proper voice either. I hoped that she would not cry, fear breaking up her voice like twigs underfoot. She sounded as if she were trying to sing through weeping and strangling. She did not pause or stop to end the embarrassment. She kept going until she said the last word, and then she sat down. When it was my turn, the same voice came out, a crippled animal running on broken legs. You could hear splinters in my voice, bones rubbing jagged against one another. I was loud, though. I was glad I didn't whisper.

How strange that the emigrant villagers are shouters, hollering face to face. My father asks, "Why is it I can hear Chinese from blocks away? Is it that I understand the language? Or is it they talk loud?" They turn the radio up full blast to hear the operas, which do not seem to hurt their ears. And they yell over the singers that wail over the drums, everybody talking at once, big arm gestures, spit flying. You can see the disgust on American faces looking at women like that. It isn't just the loudness. It is the way Chinese sounds, ching-chong ugly, to American ears, not beautiful like Japanese sayonara words with the consonants and vowels as regular as Italian. We make guttural peasant noise and have Ton Duc Thang names you can't remember. And the Chinese can't hear Americans at all; the language is too soft and western music unhearable. I've watched a Chinese audience laugh, visit, talk-story, and holler during a piano recital, as if the musician could not hear them. A Chinese American, somebody's son, was playing Chopin, which has no punctuation, no cymbals, no gongs. Chinese piano music is five black keys. Normal Chinese women's voices are strong and bossy. We American-Chinese girls had to whisper to make ourselves American-feminine. Apparently we whispered even more softly than the Americans. Once a year the teachers referred my sister and me to speech therapy, but our voices would straighten out, unpredictably normal, for the therapists. Some of us gave up, shook our heads, and said nothing, not one word. Some of us could not even shake our heads. At times shaking my head no is more self-assertion than I can manage. Most of us eventually found some voice, however faltering. We invented an American-feminine speaking personality.

Respond: Thinking Independently

1. Tell a story in your journal of a difficult time you had in elementary school. Try to capture your feelings about the event as well as what happened.
2. Write a response statement to this essay: One part of Kingston's essay that touched me/surprised me/angered me was _____.
3. What misunderstandings between Kingston and her teachers were there? Do you think they could have been prevented? How?

Reconsider: Thinking Collaboratively

1. Compare your classmates' reactions to the essay. Were they much the same? Why or why not?
2. Why do you think Kingston begins her essay (after the statement about kindergarten) with her current speech habits?

3. Discuss how Kingston reacts to other Chinese students, black students, Japanese students. (The concentration camp for Japanese she refers to was one of the relocation camps for Japanese-American citizens created in the western United States during World War II. Highly controversial for over 50 years, these camps have been the subject of lawsuits brought by Japanese Americans, who request compensation for seized land and businesses and emotional and physical damage.) Given the background, can you account for the Japanese students' behavior?
4. What were some differences between the Chinese and American schools?

Review: Thinking Critically

1. What should public policy be toward students who speak a language other than English? Should they be required to speak English or be taught in their own language?
2. Kingston tries to make readers hear her voice in the way she describes it: her voice "cracks," is "broken," and "squeaks." At one point near the end of the essay, she uses a metaphor, or comparison, calling her voice "a crippled animal running on broken legs. You could hear splinters in my voice, bones rubbing jagged against one another." Since a voice does not have bones, we have to think of this figuratively. How do you imagine she sounded? Do her descriptions help you to "hear" her even though you are reading with your eyes? What other examples can you find of such comparisons?
3. At the end of this selection, Kingston says that Chinese sounds ugly to American ears. On what does she base her opinion?

READING TO WRITE

Understanding Narration: Using Contrast Within a Narrative

Maxine Hong Kingston tells us the story of her early schooling in a rough chronological order (kindergarten, first grade, second grade), but within this overall organization she also presents the contrasts between the Chinese school and the American school. While sometimes as students in writing classes you write papers that reflect one way of organizing your thoughts, you need to be aware that skillful writers frequently combine these methods, as is done here.

Writing Applications: Narration

1. Take the journal entry you wrote about an incident in elementary school and revise it to hand in.
2. Tell about a misunderstanding you have had with a teacher or other adult.

For My Indian Daughter

Lewis P. Johnson

Preview: Thinking Ahead

*Depending on the area of the country in which you live, you may or may not
know much about the first people to live in North America, the Native Americans or "Indians" as Lewis Johnson refers to them. Johnson, in this 1983 essay
originally appearing in* Newsweek, *thinks about his identity as a Native
American and the prejudices he has encountered. He thinks too about what he
should tell his baby daughter to protect her or prepare her. As you read Johnson's essay, think about what you have seen or read about Native Americans.
What are the popular stereotypes? Are these ideas changing? Will Johnson's
daughter face a different kind of society than the author did?*

My little girl is singing herself to sleep upstairs, her voice mingling with the
sounds of the birds outside in the old maple trees. She is two and I am
nearly 50, and I am very taken with her. She came along late in my life, un-
expected and unbidden, a startling gift.

Today at the beach my chubby-legged, brown-skinned daughter ran
laughing into the water as fast as she could. My wife and I laughed watching her, until we heard behind us a low guttural curse and then an unpleas-
ant voice raised in an imitation war whoop.

I turned to see a fat man in a bathing suit, white and soft as a grub, as he
covered his mouth and prepared to make the Indian war cry again. He was
middle-aged, younger than I, and had three little children lined up next to
him, grinning foolishly. My wife suggested we leave the beach, and I agreed.

I knew the man was not unusual in his feelings against Indians. His
beach behavior might have been socially unacceptable to more civilized
whites, but his basic view of Indians is expressed daily in our small town,
frequently on the editorial pages of the country newspaper, as white people
speak out against Indian fishing rights and land rights, saying in essence,
"Those Indians are taking are fish, our land." It doesn't matter to them that
we were here first, that the U.S. Supreme Court has ruled in our favor. It
matters to them that we have something they want, and they hate us for it.
Backlash is the common explanation of the attacks on Indians, the bumper
stickers that say, "Spear an Indian, Save a Fish," but I know better. The hatred of Indians goes back to the beginning when white people came to this
country. For me it goes to my childhood in Harbor Springs, Michigan.

Theft

Harbor Springs is now a summer resort for the very affluent, but a hundred
years ago it was the Indian village of my Ottawa ancestors. My grandmother, Anna Showanessy, and other Indians like her, had their land there

taken by treaty, by fraud, by violence, by theft. They remembered how whites had burned down the village at Burt Lake in 1900 and pushed the Indians out. These were the stories in my family.

When I was a boy my mother told me to walk down the alleys in Harbor Springs and not to wear my orange football sweater out of the house. This way I would not stand out, not be noticed, and not be a target.

I wore my orange sweater anyway and deliberately avoided the alleys. I was the biggest person I knew and wasn't really afraid. But I met my comeuppance when I enlisted in the U.S. Army. One night all the men in my barracks gathered together and, gang-fashion, pulled me into the shower and scrubbed me down with rough brushes used for floors, saying "We won't have any dirty Indians in our outfit." It is a point of irony that I was cleaner than any of them. Later in Korea I learned how to kill, how to bully, how to hate Koreans. I came out of the war tougher than ever and, strangely, white.

I went to college, got married, lived in La Porte, Indiana, worked as a surveyor and raised three boys. I headed Boy Scout groups, never thinking it odd when the Scouts did imitation Indian dances, imitation Indian lore.

One day when I was 35 or thereabouts I heard about an Indian powwow. My father used to attend them and so with great curiosity and a strange joy at discovering a part of my heritage, I decided the thing to do to get ready for this big event was to have my friend make me a spear in his forge. The steel was fine and blue and iridescent. The feathers on the shaft were bright and proud.

In a dusty state fairground in southern Indiana, I found white people dressed as Indians. I learned they were "hobbyists," that is, it was their hobby and leisure pastime to masquerade as Indians on weekends. I felt ridiculous with my spear, and I left.

It was years before I could tell anyone of the embarrassment of this weekend and see any humor in it. But in a way it was that weekend, for all its silliness, that was my awakening. I realized I didn't know who I was. I didn't have an Indian name. I didn't speak the Indian language. I didn't know the Indian customs. Dimly I remembered the Ottawa word for dog, but it was a baby word, *kahgee*, not the full word, *muhkahgee*, which I was later to learn. Even more hazily I remembered a naming ceremony (my own). I remembered legs dancing around me, dust. Where had that been? Who had I been? "Suwaukquat," my mother told me when I asked, "where the tree begins to grow."

That was 1968, and I was not the only Indian in the country who was feeling the need to remember who he or she was. There were others. They had powwows, real ones, and eventually I found them. Together we researched our past, a search that for me culminated in the Longest Walk, a march on Washington in 1978. Maybe because I now know what it means to be Indian, it surprises me that others don't. Of course there aren't very many of us left. The chances of an average person knowing an average Indian in an average lifetime are pretty slim.

Circle

Still, I was amused one day when my small, four-year-old neighbor looked at me as I was hoeing in my garden and said, "You aren't a real Indian, are you?" Scotty is little, talkative, likable. Finally I said, "I'm a real Indian." He looked at me for a moment and then said, squinting into the sun. "Then where's your horse and feathers?" The child was simply a smaller, whiter version of my own ignorant self years before. We'd both seen too much TV, that's all. He was not to be blamed. And so, in a way, the moronic man on the beach today is blameless. We come full circle to realize other people are like ourselves, as discomfiting as that may be sometimes.

As I sit in my old chair on my porch, in a light that is fading so the leaves are barely distinguishable against the sky, I can picture my girl asleep upstairs. I would like to prepare her for what's to come, take her each step of the way saying, there's a place to avoid, here's what I know about this, but much of what's before her she must go through alone. She must pass through pain and joy and solitude and community to discover her own inner self that is unlike any other and come through that passage to the place where she sees all people are one, and in so seeing may live her life in a brighter future.

Respond: Thinking Indpendently

1. Write your reactions to what happened to Lewis Johnson and his family on the beach. What would you have done? Why did he and his wife leave the beach?
2. Write a response statement to the section called "Theft": _____
   _____ and to the one
   called "Circle": _____
   _____

3. What interest do you or your family take in your racial or ethnic heritage? Have you looked into your past, researched your family tree, or preserved family or cultural customs?

Reconsider: Thinking Collaboratively

1. Compare your response statements with classmates in order to determine the definitions of "Theft" and "Circle." Clear up each others' questions.
2. Discuss whether parents can protect their children from misunderstanding and prejudice. What reaction does the class have to Johnson's hope that his daughter will see "all people are one"?
3. Is it important for Americans to keep their cultural backgrounds or should the ideal be assimilation? Why does Johnson say he has a "need to remember who he . . . was?"
4. Why does Johnson make a point of saying that the man on the beach was "white and soft as a grub"? What is a grub?
5. Why does Johnson say that his experiences in Korea made him "strangely white"?

Review: Thinking Critically

1. Why is the powwow in Indiana with the "hobbyists" included in the section called "Theft"? What could be said to be "stolen" by such people?
2. Why does Johnson say that the powwow weekend was his "awakening"?
3. Why does Johnson say that both his 4-year-old neighbor and the man on the beach are "blameless" for their stereotypes of Indians? Do you agree?

READING TO WRITE

Understanding Definition: Using a Frame Structure

Lewis Johnson begins and ends his essay with his young daughter falling asleep upstairs. He then "flashes back" to the incident on the beach, his childhood in Michigan, his army experiences, his early adult life, and finally his realization of his culture and identity. The frame, like that around a picture, ties together the essay and gives a reason for the reminiscences.

Writing Application: Definition

1. Is there a moment in your life that defined for you who and what you are, either connected to your cultural heritage or not? If so, recreate the moment and explain how it defined you.

The Enemy's Eyes
EMMA LEE WARRIOR

Preview: Thinking Ahead

While Lewis Johnson has achieved a measure of understanding of the relationship of Native Americans and white society, not all Native American writers share his attitude. In the following poem the Native American speaker attacks the source of her blue eyes as the enemy, the spoiler, the invader. How has carrying the evidence of another culture affected her identity or self-esteem?

My eyes are the enemy's eyes,
stigma of the spoiler,
invader of lands, bodies
who left behind his eyes.

Chameleonlike, their shades
mock my Indian pride:

"Don't play with cat eyes!
Go away, blue eyes!"

Those taunts forged my hate
for the tainter gone home to hell.

I must pay for that wretch's sins;
my eyes are his; his eyes are mine.

Respond: Thinking Independently

1. Write in your journal your reaction to the poem. Why do children taunt the speaker? Why does the speaker hate her eyes? What does "stigma" mean?
2. Write a response statement about something you learned from the poem or a question about something you don't understand in the poem: ____

_____.

Reconsider: Thinking Collaboratively

1. Discuss your response statements or questions.
2. Discuss the meaning of "spoiler," "invader," "tainter," "wretch": why does the poet use these words?
3. What do your classmates think the word "chameleonlike" means in this poem?

Review: Thinking Critically

1. Look at the poem's last line, "my eyes are his; his eyes are mine." Is there a possibility that the speaker may reach an understanding of her heritage? How do you interpret the last two lines?

READING TO WRITE

Understanding Poetry: Paradox

Paradox is a figure a speech sometimes used in poetry to make readers think. Paradox is a statement that at first seems contradictory but could be true or least makes some sense. When Emma Lee Warrior writes, "My eyes are the enemy's eyes," a reader may think at first that this can't be true because no one can have another person's eyes—literally. But we all have heard someone say of a child that she has her mother's eyes and realize that it means the eyes look like the mother's. As one reads this poem, one begins to see that the heritage of a Caucasian invader with his blue eyes has resulted in a young Native American having eye color different from the other children of the tribe. The paradox is thereby shown to be true.

Writing Application

1. Playground taunts, though common, are nevertheless damaging. Write about (a) why children choose certain other children to taunt or (b) how taunts against you or a friend affected you.

The Red Convertible
LOUISE ERDRICH

Preview: Thinking Ahead

Louise Erdrich grew up in North Dakota, where her parents taught for the Bureau of Indian Affairs and her grandparents still lived on a reservation. After graduating from Dartmouth in 1976 with a B.A., Erdrich received an M.A. in creative writing in 1977 from Johns Hopkins. Her poems, short stories, and novels are set in North Dakota and many, but not all, center on the experiences of Chippewa families. "The Red Convertible" was originally published as a short story, but then appeared in 1984 as one of 14 related stories in the novel Love Medicine, *which won Erdrich the National Book Critics Circle Award in 1984. As you read, think about the relationship between two brothers, life's difficulties, and a favorite car.*

Lyman Lamartine

I was the first one to drive a convertible on my reservation. And of course it was red, a red Olds. I owned that car along with my brother Henry Junior. We owned it together until his boots filled with water on a windy night and he bought out my share. Now Henry owns the whole car, and his younger brother Lyman (that's myself), Lyman walks everywhere he goes.

How did I earn enough money to buy my share in the first place? My one talent was I could always make money. I had a touch for it, unusual in a Chippewa. From the first I was different that way, and everyone recognized it. I was the only kid they let in the American Legion Hall to shine shoes, for example, and one Christmas I sold spiritual bouquets for the mission door to door. The nuns let me keep a percentage. Once I started, it seemed the more money I made the easier the money came. Everyone encouraged it. When I was fifteen I got a job washing dishes at the Joliet Café, and that was where my first big break happened.

It wasn't long before I was promoted to bussing tables, and then the short-order cook quit and I was hired to take her place. No sooner than you know it I was managing the Joliet. The rest is history. I went on managing. I soon became part owner, and of course there was no stopping me then. It wasn't long before the whole thing was mine.

After I'd owned the Joliet for one year, it blew over in the worst tornado ever seen around here. The whole operation was smashed to bits. A total loss. The fryalator was up in a tree, the grill torn in half like it was paper. I was only sixteen. I had it all in my mother's name, and I lost it quick, but before I lost it I had every one of my relatives, and their relatives, to dinner, and I also brought that red Olds I mentioned, along with Henry.

The first time we saw it! I'll tell you when we first saw it. We had gotten a ride up to Winnipeg, and both of us had money. Don't ask me why, because we never mentioned a car or anything, we just had all our money.

Mine was cash, a big bankroll from the Joliet's insurance. Henry had two checks—a week's extra pay for being laid off, and his regular check from the Jewel Bearing Plant.

We were walking down Portage anyway, seeing the sights, when we saw it. There it was, parked, large as life. Really as *if* it was alive. I thought of the word *repose,* because the car wasn't simply stopped, parked, or whatever. That car reposed, calm and gleaming, a FOR SALE sign in its left front window. Then, before we had thought it over at all, the car belonged to us and our pockets were empty. We had just enough money for gas back home.

We went places in that car, me and Henry. We took off driving all one whole summer. We started off toward the Little Knife River and Mandaree in Fort Berthold and then we found outselves down in Wakpala somehow, and then suddenly we were over in Montana on the Rocky Boys, and yet the summer was not even half over. Some people hang on to details when they travel, but we didn't let them bother us and just lived our everyday lives here to there.

I do remember this one place with willows. I remember I laid under those trees and it was comfortable. So comfortable. The branches bent down all around me like a tent or a stable. And quiet, it was quiet, even though there was a powwow close enough so I could see it going on. The air was not too still, not too windy either. When the dust rises up and hangs in the air around the dancers like that, I feel good, Henry was asleep with his arms thrown wide. Later on, he woke up and we started driving again. We were somewhere in Montana, or maybe on the Blood Reserve—it could have been anywhere. Anyway it was where we met the girl.

All her hair was in buns around her ears, that's the first thing I noticed about her. She was posed alongside the road with her arm out, so we stopped. That girl was short, so short her lumber shirt looked comical on her, like a nightgown. She had jeans on and fancy moccasins and she carried a little suitcase.

'Hop on in," says Henry. So she climbs in between us.

"We'll take you home," I says. "Where do you live?"

"Chicken," she says.

"Where the hell's that?" I ask her.

"Alaska."

Okay," says Henry, and we drive.

We got up there and never wanted to leave. The sun doesn't truly set there in summer, and the night is more a soft dusk. You might doze off, sometimes, but before you know it you're up again, like an animal in nature. You never feel like you have to sleep hard or put away the world. And things would grow up there. One day just dirt or moss, the next day flowers and long grass. The girl's name was Susy. Her family really took to us. They fed us and put us up. We had our own tent to live in by their house, and the kids would be in and out of there all day and night. They couldn't get over me and Henry being brothers, we looked so different. We told them we knew we had the same mother, anyway.

One night Susy came in to visit us. We sat around in the tent talking of this thing and that. The season was changing. It was getting darker by that time, and the cold was even getting just a little mean. I told her it was time for us to go. She stood up on a chair.

"You never seen my hair," Susy said.

That was true. She was standing on a chair, but still, when she unclipped her buns the hair reached all the way to the ground. Our eyes opened. You couldn't tell how much hair she had when it was rolled up so neatly. Then my brother Henry did something funny. He went up to the chair and said, "Jump on my shoulders." So she did that, and her hair reached down past his waist, and he started twirling, this way and that, so her hair was flung out from side to side.

"I always wondered what it was like to have long pretty hair," Henry says. Well we laughed. It was a funny sight, the way he did it. The next morning we got up and took leave of those people.

On to greener pastures, as they say. It was down through Spokane and across Idaho then Montana and very soon we were racing the weather right along under the Canadian border through Columbus, Des Lacs, and then we were in Bottineau County and soon home. We'd made most of the trip, that summer, without putting up the hood at all. We got home just in time, it turned out, for the army to remember Henry had signed up to join it.

I don't wonder that the army was so glad to get my brother that they turned him into a Marine. He was built like a brick outhouse anyway. We liked to tease him that they really wanted him for his Indian nose. He had a nose big and sharp as a hatchet, like the nose on Red Tomahawk, the Indian who killed Sitting Bull, whose profile is on signs all along the North Dakota highways. Henry went off to training camp, came home once during Christmas, then the next thing you know we got an overseas letter from him. It was 1970, and he said he was stationed up in the northern hill country. Whereabouts I did not know. He wasn't such a hot letter writer, and only got off two before the enemy caught him. I could never keep it straight, which direction those good Vietnam soldiers were from.

I wrote him back several times, even though I didn't know if those letters would get through. I kept him informed all about the car. Most of the time I had it up on blocks in the yard or half taken apart, because that long trip did a hard job on it under the hood.

I always had good luck with numbers, and never worried about the draft myself. I never even had to think about what my number was. But Henry was never lucky in the same way as me. It was at least three years before Henry came home. By then I guess the whole war was solved in the government's mind, but for him it would keep on going. In those years I'd put his car into almost perfect shape. I always thought of it as his car while he was gone, even though when he left he said, "Now it's yours," and threw me his key.

"Thanks for the extra key," I'd said. "I'll put it up in your drawer just in case I need it." He laughed.

When he came home, though, Henry was very different, and I'll say this: the change was no good. You could hardly expect him to change for the better, I know. But he was quiet, so quiet, and never comfortable sitting still anywhere but always up and moving around. I thought back to times we'd sat still for whole afternoons, never moving a muscle, just shifting our weight along the ground, talking to whoever sat with us, watching things. He'd always had a joke, then, too, and now you couldn't get him to laugh, or when he did it was more the sound of a man choking, a sound that stopped up the throats of other people around him. They got to leaving him alone most of the time, and I didn't blame them. It was a fact: Henry was jumpy and mean.

I'd bought a color TV set for my mom and the rest of us while Henry was away. Money still came very easy. I was sorry I'd ever bought it though, because of Henry. I was also sorry I'd bought color, because with black-and-white the pictures seem older and farther away. But what are you going to do? He sat in front of it, watching it, and that was the only time he was completely still. But it was the kind of stillness that you see in a rabbit when it freezes and before it will bolt. He was not easy. He sat in his chair gripping the armrests with all his might, as if the chair itself was moving at a high speed and if he let go at all he would rocket forward and maybe crash right through the set.

Once I was in the room watching TV with Henry and I heard his teeth click at something. I looked over, and he'd bitten through his lip. Blood was going down his chin. I tell you right then I wanted to smash that tube to pieces. I went over to it but Henry must have known what I was up to. He rushed from his chair and shoved me out of the way, against the wall. I told myself he didn't know what he was doing.

My mom came in, turned the set off real quiet, and told us she had made something for supper. So we went and sat down. There was still blood going down Henry's chin, but he didn't notice it and no one said anything, even though every time he took a bite of his bread his blood fell onto it until he was eating his own blood mixed in with the food.

While Henry was not around we talked about what was going to happen to him. There were no Indian doctors on the reservation, and my mom was afraid of trusting Old Man Pillager because he courted her long ago and was jealous of her husbands. He might take revenge through her son. We were afraid that if we brought Henry to a regular hospital they would keep him.

"They don't fix them in those places," Mom said; "they just give them drugs."

"We wouldn't get him there in the first place," I agreed, "so let's just forget about it."

Then I thought about the car.

Henry had not even looked at the car since he'd gotten home, though like I said, it was in tip-top condition and ready to drive. I thought the car might bring the old Henry back somehow. So I bided my time and waited for my chance to interest him in the vehicle.

One night Henry was off somewhere. I took myself a hammer. I went out to that car and I did a number on its underside. Whacked it up. Bent the tail pipe double. Ripped the muffler loose. By the time I was done with the car it looked worse than any typical Indian car that has been driven all its life on reservation roads, which they always say are like government promises—full of holes. It just about hurt me, I'll tell you that! I threw dirt in the carburetor and I ripped all the electric tape off the seats. I made it look just as beat up as I could. Then I sat back and waited for Henry to find it.

Still, it took him over a month. That was all right, because it was just getting warm enough, not melting, but warm enough to work outside.

"Lyman," he says, walking in one day, "that red car looks like shit."

"Well it's old," I says. "You got to expect that."

"No way!" says Henry. "That car's a classic! But you went and ran the piss right out of it, Lyman, and you know it don't deserve that. I kept that car in A-one shape. You don't remember. You're too young. But when I left, that car was running like a watch. Now I don't even know if I can get it to start again, let alone get it anywhere near its old condition."

"Well you try," I said, like I was getting mad, "but I say it's a piece of junk."

Then I walked out before he could realize I knew he'd strung together more than six words at once.

After that I thought he'd freeze himself to death working on that car. He was out there all day, and at night he rigged up a little lamp, ran a cord out the window, and had himself some light to see by while he worked. He was better than he had been before, but that's still not saying much. It was easier for him to do the things the rest of us did. He ate more slowly and didn't jump up and down during the meal to get this or that or look out the window. I put my hand in the back of the TV set, I admit, and fiddled around with it, so that it was almost impossible now to get a clear picture. He didn't look at it very often anyway. He was always out with that car or going off to get parts for it. By the time it was really melting outside, he had it fixed.

I had been feeling down in the dumps about Henry around this time. We had always been together before. Henry and Lyman. But he was such a loner now that I didn't know how to take it. So I jumped at the chance one day when Henry seemed friendly. It's not that he smiled or anything. He just said, "Let's take that old shitbox for a spin." Just the way he said it made me think he could be coming around.

We went out to the car. It was spring. The sun was shining very bright. My only sister, Bonita, who was just eleven years old, came out and made us stand together for a picture. Henry leaned his elbow on the red car's wind-shield, and he took his other arm and put it over my shoulder, very carefully, as though it was heavy for him to lift and he didn't want to bring the weight down all at once.

"Smile," Bonita said, and he did.

That picture. I never look at it anymore. A few months ago, I don't know why, I got his picture out and tacked it on the wall. I felt good about Henry at the time, close to him. I felt good having his picture on the wall, until one night when I was looking at television. I was a little drunk and stoned. I looked up at the wall and Henry was staring at me. I don't know what it was, but his smile had changed, or maybe it was gone. All I know is I couldn't stay in the same room with that picture. I was shaking. I got up, closed the door, and went into the kitchen. A little later my friend Ray came over and we both went back into that room. We put the picture in a brown bag, folded the bag over and over tightly, then put it way back in a closet.

I still see that picture now, as if it tugs at me, whenever I pass that closet door. The picture is very clear in my mind. It was so sunny that day Henry had to squint against the glare. Or maybe the camera Bonita held flashed like a mirror, blinding him, before she snapped the picture. My face is right out in the sun, big and round. But he might have drawn back, because the shadows on his face are deep as holes. There are two shadows curved like little hooks around the ends of his smile, as if to frame it and try to keep it there—that one, first smile that looked like it might have hurt his face. He has his field jacket on and the worn-in clothes he'd come back in and kept wearing ever since. After Bonita took the picture, she went into the house and we got into the car. There was a full cooler in the trunk. We started off, east, toward Pembina and the Red River because Henry said he wanted to see the high water.

The trip over there was beautiful. When everything starts changing, drying up, clearing off, you feel like your whole life is starting. Henry felt it, too. The top was down and the car hummed like a top. He'd really put it back in shape, even the tape on the seats was very carefully put down and glued back in layers. It's not that he smiled again or even joked, but his face looked to me as if it was clear, more peaceful. It looked as though he wasn't thinking of anything in particular except the bare fields and windbreaks and houses we were passing.

The river was high and full of winter trash when we got there. The sun was still out, but it was colder by the river. There were still little clumps of dirty snow here and there on the banks. The water hadn't gone over the banks yet, but it would, you could tell. It was just at its limit, hard swollen, glossy like an old gray scar. We made ourselves a fire, and we sat down and watched the current go. As I watched it I felt something squeezing inside me and tightening and trying to let go all at the same time. I knew I was not just feeling it myself; I knew I was feeling what Henry was going through at that moment. Except that I couldn't stand it, the closing and opening. I jumped to my feet. I took Henry by the shoulders and I started shaking him. "Wake up," I says, "wake up, wake up, wake up!" I didn't know what had come over me. I sat down beside him again.

His face was totally white and hard. Then it broke, like stones break all of a sudden when water boils up inside them.

"I know it," he says. "I know it. I can't help it. It's no use."

We started talking. He said he knew what I'd done with the car. It was obvious it had been whacked out of shape and not just neglected. He said he wanted to give the car to me for good now, it was no use. He said he'd fixed it just to give it back and I should take it.

"No way," I says, "I don't want it."

"That's okay," he says, "you take it."

"I don't want it, though," I says back to him, and then to emphasize, just to emphasize, you understand, I touch his shoulder. He slaps my hand off.

"Take that car," he says.

"No," I say, "make me," I say, and then he grabs my jacket and rips the arm loose. That jacket is a class act, suede with tags and zippers. I push Henry backwards, off the log. He jumps up and bowls me over. We go down in a clinch and come up swinging hard, for all we're worth, with our fists. He socks my jaw so hard I feel like it swings loose. Then I'm at his ribcage and land a good one under his chin so his head snaps back. He's dazzled. He looks at me and I look at him and then his eyes are full of tears and blood and at first I think he's crying. But no, he's laughing. "Ha! Ha!" he says. "Ha! Ha! Take good care of it."

"Okay," I says "okay, no problem, Ha! Ha!"

I can't help it, and I start laughing too. My face feels fat and strange, and after a while I get a beer from the cooler in the trunk, and when I hand it to Henry he takes his shirt and wipes my germs off. "Hoof-and-mouth disease," he says. For some reason this cracks me up, and so we're really laughing for a while, and then we drink all the rest of the beers one by one and throw them in the river and see how far, how fast, the current takes them before they fill up and sink.

"You want to go on back?" I ask after a while. "Maybe we could snag a couple nice Kashpaw girls."

He says nothing. But I can tell his mood is turning again.

"They're all crazy, the girls up here, every damn one of them."

"You're crazy too," I say, to jolly him up. "Crazy Lamartine boys!"

He looks as though he will take this wrong at first. His face twists, then clears, and he jumps up on his feet. "That's right!" he says. "Crazier 'n hell. Crazy Indians!"

I think it's the old Henry again. He throws off his jacket and starts swinging his legs out from the knees like a fancy dancer. He's down doing something between a grouse dance and a bunny hop, no kind of dance I ever saw before, but neither has anyone else on all this green growing earth. He's wild. He wants to pitch whoopee! He's up and at me and all over. All this time I'm laughing so hard, so hard my belly is getting tied up in a knot.

"Got to cool me off!" he shouts all of a sudden. Then he runs over to the river and jumps in.

There's boards and other things in the current. It's so high. No sound comes from the river after the splash he makes, so I run right over. I look around. It's getting dark. I see he's halfway across the water already, and I know he didn't swim there but the current took him. It's far. I hear his voice, though, very clearly across it.

"My boots are filling," he says.

He says this in a normal voice, like he just noticed and he doesn't know what to think of it. Then he's gone. A branch comes by. Another branch. And I go in.

By the time I get out of the river, off the snag I pulled myself onto, the sun is down. I walk back to the car, turn on the high beams, and drive it up the bank. I put it in first gear and then I take my foot off the clutch. I get out, close the door, and watch it plow softly into the water. The headlights reach in as they go down, searching, still lighted even after the water swirls over the back end. I wait. The wires short out. It is all finally dark. And then there is only the water, the sound of it going and running and going and running and running.

Respond: Thinking Independently

1. Write in your journal your reaction to the relationship between the two brothers.
2. Write a response statement: Lyman was/was not a good brother to Henry because _____.
3. Have you ever fought physically with a brother or sister? If so, why? Why do you think Henry and Lyman fought down by the river?

Reconsider: Thinking Collaboratively

1. Discuss with classmates their views of the brothers' relationship.
2. How do your classmates account for the change in Henry?
3. How much does being Native American have an effect on Lyman and Henry or on the outcome of the story?
4. Why does Lyman beat up the car? Why does he send the car into the river at the end of the story?
5. At what point in the story did you guess how it would end, or were you surprised by the ending?

Review: Thinking Critically

1. Why does Erdrich include the incident of Susy, the Alaskan girl with the long hair? What does it show about Lyman or Henry?
2. How is the red convertible linked to Lyman and Henry? Of what significance is Lyman's statement at the beginning that "Henry owns the whole car, and . . . Lyman . . . walks everywhere he goes"?
3. What do you think Lyman's reaction to the picture of Henry means?
4. In your opinion, did Henry mean to drown himself?

Understanding Fiction: Foreshadowing

If you go to many movies, you probably have gotten pretty good at predicting what is going to happen. First of all, many movies follow a predictable formula so if you've seen one *Die Hard*, you know what will happen in a similar picture. Also, there is the music. In a thriller or horror picture, you just know from the music that the bad guy or monster is about to pounce on a victim. These hints or clues are not necessarily faults in the film. Audiences may like to be tricked or fooled temporarily, but if a picture ends completely illogically without any prior buildup, they'll feel misled, exploited, or cheated.

Short story writers and novelists do not have music, of course, to foreshadow what is to come, and they don't want to be too predictable. But they also don't want readers to accuse them of false or misleading endings. So writers frequently drop hints of what is to come. In "Where Are You Going, Where Have You Been?" Joyce Carol Oates creates an evil atmosphere around Arnold Friend and his sidekick Ellie that certainly doesn't bode well for the young girl Connie. In this story, Erdrich drops clues when she mentions Henry's "boots filled with water on a windy night and he bought out my share." A reader is not expected to understand that line completely when the story opens, but as Henry sinks deeper and deeper into depression after returning from Vietnam, we readers begin to think that something bad will happen to Henry, and the earlier line begins to make sense. Active readers pay attention to these hints and clues as they read.

Writing Applications

1. Tell about a friend or family member who changed and how it affected you.
2. Write a character description of Lyman or Henry, drawing conclusions from their behavior in the story.

Jon Will's Aptitudes

GEORGE F. WILL

Preview: Thinking Ahead

We often think of outsiders in our society as those in minority racial, religious, or ethnic groups, but this essay by a father of a young man with Down syndrome reminds us that other conditions may also pose problems for people in our society. As you read this 1993 essay, think about what you, your family, the community, and society value in a individual.

Jon Will, the oldest of my four children, turns 21 this week and on this birthday, as on every other workday, he will commute by subway to his job delivering mail and being useful in other ways at the National Institutes of Health. Jon is a taxpayer, which serves him right: he voted for Bill Clinton (although he was partial to Pat Buchanan in the primaries).

The fact that Jon is striding into a productive adulthood with a spring in his step and Baltimore's Orioles on his mind is a consummation that could not have been confidently predicted when he was born. Then a doctor told his parents that their first decision must be whether or not to take Jon home. Surely 21 years later fewer doctors suggest to parents of handicapped newborns that the parental instinct of instant love should be tentative or attenuated, or that their commitment to nurturing is merely a matter of choice, even a question of convenience.

Jon has Down syndrome, a chromosomal defect involving varying degrees of mental retardation and physical abnormalities. Jon lost, at the instant he was conceived, one of life's lotteries, but he also was lucky: his physical abnormalities do not impede his vitality and his retardation is not so severe that it interferes with life's essential joys—receiving love, returning it, and reading baseball box scores.

One must mind one's language when speaking of people like Jon. He does not "suffer from" Down syndrome. It is an affliction, but he is happy— as happy as the Orioles' stumbling start this season will permit. You may well say that being happy is easy now that ESPN exists. Jon would agree. But happiness is a species of talent, for which some people have superior aptitudes.

Jon's many aptitudes far exceed those few that were dogmatically ascribed to people like him not long ago. He was born when scientific and social understanding relevant to him was expanding dramatically. We know much more about genetically based problems than we did when, in the early 1950s, James Watson and Francis Crick published their discoveries concerning the structure of DNA, the hereditary molecule, thereby beginning the cracking of the genetic code. Jon was born the year before *Roe v. Wade* and just as prenatal genetic tests were becoming routine. Because of advancing science and declining morals, there are fewer people like Jon than there should be. And just in Jon's generation much has been learned about unlocking the hitherto unimagined potential of the retarded. This begins with early intervention in the form of infant stimulation. Jon began going off to school when he was three months old.

Because Down syndrome is determined at conception and leaves its imprint in every cell of the person's body, it raises what philosophers call ontological questions. It seems mistaken to say that Jon is less than he would be without Down syndrome. When a child suffers a mentally limiting injury after birth we wonder sadly about what might have been. But a Down person's life never had any other trajectory. Jon was Jon from conception on. He has seen a brother two years younger surpass him in size, get a driver's license and leave for college, and although Jon would be forgiven for shaking his fist at the universe, he has been equable. I believe his serenity is grounded in his sense that he is a complete Jon and that is that.

Shadow of Loneliness

Some of life's pleasures, such as the delights of literature, are not accessible to Jon, but his most poignant problem is that he is just like everyone else, only a bit more so. A shadow of loneliness, an irreducible apartness from others, is inseparable from the fact of individual existence. This entails a sense of incompleteness—we *are* social creatures—that can be assuaged by marriage and other friendships, in the intimacy of which people speak their hearts and minds. Listen to the wisdom whispered by common locutions: We speak of "unburdening ourselves" when we talk with those to whom we talk most freely.

Now, try to imagine being prevented, by mental retardation and by physical impediments to clear articulation, from putting down, through conversation, many burdens attendant on personhood. The shadow of loneliness must often be somewhat darker, the sense of apartness more acute, the sense of incompleteness more aching for people like Jon. Their ability to articulate is, even more than for everyone else, often not commensurate with their abilities to think and feel, to be curious and amused, and to yearn.

Because of Jon's problems of articulation, I marvel at his casual everyday courage in coping with a world that often is uncomprehending. He is intensely interested in major league baseball umpires, and is a friend of a few of them. I think he is fascinated by their ability to make themselves understood, by vigorous gestures, all the way to the back row of the bleachers. From his season-ticket seat behind the Orioles dugout, Jon relishes rhubarbs, but I have never seen him really angry. The closest he comes is exasperation leavened by resignation. It is an interesting commentary on the human condition that one aspect of Jon's abnormality—a facet of his disability—is the fact that he is gentleness straight through. But must we ascribe a sweet soul to a defective chromosome? Let us just say that Jon is an adornment to a world increasingly stained by anger acted out.

Like many handicapped people, Jon frequently depends on the kindness of strangers. He almost invariably receives it, partly because Americans are, by and large, nice, and because Jon is, too. He was born on his father's birthday, a gift that keeps on giving.

Respond: Thinking Independently

1. Write in your journal your reaction to George Will's definition of his son's abilities and qualities.
2. Write a response statement: I was touched/surprised/angered by _____
   _____.
3. If you have known someone who has a disability, describe the person and his/her qualities.

Reconsider: Thinking Collaboratively

1. Compare response statements with your classmates. Did any of them respond to George Will's statement of his own moral judgments? If not consider his statement, "Because of advancing science and declining morals, there are fewer people like Jon than there should be." In the class's opinion, does Will make his essay stronger or weaker with such statements?
2. What are Jon Will's aptitudes?

Review: Thinking Critically

1. What does Will mean "his most poignant problem is that he is just like everyone else, only a bit more so"?
2. What is the effect of Will's references to baseball?
3. Will's statement that "Jon frequently depends on the kindness of strangers" is an echo of a line from the play *A Streetcar Named Desire* by Tennessee Williams. To what extent do you think that all of us sometimes depend on the kindness of strangers?

READING TO WRITE

Understanding Definition: Using One to Stand for Many

George Will wants readers to understand his son's abilities in order to broaden their horizons on what being "retarded" may mean. To do this he examines many facets of his son: his occupation, his hobbies, his early diagnosis and education, his problems with articulation (expressing himself). Though he focuses on his son, his unspoken purpose is for readers to define other retarded citizens in a more understanding way. Thus defining one case may extend to a broader definition of all cases.

Writing Applications: Definition

1. Define the qualities of one teacher, police officer, parent, or other person in a way that shows what the ideal teacher, police officer, or parent should be.
2. Try to broaden the understanding of readers by defining the qualities of a misunderstood group: tatoo wearers, body jewelry fanciers, rap or rock groups, or other groups.

THREE

The Meaning of Male and Female: Establishing Identity in the Face of Gender Conflicts

The open discussion of gender conflicts and sexual preference as they affect a person's self-image and even his or her identity is relatively recent. While it is true that women's suffrage and other feminist issues surfaced in the 1820s in the United States, most of the time these issues focused on public policy, such as women's right to vote and equal pay for equal work. Early pioneers for birth control like Emma Goldman and Margaret Sanger recognized that women's control over their reproductive functions had a direct bearing on their economic and political lives as well, but for the most part, there was little public talk about private issues until the birth control pill was introduced in the 1960s and the *Roe* v. *Wade* abortion decision was issued by the Supreme Court in 1973.

In much of the United States prior to this time, men and women accepted roles that few dared question. A boy grew up to marry a woman and become the "breadwinner," or jobholder, in the family. His wife, whether educated beyond high school or not, whether she had held a job or not, now stayed home to take care of the house and then the children. People who didn't marry felt society's displeasure or were the source of jokes: "the old maid" or "the mama's boy." Married women who worked were thought to be irresponsible to husbands and children or were a poor reflection on their husbands' earning capacity. Birth control and abortion were not discussed, since both were illegal in some states (such as Connecticut), and abortion was illegal in all states. Sexuality and sex education were generally mysteries that young people discovered on their own. Homosexuality was a taboo subject. Very few people were openly "gay," a term not publically used until recently.

Much has changed both legally and culturally in the area of gender issues. Besides women's increased control over their reproductive capacity, women have voiced dissatisfaction with the one accepted woman's role and have entered into many previously all-male occupations including police and fire fighting work, construction, and some military combat roles, to name a few. Changes have occurred in all aspects of art and culture: rock and roll music, more sexually explicit films, unconventional art, and protest theater.

These changes have produced many options for men and women in the way they see themselves and the ways they relate to each other. However, many options also lead to some confusion in sorting out just what one's identity is. The selections in this chapter explore several aspects of gender questions in order to shed some light on both the possibilities and the difficulties that modern life poses.

Abortion Fight Is over Choice

VICTORIA BISSELL BROWN

Preview: Thinking Ahead

Abortion is an issue that produces sharp debate. In this 1988 essay a mom who grew up in the 1960s and her 13-year-old daughter find themselves on opposite sides of the question. Their discussion raises the central issues of this debate. As you read, try to understand both the mother's and daughter's positions.

The local broadcaster announced that after the commercial he would be interviewing a leader in the anti-abortion movement. "Turn it off," I snapped at my daughter, "I can't bear to listen to that."

She gave me the kind of look children in the 1960s gave parents who refused to watch anti-war demonstrations on TV news. That look asked how could I have such a closed mind? How could I be so Establishment? And how could I be so curt, so final, so decisive about what my 13-year-old daughter says she regards as possibly the killing of babies?

Standing there in my kitchen, biscuit dough on my hands, I felt the full force of the abortion backlash. At that moment, my daughter saw me not as a soft-hearted liberal—a political persona I've grown comfortable with—but as a cold-hearted killer, one who sacrifices the unborn in the name of some abstract right to privacy. It was not the fact that she disagreed with me that was so disturbing. She's a teen-ager, she disagrees with me every day. What was so disturbing was the success of the anti-abortion movement at depicting people like me as heartless, amoral abstractionists who care more about rights than about life.

It seems to me that this is where I came in some 20 years ago. Only back then the opponents of abortion laws were the ones who were the heartless killers. Back then, we charged them with caring more about abstract principles than real life. Back then, we were the ones who showed the gruesome pictures—of women butchered on dirty kitchen tables, of women dead from unnecessary infections, of fetuses punctured by coat hangers, of women poisoned from drinking lye.

The movement for abortion rights did not begin and was not fueled by a passion for the right to privacy. That is the principle that convinced the Supreme Court, but the heart of this government is nothing so anemic as a legalistic principle. The heart of this movement is a deep concern for the lives, the health and the well-being of American women.

That is the point I tried to make to my daughter. As the biscuits cooked and the interview came on the television, we sat and discussed the matter as only a mother and adolescent daughter can. Which is to say that we were alternately snarly and sensitive; there were bursts of honesty as well as of anger; there were questions and accusations; there were tears and occasional smiles. We were momentarily locked in a primal tug of wills over the most primal of issues.

We began, of course, with the fundamentals. "How do you know you're not killing a person?" she asked. Because I know that a 10-week-old fetus cannot survive outside a woman's womb, I know that it has no cognitive abilities. I know that it has no capacity for love or work, I know that it has no relationships or responsibilities. And I weigh that knowledge against the certitude that a pregnant women is, most definitely, a person with relationships and responsibilities that only she can calculate.

I know that the research on women considering abortions shows that they aren't consumed with the question of privacy rights; they're consumed with the question of responsibilities—to their other children, to their parents, to their employers or teachers, to their husbands or lovers, to themselves, to that embryo. Few women make this decision casually; no women make it because they want to assert their right to privacy. Women decide to abort pregnancies because the ties that bind them in every other corner of their lives take priority over the very tenuous tie that binds them to that very tenuous bit of life in their wombs.

My daughter paid attention to these remarks, but seemed unmoved.

The television interview intruded. "What advice do you give to single women?" asked the interviewer. "We advise chastity," responded the pretty, powdered, softly bow-tied lady on the screen. I looked sideways at my daughter.

"What do you think of that?" I asked her. "Well," she sniffed, "I don't think people should be irresponsible about sex." That answer should have warmed the cockles of my maternal heart, but it didn't. It sounded cold-hearted, abstract—a principle unrelated to real life uttered by one who has yet to experience her first kiss.

My innocent child holds the conviction that women are—or should be—sufficiently in control of their lives so that they could always prevent pregnancy, either through contraception or by simply saying "no." It seems that she is, after all, the daughter of a feminist. This child of the women's movement expects women to be in charge of their lives. After all, her mother had only one child and no abortions—why can't everyone else be similarly well regulated? So great is women's progress (on TV and among the privileged white elite of my daughter's experience) that she simply cannot imagine women as victims of either the law or contraceptive failure or male sexual demands.

In abstract principle, she's right of course. In the best of all possible worlds, women would have the personal socialization and the economic independence that would allow them to say "no," and they would have medical and legal protections against unwanted pregnancies. But we don't live in abstract principle, and this isn't the best of all possible worlds, and despite what the softly bow-tied lady on TV said, making abortion illegal will not decrease premarital—or "irresponsible"—sex. It will only bring back all those couples who "had" to get married and all those women who were maimed or killed by underworld abortionists and all those mothers who abandoned all personal goals and resigned themselves to the vagaries of reproductive chance.

My daughter's eyes glazed over a bit, the way they do when I started sounding like a history professor. This story doesn't end with her throwing her arms around me and swearing her allegiance to my politics. It ends with my husband serving some almost-burned biscuits and my daughter and me making amends at a funny matinee.

She's not going to acquiesce to me on this. She wants the autonomy to make her own choice about abortion. And in that, she is true to the proud tradition of the abortion rights movement.

Respond: Thinking Independently

1. Write in your journal your reaction to this mother-daughter discussion.
2. Write a response statement: The statement in the essay that I agree/disagree with most is _____ because _____
_____.

Reconsider: Thinking Collaboratively

1. Compare your responses statements with your classmates. How divided is the class on this issue?
2. What part does history play in the mother's point of view?
3. Discuss the ending statement: "She's [the daughter is] not going to acquiesce to me on this. She wants the autonomy to make her own choice about abortion. And in that, she is true to the proud tradition of the abortion rights movement."

Review: Thinking Critically

1. Summarize the mother's arguments briefly. Summarize the daughter's position.
2. What does the author say the principle guiding the Supreme Court's decision was? What does she say the concern of the abortion rights movement is?
3. Why does the mother consider the daughter's argument about sexual responsibility "a principle unrelated to real life"? What do you think?

Understanding Comparison and Contrast: Using a Scenario to Explain a Contrast

When an essay writer wishes to explore the differences between two things or two ideas, she may wish to try a more creative approach than the typical alternating method or whole method of contrast. In this essay the reader is put in the middle of a scene taking place between a mother and her daughter which begins with a request to turn off the TV. The discussion between the mother and daughter on their views of abortion and sexual responsibility does alternate sides, but in a way that presents their views very conversationally. The mother does present a little background for her attitudes, but most of the debate centers on the conversation. Think about other possible scenarios: between a logger and an environmental protectionist, between a person for and one against gun control. Can you think of a situation that could bring these two together to argue their respective sides? Experiment with different ways to present the contrast.

Writing Applications: Comparison and Contrast

1. Write about a contemporary issue like welfare reform, health care, abortion, or changing the drinking age by constructing a conversation between two people who are on opposite sides of the issue.
2. Write about a topic on which you and your parents disagree. The topic need not be a major national issue but may be anything from how to pay for college to your choice of friends. You may summarize their position first and then write your own, or you may proceed point for point, explaining first their idea and then your own.

Hills Like White Elephants

ERNEST HEMINGWAY

Preview: Thinking Ahead

Ernest Hemingway, one of America's best-known writers, explores in many of his novels and short stories the different kinds of relationships men and women have with each other. This 1938 short story has intrigued many readers because the conversation between the man and the woman does not specifically state the subject. See if you can construct a plausible interpretation of their discussion based on clues in the story, as you would have to if you were in a cafe overhearing two people talk. Pay attention, too, to how they seem to relate to one another. Is their relationship, in your opinion, a healthy male-female relationship?

The hills across the valley of the Ebro were long and white. On this side there was no shade and no trees and the station was between two lines of rails in the sun. Close against the side of the station there was the warm shadow of the building and a curtain, made of strings of bamboo beads, hung across the open door into the bar, to keep out flies. The American and the girl with him sat at a table in the shade, outside the building. It was very hot and the express from Barcelona would come in forty minutes. It stopped at this junction for two minutes and went on to Madrid.

"What should we drink?" the girl asked. She had taken off her hat and put it on the table.

"It's pretty hot," the man said.

"Let's drink beer."

"Dos cervezas," the man said into the curtain.

"Big ones?" a woman asked from the doorway.

"Yes. Two big ones."

The woman brought two glasses of beer and two felt pads. She put the felt pads and the beer glasses on the table and looked at the man and the girl. The girl was looking off at the line of hills. They were white in the sun and the country was brown and dry.

"They look like white elephants," she said.

"I've never seen one," the man drank his beer.

"No, you wouldn't have."

"I might have," the man said. "Just because you say I wouldn't have doesn't prove anything."

The girl looked at the bead curtain. "They've painted something on it," she said. "What does it say?"

"Anis del Toro. It's a drink."

"Could we try it?"

The man called "Listen" through the curtain. The woman came out from the bar.

"Four reales."

"We want two Anis del Toro."

"With water?"

"Do you want it with water?"

"I don't know," the girl said. "Is it good with water?"

"It's all right."

"You want them with water?" asked the woman.

"Yes, with water."

"It tastes like licorice," the girl said and put the glass down.

"That's the way with everything."

"Yes," said the girl. "Everything tastes of licorice. Especially all the things you've waited so long for, like absinthe."

"Oh, cut it out."

"You started it," the girl said. "I was being amused. I was having a fine time."

"Well, let's try and have a fine time."

"All right. I was trying. I said the mountains looked like white elephants. Wasn't that bright?"

"That was bright."

"I wanted to try this new drink. That's all we do, isn't it—look at things and try new drinks?"

"I guess so."

The girl looked across at the hills.

"They're lovely hills," she said. "They don't really look like white elephants. I just meant the coloring of their skin through the trees."

"Should we have another drink?"

"All right."

The warm wind blew the bead curtain against the table.

"The beer's nice and cool," the man said.

"It's lovely," the girl said.

"It's really an awfully simple operation, Jig," the man said. "It's not really an operation at all."

The girl looked at the ground the table legs rested on.

"I know you wouldn't mind it, Jig. It's really not anything. It's just to let the air in."

The girl did not say anything.

"I'll go with you and I'll stay with you all the time. They just let the air in and then it's all perfectly natural."

"Then what will we do afterward?"

"We'll be fine afterward. Just like we were before."

"What makes you think so?"

"That's the only thing that bothers us. It's the only thing that's made us unhappy."

The girl looked at the bead curtain, put her hand out and took hold of two of the strings of beads.

"And you think then we'll be all right and be happy."

"I know we will. You don't have to be afraid. I've known lots of people that have done it."

"So have I," said the girl. "And afterward they were all so happy."

"Well," the man said, "if you don't want to you don't have to. I wouldn't have you do it if you didn't want to. But I know it's perfectly simple."

"And you really want to?"

"I think it's the best thing to do. But I don't want you to do it if you don't really want to."

"And if I do you'll be happy and things will be like they were and you'll love me?"

"I love you now. You know I love you."

"I know. But if I do it, then it will be nice again if I say things are like white elephants, and you'll like it?"

"I'll love it. I love it now but I just can't think about it. You know how I get when I worry."

"If I do it you won't ever worry?"

"I won't worry about that because it's perfectly simple."

"Then I'll do it. Because I don't care about me."

"What do you mean?"

"I don't care about me."

"Well, I care about you."

"Oh, yes. But I don't care about me. And I'll do it and then everything will be fine."

"I don't want you to do it if you feel that way."

The girl stood up and walked to the end of the station. Across, on the other side, were fields of grain and trees along the banks of the Ebro. Far away, beyond the river, were mountains. The shadow of a cloud moved across the field of grain and she saw the river through the trees.

"And we could have all this," she said. "And we could have everything and every day we make it more impossible."

"What did you say?"

"I said we could have everything."

"We can have everything."

"No, we can't."

"We can have the whole world."

"No, we can't."

"We can go everywhere."

"No, we can't. It isn't ours any more."

"It's ours."

"No, it isn't. And once they take it away, you never get it back."

"But they haven't taken it away."

"We'll wait and see."

"Come on back in the shade," he said. "You mustn't feel that way."

"I don't feel any way," the girl said. "I just know things."

"I don't want you to do anything that you don't want to do——"

"Nor that isn't good for me," she said. "I know. Could we have another beer?"

"All right. But you've got to realize——"

"I realize," the girl said. "Can't we maybe stop talking?"

They sat down at the table and the girl looked across at the hills on the dry side of the valley and the man looked at her and the table.

"You've got to realize," he said, "that I don't want you to do it if you don't want to. I'm perfectly willing to go through with it if it means anything to you."

"Doesn't it mean anything to you? We could get along."

"Of course it does. But I don't want anybody but you. I don't want any one else. And I know it's perfectly simple."

"Yes, you know it's perfectly simple."

"It's all right for you to say that, but I do know it."

"Would you do something for me now?"

"I'd do anything for you."

"Would you please please please please please please please stop talking?"

He did not say anything but looked at the bags against the wall of the station. There were labels on them from all the hotels where they had spent nights.

"But I don't want you to," he said, "I don't care anything about it."

"I'll scream," the girl said.

The woman came out through the curtains with two glasses of beer and put them down on the damp felt pads. "The train comes in five minutes," she said.

"What did she say?" asked the girl.

"That the train is coming in five minutes."

The girl smiled brightly at the woman, to thank her.

"I'd better take the bags over to the other side of the station," the man said. She smiled at him.

"All right. Then come back and we'll finish the beer."

He picked up the two heavy bags and carried them around the station to the other tracks. He looked up the tracks but could not see the train. Coming back, he walked through the barroom, where people waiting for the train were drinking. He drank an Anis at the bar and looked at the people. They were all waiting reasonably for the train. He went out through the bead curtain. She was sitting at the table and smiled at him.

"Do you feel better?" he asked.

"I feel fine," she said. "There nothing wrong with me. I feel fine."

Respond: Thinking Independently

1. In your journal write what you think the couple is talking about. How well do you think they relate to each other?
2. Write a response statement or question: _____
3. Briefly describe the characters of the man and woman.

Reconsider: Thinking Collaboratively

1. Compare your analysis of the couple's conversations with your classmates. What interpretations are there? What support from the story is there for each interpretation?
2. Help answer your classmates' questions.
3. Discuss a few of the man's statements: "We'll be fine afterward. Just like we were before"; "I don't want you to do it if you feel that way"; "We can have everything. . . . We can have the whole world."

Discuss what the woman says: "And if I do it you'll be happy and things will be like they were and you'll love me?"; "I don't care about me"; "And we could have all this. . . And we could have everything and every day we make it more impossible."

What do these statements show about the two people?

Review: Thinking Critically

1. Since this story is told almost entirely by dialogue, the active reader needs to consider how each statement by the woman is reacted to by the man and vice versa. That is, a reader must read "between the lines." Choose any pair of lines, one from the woman, the other from the man and discuss what they mean.
2. Why does the woman, not the man, notice and remark on the hills, the fields of grain, the river? What does the title of the story mean?

3. Why do you think that the couple "talks around" the subject, never actually defining it?
4. How do you interpret the last line of the story? Do you think the woman is being ironic? (See below.)

READING TO WRITE

Understanding Fiction: Irony

Sometimes a character in a story or a person in real life says one thing but means another. Friends tease friends, saying "that's a great haircut" when they mean just the opposite. The term for these opposite meaning statements is irony. We say the person is being ironic. In literature, and life, it is not always easy to tell when someone is being ironic, but in life, we pick up cues from someone's facial expressions or tone of voice that he/she is not saying exactly what is meant. In literature, we have to depend on the surrounding context or the exact wording to tell us that the person means something different from what is being said. Examine this section of dialogue:

"And you think then we'll be all right and be happy."
"I know we will. You don't have to be afraid. I've known lots of people that have done it."
"So have I," said the girl. "And afterward they were all so happy."
"Well," the man said, "if you don't want to you don't have to. . . ."

What might tell you that the woman is being ironic when she says that "afterward they were all so happy"? Find other places in the story where someone is being ironic.

Writing Applications

1. A well-known line from Shakespeare's *Hamlet* says, "The lady doth protest too much, methinks." In your opinion, do either the man or the woman in this story protest anything too much? Write about your ideas.
2. Write a dialogue between two people about a subject that is never revealed. Begin a new line and indent slightly when you shift from speaker to speaker. You may also use dialogue tags (he said, she said), but try to vary them, and use them sparingly.

The Most Influential Investment
LAWRENCE SUMMERS

Preview: Thinking Ahead

Why does an economist write about education for women? Lawrence Summers, the chief economist at the World Bank, looks at education for women as a

very practical investment (not discounting the social implications). Examine
Summers's evidence supporting his argument in this 1992 essay.

Educating girls quite possibly yields a higher rate of return than any other investment available in the developing world. Women's education may be unusual territory for economists, but enhancing women's contribution to development is actually as much an economic as a social issue. And economics, with its emphasis on incentives, provides guideposts that point to an explanation for why so many young girls are deprived of an education.

Parents in low-income countries fail to invest in their daughters because they do not expect them to make an economic contribution to the family: girls grow up only to marry into somebody else's family and bear children. Girls are thus less valuable than boys and are kept at home to do chores while their brothers are sent to school—the prophecy becomes self-fulfilling, trapping women in a vicious cycle of neglect.

An educated mother, on the other hand, has greater earning abilities outside the home and faces an entirely different set of choices. She is likely to have fewer, healthier children and can insist on the development of all her children, ensuring that her daughters are given a fair chance. The education of her daughters then makes it much more likely that the next generation of girls, as well as of boys, will be educated and healthy. The vicious cycle is thus transformed into a virtuous circle.

Few will dispute that educating women has great social benefits. But it has enormous economic advantages as well. Most obviously, there is the direct effect of education on the wages of female workers. Wages rise by 10 to 20 percent for each additional year of schooling. Returns of this magnitude are impressive by the standard of other available investments, but they are just the beginning. Educating women also has an impressive impact on health practices, including family planning.

Let us look at some numbers in one country as an illustration of the savings from improved hygiene and birth control. In Pakistan, educating an extra 1,000 girls an additional year would have cost approximately $40,000 in 1990. Each year of schooling is estimated to reduce mortality of children younger than five years by up to 10 percent. Since an average woman in Pakistan has 6.6 children, it follows that providing 1,000 women with an extra year of schooling would prevent roughly 60 infant deaths. Saving 60 lives with health care interventions would cost an estimated $48,000.

Educated women also choose to have fewer children. Econometric studies find that an extra year of schooling reduces female fertility by approximately 10 percent. Thus, a $40,000 investment in educating 1,000 women in Pakistan would avert 660 births. A typical family-planning evaluation concludes that costs run approximately $65 for each birth averted, or $43,000 for 660 births.

Even beyond those savings, one can calculate that an additional year of schooling for 1,000 women will prevent the deaths of four women during childbirth. Achieving similar gains through medical interventions would cost close to $10,000.

These estimates are of course crude. On one hand, I have failed to discount benefits to reflect the fact that female education operates with a lag. On the other, I have neglected the add-on gains as healthier, better educated mothers have not only healthier, better educated children but healthier, better educated grandchildren. (When the average mother in Pakistan has nearly 40 grandchildren, this is no small thing.)

Even with these caveats, the social improvements brought about by educating women are more than sufficient to cover its costs. Given that education also yields higher wages, it seems reasonable to conclude that the return on getting more girls into school is in excess of 20 percent, and probably much greater. In fact, it may well be the single most influential investment that can be made in the developing world.

So what can we do to promote investment in the education of girls? Scholarship funds should be established and more free books and other supplies given to girls. Providing schooling that responds to cultural and practical concerns is also essential: female enrollment depends heavily on schools' being nearby, on the provision of appropriate sanitation facilities and on the hiring of female teachers. Flexible hours and care for younger siblings can also be helpful.

Raising the primary school enrollment of girls to equal that of boys in the world's low-income countries would involve educating an extra 25 million girls every year at a total cost of approximately $938 million. Equalizing secondary school enrollment would mean educating an additional 21 million girls at a total cost of $1.4 billion. Eliminating educational discrimination in the low-income countries would thus cost a total of $2.4 billion. This sum represents less than one quarter of 1 percent of the gross domestic product of the low-income countries, less than 1 percent of their investment in new capital goods and less than 10 percent of their defense spending.

When compared with investments outside the social sector, education looks even more attractive. Take power generation as an example. Projections suggest that developing countries will spend approximately $1 trillion on power plants over the next 10 years. Because of poor maintenance and pricing problems, many of these nations use less than 50 percent of the capability of existing power plants. In a sample of 57 developing countries, the overall return on power-plant physical assets averaged less than 4 percent over the past three years and less than 6 percent over the past decade—returns that cannot even compare with those of 20 percent or more from providing education for females.

No doubt developing countries will improve their efficiency in generating power. And I have probably understated somewhat the difficulty of raising enrollment rates by neglecting capital costs and not taking explicit account of the special costs incurred in targeting girls. Nevertheless, it is hard to believe that building 19 out of every 20 planned power plants and using the savings to finance equal educational opportunity for girls would not be desirable.

There are those who say educating girls is a strategy that pays off only in the long run. This argument reminds me of a story, which John F.

Kennedy used to tell, of a man asking his gardener how long it would take for a certain seed to grow into a tree. The gardener said it would take 100 years, to which the man replied, "Then plant the seed this morning. There is no time to lose."

Respond: Thinking Independently

1. How did you react to Summers's point of view? Did anything surprise you? Did it confirm an opinion you already held or change your views?
2. Write a response statement: _____
3. What attitudes do your friends and family have on education for women? Have those attitudes changed since the time when your mother was your age?
4. Whether you are male or female, how do you think education for women affects us here in the United States?

Reconsider: Thinking Collaboratively

1. Compare classmates' reactions to Summers's essay.
2. How does Summers support his argument? Briefly list and discuss his evidence.
3. Why does he use the example of Pakistan? Why does he use the example of the cost of building power plants?

Review: Thinking Critically

1. Where does Summers first state his main point, his thesis sentence?
2. What is the purpose of the second paragraph?
3. Writers frequently keep their opponents' arguments in mind as they write in order to refute them. What opposing arguments does Summers raise? How does he refute them?
4. Where does Summers admit any weaknesses in his evidence? Why does he do that?

READING TO WRITE

Understanding Causal Analysis: Combining Rhetorical Methods

If you are reading this text in connection with a writing course and following the rhetorical table of contents, you probably notice that this essay is listed under "Causal Analysis." That is, it argues that a cause, women's education, has several desirable economic effects. However, the writer, like almost all writers, makes use of other rhetorical elements in this essay. For example, paragraph 5 begins, "Let us look at some numbers in one country as an illustration of the savings. . . ." Summers chooses to use the illustration or example of Pakistan as part of his support for his argument about the economic benefits of educating women. Another example in paragraph 12 is used to provide a comparison in the rate of return of building new power plants or educating more women.

Few writers, even experienced ones, sit down to write thinking, "Here I'll use examples, there I'll compare." Rather these ways of presenting information are tools to use whenever they seem appropriate, much the same way a builder reaches automatically for the proper screwdriver, or a cook for a wire whisk. However, builders, cooks, and writers had to learn to use the tools the first time they were introduced. So if all these rhetorical patterns are confusing at first, soon, with practice, you will recognize and use them easily.

Writing Applications: Cause and Effect

1. Write about the investment you have made in education so far—in money, time, and/or effort. What effects has your investment had on your life? What future effects do you hope for or expect?
2. Write your own opinion essay on education for women.

Hidden Lessons: Do Little Boys Get a Better Education Than Little Girls?
CLAIRE SAFRAN

Preview: Thinking Ahead

In the previous essay, Lawrence Summers makes the point that educating women in developing countries makes economic sense. In the United States boys and girls go to school, but is their education there equal? That question is the subject of Claire Safran's 1983 report on gender bias in education. Think about your own school experiences as you read the essay. How were the boys and girls treated in your school?

Our public school teachers are targets once again of the researchers. This time, they have been charged with sex-biased instructional methods.

Drs. David and Myra Sadker of American University in Washington, D.C., sent observers to 100 classrooms in five states to sit in on teaching sessions. The Sadkers' researchers cited instances of boys being taught differently from girls in elementary schools, where women teachers far outnumber men, through secondary schools, where more than half the teachers are male.

The bias generally is unintentional and unconscious, says Myra Sadker, dean of the School of Education at American University. She notes: "We've met teachers who call themselves feminists. They show me their nonsexist textbooks and nonsexist bulletin boards. They insist there is equity in their classrooms. Then," she continues, "I videotape them as they're teaching—

and they're amazed. If they hadn't seen themselves at work on film, they'd never have believed that they were treating boys and girls so differently."

Such videotaping of teachers is among the functions of 12 U.S. Department of Education Centers for Sex Equity in educational districts across the country.

From nursery school to beyond graduate school, studies show that teachers call on male students in class far more often than they call on female students. That difference in involvement in the learning process is crucial, say educators, who add that the students who are active in class are the ones who go on to higher achievement and a more positive attitude.

Many teachers unwittingly hinder girls from being active in class. Dr. Lisa Serbin of Concordia University in Montreal studied nursery schools in Suffolk County, N.Y. She tells how a teacher poured water into containers of different heights and widths, then told a little boy to try it—to learn for himself how water can change its shape without changing its amount.

"Can I do it?" a little girl asked.

"You'll have to wait your turn," the teacher replied, giving the pitcher to a second boy. The girl asked again, but it was time to put the materials away.

"You can help me do that," the teacher offered.

Who gets to pour the water is important. Learning is connected to instruction and direction, and boys get more of that than girls do all through school. Why? Partly because teachers tend to question the students they expect will have the answers. Since girls traditionally don't do so well as boys in such "masculine" subjects as math and science, they're called on least in those classes. But girls are called on most in verbal and reading classes, where boys are expected to have the trouble. The trouble is in our culture, not in our chromosomes. In Germany, everything academic is considered masculine, most teachers are men, and girls have the reading problems. In Japan, there's no sex bias about reading, and neither sex has special problems with it.

In most U.S. schools, there are remedial classes for reading—the "boys' problem"—and boys quickly catch up to the girls. But there are very few remedial classes in math and science—the "girls' problems." Thus boys have the most skill in these subjects, which can lead to better-paying jobs later.

According to the National Assessment of Educational Progress, an organization in Denver that surveys both public and private schools nationally, girls get better math grades than boys do at age 9, but their scores decline as they progress while boys' math scores rise. Researchers say such things happen because boys are taught to take a more active part in learning than girls.

This differing of the educational process for the sexes starts at home. For example, in one study, preschool youngsters were shown a drawing of a house and asked, "How far can you go from your own house?" Most girls pointed to an area quite near the house and said that was how far their parents permitted them to go and how far they actually went. Most boys pointed to a much wider perimeter of permission and generally said they exceeded it. In the classroom, unconscious sex bias takes various forms:

- Girls tend to be called on if they sit close to the teacher—first row—right under his or her nose. Boys tend to be called on wherever they sit. (*Girls' Lesson:* Be dependent—stay close to the teacher, and you'll be rewarded. *Boys' Lesson:* Be independent—sit anywhere; you'll be rewarded.)
- The Sadkers report this interchange. Fourth-grade teacher to a girl: "That's a neat paper. The margins are just right." To a boy: "That's a good analysis of the cause of the Civil War." (*Girl's Lesson:* Form, not content, is all that's expected of you. *Boy's Lesson:* Analytical thinking is what's expected of you.)
- Dr. Carol Dweck, professor of education at Harvard University, cites these comments by a teacher to students who have given incorrect answers. To a girl: "That's wrong." To a boy: "You'd know the right answer if you'd done your homework." (Girl's Lesson: The failure may be due to your own lack of ability. Boy's Lesson: You can do better if you make the effort.) Told that effort brings success, both sexes try—and succeed. Otherwise, both stop trying. Educators call this concept "attribution to effort."

Some teacher are learning to recognize—and then change—their methods. And small changes can make large differences. The Sadkers, for example, found that if teachers wait a few seconds after asking a question before they call on a student, more students will participate and their answers will be more complete.

Parents disturbed by sex bias in classrooms might first test themselves for it at home. Those who want to help combat teachers' sex bias might arrange to observe classes in their children's schools, and they might discuss sex bias at PTA meetings. On this issue, awareness is the first step.

Respond: Thinking Independently

1. Write your reactions to the essay in your journal. Do you find the study findings convincing? How does your own experience compare with the research findings?
2. Write a response statement: I agree/disagree with _____ _____ because _____.

Reconsider: Thinking Collaboratively

1. Compare reactions and response statements with your classmates. Is there any difference in the reaction from male or female students?
2. Discuss the study showing that parents give boys and girls differing levels of permission to explore. Was that true in your classmates' experience? What are some possible reasons? Do you agree that such differences have negative effects on girls' education?
3. What do the studies of reading problems in Germany and Japan reveal? What conclusion did Safran come to? Did the conclusion seem warranted?

Review: Thinking Critically

1. How was the Sadker study conducted? What are the advantages and disadvantages of the method?
2. Who do you think Safran was writing her essay for originally? How can you tell?
3. What does the author mean by "hidden lessons"? Give one or two examples from the essay.

READING TO WRITE

Understanding Comparison and Contrast: Using Sources in an Essay

This article by Claire Safran reports on a number of studies done by educational researchers. In order to use these sources responsibly and effectively, Safran has to do several things. First, she needs to let her readers know which ideas come from her sources and which ideas are her own conclusions. She does this often by introducing ideas coming from her sources by using their names and background: "Drs. David and Myra Sadker of American University in Washington, D.C., sent observers to 100 classrooms. . . ." She also quotes them directly, using quotation marks around what the sources say. Because this is a popular magazine article, not an academic research paper, there are no page numbers, footnotes, or bibliography, and sometimes Safran reports ideas from unnamed sources or studies which she probably wouldn't do in an academic paper.

Second, Safran wants to present the sources in her essay smoothly and effectively, so she usually introduces the subject of the study before the actual quotation. For example, the sixth paragraph begins, "Many teachers unwittingly hinder girls from being active in class." Then Safran introduces a study by Dr. Lisa Serbin to show this idea. She tries to comment on the quotation afterwards as well, to show readers how the study fits with the larger point she is making. For example, after the above mentioned study by Dr. Serbin, Safran underscores it by writing, "Who gets to pour water [the subject of Dr. Serbin's observation] is important. Learning is connected to instruction and direction. . . ." Those of you who have written research assignments know that integrating the outside sources with your own ideas responsibly and effectively is difficult, but gets easier with each attempt.

Writing Applications: Comparison and Contrast

1. Based on your own educational experiences, compare the treatment of boys and girls.
2. Argue for or against the idea that while gender differences in schools exist, they even out in the end with girls and boys suffering or benefiting equally.

Teachers' Classroom Strategies Should Recognize That Men and Women Use Language Differently

DEBORAH TANNEN

Preview: Thinking Ahead

In the previous selection, Claire Safran suggested ways that teachers could treat the genders more equally. In this 1991 essay Deborah Tannen, linguistics professor at Georgetown University and author of the best-selling You Just Don't Understand: Women and Men in Conversation, *acknowledges the differences in the ways men and women communicate. As you read, try to solve the dilemma, can a teacher treat genders equally and still acknowledge the differences between them?*

When I researched and wrote my latest book, *You Just Don't Understand: Women and Men in Conversation,* the furthest thing from my mind was reevaluating my teaching strategies. But that has been one of the direct benefits of having written the book.

The primary focus of my linguistic research always has been the language of everyday conversation. One facet of this is conversational style: how different regional, ethnic, and class backgrounds, as well as age and gender, result in different ways of using language to communicate. *You Just Don't Understand* is about the conversational styles of women and men. As I gained more insight into typically male and female ways of using language, I began to suspect some of the causes of the troubling facts that women who go to single-sex schools do better in later life, and that when young women sit next to young men in classrooms, the males talk more. This is not to say that all men talk in class, nor that no women do. It is simply that a greater percentage of discussion time is taken by men's voices.

The research of sociologists and anthropologists such as Janet Lever, Marjorie Harness Goodwin, and Donna Eder has shown that girls and boys learn to use language differently in their sex-separate peer groups. Typically, a girl has a best friend with whom she sits and talks, frequently telling secrets. It's the telling of secrets, the fact and the way that they talk to each other, that makes them best friends. For boys, activities are central: Their best friends are the ones they do things with. Boys also tend to play in larger groups that are hierarchical. High-status boys give orders and push low-status boys around. So boys are expected to use language to seize center stage: by exhibiting their skill, displaying their knowledge, and challenging and resisting challenges.

These patterns have stunning implications for classroom interaction. Most faculty members assume that participating in class discussion is a necessary part of successful performance. Yet speaking in a classroom is more congenial to boys' language experience than to girls', since it entails putting oneself forward in front of a large group of people, many of whom are strangers and at least one of whom is sure to judge speakers' knowledge and intelligence by their verbal display.

Another aspect of many classrooms that makes them more hospitable to most men than to most women is the use of debate-like formats as a learning tool. Our educational system, as Walter Ong argues persuasively in his book *Fighting for Life* (Cornell University Press, 1981), is fundamentally male in that the pursuit of knowledge is believed to be achieved by ritual opposition: public display followed by argument and challenge. Father Ong demonstrates that ritual opposition—what he calls "adversativeness" or "agonism"—is fundamental to the way most males approach almost any activity. (Consider, for example, the little boy who shows he likes a little girl by pulling her braids and shoving her.) But ritual opposition is antithetical to the way most females learn and like to interact. It is not that females don't fight, but that they don't fight for fun. They don't *ritualize* opposition.

Anthropologists working in widely disparate parts of the world have found contrasting verbal rituals for women and men. Women in completely unrelated cultures (for example, Greece and Bali) engage in ritual laments: spontaneously produced rhyming couplets that express their pain, for example, over the loss of loved ones. Men do not take part in laments. They have their own, very different verbal ritual: a contest, a war of words in which they vie with each other to devise clever insults.

When discussing these phenomena with a colleague, I commented that I see these two styles in American conversation: Many women bond by talking about troubles, and many men bond by exchanging playful insults and put-downs, and other sorts of verbal sparring. He exclaimed: "I never thought of this, but that's the way I teach: I have students read an article, and then I invite them to tear it apart. After we've torn it to shreds, we talk about how to build a better model."

This contrasts sharply with the way I teach: I open the discussion of readings by asking, "What did you find useful in this? What can we use in our own theory building and our own methods?" I note what I see as weaknesses in the author's approach, but I also point out that the writer's discipline and purposes might be different from ours. Finally, I offer personal anecdotes illustrating the phenomena under discussion and praise students' anecdotes as well as their critical acumen.

These different teaching styles must make our classrooms widely different places and hospitable to different students. Male students are more likely to be comfortable attacking the readings and might find the inclusions of personal anecdotes irrelevant and "soft." Women are more likely to resist discussion they perceive as hostile, and, indeed, it is women in my classes who are most likely to offer personal anecdotes.

A colleague who read my book commented that he had always taken for granted that the best way to deal with students' comments is to challenge them; this, he felt it was self-evident, sharpens their minds and helps them develop debating skills. But he had noticed that women were relatively silent in his classes, so he decided to try beginning discussion with relatively open-ended questions and letting comments go unchallenged. He found, to his amazement and satisfaction, that more women began to speak up.

Though some of the women in his class clearly liked this better, perhaps some of the men liked it less. One young man in my class wrote in a questionnaire about a history professor who gave students questions to think about and called on people to answer them: "He would then play devil's advocate . . . *i.e.*, he debated us. . . . That class *really* sharpened me intellectually. . . . We as students do need to know how to defend ourselves." This young man valued the experience of being attacked and challenged publicly. Many, if not most, women would shrink from such "challenge," experiencing it as public humiliation.

A professor at Hamilton College told me of a young man who was upset because he felt his class presentation had been a failure. The professor was puzzled because he had observed that class members had listened attentively and agreed with the student's observations. It turned out that it was this very agreement that the student interpreted as failure: Since no one had engaged his ideas by arguing with him, he felt they had found them unworthy of attention.

So one reason men speak in class more than women is that many of them find the "public" classroom setting more conducive to speaking, whereas most women are more comfortable speaking in private to a small group of people they know well. A second reason is that men are more likely to be comfortable with the debate-like form that discussion may take. Yet another reason is the different attitudes toward speaking in class that typify women and men.

Students who speak frequently in class, many of whom are men, assume that it is their job to think of contributions and try to get the floor to express them. But many women monitor their participation not only to get the floor but to avoid getting it. Women students in my class tell me that if they have spoken up once or twice, they hold back for the rest of the class because they don't want to dominate. If they have spoken a lot one week, they will remain silent the next. These different ethics of participation are, of course, unstated, so those who speak freely assume that those who remain silent have nothing to say, and these who are reining themselves in assume that the big talkers are selfish and hoggish.

When I looked around my classes, I could see these differing ethics and habits at work. For example, my graduate class in analyzing conversation had 20 students, 11 women and 9 men. Of the men, four were foreign students: two Japanese, one Chinese, and one Syrian. With the exception of the three Asian men, all the men spoke in class at least occasionally. The biggest talker in the class was a woman, but there were also five women who never spoke at all, only one of whom was Japanese. I decided to try something different.

I broke the class into small groups to discuss the issues raised in the readings and to analyze their own conversational transcripts. I devised three ways of dividing the students into groups: one by the degree program they were in, one by gender, and one by conversational style, as closely as I could guess it. This meant that when the class was grouped according to conversational style, I put Asian students together, fast talkers together, and quiet students together. The class split into groups six times during the semester, so they met in each grouping twice. I told students to regard the groups as examples of interactional data and to note the different ways they participated in the different groups. Toward the end of the term, I gave them a questionnaire asking about their class and group participation.

I could see plainly from my observation of the groups at work that women who never opened their mouths in class were talking away in the small groups. In fact, the Japanese woman commented that she found it particularly hard to contribute to the all-woman group she was in because "I was overwhelmed by how talkative the female students were in the female-only group." This is particularly revealing because it highlights that the same person who can be "oppressed" into silence in one context can become the talkative "oppressor" in another. No one's conversational style is absolute: everyone's style changes in response to the context and others' styles.

Some of the students (seven) said they preferred the same-gender groups; others preferred the same-style groups. In answer to the question "Would you have liked to speak in class more than you did?" six of the seven who said Yes were women; the one man was Japanese. Most startlingly, this response did not come only from quiet women; it came from women who had indicated they had spoken in class never, rarely, sometimes, and often. Of the 11 students who said the amount they had spoken was fine, 7 were men. Of the four women who checked "fine," two added qualifications indicating it wasn't completely fine: One wrote in "maybe more," and one wrote, "I have an urge to participate but often feel I should have something more interesting/relevant/wonderful/intelligent to say!!"

I counted my experiment a success. Everyone in the class found the small groups interesting, and no one indicated he or she would have preferred that the class not break into groups. Perhaps most instructive, however, was the fact that the experience of breaking into groups, and of talking about participation in class, raised everyone's awareness about classroom participation. After we had talked about it, some of the quietest women in the class made a few voluntary contributions, though sometimes I had to insure their participation by interrupting the students who were exuberantly speaking out.

Americans are often proud that they discount the significance of cultural differences: "We're are all individuals," many people boast. Ignoring such issues are gender and ethnicity becomes a source of pride: "I treat everyone the same." But treating people the same is not equal treatment if they are not the same.

The classroom is a different environment for those who feel comfortable putting themselves forward in a group than it is for those who find the prospect of doing so chastening, or even terrifying. When a professor asks, "Are there any questions?" students who can formulate statements the fastest have the greatest opportunity to respond. Those who need significant time to do so have not really been given a chance at all, since by the time they are ready to speak, someone else has the floor.

In a class where some students speak out without raising hands, those who feel they must raise their hands and wait to be recognized do not have equal opportunity to speak. Telling them to feel free to jump in will not make them feel free; one's sense of timing, of one's rights and obligations in a classroom, are automatic, learned over years of interaction. They may be changed over time, with motivation and effort, but they cannot be changed on the spot. And everyone assumes his or her own way is best. When I asked my students how the class could be changed to make it easier for them to speak more, the most talkative woman said she would prefer it if no one had to raise hands, and a foreign student said he wished people would raise their hands and wait to be recognized.

My experience in this class has convinced me that small-group interaction should be part of any class that is not a small seminar. I also am convinced that having the students become observers of their own interaction is a crucial part of their education. Talking about ways of talking in class makes students aware that their ways of talking affect other students, that the motivations they impute to others may not truly reflect others' motives, and that the behaviors they assume to be self-evidently right are not universal norms.

The goal of complete equal opportunity in class may not be attainable, but realizing that one monolithic classroom-participation structure is not equal opportunity is itself a powerful motivation to find more diverse methods to serve diverse students—and every classroom is diverse.

Respond: Thinking Independently

1. Write your reactions to Tannen's analysis of class discussion. What do you think of small group discussions? How do you react to the read and tear it apart approach?
2. Choose one of Tannen's statements that you highlighted, and write it here: _____
   Explain what you thought important or did not understand about this statement.
3. Describe the way the ideal class would be taught.

Reconsider: Thinking Collaboratively

1. Try Tannen's experiment in your class: Group yourselves in a different way from the previous small groups you were in. Choose a grouping by gender or conversational style (for the latter, perhaps get the help of

your instructor). Discuss your reactions to Tannen's essay and record your level of participation in this type of group.

2. Discuss in your new groups Tannen's statement: "But treating people the same is not equal treatment if they are not the same." How can society best balance the need for equality with the need to recognize individual differences?

3. What insights into male–female differences in conversation did you get from reading this essay?

Review: Thinking Critically

1. A dilemma is a problem with no completely satisfactory solution. One way to describe it in a cliche borrowed by the Rolling Stones is "between a rock and a hard place." Describe the dilemma of the teacher who wants to treat everyone equally.

2. What does Tannen suggest as at least a partial solution to the classroom participation question?

3. What evidence is there in this essay that gender differences in conversations exist in different cultures, not just in America? What is the importance of these cross-culture studies?

READING TO WRITE

Understanding Comparison and Contrast: A Closer Look at the Alternating Method

Earlier in this text, you were introduced to two main methods of organizing a comparison/contrast essay, the whole method which takes up one subject for half the essay and then the other subject, and the alternating method, which alternates discussion of both subjects throughout the essay. As you can see in this essay, Deborah Tannen alternates her discussion of women's and men's conversation styles. Look, for example, at the third paragraph. Tannen cites a study that first shows how girls talk and relate to friends and next how boys focus their relationships on activities and challenges to each other. Find other instances of paragraphs that first take up one gender's qualities and then the other.

As Tannen moves through her essay, she applies the general differences between men and women's talk styles to the specific situation of the classroom, beginning with a male colleague's description of his teaching as "tearing" an article apart contrasted with her own method of asking open-ended questions. Tannen departs from her contrast organization a few times, notably to discuss the process she used in splitting students into experimental groups. As observed before, essayists use the tools of writing patterns as they need them to convey their thoughts, in this case, moving from contrast to process analysis and back to contrast to report the results.

Writing Application: Comparison and Contrast

1. Analyze your own participation style, contrasting examples of classes you have felt comfortable participating in and those in which you were ill at ease. Try to explain your reactions.

Other Writing Applications

1. Argue for or against any one of Tannen's statements that you or a classmate identified and discussed earlier.
2. Revise your description of the ideal class to hand in.

Miss U.S.A.: Emma Knight
Studs Terkel

Preview: Thinking Ahead

For some people the ultimate success is to win a beauty contest, but few know what goes into winning. Fewer still reflect on what these contests and their messages mean to American culture. Studs Terkel (b. 1912), lawyer, radio interview host, reporter, and writer, has written a series of books interviewing people to learn their thoughts on a variety of subjects, from Hard Times *(1966) in the Depression to* Working *(1974). Emma Knight's interview appeared in* American Dreams: Lost and Found *(1980). Think about Emma Knight's experience and the importance of beauty in American culture.*

Miss U.S.A., 1973. She is twenty-nine.

I wince when I'm called a former beauty queen or Miss U.S.A. I keep thinking they're talking about someone else. There are certain images that come to mind when people talk about beauty queens. It's mostly what's known as t and a, tits and ass. No talent. For many girls who enter the contest, it's part of the American Dream. It was never mine.

You used to sit around the TV and watch Miss America and it was exciting, we thought, glamorous. Fun, we thought. But by the time I was eight or nine, I didn't feel comfortable. Soon I'm hitting my adolescence, like fourteen, but I'm not doing any dating and I'm feeling awkward and ugly. I'm much taller than most of the people in my class. I don't feel I can compete the way I see girls competing for guys. I was very much of a loner. I felt intimidated by the amount of competition females were supposed to go through with each other. I didn't like being told by *Seventeen* magazine: Subvert your interests if you have a crush on a guy, be interested in what he's interested in. If you play cards, be sure not to beat him. I was very bad at these social games.

After I went to the University of Colorado for three and a half years, I had it. This was 1968 through '71. I came home for the summer. An agent met me and wanted me to audition for commercials, modeling, acting jobs. I started auditioning and winning some.

I did things actors do when they're starting out. You pass out literature at conventions, you do print ads, you pound the pavements, you send out your resumés. I had come to a model agency one cold day, and an agent came out and said: "I want you to enter a beauty contest." I said: "No, uh-uh, never, never, never. I'll lose, how humiliating." She said: "I want some girls to represent the agency, might do you good." So I filled out the application blank: hobbies, measurements, blah, blah, blah. I got a letter: "Congratulations. You have been accepted as an entrant into the Miss Illinois-Universe contest." Now what do I do? I'm stuck.

You have to have a sponsor. Or you're gonna have to pay several hundred dollars. So I called up the lady who was running it. Terribly sorry, I can't do this. I don't have any money. She calls back a couple of days later: "We found you a sponsor, it's a lumber company."

It was in Decatur. There were sixty-six contestants from all over the place. I went as a lumberjack: blue jeans, hiking boots, a flannel shirt, a pair of suspenders, and carrying an axe. You come out first in your costume and you introduce yourself and say your astrological sign or whatever it is they want you to say. You're wearing a banner that has the sponsor's name on it. Then you come out and do your pirouettes in your one-piece bathing suit, and the judges look at you a lot. Then you come out in your evening gown and pirouette around for a while. That's the first night.

The second night, they're gonna pick fifteen people. In between, you had judges' interviews. For three minutes, they ask you anything they want. Can you answer questions? How do you handle yourself? Your poise, personality, blah, blah, blah. They're called personality judges.

I thought: This will soon be over, get on a plane tomorrow, and no one will be the wiser. Except that my name got called as one of the fifteen. You have to go through the whole thing all over again.

I'm thinking: I don't have a prayer. I'd come to feel a certain kind of distance, except that they called my name. I was the winner, Miss Illinois. All I could do was laugh. I'm twenty-two, standing up there in a borrowed evening gown, thinking: What am I doing here? This is like Tom Sawyer becomes an altar boy.

I was considered old for a beauty queen, which is a little horrifying when you're twenty-two. That's very much part of the beauty queen syndrome: the young, untouched, unthinking human being.

I had to go to this room and sign the Miss Illinois-Universe contract right away. Miss Universe, Incorporated, is the full name of the company. It's owned by Kaiser-Roth, Incorporated, which was bought out by Gulf & Western. Big business.

I'm sitting there with my glass of champagne and I'm reading over this contract. They said: "Oh, you don't have to read it." And I said: "I never sign anything that I don't read." They're all waiting to take pictures, and I'm sitting there reading this long document. So I signed it and the phone rang and the guy was from a Chicago paper and said: "Tell me, is it Miss or Ms.?" I said: "It's Ms." He said: "You're kidding." I said: "No, I'm not." He wrote an article the next day saying something like it finally happened: a beauty queen, a feminist. I thought I was a feminist before I was a beauty queen, why should I stop now?

Then I got into the publicity and training and interviews. It was a throwback to another time where crossed ankles and white gloves and teacups were present. I was taught how to walk around with a book on my head, how to sit daintily, how to pose in a bathing suit, and how to frizz my hair. They wanted curly hair, which I hate.

One day the trainer asked me to shake hands. I shook hands. She said: "That's wrong. When you shake hands with a man, you always shake hands ring up." I said: "Like the pope? Where my hand is up, like he's gonna kiss it?" Right. I thought: Holy mackerel! It was a very long February and March and April and May.

I won the Miss U.S.A. pageant. I started to laugh. They tell me I'm the only beauty queen in history that didn't cry when she won. It was on network television. I said to myself: "You're kidding." Bob Barker, the host, said: "No, I'm not kidding." I didn't know what else to say at that moment. In the press releases, they call it the great American Dream. There she is, Miss America, your ideal. Well, not my ideal, kid.

The minute you're crowned, you become their property and subject to whatever they tell you. They wake you up at seven o'clock next morning and make you put on a negligee and serve you breakfast in bed, so that all the New York papers can come in and take your picture sitting in bed, while you're absolutely bleary-eyed from the night before. They put on the Kaiser-Roth negligee, hand you the tray, you take three bites. The photographers leave, you whip off the negligee, they take the breakfast away, and that's it. I never did get any breakfast that day. (Laughs.)

You immediately start making personal appearances. The Jaycees or the chamber of commerce says: "I want to book Miss U.S.A. for our Christmas Day parade." They pay, whatever it is, seven hundred fifty dollars a day, first-class air fare, round trip, expenses, so forth. If the United Fund calls and wants me to give a five-minute pitch on queens at a luncheon, they still have to pay a fee. Doesn't matter that it's a charity. It's one hundred percent to Miss Universe, Incorporated. You get your salary. That's your prize money for the year. I got fifteen thousand dollars, which is all taxed in New York. Maybe out of a check of three thousand dollars, I'd get fifteen hundred dollars.

From the day I won Miss U.S.A. to the day I left for Universe, almost two months, I got a day and a half off. I made about two hundred fifty appearances that year. Maybe three hundred. Parades, shopping centers, and things. Snip ribbons. What else do you do at a shopping center? Model clothes. The nice thing I got to do was public speaking. They said: "You want a ghost writer?" I said: "Hell, no, I know how to talk." I wrote my own speeches. They don't trust girls to go out and talk because most of them can't.

One of the big execs from General Motors asked me to do a speech in Washington, D. C., on the consumer and the energy crisis. It was the fiftieth anniversary of the National Management Association. The White House, for some reason, sent me some stuff on it. I read it over, it was nonsense. So I stood up and said: "The reason we have an energy crisis is because we are, industrially and personally, pigs. We have a short-term view of the resources available to us; and unless we wake up to what we're doing to our air and water, we'll have a dearth, not just a crisis." Oh, they weren't really pleased. (Laughs.)

What I resent most is that a lot of people didn't expect me to live this version of the American Dream for myself. I was supposed to live it their way.

When it came out in a newspaper interview that I said Nixon should resign, that he was a crook, oh dear, the fur flew. They got very upset until I got an invitation to the White House. They wanted to shut me up. The Miss Universe corporation had been trying to establish some sort of liaison with the White House for several years. I make anti-Nixon speeches and get this invitation.

I figured they're either gonna take me down to the basement and beat me up with a rubber hose or they're gonna offer me a cabinet post. They had a list of fifteen or so people I was supposed to meet. I've never seen such a bunch of people with raw nerve endings. I was dying to bring a tape recorder but thought if you mention the word "Sony" in the Nixon White House, you're in trouble. They'd have cardiac arrest. But I'm gonna bring along a pad and a paper. They were patronizing. And when one of 'em got me in his office and talked about all the journalists and television people being liberals, I brought up blacklisting, *Red Channels*, and the TV industry. He changed the subject.

Miss Universe took place in Athens, Greece. The junta was still in power. I saw a heck of a lot of jeeps and troops and machine guns. The Americans were supposed to keep a low profile. I had never been a great fan of the Greek junta, but I knew darn well I was gonna have to keep my mouth shut. I was still representing the United States, for better or for worse. Miss Philippines won. I ran second.

At the end of the year, you're run absolutely ragged. That final evening, they usually have several queens from past years come back. Before they crown the new Miss U.S.A., the current one is supposed to take what they call the farewell walk. They call over the PA: Time for the old queen's walk. I'm now twenty-three and I'm an old queen. And they have this idiot farewell speech playing over the airwaves as the old queen takes the walk. And you're sitting on the throne for about thirty seconds, then you come down and they announce the name of the new one and you put the crown on her head. And then you're out.

As the new one is crowned, the reporters and photographers rush on the stage. I've seen photographers shove the girl who has just given her reign up thirty seconds before, shove her physically. I was gone by that time, I had jumped off the stage in my evening gown. It is very difficult for girls who are terrified of this ending. All of a sudden (snaps fingers), you're out. Nobody gives a damn about the old one.

Miss U.S.A. and remnants thereof is the crown stored in the attic in my parents' home. I don't even know where the banners are. It wasn't me the fans of Miss U.S.A. thought was pretty. What they think is pretty is the banner and crown. If I could put the banner and crown on that lamp, I swear to God ten men would come in and ask it for a date. I'll think about committing an ax murder if I'm not called anything but a former beauty queen. I can't stand it any more.

Several times during my year as what's-her-face I had seen the movie *The Sting*. There's a gesture the characters use which means the con is on: they rub their nose. In my last fleeting moments as Miss U.S.A., as they were playing that silly farewell speech and I walked down the aisle and stood by the throne, I looked right into the camera and rubbed my finger across my nose. The next day, the pageant people spent all their time telling people that I hadn't done it. I spent the time telling them that, of course, I had. I simply meant: the con is on. (Laughs.)

Miss U.S.A. is in the same graveyard that Emma Knight the twelve-year-old is. Where the sixteen-year-old is. All the past selves. There comes a time when you have to bury those selves because you've grown into another one. You don't keep exhuming the corpses.

If I could sit down with every young girl in America for the next fifty years, I could tell them what I liked about the pageant, I could tell them what I hated. It wouldn't make any difference. There're always gonna be girls who want to enter the beauty pageant. That's the fantasy: the American Dream.

Respond: Thinking Independently

1. Write your reactions to "Miss U.S.A." in your journal.
2. Write a response statement: Emma Knight's main point seemed to be

   _____.

3. How much are beauty pageants a part of American girls' fantasies today?

Reconsider: Thinking Collaboratively

1. Compare responses with your classmates. Do they admire Emma Knight's point of view? Explain.
2. Discuss what Emma Knight means by the "social games" she learned from Seventeen magazine. Have "social games" changed? Are they still being played? Explain.
3. What expectations did pageant officials have about their winners? That is, what kind of thoughts, behavior, and appearance was Emma Knight supposed to have?
4. Emma Knight says, "There comes a time when you have to bury those selves because you've grown into another one." What does she mean? Do you agree?

Review: Thinking Critically

1. Emma Knight says, "It wasn't me the fans of Miss U.S.A. thought was pretty. What they think is pretty is the banner and the crown." What does she mean? Are there other examples of fans' worshipping the image or the position but not the person?
2. Knight says that her story is not going to make a difference in young women's attitudes toward beauty contests. Do you agree? Why or why not?
3. What does Knight mean that "people didn't expect me to live this version of the American Dream for myself. I was supposed to live it their way?

READING TO WRITE

Understanding Description: The Vignette

Writers sometimes describe a moment in time and place that captures their view of an entire experience. Such a glimpse, or vignette, can capture a reader's interest because it is very specific and makes the reader feel like an eyewitness. Emma Knight's description of her signing the contract, her training, her "breakfast in bed," or her rubbing her nose during her final farewell walk are examples of these moments in time.

Writing Application: Description

1. Write a paragraph describing a particular moment that seemed to stand for a larger experience: childhood, high school, family life, your identity.

Writing Application

1. Write about how Americans act toward celebrities. Try to account for that behavior. (Note: Choose a celebrity and read articles in magazines or newspapers about his or her life and relationships with fans.)

Daystar
RITA DOVE

Preview: Thinking Ahead

The need to maintain one's identity in a marriage with children requires creative solutions sometimes. In this 1986 poem a woman finds her own space to focus only on her own concerns. Rita Dove is an African American born and raised in Akron, Ohio. Educated at Miami University in Ohio, Dove was

*awarded a Fullbright for study in Germany and then earned a master of Fine
Arts in Writing at the University of Iowa. The author of several books of poetry, Dove teaches creative writing and in 1993 was named Poet Laureate of
the United States.*

She wanted a little room for thinking:
but she saw diapers steaming on the line,
a doll slumped behind the door.

So she lugged a chair behind the garage
to sit out the children's naps.

Sometimes there were things to watch—
the pinched armor of a vanished cricket,
a floating maple leaf. Other days
she stared until she was assured
when she closed her eyes
she'd see only her own vivid blood.

She had an hour, at best, before Liza appeared
pouting from the top of the stairs.
And just *what* was mother doing
out back with the field mice? Why,

building a palace. Later
that night when Thomas rolled over and
lurched into her, she would open her eyes
and think of the place that was hers
for an hour—where
she was nothing,
pure nothing, in the middle of the day.

Respond: Thinking Independently

1. How do you react to "She wanted a little room for thinking"?
2. Choose a line that means something to you and explain its meaning:
   _____
3. What's American culture's attitude toward being alone?

Reconsider: Thinking Collaboratively

1. Discuss the mother's need to be alone. Is she being selfish?
2. Discuss the lines classmates have chosen and their interpretations.

Review: Thinking Critically

1. Why does she answer Liza's question with "building a palace"?
2. What does she mean when she says that she was "pure nothing"? Is this
   a negative thing for her?
3. Why does she observe some days and just stare at other times?
4. What can you tell about her relationship with Thomas, her husband?

READING TO WRITE

Understanding Poetry: The Power of Specific Details

Because poets must make every word count in the compressed poetic form, they know the specific detail will make a powerful impression on the reader. In this poem Rita Dove uses specific word pictures to convey her speaker's mood and ideas. For example, to express the young mother's frustrations over never having any time to herself, she writes "She wanted a little room for thinking: / but she saw diapers steaming on the line," the drying diapers representing her all-consuming motherhood. To emphasize that the speaker simply wants to meditate, Dove says that she watches "the pinched armor of a vanished cricket," which is just a brown paper-thin shell left behind when the insect molts, or a "floating maple leaf." She knows these are not much to watch, which emphasizes the speaker's need to get away and be "nothing."

Prose writers also know the power of specific detail, as has been mentioned earlier in the text. Sharp observing and exact wording create such details. If a person is smiling, how does she smile? Slyly? Flirtingly? Knowingly? If a person frowns, how does he frown? Disapprovingly? Fearfully? Distractedly? If a vacant lot is strewn with trash, just what is the trash? If it's old baseball programs and hot dog wrappers, that gives the reader a different image than if the trash is broken beer bottles and empty crack vials. Use the power of detail in your writing.

Writing Applications: Specific Details

1. Write about the importance you feel about being with people or being alone. Make your readers understand your feelings through the details you use.
2. Take some time to sit and observe a natural scene and record in as much detail as you can what you see, hear, and smell.

This Is Just to Say

WILLIAM CARLOS WILLIAMS

Preview: Thinking Ahead

William Carlos Williams combined being a physician and a poet from the time he graduated from the University of Pennsylvania Medical School in 1906. Later he added novels, short stories, and plays to his growing collection of published works. He won the first National Book Award for poetry in 1950 and is considered to be one of the best twentieth-century writers. In this very short poem, try to think who the speaker (I) might be and the person the speaker is writing to (you) might be. What is their relationship? Why does the speaker write to the other person?

I have eaten
the plums
that were in
the icebox

and which
you were probably
saving
for breakfast

Forgive me
they were delicious
so sweet
and so cold

Respond: Thinking Independently

1. Write your response to the poem and the relationship between the speaker and the one receiving the message.

Reconsider: Thinking Collaboratively

1. Compare responses with your classmates. Does everyone have the same interpretation? Account for the differences, if any.
2. If the speaker thought the plums were "probably" being saved for breakfast, why did he/she eat them? What does this act tell about the speaker?
3. How does the class react to the apology "Forgive me"?
4. Why does the speaker describe the already eaten plums?

Review: Thinking Critically

1. Speculate upon the relationship between the "I" and "you" of the poem.

READING TO WRITE

Understanding Poetry: Drawing Inferences

Earlier in the text you read about using inferences in understanding an essay. Here this skill is being applied to reading poetry, but we all use this skill in our everyday lives. For example, if you walk into a room where two people have been talking, you may sense that they have been quarreling by their facial expressions, body language, or a few curt remarks, even if you did not hear the quarrel. You have inferred something about their conversation from their outward appearance.

In something written such as a poem or a short story, readers frequently infer what is going on by thinking about the written lines and what might be going on in the background to produce the written lines. So, for example, if you read "Hills Like White Elephants," you needed to figure out what the man and woman were discussing and what was happening to their relationship by interpreting what they were saying in the written dialogue. In this poem, the action is simply the eating of plums, but can we infer something about the relationship between the speaker of the poem and the "you" to whom dialogue is directed? One reviewer of this text wondered why I put this poem in Chapter III, The Meaning of Male and Female, since there was no obvious connection with the theme. Can you guess what I inferred about the "I" and "you" in the poem to account for my including the poem here? Do you agree?

Writing Application

1. In response to the poems in this chapter, write an essay examining what each partner in a relationship owes to the other. Use the poems, other selections, or your own reading and experience.

Why Marriages Fail
ANNE ROIPHE

Preview: Thinking Ahead

Popular novelist and essayist Anne Roiphe examines the causes for America's high divorce rate. This article, which appeared in Family Weekly, *February 27, 1983, draws together ideas from psychology, current trends, and examples of others' experiences to explain how two identities which come together in a marriage may break apart. Compare her analysis with your own experience and other reading you have done.*

These days so many marriages end in divorce that our most sacred vows no longer ring with truth. "Happily ever after" and "Till death do us part" are expressions that seem on the way to becoming obsolete. Why has it become so hard for couples to stay together? What goes wrong? What has happened to us that close to one-half of all marriages are destined for the divorce courts? How could we have created a society in which 42 percent of our children will grow up in single-parent homes? If statistics could only measure loneliness, regret, pain, loss of self-confidence and fear of the future, the numbers would be beyond quantifying.

Even though each broken marriage is unique, we can still find the common perils, the common causes for marital despair. Each marriage has crisis points and each marriage tests endurance, the capacity for both intimacy and change. Outside pressures such as job loss, illness, infertility, trouble with a child, care of aging parents and all the other plagues of life hit marriage the way hurricanes blast our shores. Some marriages survive these storms and others don't. Marriages fail, however, not simply because of the outside weather but because the inner climate becomes too hot or too cold, too turbulent or too stupefying.

When we look at how we choose our partners and what expectations exist at the tender beginnings of romance, some of the reasons for disaster become quite clear. We all select with unconscious accuracy a mate who will recreate with us the emotional patterns of our first homes. Dr. Carl A. Whitaker, a marital therapist and emeritus professor of psychiatry at the University of Wisconsin explains, "From early childhood on, each of us carried models for marriage, femininity, masculinity, motherhood, fatherhood and all the other family roles." Each of us falls in love with a mate who has qualities of our parents, who will help us rediscover both the psychological happiness and miseries of our past lives. We may think we have found a man unlike Dad, but then he turns to drink or drugs, or loses his job over and over again or sits silently in front of the T.V. just the way Dad did. A man may choose a woman who doesn't like kids just like his mother or who gambles away the family savings just like his mother. Or he may choose a slender wife who seems unlike his obese mother but then turns out to have other addictions that destroy their mutual happiness.

A man and a woman bring to their marriage bed a blended concoction of conscious and unconscious memories of their parents' lives together. The human way is to compulsively repeat and recreate the patterns of the past. Sigmund Freud so well described the unhappy design that many of us get trapped in: the unmet needs of childhood, the angry feelings left over from frustrations of long ago, the limits of trust and the reoccurrence of old fears. Once an individual senses this entrapment, there may follow a yearning to escape, and the result could be a broken, splintered marriage.

Of course people can overcome the habits and attitudes that developed in childhood. We all have hidden strengths and amazing capacities for growth and creative change. Change, however, requires work—observing your part in a rotten pattern, bringing difficulties out into the open—and work runs counter to the basic myth of marriage: "When I wed this person all my problems will be over. I will have achieved success and I will become the center of life for this other person and this person will be my center, and we will mean everything to each other forever." This myth, which every marriage relies on, is soon exposed. The coming of children, the pulls and tugs of their demands on affection and time, place a considerable strain on that basic myth of meaning everything to each other, of merging together and solving all of life's problems.

Concern and tension about money take each partner away from the other. Obligations to demanding parents or still-depended-upon parents create further strain. Couples today must also deal with all the cultural changes brought on in recent years by the women's movement and the sexual revolution. The altering of roles and the shifting of responsibilities have been extremely trying for many marriages.

These and other realities of life erode the visions of marital bliss the way sandstorms eat at rock and the ocean nibbles away at the dunes. Those eu-

phoric, grand feelings that accompany romantic love are really self-delu-
sions, self-hypnotic dreams that enable us to forge a relationship. Real life,
failure at work, disappointments, exhaustion, bad smells, bad colds and
hard times all puncture the dream and leave us stranded with our mate,
with our childhood patterns pushing us this way and that, with our unfulfilled expectations.

The struggle to survive in marriage requires adaptability, flexibility,
genuine love and kindness and an imagination strong enough to feel what
the other is feeling. Many marriages fall apart because either partner cannot
imagine what the other wants or cannot communicate what he or she needs
or feels. Anger builds until it erupts into a volcanic burst that buries the
marriage in ash.

It is not hard to see, therefore, how essential communication is for a
good marriage. A man and a woman must be able to tell each other how
they feel and why they feel the way they do; otherwise they will impose on
each other roles and actions that lead to further unhappiness. In some cases,
the communication patterns of childhood—of not talking, of talking too
much, of not listening, of distrust and anger, of withdrawal—spill into the
marriage and prevent a healthy exchange of thoughts and feelings. The answer is to set up new patterns of communication and intimacy.

At the same time, however, we must see each other as individuals. "To
achieve a balance between separateness and closeness is one of the major
psychological tasks of all human beings at every stage of life," says Dr. Stu-
art Bartle, a psychiatrist at the New York University Medical Center.

If we sense from our mate a need for too much intimacy, we tend to
push him or her away, fearing that we may lose our identities in the merging of marriage. One partner may suffocate the other partner in a childlike
dependency.

A good marriage means growing as a couple but also growing as individuals. This isn't easy. Richard gives up his interest in carpentry because
his wife, Helen, is jealous of the time he spends away from her. Karen quits
her choir group because her husband dislikes the friends she makes there.
Each pair clings to each other and are angry with each other as life closes in
on them. This kind of marital balance is easily thrown as one or the other
pulls away and divorce follows.

Sometimes people pretend that a new partner will solve the old problems. Most often extramarital sex destroys a marriage because it allows an
artificial split between the good and the bad—the good is projected on the
new partner and the bad is dumped on the head of the old. Dishonesty, hiding and cheating create walls between men and women. Infidelity is just a
symptom of trouble. It is a symbolic complaint, a weapon of revenge, as well
as an unraveler of closeness. Infidelity is often that proverbial last straw that
sinks the camel to the ground.

All right—marriage has always been difficult. Why then are we seeing
so many divorces at this time? Yes, our modern social fabric is thin, and yes
the permissiveness of society has created unrealistic expectations and

thrown the family into chaos. But divorce is so common because people today are unwilling to exercise the self-discipline that marriage requires. They expect easy joy, like the entertainment on TV, the thrill of a good party.

Marriage takes some kind of sacrifice, not dreadful self-sacrifice of the soul, but some level of compromise. Some of one's fantasies, some of one's legitimate desires have to be given up for the value of the marriage itself. "While all marital partners feel shackled at times, it is they who really choose to make the marital ties into confining chains or supporting bonds," says Dr. Whitaker. Marriage requires sexual, financial and emotional discipline. A man and a woman cannot follow every impulse, cannot allow themselves to stop growing or changing.

Divorce is not an evil act. Sometimes it provides salvation for people who have grown hopelessly apart or were frozen in patterns of pain or mutual unhappiness. Divorce can be, despite its initial devastation, like the first cut of the surgeon's knife, a step toward new health and a good life. On the other hand, if the partners can stay past the breaking up of the romantic myths into the development of real love and intimacy, they have achieved a work as amazing as the greatest cathedrals of the world. Marriages that do not fail but improve, that persist despite imperfections, are not only rare these days but offer a wondrous shelter in which the face of our mutual humanity can safely show itself.

Respond: Thinking Independently

1. React to Roiphe's list of the reasons why marriages fail. Which do you agree with? Disagree with?
2. Choose a sentence to discuss later with the class, either because you think it is true, not true, or because you are not sure what it means:
3. What do you think is the most important reason for a failed marriage?

Reconsider: Thinking Collaboratively

1. On what do classmates agree and disagree?
2. Discuss the sentences you chose earlier as a focus of discussion.
3. Discuss this sentence: "Divorce is so common because people today are unwilling to exercise the self-discipline that marriage requires."
4. Discuss what Roiphe calls the "basic myth of marriage."

Review: Thinking Critically

1. What support (or evidence) does Roiphe cite? Is it adequate? Explain.
2. What outside pressures on marriages does Roiphe list? What others would you add?
3. Summarize Roiphe's explanation of how childhood influences our choices of marriage partners.
4. Discuss what Roiphe sees as the need for communication and intimacy balanced by the need to "see each other as individuals."
5. What is Roiphe's overall attitude toward marriage and divorce?

READING TO WRITE

Understanding Causal Analysis: Emphasizing Causes

As has been explained in earlier selections, a writer can emphasize the causes of a particular situation, its effects, or causes and effects equally, often in a kind of chain with each cause leading to an effect which then becomes another cause. This selection by Anne Roiphe emphasizes the causes of failed marriages and only looks at the effects of divorce at the beginning and at the end of the essay. Roiphe looks both at immediate causes for divorce such as life's pressures caused by job loss and at deeper, more psychologically rooted causes like the influence of one's childhood on the choice of a mate. As she discusses these causes, note that she qualifies her statements saying "in some cases," "sometimes," "most often." The causes of divorce are so complex that no one could name just one with absolute certainty.

Writing Applications: Causal Analysis

1. Examine the causes of a broken relationship in your life.
2. Analyze the causes of any local or campus situation. While you may refer to the effects, emphasize the search for causes.

A Serious Talk

RAYMOND CARVER

Preview: Thinking Ahead

Tension between separated or divorced couples create situations frequently leading to arguments and all too often to domestic violence. As you read this 1981 story, try to understand Burt's feelings as well as his actions. Try to understand Vera's feelings and concerns also. Raymond Carver writes poems and stories about working-class people he knew firsthand while growing up as the son of a sawmill worker. He married at 18, went to school at night, and worked at many dead-end jobs. By 1967, however, his poetry and stories were being published, and "Will You Please Be Quiet, Please?" was selected for the Best American Short Stories in that year. In 1993, a collection of his stories was made into Short Cuts, *a Robert Altman film.*

Vera's car was there, no others, and Burt gave thanks for that. He pulled into the drive and stopped beside the pie he'd dropped the night before. It was still there, the aluminum pan upside down, a halo of pumpkin filling on the pavement. It was the day after Christmas.

He'd come on Christmas day to visit his wife and children. Vera had warned him beforehand. She'd told him the score. She'd said he had to be out by six o'clock because her friend and his children were coming for dinner.

They had sat in the living room and solemnly opened the presents Burt had brought over. They had opened his packages while other packages wrapped in festive paper lay piled under the tree waiting for after six o'clock.

He had watched the children open their gifts, waited while Vera undid the ribbon on hers. He saw her slip off the paper, lift the lid, take out the cashmere sweater.

"It's nice," she said. "Thank you, Burt."

"Try it on," his daughter said.

"Put it on," his son said.

Burt looked at his son, grateful for his backing him up.

She did try it on. Vera went into the bedroom and came out with it on.

"It's nice," she said.

"It's nice on *you*," Burt said, and felt a welling in his chest.

He opened his gifts. From Vera, a gift certificate at Sondheim's men's store. From his daughter, a matching comb and brush. From his son, a ballpoint pen.

Vera served sodas, and they did a little talking. But mostly they looked at the tree. Then his daughter got up and began setting the dining-room table, and his son went off to his room.

But Burt liked it where he was. He liked it in front of the fireplace, a glass in his hand, his house, his home.

Then Vera went into the kitchen.

From time to time his daughter walked into the dining room with something for the table. Burt watched her. He watched her fold the linen napkins into the wine glasses. He watched her put a slender vase in the middle of the table. He watched her lower a flower into the vase, doing it ever so carefully.

A small wax and sawdust log burned on the grate. A carton of five more sat ready on the hearth. He got up from the sofa and put them all in the fireplace. He watched until they flamed. Then he finished his soda and made for the patio door. On the way, he saw the pies lined up on the sideboard. He stacked them in his arms, all six, one for every ten times she had ever betrayed him.

In the driveway in the dark, he'd let one fall as he fumbled with the door.

The front door was permanently locked since the night his key had broken off inside it. He went around to the back. There was a wreath on the patio door. He rapped on the glass. Vera was in her bathrobe. She looked out at him and frowned. She opened the door a little.

Burt said, "I want to apologize to you for last night. I want to apologize to the kids, too."

Vera said, "They're not here."

She stood in the doorway and he stood on the patio next to the philodendron plant. He pulled at some lint on his sleeve.

She said, "I can't take any more. You tried to burn the house down."

"I did not."

"You did. Everybody here was a witness."

He said, "Can I come in and talk about it?"

She drew the robe together at her throat and moved back inside.

She said, "I have to go somewhere in an hour."

He looked around. The tree blinked on and off. There was a pile of colored tissue paper and shiny boxes at one end of the sofa. A turkey carcass sat on a platter in the center of the dining-room table, the leathery remains in a bed of parsley as if in a horrible nest. A cone of ash filled the fireplace. There were some empty Shasta cola cans in there too. A trail of smoke stains rose up to the bricks to the mantel, where the wood that stopped them was scorched black.

He turned around and went back to the kitchen.

He said, "What time did your friend leave last night?"

She said, "If you're going to start that, you can go right now."

He pulled a chair out and sat down at the kitchen table in front of the big ashtray. He closed his eyes and opened them. He moved the curtain aside and looked out at the backyard. He saw a bicycle without a front wheel standing upside down. He saw weeds growing along the redwood fence.

She ran water into a saucepan. "Do you remember Thanksgiving?" she said. "I said then that was the last holiday you were going to wreck for us. Eating bacon and eggs instead of turkey at ten o'clock at night."

"I know it," he said. "I said I'm sorry."

"Sorry isn't good enough."

The pilot light was out again. She was at the stove trying to get the gas going under the pan of water.

"Don't burn yourself," he said. "Don't catch yourself on fire."

He considered her robe catching fire, him jumping up from the table, throwing her down onto the floor and rolling her over and over into the living room, where he would cover her with his body. Or should he run to the bedroom for a blanket?

"Vera?"

She looked at him.

"Do you have anything to drink? I could use a drink this morning."

"There's some vodka in the freezer."

"When did you start keeping vodka in the freezer?"

"Don't ask."

"Okay," he said, "I won't ask."

He got out the vodka and poured some into a cup he found on the counter.

She said, "Are you just going to drink it like that, out of a cup?" She said, "Jesus Burt. What'd you want to talk about, anyway? I told you I have someplace to go. I have a flute lesson at one o'clock."

"Are you still taking flute?"

"I just said so. What is it? Tell me what's on your mind, and then I have to get ready."

"I wanted to say I was sorry."

She said, "You said that."

He said, "If you have any juice, I'll mix it with this vodka."

She opened the refrigerator and moved things around.

"There's cranapple juice," she said.

"That's fine," he said.

"I'm going to the bathroom," she said.

He drank the cup of cranapple juice and vodka. He lit a cigarette and tossed the match into the big ashtray that always sat on the kitchen table. he studied the butts in it. Some of them were Vera's brand, and some of them weren't. Some even were lavender-colored. He got up and dumped it all under the sink.

The ashtray was not really an ashtray. It was a big dish of stoneware they'd bought from a bearded potter on the mall in Santa Clara. He rinsed it out and dried it. He put it back on the table. And then he ground out his cigarette in it.

The water on the stove began to bubble just as the phone began to ring.

He heard her open the bathroom door and call to him through the living room.

"Answer that! I'm about to get into the shower."

The kitchen phone was on the counter in a corner behind the roasting pan. He moved the roasting pan and picked up the receiver.

"Is Charlie there?" the voice said.

"No," Burt said.

"Okay," the voice said.

While he was seeing to the coffee, the phone rang again.

"Charlie?"

"Not here," Burt said.

This time he left the receiver off the hook.

Vera came back into the kitchen wearing jeans and a sweater and brushing her hair.

He spooned the instant into the cups of hot water and then spilled some vodka into his. He carried the cups over to the table.

She picked up the receiver, listened. She said, "What's this? Who was on the phone?"

"Nobody," he said. "Who smokes colored cigarettes?"

"I do."

"I didn't know you did that."

"Well, I do."

She sat across from him and drank her coffee. They smoked and used the ashtray.

There were things he wanted to say, grieving things, consoling things, things like that.

"I'm smoking three packs a day," Vera said. "I mean, if you really want to know what goes on around here."

"God almighty," Burt said.

Vera nodded.

"I didn't come over here to hear that," he said.

"What did you come over here to hear, then? You want to hear the house burned down?"

"Vera," he said. "It's Christmas. That's why I came."

"It's the day after Christmas," she said. "Christmas has come and gone," she said. "I don't ever want to see another one."

"What about me?" he said. "You think I look forward to holidays?"

The phone rang again. Burt picked it up.

"It's someone wanting Charlie," he said.

"What?"

"Charlie," Burt said.

Vera took the phone. She kept her back to him as she talked. Then she turned to him and said, "I'll take this call in the bedroom. So would you please hang up after I've picked it up in there? I can tell, so hang it up when I say."

He took the receiver. She left the kitchen. He held the receiver to his ear and listened. He heard nothing. Then he heard a man clear this throat. Then he heard Vera pick up the other phone. She shouted, "Okay, Burt! I have it now, Burt!"

He put down the receiver and stood looking at it. He opened the silverware drawer and pushed things around inside. He opened another drawer. He looked in the sink. He went into the dining room and got the carving knife. He held it under hot water until the grease broke and ran off. He wiped the blade on his sleeve. He moved to the phone, doubled the cord, and sawed through without any trouble at all. He examined the ends of the cord. Then he shoved the phone back into its corner behind the roasting pan.

She came in. She said, "The phone went dead. Did you do anything to the telephone?" She looked at the phone and then picked it up from the counter.

"Son of a bitch!" she screamed. She screamed, "Out, out, where you belong!" She was shaking the phone at him. "That's it! I'm going to get a restraining order, that's what I'm going to get!"

The phone made a *ding* when she banged it down on the counter.

"I'm going next door to call the police if you don't get out of here now!"

He picked up the ashtray. He held it by its edge. He posed with it like a man preparing to hurl the discuss.

"Please," she said. "That's our ashtray."

He left through the patio door. He was not certain, but he thought he had proved something. He hoped he had made something clear. The thing was, they had to have a serious talk soon. There were things that needed talking about, important things that had to be discussed. They'd talk again. Maybe after the holidays were over and things got back to normal. He'd tell her the goddamn ashtray was a goddamn dish, for example.

He stepped around the pie in the driveway and got back into his car. He started the car and put it into reverse. It was hard managing until he put the ashtray down.

Respond: Thinking Independently

1. Write your reactions to Burt and Vera in your journal.
2. Write a response statement: I was surprised/angered/saddened by _____ because _____.
3. React to the way Burt and Vera's children interact with their parents on Christmas Day.

Reconsider: Thinking Collaboratively

1. Compare classmates' reactions to the story. Do they divide along gender lines?
2. Discuss the family: What feelings can you infer from the conversations and the actions?
3. How does Burt show his jealousy? His love? His failure to grasp the reality of the situation?
4. Why does Burt take the ashtray?

Review: Thinking Critically

1. Though the story is told in the third person, whose point of view does the reader see? Of what significance is this choice of point of view? If any other character told the story, what difference would there be?
2. Notice the time organization of the story: When does it open? What has already happened?
3. Certain actions are described specifically, like cutting the phone cord, and others are more casually described like trying to burn the house down. Why?
4. What things seem to set Burt off? Why does he react that way?
5. What does Burt mean when he thinks, "they had to have a serious talk soon."

READING TO WRITE

Understanding Fiction: Reading Between the Lines

As we have seen, "reading between the lines" is a skill needed by the active reader. Fiction writers frequently convey feelings or even whole events by inference and indirection, or they may juxtapose two scenes (that is, present two scenes without comment, allowing the reader to draw conclusions about what they mean). In this story Raymond Carver invites the reader to read between the lines when he mentions the pie in the driveway and the excess logs put on the fire. That is, Carver tells us that Burt takes the pies, dropping one, and puts the waxed logs on the fire but not why he does it.

The reader needs to pay close attention to what was going on in the house just before the pie and log incident to interpret Burt's actions. Why do you think he did these things? Does severing the telephone cord later in the story fit with his reason for these earlier actions?

Writing Applications: Reading Between the Lines

1. Understanding a person's motivations is difficult but sometimes helps us make sense of otherwise senseless actions. Choose an action of your own, a family member, a friend, a boss, or a co-worker, and try to account for the reasons behind it.
2. Write an analysis of Burt and Vera's relationship. Does it have a future?

Escaping the Daily Grind for Life as a House Father
RICK GREENBERG

Preview: Thinking Ahead

Reversing roles and becoming the stay-at-home house father, Rick Greenberg finds, requires adjustments from society and himself. As he examines these adjustments, he admits to himself some qualms about making this a permanent move. His situation may become less unusual, however, as more Americans will have it "both ways," working out of their homes electronically. No doubt, that circumstance will raise new questions and further reevaluation of work as well as of individual's roles.

"You on vacation?" my neighbor asked.

My 15-month-old son and I were passing her yard on our daily hike through the neighborhood. It was a weekday afternoon and I was the only working-age male in sight.

"I'm uh . . . working out of my house now," I told her.

Thus was born my favorite euphemism for house fatherhood, one of those new life-style occupations that is never merely mentioned. Explained, yes. Defended. Even rhapsodized about. I was tongue-tied then, but no longer. People are curious and I've learned to oblige.

I joined up earlier this year when I quit my job—a dead-end, ulcer-producing affair that had dragged on interminably. I left to be with my son until something better came along. And if nothing did, I'd be with him indefinitely.

This was no simple transition. I had never known a house father, never met one. I'd only read about them. They were another news magazine trend. Being a traditionalist, I never dreamed I'd take the plunge.

But as the job got worse, I gave it serious thought. And more thought. And in the end, I still felt ambivalent. This was a radical change that seemed to carry as many drawbacks as benefits. My dislike for work finally pushed me over the edge. That, and the fact that we had enough money to get by.

Escaping the treadmill was a bold stroke. I had shattered my lethargy and stopped whining, and for that I was proud.

Some friends said they were envious. Of course they weren't quitting one job without one waiting—the ultimate in middle-class taboos. That ran through my mind as I triumphantly, and without notice, tossed the letter of resignation on my boss' desk. Then I walked away wobbly-kneed.

The initial trauma of quitting, however, was mitigated by my eagerness to raise our son. Mine was the classic father's lament. I felt excluded. I had become "the man who got home after dark," that other person besides Mama. It hurt when I couldn't quiet his crying.

I sensed that staying home would be therapeutic. The chronic competitiveness and aggressiveness that had served me well as a daily journalist would subside. Something better would emerge, something less obnoxious. My ulcer would heal. Instead of beating deadlines, I'd be doing something important for a change. This was heresy coming from a newspaper gypsy, but it rang true.

There was unease, too. I'd be adrift, stripped of the home-office-home routine that had defined my existence for more than a decade. No more earning a living. No benchmarks. Time would be seamless. Would Friday afternoons feel the same?

The newness of it was scary.

Until my resignation, my wife and I typified today's baby-boomer couples, the want-it-all generation. We had two salaries, a full-time nanny and guilt pangs over practicing parenthood by proxy.

Now, my wife brings home the paychecks, the office problems and thanks for good work on the domestic front. With me at home, her work hours are more flexible. Nanny-less, I change diapers, prepare meals and do all the rest. And I wonder what comes next.

What if I don't find another job? My field is tight. At 34, I'm not getting any more marketable and being out of work doesn't help.

As my father asked incredulously: "Is this going to be what you do?"

Perhaps. I don't know. I wonder myself. It's even more baffling to my father, the veteran of a long and traditional 9-to-5 career. For most of it, my mother stayed home. My father doesn't believe in trends. All he knows is that his only son—with whom he shares so many traits—has violated the natural order of men providing and women raising children. In his view, I've shown weakness and immaturity by succumbing to a bad job.

But he's trying to understand, and I think he will.

I'm trying to understand it myself. House fatherhood has been humbling, rewarding and unnerving.

"It's different," I tell friends. "Different."

Imagine never having to leave home for the office in the morning. That's how different. No dress-up, no commute. Just tumble out of bed and you're there. House fathering is not for claustrophobics.

I find myself enjoying early morning shopping. My son and I arrive right after the supermarket opens. The place is almost empty. For the next hour we glide dreamily, cruising the aisles to a Muzak accompaniment. This is my idyll. My son likes it, too; he's fascinated by the spectacle.

Housekeeping still doesn't seem like work, and that's by design. I've mastered the art of doing just enough chores to get by. This leaves me enough free time. Time to read and write and daydream. Time with my son. Time to think about the structure.

So much time, and so little traditional structure, that the days sometimes blur together. I remember on Sunday nights literally dreading the approaching work week, the grind. Today, the close of the weekend still triggers a shiver of apprehension; I now face the prospect of a week without tangible accomplishments, a void.

On our hikes to the playground, I can feel my old identity fading. All around are people with a mission, a sense of purpose. Workers. And then there's the rest of us—the stroller and backpack contingent. The moms, the nannies, and me. I wonder if I've crossed over a line never to return.

Still, the ulcer seems to be healing. I take pride in laying out a good dinner for the family and in pampering my wife after a tough day at the office. I love reading to my son. Running errands isn't even so bad. A lot of what had been drudgery or trivia is taking on new meaning; maybe I'm mellowing.

Which is ironic. To be a truly committed and effective at-home parent, there must be this change—a softening, a contentment with small pleasures, the outwardly mundane. This is a time of reduced demands and lowered expectations. Progress is gradual, often agonizingly so. Patience is essential. Ambition and competitiveness are anathema. Yet eliminating these last two qualities—losing the edge—could ruin my chances of resurrecting my career. I can't have it both ways.

The conflict has yet to be resolved. And it won't be unless I make a firm commitment and choose one life style over the other. I'm not yet ready for that decision.

In the meantime, a wonderful change is taking place in our home. Amid all the uncertainties, my son and I have gotten to know each other. He can't put a phrase together, but he confides in me. It can be nothing more than a grin or a devilish look. He tries new words on me, new shtick. We roll around a lot; we crack each other up. I'm no longer the third wheel, the man who gets home after dark. Now, I'm as much a part of his life as his mother is. I, too, can stop his crying. So far, that has made the experiment worthwhile.

Respond: Thinking Independently

1. Write your reaction to Greenberg's essay.
2. Write a response statement: One thing I learned from Greenberg's reactions to being at home was _____.
3. What do you think the ideal blend of career and home is?

Reconsider: Thinking Collaboratively

1. Compare reactions of classmates to the essay.
2. Compare your definitions of the ideal blend of career and home. How possible are these ideals?
3. What are the hardest aspects of Greenberg's adjustments? The easiest?

Review: Thinking Critically

1. Describe the pressures (causes) that made Greenberg quit his job. Was he "whining," as he puts it?
2. What point does he make about ambition and competitiveness?
3. What beneficial effects does he explain?
4. What bad effects does he fear?

READING TO WRITE

Understanding Causal Analysis: Using Sentence Fragments on Purpose

Nearly every writing student has been warned against writing incomplete sentences, often called sentence fragments. Grammar handbooks contain explanations and exercises to help students write complete sentences. (See section A2 in this text's Appendix, for example.) However, when students read an essay, such as the one above by Rick Greenberg, they find many such fragments, and he's getting paid for writing that way!

The difference is not so much that they are students, and he is a professional writer and can get away with it. The difference lies in the nature of the fragment. Writers use fragments on purpose to show nervousness, or hurry, or to mimic a person's conversation. To be effective the fragment has to be clearly understood. Student fragments are usually accidental, are not used to create any kind of effect, and cause confusion in the reader.

Look at some of Greenberg's fragments. In the first part of the essay, Greenberg says, "Thus was born my favorite euphemism for house fatherhood, one of those new life-style occupations that is never merely mentioned. Explained, yes. Defended. Even rhapsodized about." Notice that the verb in the complete sentence is followed by three more verb fragments (explained, defended, and rhapsodized about), each of which is a more intense word. Explaining is more intense than mentioning, defending is more intense than explaining, and so on. It is clear that all three verb fragments are related to "mentioned" in the complete sentence. Find other fragments in Greenberg's essay and see if you can discover his purpose for using them.

If you would like to attempt to use fragments on purpose, ask your instructor if you can use them if you star them like this (*). Then your instructor will know that you know what you are doing and will be able to tell you whether your experiment was effective.

Writing Application: Causal Analysis

1. Discuss the effects for either gender of working out of the home, as more people are now able to do with the use of the computer, modem, and fax machine. Will this development break down the traditional differences between home and work?

Other Writing Application

1. Revise your description of the ideal blend of home and career into an essay.

The Androgynous Male
NOEL PERRIN

Preview: Thinking Ahead

One of the challenges of establishing identity in the face of gender conflicts is that very few of us, male or female, live up to the cultural stereotype of ideal woman or man. That is, we are not all Cindy Crawford or Arnold Schwartzenegger. Further, we may have confusing feelings about our sexuality or even our sexual preference that American culture does not easily acknowledge. In this 1984 essay Noel Perrin explores the notion of a gender that has both masculine and feminine characteristics.

The summer I was 16, I took a train from New York to Steamboat Springs, Colo., where I was going to be assistant horse wrangler at a camp. The trip took three days, and since I was much too shy to talk to strangers, I had quite a lot of time for reading. I read all of *Gone with the Wind*. I read all the interesting articles in a couple of magazines I had, and then I went back and read all the dull stuff. I also took all the quizzes, a thing of which magazines were even fuller then than now.

The one that held my undivided attention was called "How Masculine/Feminine Are You?" It consisted of a large number of inkblots. The reader was supposed to decide which of four objects each blot most resembled. The choices might be a cloud, a steam engine, a caterpillar and a sofa.

When I finished the test, I was shocked to find that I was barely masculine at all. On a scale of 1 to 10, I was about 1.2. Me, the horse wrangler? (And not just wrangler, either. That summer, I had to skin a couple of horses that died—the camp owner wanted the hides.)

The results of that test were so terrifying to me that for the first time in my life I did a piece of original analysis. Having unlimited time on the train, I looked at the "masculine" answers over and over, trying to find what it was that distinguished real men from people like me—and eventually I discovered two very simple patterns. It was "masculine" to think the blots looked like man-made objects, and "feminine" to think they looked like natural objects. It was masculine to think they looked like things capable of causing harm, and feminine to think of innocent things.

Even at 16, I had the sense to see that the compilers of the test were using rather limited criteria—maleness and femaleness are both more complicated than *that*—and I breathed a huge sigh of relief. I wasn't necessarily a wimp, after all.

That the test did reveal something other than the superficiality of its makers I realized only many years later. What it revealed was that there is a large class of men and women both, to which I belong, who are essentially androgynous. That doesn't mean we're gay, or low in the appropriate hormones, or uncomfortable performing the jobs traditionally assigned our sexes. (A few years after that summer, I was leading troops in combat and, unfashionable as it now is to admit this, having a very good time. War is exciting. What a pity the 20th century went and spoiled it with high-tech weapons.)

What it does mean to be spiritually androgynous is a kind of freedom. Men who are all-male, or he-man, or 100 percent red-blooded Americans, have a little biological set that causes them to be attracted to physical power, and probably also to dominance. Maybe even to watching football. I don't say this to criticize them. Completely masculine men are quite often wonderful people: good husbands, good (though sometimes overwhelming) fathers, good members of society. Furthermore, they are often so unself-consciously at ease in the world that other men seek to imitate them. They just aren't as free as us androgynes. They pretty nearly have to be what they are; we have a range of choices open.

The sad part is that many of us never discover that. Men who are not 100 percent red-blooded Americans—say, those who are only 75 percent red-blooded—often fail to notice their freedom. They are too busy trying to copy the he-men ever to realize that men, like women, come in a wide variety of acceptable types. Why this frantic imitation? My answer is mere speculation, but not casual. I have speculated on this for a long time.

Partly they're just envious of the he-man's unconscious ease. Mostly they're terrified of finding that there may be something wrong with them deep down, some weakness at the heart. To avoid discovering that, they spend their lives acting out the role that the he-man naturally lives. Sad.

One thing that men owe to the women's movement is that this kind of failure is less common than it used to be. In releasing themselves from the single ideal of the dependent woman, women have more or else incidentally released a lot of men from the single ideal of the dominant male. The one mistake the feminists have made, I think, is in supposing that *all* men need this release, or that the world would be a better place if all men achieved it. It wouldn't. It would just be duller.

So far I have been pretty vague about just what the freedom of the androgynous man is. Obviously it varies with the case. In the case I know best, my own, I can be quite specific. It has freed me most as a parent. I am, among other things, a fairly good natural mother. I like the nurturing role. It makes me feel good to see a child eat—and it turns me to mush to see a 4-year-old holding a glass with both small hands, in order to drink. I even enjoyed sewing patches on the knees of my daughter Amy's Dr. Dentons when she was at the crawling stage. All that pleasure I would have lost if I had made myself stick to the notion of the paternal role that I started with.

Or take a smaller and rather ridiculous example. I feel free to kiss cats. Until recently it never occurred to me that I would want to, though my daughters have been doing it all their lives. But my elder daughter is now 22, and in London. Of course, I get to look after her cat while she is gone. He's a big, handsome farm cat named Petrushka, very unsentimental, though used from kittenhood to being kissed on the top of the head by Elizabeth. I've gotten very fond of him (he's the adventurous kind of cat who likes to climb hills with you), and one night I simply felt like kissing him on the top of the head, and did. Why did no one tell me sooner how silky cat fur is?

Then there's my relation to cars. I am completely unembarrassed by my inability to diagnose even minor problems in whatever object I happened to be driving, and don't have to make some insider's remark to mechanics to try to establish that I, too, am a "Man with His Machine."

The same ease extends to household maintenance. I do it, of course. Service people are expensive. But for the last decade my house has functioned better than it used to because I've had the aid of a volume called "Home Repairs Any Woman Can Do," which is pitched just right for people at my technical level. As a youth, I'd as soon have touched such a book as I would have become a transvestite. Even though common sense says there is really nothing sexual whatsoever about fixing sinks.

Or take public emotion. All my life I have easily been moved by certain kinds of voices. The actress Siobhan McKenna's, to take a notable case. Give her an emotional scene in a play, and within 10 words my eyes are full of tears. In boyhood, my great dread was that someone might notice. I struggled manfully, you might say, to suppress this weakness. Now, of course, I don't see it as a weakness at all, but as a kind of fulfillment. I even suspect that the true he-men feel the same way, or one kind of them does, at least, and it's only the poor imitators who have to struggle to repress themselves.

Let me come back to the inkblots, with their assumption that masculine equates with machinery and science, and feminine with art and nature. I have no idea whether the right pronoun for God is He, She, or It. But this I'm pretty sure of. If God could somehow be induced to take that test, God would not come out macho, and not feminismo, either, but right in the middle. Fellow androgynes, it's a nice thought.

Respond: Thinking Independently

1. Write your reaction to Perrin's essay.
2. Write your own definition of androgyny: _____
3. What would make establishing one's gender identity easier in American culture?

Reconsider: Thinking Collaboratively

1. Discuss Perrin's concept of androgyny. Is it freer than the stereotype?
2. Discuss Perrin's assertion that many men force themselves to act the "he-man" because they are "terrified of finding that there may be something wrong with them deep down. . . ." What might the "something wrong" refer to?
3. Why does Perrin tell us in parentheses about his skinning a horse and leading men into combat? Does his telling us these things contradict his statement of feeling free?
4. What advantage has the women's movement had for men, according to Perrin? Do you agree?

Review: Thinking Critically

1. In this essay, Perrin tries to define an androgynous character in part by listing the things he likes and feels comfortable doing and the things that he is not good at or feels uncomfortable with. Which things does he place in each category? Do you agree with the way he characterizes them?
2. Several times Perrin seems to include the reader in his assessment of gender: "us androgynes," "we have a range of choices." What advantages and disadvantages are there to this appeal to the reader?

READING TO WRITE

Understanding Definition: Personal Experience as Evidence

Noel Perrin's definition of "androgyne" is based largely on his own experience and thinking. He tells the reader, "So far I have been pretty vague about just what the freedom of the androgynous man is. Obviously it varies with the case. In the case I know best, my own, I can be quite specific." What examples of this freedom does he then cite from his own life? Whether Perrin succeeds in getting across his definition to readers depends on their understanding of his examples, and perhaps thinking of similar androgynous experiences in their own lives. Personal experience, then, is most effective in enlightening readers on a personal definition of a word, but if the definition is to serve an academic reason, such as a discussion of the range of masculine or feminine behaviors in a psychology journal, then studies of many subjects and presentation of the data would be required.

Writing Applications: Definitions

1. How stereotyped were gender definitions when you were growing up? Think about your toys, activities, friends, games at school, and behavior. If there were quite clear differences between the genders, where did they come from: parents, peers, teachers, from within the individual? What problems were there if someone did not fit the expected definition?
2. Write your own definitions of masculine and/or feminine roles as you see them evolving.

FOUR

A Changing Sense of Self: Redefining Identity in Mid-Life

Even when a person has achieved a sense of who he or she is, circumstances can challenge that identity. If you have incorporated being a wife or husband into your sense of self, a divorce or death of a spouse may change the way you see yourself and your relationship to others. In the 1990s, corporate downsizing resulted in layoffs and unemployment for many Americans from the factory floor to the executive offices, causing a reassessment of the part work plays in one's identity. Because some middle-aged people found getting a new job difficult, they were forced to consider changing occupations, many returning to college or technical institutes for retraining.

Getting older forces many people to reevaluate their goals and perhaps strike out for a new destination, as Eddy Harris decides to do in "Mississippi Solo." Or as Gloria Steinem has experienced, getting older may make someone more radical, more likely to challenge tradition than she did when she was younger.

Identity, as we learned from Gail Sheehy in a previous selection, is not a fixed entity but changes as one meets the challenges of life. As you read the selections in this chapter, note the ways the writers see people coping, or failing to cope, with these challenges.

The Three Calendar Cafe*
WILLIAM LEAST HEAT MOON

Preview: Thinking Ahead
William Least Heat Moon, a writer of Native American descent also known as William Trogdon, decided to explore America's back roads or Blue Highways, *as he called the 1982 book from which this excerpt is taken. Moon thus*

*Editor's title

joins a long tradition of American wanderers and chroniclers from the fictional Huckleberry Finn to writers like Jack Kerouac and John Steinbeck to CBS television's Charles Kuralt. Typically, such wanderers are looking at their own identities in their journeys as well as looking at the character of the Americans they meet along the way. As you read this selection, try to determine what Moon values most in these small towns he visits. And note too the way other people relate to him.

Had it not been raining hard that morning on the Livingston square, I never would have learned of Nameless, Tennessee. Waiting for the rain to ease, I lay on my bunk and read the atlas to pass time rather than to see where I might go. In Kentucky were towns with fine names like Boreing, Bear Wallow, Decoy, Subtle, Mud Lick, Mummie, Neon; Belcher was just down the road from Mouthcard, and Minnie only ten miles from Mousie.

I looked at Tennessee. Turtletown eight miles from Ducktown. And also: Peavine, Wheel, Milky Way, Love Joy, Dull, Weakly, Fly, Spot, Miser Station, Only, McBurg, Peeled Chestnut, Clouds, Topsy, Isoline. And the best of all, Nameless. The logic! I was heading east, and Nameless lay forty-five miles west. I decided to go anyway.

The rain stopped, but things looked saturated, even bricks. In Gainesboro, a hill town with a square of businesses around the Jackson County Courthouse, I stopped for directions and breakfast. There is one almost infallible way to find honest food at just prices in blue-highway America: count the wall calendars in a cafe.

No calendar: Same as an interstate pit stop.
One calendar: Preprocessed food assembled in New Jersey
Two calendars: Only if fish trophies present.
Three calendars: Can't miss on the farm-boy breakfasts.
Four calendars: Try the ho-made pie too.
Five calendars: Keep it under your hat, or they'll franchise.

One time I found a six-calendar cafe in the Ozarks, which served fried chicken, peach pie, and chocolate malts, that left me searching for another ever since. I've never seen a seven-calendar place. But old-time travelers— road men in a day when cars had running boards and lunchroom windows said AIR COOLED in blue letters with icicles dripping from the tops—those travelers have told me the golden legends of seven-calendar cafes.

To the rider of back roads, nothing shows the tone, the voice of a small town more quickly than the breakfast grill or the five-thirty tavern. Much of what the people do and believe and share is evident then. The City Cafe in Gainesboro had three calendars that I could see from the walk. Inside were no interstate refugees with full bladders and empty tanks, no wild-eyed children just released from the glassy cell of a stationwagon backseat, no longhaul truckers talking in CB numbers. There were only townspeople wearing overalls, or catalog-order suits with five-and-dime ties, or uniforms. That is, here were farmers and mill hands, bank clerks, the dry goods merchant, a policeman, and chiropractor's receptionist. Because it was Saturday, there were also mothers and children.

I ordered my standard on-the-road breakfast: two eggs up, hashbrowns, tomato juice. The waitress, whose pale, almost translucent skin shifted hue in the gray light like a thin slice of mother of pearl, brought the food. Next to the eggs was a biscuit with a little yellow Smiley button stuck in it. She said, "You from the North?"

"I guess I am." A Missourian gets used to Southerners thinking him a Yankee, a Northerner considering him a cracker, a Westerner sneering at his effete Easternness, and the Easterner taking him for a cowhand.

"So whata you doin' in the mountains?"

"Talking to people. Taking some pictures. Looking mostly."

"Lookin' for what?"

"A three-calendar cafe that serves Smiley buttons on the biscuits."

"You needed a smile. Tell me really."

"I don't know. Actually, I'm looking for some jam to put on this biscuit now that you've brought one."

She came back with grape jelly. In a land of quince jelly, apple butter, apricot jam, blueberry preserves, pear conserves, and lemon marmalade, you always get grape jelly.

"Whata you lookin' for?"

Like anyone else, I'm embarrassed to eat in front of a watcher, particularly if I'm getting interviewed. "Why don't you have a cup of coffee?"

"Cain't right now. You gonna tell me?"

"I don't know how to describe it to you. Call it harmony."

She waited for something more. "Is that it?" Someone called her to the kitchen. I had managed almost to finish by the time she came back. She sat on the edge of the booth. "I started out in life not likin' anything, but then it grew on me. Maybe that'll happen to you." She watched me spread the jelly. "Saw your van." She watched me eat the biscuit. "You sleep in there?" I told her I did. "I'd love to do that, but I'd be scared spitless."

"I don't mind being scared spitless. Sometimes."

"I'd like to take off cross country. I like to look at different license plates. But I'd take a dog. You carry a dog?"

"No dogs, no cats, no budgie birds. It's a one-man campaign to show Americans a person can travel alone without a pet."

"Cain't travel without a dog!"

"I like to do things the hard way."

"Shoot! I'd take me a dog to talk to. And for protection."

"It isn't traveling to cross the country and talk to your pug instead of people along the way. Besides, being alone on the road makes you ready to meet someone when you stop. You get sociable traveling alone."

She looked out toward the van again. "Time I get the nerve to take a trip, gas'll cost five dollars a gallon."

"Could be. My rig might go the way of the steamboat." I remembered why I'd come to Gainesboro. "You know the way to Nameless?"

"Nameless? I've heard of Nameless. Better ask the amlance driver in the corner booth." She pinned the Smiley on my jacket. "Maybe I'll see you on the road somewhere. His name's Bob, by the way."

"The ambulance driver?"

"The Smiley. I always name my Smileys—otherwise they all look alike. I'd talk to him before you go."

"The Smiley?"

"The amlance driver."

And so I went looking for Nameless, Tennessee, with a Smiley button named Bob.

Respond: Thinking Independently

1. Respond in your journal to Moon's visit to Gainesboro. Would you be "scared spitless" to take such a journey?
2. What do you think Moon means when he answers the waitress's question "Whata you lookin' for?" with "Call it harmony"?

Reconsider: Thinking Collaboratively

1. Compare class reactions to Moon's journey. What different opinions are there?
2. Discuss your individual interpretations of Moon's "harmony."
3. What things does Moon praise and what does he criticize? Why?
4. Discuss Moon's classification of cafes according to the number of calendars. Why do you think the number of wall calendars might say something about the quality of the food served?

Review: Thinking Critically

1. What does the waitress's questioning tell about the waitress? What do you think she means by, "I started out in life not likin' anything, but then it grew on me. Maybe that'll happen to you"? What is she assuming about the reason for Moon's journey? Is that assumption supported in this selection?
2. Why doesn't Moon travel with a dog or other pet?
3. What is Moon's comment about people taking him, a Missourian, for a Northerner in some places and seeing him quite differently in other places?
4. Why do you think Moon wants to find Nameless?

READING TO WRITE

Understanding Classification: Combining Methods

As you can see in this essay, the classification of small town cafes by how many calendars they have on the walls is only a small part of this selection. But Moon's description of this cafe, a three-calendar one, and the people in it are helped by explaining his overall system. Therefore, classifying cafes has become just a part of moon's overall essay. Writers frequently combine elements from several rhetorical techniques in order to express themselves. In fact, it may be helpful to think of these techniques as tools to use to express ideas rather than ends in themselves. Few writers sit down to write a "classification essay." Instead they have ideas that can best be expressed by classifying something or comparing something or describing something. One learns scales on a piano or chords on a guitar, but soon combines the notes in many different ways to produce meaningful music.

Writing Application: Classification

1. Choose a kind of restaurant (pizza place, deli, pancake palace, hot dog stand, coffee house, etc.) and try to capture its character. You may compare it with others of the same sort or even fit it into your own classification scheme.

Other Writing Application

1. Write about what traveling has meant to you, what it contributed to your sense of yourself or your understanding of others.

Mississippi Solo
EDDY HARRIS

Preview: Thinking Ahead

What would your friends and family say if you announced you were going to canoe down the Mississippi River from Minnesota to Louisiana? Too much Mark Twain? Too much Ernest Hemingway, as the journalist Eddy Harris admits might be true? This excerpt from the 1988 book of the same title is part of a true account of Harris's voyage as he tries to explain to himself and others why a Stanford-educated African American who never was that much for the outdoor life-style would undertake such a journey. As you read, try to understand the identity questions Harris is asking.

In the night the mind voices what was only a creepy suspicion during the day. *What in the world am I doing out here?*

I'm a city fellow, urbane and civilized. I always use the correct fork. I keep my napkin in my lap. And like a good little boy who does what his mommy tells him, I chew my food fifty-six times before swallowing. My idea of travel and good fun is shooting craps in Las Vegas or playing roulette in the Grand Casino at Monte Carlo, fishing for marlin off Bimini, scuba diving the reefs of the Caribbean, hiking the Swiss Alps and skiing the

Austrian, dining and wining in Paris, bicycling through Scotland. I see my-self wearing tuxedoes and drinking champagne, not eating beans and wee-nies and wearing the same smelly clothes for weeks.

And I'm no expert in a canoe. That much is evident now. I think I'd been in a canoe maybe five times before. Floating the Black River a couple of times—mostly just an easy stream but I still managed to tip over and fall in. One time canoeing leisurely in the summer sun on the Thames not far from London. Once on a lake just drifting lazily with a fishing rod in hand but not even a nibble to worry about, only the weeds and the marsh and the water lilies snagging the canoe and forcing me to work. And once on the Severån, a lazy little river in the north of Sweden. Not exactly training for the proving ground of the Mississippi.

Nor was I any more experienced as a camper. Not an outdoorsman at all. Cleaning fish is not one of my favorite things. I don't like snakes, can't stand mosquitoes, and creatures that growl in the night scare me.

And yet. . . .

I'm haunted by the ghost of Ernest Hemingway. All writers—American male—probably are. His style of writing, sure, but mostly his zesty style of living—big-game hunter, deep-sea fisher, hard drinker. Lover of man and women and good times and travel to exotic locales. A courter of danger.

It was a different world then, though. Everything wasn't taken so much for granted. A punch in the nose risked a return punch in the nose, a few moments' sweat and adrenaline, not a lawsuit. Air travel was an adventure. Getting there—anywhere—was as thrilling as being there. Skiing was not chic, the thing to do, but rather hard work down the mountain, harder work back up, an exhilaration, an exotic adventure. Your tales had zing in those days because everyone you know hadn't already been to Europe. Living was an adventure. And Paris was really Paris.

It was a different world all right.

Now life is a media event. Well publicized, well sign-posted, the paths well worn and all the right things to do and places to go marked out. And absolutely everyone has a ticket to watch.

Is that what we've become? Mere spectators at a zoo? With real living removed from us and kept safely behind bars?

I hope to God I'm not out here because I miss the Good Old Days.

What good old days? Twenty years from now, these will be the good old days.

And not because I wanted to be Ernest Hemingway.

I want to be Eddy Harris. I want to live a life of my own adventures, my own tryings, triumphs—even failures.

I look at the Mississippi and I see a symbol of America, the spine of the nation, a symbol of strength and freedom and pride, wanderlust and his-tory and imagination. The river is also a symbol of our times, for the river fights in a desperate battle against the US Army Corps of Engineers who refuse to let the river find its own way. The Corps of Engineers fights the river with technology and brute brain power to bend the river, make it conform to the needs of society in order to save homes that would otherwise be flooded, to aid shipping, to strip the river of its power and its will and its natural dignity. Nobody has asked the river. The river which yearns to be free, rages for it.

Alas! Time runs out—for the river, for me, for us all. The world around closes in.

Computerized, mechanized, itemized, formalized, and most dangerously, standardized. Laws hemming us in and fencing us out, stripping us down and standardizing behavior. Hotel chains and fast food joints standardize travel and eating. Dallas looks like Denver looks like Tacoma looks like Tallahassee. Traveling is truly home away from home. No surprises, no disasters at mealtime, no disappointments, no thrills. Just a steady heartbeat and a blank look.

Doesn't it make you mad enough to holler and spit?

Taking chances. Isn't that what life is all about? Sometimes you come up winners, sometimes you lose. But without the risk of defeat, where is the triumph? Without death hanging over the head, what value is life?

And *that* is why I wanted to do this foolish thing. If I were expert with canoe, fishing gear, bow and arrow and rifle, if I were the Daniel Boone type used to spending weeks at a time in the same clothes, in the woods, if I loved gutting rabbits and sleeping out in the rain, a trip down the big river would have been a simple thing. Fun, but little more than routine. Only half an adventure.

This voyage, on the other hand, was a true adventure.

Respond: Thinking Independently

1. Write in your journal about the reasons Harris has for undertaking this adventure and your reactions to them.
2. Write a response statement choosing a quotation from Harris that you either agree or disagree with and then explaining why.
3. Describe your dream journey. Why do you want to make this trip?

Reconsider: Thinking Collaboratively

1. Compare reactions to the essay with your classmates.
2. Discuss what Harris means by, "Now life is a media event."
3. Discuss Harris's view of taking chances and possible failure. Is he being foolish? Explain.

Review: Thinking Critically

1. Harris says, "The river is also a symbol of our times." In what ways does he mean this?
2. What point about modern life does he make? Is there a connection between his views and those expressed by William Least Heat Moon? Do you agree?
3. What issues of identity does Harris explore in this short excerpt?

Understanding Causal Analysis: Finding Immediate and Remote Causes

Eddy Harris explores why he undertakes to canoe the Mississippi River. That is, he is looking for the causes of his own actions. Causes may be immediate, which spring from present circumstances, or remote, which may lie in a person's past. List the causes that you find in the essay. Are they immediate or remote causes? Now assess which causes seem the strongest, the most likely ones to get him to go on this voyage. Which causes did Harris hope he wasn't listening to? Why not? Are there other causes that Harris doesn't state but that you think might be operating?

Writing Applications: Causal Analysis

1. Analyze Harris's reasons for taking his journey, paying attention to the reasons he gives but also to other reasons that you think may be operating.
2. Discuss risk taking in yourself or others. What causes people to take physical risks? What do they get out of it?
3. Do you agree that modern life has become mechanized, controlled, and standardized? If so, is that bad? If so, what can we do about it?

The Road Not Taken
Robert Frost

Preview: Thinking Ahead

Robert Frost is perhaps the most popular poet among most Americans. Nearly everyone has read at least one of his poems in school, and his poetry is generally not difficult to read. That is, the poems are usually written in conversational language about subjects many people have experienced, such as walking in the woods or picking apples. However, Frost's poems also have the capacity to make us think about our lives and have enough complexity to keep people interpreting his meanings. As you read this poem, think about what Frost is saying about the paths people take in their lives.

Two roads diverged in a yellow wood,
And sorry I could not travel both
And be one traveler, long I stood

And looked down one as far as I could
To where it bent in the undergrowth;

Then took the other, as just as fair,
And having perhaps the better claim,
Because it was grassy and wanted wear;
Though as for that the passing there
Had worn them really about the same,

And both that morning equally lay
In leaves no step had trodden black.
Oh, I kept the first for another day!
Yet knowing how way leads on to way,
I doubted if I should ever come back.

I shall be telling this with a sigh
Somewhere ages and ages hence:
Two roads diverged in a wood, and I—
I took the one less traveled by,
And that has made all the difference.

Respond: Thinking Independently

1. Write in your journal your interpretation of the poem.
2. Choose a line in the poem that means something to you and then explain what it means to you: _____

Reconsider: Thinking Collaboratively

1. Compare the individual interpretations of the poem. Do they differ? If so, how do the words of the poem support multiple interpretations? Is that a strength or weakness of poetry?
2. Examine the lines describing the two roads. Is one road clearly "less traveled by"? If not, what is one to make of the last two lines of the poem?
3. When the speaker in the poem chooses a road, he/she says, "Oh, I kept the first for another day." But what does the speaker say about going back to that first road? Do you find this observation to be generally true?

Review: Thinking Critically

1. Think about the two roads again and the end of the poem. Why does the speaker say, "I shall be telling this with a sigh"? Who would he/she be telling this to? Why "with a sigh"? And why would the telling be "ages and ages hence"? Does the passage of time and the telling of one's life choices influence one's memory of the event?

2. In the last line, the speaker says that the choice of roads "has made all the difference." Could that be true no matter how the original choice was made? In your experience, are there milestone decisions that, however they were made, continue to affect a person's life? Explain.

READING TO WRITE

Understanding Poetry: A Poet's Pattern

Robert Frost said "a poem begins in delight and ends in wisdom." A reader of Frost may be able to see that pattern in his poetry. That is, he often begins with a scene in nature, skillfully described, and then as the poem ends he seems to interpret the scene, leaving the reader with a thought to ponder. Does this poem follow the pattern? Read other Frost poems and see what you find. Do other poems in this anthology follow the pattern?

Writing Applications

1. Tell how, in your life, one situation led to another situation which created a direction or path in your life ("how way leads on to way," in Frost's words).
2. Argue that people can go back and revisit a decision.

I Stand Here Ironing

Tillie Olsen

Preview: Thinking Ahead

Parents often undergo a self-examination when they see their children emerging from childhood into adulthood. Few parents are perfect, and few children's life circumstances are perfect, so inevitably there are feelings of guilt, regret, and wistfulness about what might have been. In this short story, Tillie Olsen wrenchingly describes a mother's attempt to understand her oldest child's life journey. Note, as you read, the combination of historical, environmental, and personal issues that impinge on the relationship between this mother and daughter.

I stand here ironing, and what you asked me moves tormented back and forth with the iron.

"I wish you would manage the time to come in and talk with me about your daughter. I'm sure you can help me understand her. She's a youngster who needs help and whom I'm deeply interested in helping."

"Who needs help." . . . Even if I came, what good would it do? You think because I am her mother I have a key, or that in some way you could use me as a key? She has lived for nineteen years. There is all that life that has happened outside of me, beyond me.

And when is there time to remember, to sift, to weigh, to estimate, to total? I will start and there will be an interruption and I will have to gather it all together again. Or I will become engulfed with all I did or did not do, with what should have been and what cannot be helped.

She was a beautiful baby. The first and only one of our five that was beautiful at birth. You do not guess how new and uneasy her tenancy in her now-loveliness. You did not know her all those years she was thought homely, or see her poring over her baby pictures, making me tell her over and over how beautiful she had been—and would be, I would tell her—and was now, to the seeing eye. But the seeing eyes were few or nonexistent. Including mine.

I nursed her. They feel that's important nowadays. I nursed all the children, but with her, with all the fierce rigidity of first motherhood, I did like the books then said. Though her cries battered me to trembling and my breasts ached with swollenness, I waited till the clock decreed.

Why do I put that first? I do not even know if it matters, or if it explains anything.

She was a beautiful baby. She blew shining bubbles of sound. She loved motion, loved light, loved color and music and textures. She would lie on the floor in her blue overalls patting the surface so hard in ecstasy her hands and feet would blur. She was a miracle to me, but when she was eight months old I had to leave her daytimes with the woman downstairs to whom she was no miracle at all, for I worked or looked for work and for Emily's father, who "could no longer endure" (he wrote in his good-bye note) "sharing want with us."

I was nineteen. It was the pre-relief, pre-WPA world of the depression. I would start running as soon as I got off the streetcar, running up the stairs, the place smelling sour, and awake or asleep to startle awake, when she saw me she would break into a clogged weeping that could not be comforted, a weeping I can hear yet.

After a while I found a job hashing at night so I could be with her days, and it was better. But it came to where I had to bring her to his family and leave her.

It took me a long time to raise the money for her fare back. Then she got chicken pox and I had to wait longer. When she finally came, I hardly knew her, walking quick and nervous like her father, looking like her father, thin, and dressed in a shoddy red that yellowed her skin and glared at the pockmarks. All the baby loveliness gone.

She was two. Old enough for nursery school they said, and I did not know then what I know now—the fatigue of the long day, and the lacerations of group life in the kinds of nurseries that are only parking places for children.

Except that it would have made no difference if I had known. It was the only place there was. It was the only way we could be together, the only way I could hold a job.

And even without knowing, I knew. I knew the teacher that was evil because all these years it has curdled into my memory, the little boy hunched in the corner, her rasp, "why aren't you outside, because Alvin hits you? that's no reason, go out, scaredy." I knew Emily hated it even if she did not clutch and implore "don't go Mommy" like the other children, mornings.

She always had a reason why we should stay home. Momma, you look sick. Momma, I feel sick. Momma, the teachers aren't there today, they're sick. Momma, we can't go, there was a fire there last night. Momma, it's a holiday today, no school, they told me.

But never a direct protest, never rebellion. I think of our others in their three-, four-year-oldness—the explosions, the tempers, the denunciations, the demands—and I feel suddenly ill. I put the iron down. What in me demanded that goodness in her? And what was the cost, the cost to her of such goodness?

The old man living in the back once said in his gentle way: "You should smile at Emily more when you look at her." What *was* in my face when I looked at her? I loved her. There were all the acts of love.

It was only with the others I remembered what he said, and it was the face of joy, and not of care or tightness or worry I turned to them—too late for Emily. She does not smile easy, let alone almost always as her brothers and sisters do. Her face is closed and sombre, but when she wants, how fluid. You must have seen it in her pantomimes, you spoke of her rare gift for comedy on the stage that rouses a laughter out of the audience so dear they applaud and applaud and do not want to let her go.

Where does it come from, that comedy? There was none of it in her when she came back to me that second time, after I had had to send her away again. She had a new daddy now to learn to love, and I think perhaps it was a better time.

Except when we left her alone nights, telling ourselves she was old enough.

"Can't you go some other time, Mommy, like tomorrow?" she would ask. "Will it be just a little while you'll be gone? Do you promise?"

The time we came back, the front door open, the clock on the floor in the hall. She rigid awake. "It wasn't just a little while. I didn't cry. Three times I called you, just three times, and then I ran downstairs to open the door so you could come faster. The clock talked loud. I threw it away, it scared me what it talked."

She said the clock talked loud again that night I went to the hospital to have Susan. She was delirious with the fever that comes before red measles, but she was fully conscious all the week I was gone and the week after we were home when she could not come near the new baby or me.

She did not get well. She stayed skeleton thin, not wanting to eat, and night after night she had nightmares. She would call for me, I would rouse from exhaustion to sleepily call back: "You're all right, darling, go to sleep, it's just a dream," and if she still called, in a sterner voice, "now go to sleep, Emily, there's nothing to hurt you." Twice, only twice, when I had to get up for Susan anyhow, I went in to sit with her.

Now when it is too late (as if she would let me hold and comfort her like I do the others) I get up and go to her at once at her moan or restless stirring. "Are you awake, Emily? Can I get you something?" And the answer is always the same: "No, I'm all right, go back to sleep, Mother."

They persuaded me at the clinic to send her away to a convalescent home in the country where "she can have the kind of food and care you can't manage for her, and you'll be free to concentrate on the new baby." They still send children to that place. I see pictures on the society page of sleek young women planning affairs to raise money for it, or dancing at the affairs, or decorating Easter eggs or filling Christmas stockings for the children.

They never have a picture of the children so I do not know if the girls still wear those gigantic red bows and the ravaged looks on the every other Sunday when parents can come to visit "unless otherwise notified"—as we were notified the first six weeks.

Oh it is a handsome place, green lawns and tall trees and fluted flower beds. High up on the balconies of each cottage the children stand, the girls in their red bows and white dresses, the boys in white suits and giant red ties. The parents stand below shrieking up to be heard and the children shriek down to be heard, and between them the invisible wall "Not To Be Contaminated by Parental Germs or Physical Affection.

There was a tiny girl who always stood hand in hand with Emily. Her parents never came. One visit she was gone. "They moved her to Rose Cottage" Emily shouted in explanation. "They don't like you to love anybody here."

She wrote once a week, the labored writing of a seven-year-old. "I am fine. How is the baby. If I write my letter nicely I will have a star. Love." There was never a star. We wrote every other day, letters she could never hold or keep but only hear read—once. "We simply do not have room for children to keep any personal possessions," they patiently explained when we pieced one Sunday's shrieking together to plead how much it would mean to Emily, who loved so to keep things, to be allowed to keep her letters and cards.

Each visit she looked frailer. "She isn't eating," they told us.

(They had runny eggs for breakfast or mush with lumps, Emily said later, I'd hold it in my mouth and not swallow. Nothing ever tasted good, just when they had chicken.)

It took us eight months to get her released home, and only the fact that she gained back so little of her seven lost pounds convinced the social worker.

I used to try to hold and love her after she came back, but her body would stay stiff, and after a while she'd push away. She ate little. Food sickened her, and I think much of life too. Oh she had physical lightness and brightness, twinkling by on skates, bouncing like a ball up and down over the jump rope, skimming over the hill; but these were momentary.

She fretted about her appearance, thin and dark and foreign-looking at a time when every little girl was supposed to look or thought she should look a chubby blonde replica of Shirley Temple. The doorbell rang for her, but no one seemed to come and play in the house or be a best friend. Maybe because we moved so much.

There was a boy she loved painfully through two school semesters. Months later she told me how she had taken pennies from my purse to buy him candy. "Licorice was his favorite and I brought him some every day, but he still liked Jennifer better'n me. Why, Mommy?" The kind of question for which there is no answer.

School was a worry to her. She was not glib or quick in a world where glibness and quickness were easily confused with ability to learn. To her overworked and exasperated teachers she was an overconscientious "slow learner" who kept trying to catch up and was absent entirely too often.

I let her be absent, though sometimes the illness was imaginary. How different from my now-strictness about attendance with the others. I wasn't working. We had a new baby, I was home anyhow. Sometimes, after Susan grew old enough, I would keep her home from school, too, to have them all together.

Mostly Emily has asthma, and her breathing, harsh and labored, would fill the house with a curiously tranquil sound. I would bring the two old dresser mirrors and her boxes of collections to her bed. She would select beads and single earrings, bottle tops and shells, dried flowers and pebbles, old postcards and scraps, all sorts of oddments; then she and Susan would play Kingdom, setting up landscapes and furniture, peopling them with with action.

Those were the only times of peaceful companionship between her and Susan. I have edged away from it, that poisonous feeling between them, that terrible balancing of hurts and needs I had to do between the two, and did so badly, those earlier years.

Oh there are conflicts between the others too, each one human, needing, demanding, hurting, taking but only between Emily and Susan, no, Emily toward Susan that corroding resentment. It seems so obvious on the surface, yet it is not obvious. Susan, the second child, golden- and curly-haired and chubby, quick and articulate and assured, everything in appearance and manner Emily was not; Susan, not able to resist Emily's precious things, losing or sometimes clumsily breaking them; Susan telling jokes and riddles to company for applause while Emily sat silent (to say to me later: that was *my* riddle, Mother, I told it to Susan); Susan, who for all the five years' difference in age was just a year behind Emily in developing physically.

I am glad for that slow physical development that widened the difference between her and her contemporaries, though she suffered over it. She was too vulnerable for that terrible world of youthful competition, of preening and parading, of constant measuring of yourself against every other, of envy, "If I had that copper hair," "If I had that skin. . . ." She tormented herself enough about not looking like the others, there was enough of the unsureness, the having to be conscious of words before you speak, the constant caring what are they thinking of me? without having it all magnified by the merciless physical drives.

Ronnie is calling. He is wet and I change him. It is rare there is such a cry now. That time of motherhood is almost behind me when the ear is not one's own but must always be racked and listening for the child cry, the child call. We sit for a while and I hold him, looking out over the city spread in charcoal with its soft aisles of light. "*Shoogily,*" he breathes and curls closer. I carry him back to bed, asleep. *Shoogily.* A funny word, a family word, inherited from Emily, invented by her to say: *comfort.*

In this and other ways she leaves her seal, I say aloud. And startle at my saying it. What do I mean? What did I start to gather together, to try and make coherent? I was at the terrible, growing years. War years. I do not remember them well. I was working, there were four smaller ones now, there was not time for her. She had to help be a mother, and housekeeper, and shopper. She had to set her seal. Mornings of crisis and near hysteria trying to get lunches packed, hair combed, coats and shoes found, everyone to school or Child Care on time, the baby ready for transportation. And always the paper scribbled on by a smaller one, the book looked at by Susan then mislaid, the homework not done. Running out to that huge school where she was one, she was lost, she was a drop; suffering over the unpreparedness, stammering and unsure in her classes.

There was so little time left at night after the kids were bedded down. She would struggle over books, always eating (it was in those years she developed her enormous appetite that is legendary in our family) and I would be ironing, or preparing food for the next day, or writing V-mail to Bill, or tending the baby. Sometimes, to make me laugh, or out of her despair, she would imitate happenings or types at school.

I think I said once, "Why don't you do something like this in the school amateur show?" One morning she phoned me at work, hardly understandable through the weeping: "Mother, I did it. I won, I won; they gave me first prize; they clapped and clapped and wouldn't let go."

Now suddenly she was Somebody, and as imprisoned in her difference as she had been in anonymity.

She began to be asked to perform at other high schools, even in colleges, then at city and statewide affairs. The first one we went to, I only recognized her that first moment when thin, shy, she almost drowned herself into the curtains. Then: Was this Emily? The control, the command, the convulsing and deadly clowning, the spell, then the roaring, stamping audience, unwilling to let this rare and precious laughter out of their lives.

Afterwards: You ought to do something about her with a gift like that— but without money or knowing how, what does one do? We have left it all to her, and the gift has as often eddied inside, clogged and clotted, as been used and growing.

She is coming. She runs up the stairs two at a time with her light grace-ful step, and I know she is happy tonight. Whatever it was that occasioned your call did not happen today.

"Aren't you ever going to finish the ironing, Mother? Whistler painted his mother in a rocker. I'd have to paint mine standing over an ironing board." This is one of her communicative nights and she tells me everything and nothing as she fixes herself a plate of food out of the icebox.

She is so lovely. Why did you want me to come in at all? Why were you concerned? She will find her way.

She starts up the stairs to bed. "Don't get me up with the rest in the morning." "But I thought you were having midterms." "Oh, those," she comes back in, kisses me, and says quite lightly, "in a couple of years when we'll all be atom-dead they won't matter a bit."

She has said it before. She *believes* it. But because I have been dredging the past, and all that compounds a human being is so heavy and meaningful in me, I cannot endure it tonight.

I will never total it all. I will never come in to say: She was a child sel-dom smiled at. Her father left me before she was a year old. I had to work her first six years when there was work, or I sent her home and to his rela-tives. There were years she had care she hated. She was dark and thin and foreign-looking in a world where the prestige went to blondeness and curly hair and dimples, she was slow where glibness was prized. She was a child of anxious, not proud, love. We were poor and could not afford for her the soil of easy growth. I was a young mother, I was a distracted mother. There were the other children pushing up, demanding. Her younger sister seemed all that she was not. There were years she did not want me to touch her. She kept too much in herself, her life was such she had to keep too much in her-self. My wisdom came too late. She has much to her and probably little will come of it. She is a child of her age, of depression, of war, of fear.

Let her be. So all that is in her will not bloom—but in how many does it? There is still enough left to live by. Only help her to know—help make it so there is cause for her to know—that she is more than this dress on the iron-ing board, helpless before the iron.

Respond: Thinking Independently

1. Write your reactions to the mother's biography of her daughter Emily.
2. Write a response statement: I was angered/saddened/surprised at ____ _____ because _____
3. What, in your opinion, could the mother have done differently?

Reconsider: Thinking Collaboratively

1. Compare reactions to the story.
2. Discuss Emily from what we are told about her by her mother, her teachers, and from what we briefly see of her at the end of the story.

3. What part do historical events (the Depression, World War II) play in this story?
4. Discuss the irony of Emily's father leaving the family because he "could no longer endure sharing want with us."
5. How well did social services serve the family? What practices would we describe today as "misguided"?

Review: Thinking Critically

1. Some years ago Francois Trauffaut, a French film director, made a movie about the difficult childhood of a young boy called *The Four Hundred Blows.* How many "blows" does Emily take in her life? What compensations have there been?
2. What significance does the clock talking to Emily have?
3. What does her mother mean by the last lines of the story that "all that is in her will not bloom" but that she is not "helpless before the iron"?

READING TO WRITE

Understanding Fiction: Interior Monologue

As you see, the mother in Tillie Olsen's story is the narrator, and therefore the point of view is first person. And yet, the story reads quite differently from Toni Cade Bambara's "The Lesson," which also has a first person narrator. In Olsen's story, the mother is speaking from her mind, remembering when her daughter Emily was growing up. In a sense while she is ironing, she is rehearsing what she might say to the counselor or school official who wants her to come in and talk about her daughter who "needs help." Her reminiscences are a kind of one-sided conversation called an "interior monologue." At the end of the story, the monologue is briefly broken when Emily comes in from school and mother and daughter have a dialogue, but the mother resumes her thoughts about Emily's future as the story ends.

A reader learns much about a character in an interior monologue, but only, of course, what the character reveals. The reader has no way to check on the narrator's story or compare other characters' versions of events. How reliable do you think the mother is in telling this story? What responsibility does she take for Emily? Should she take more? Less?

Writing Applications

1. If you are a parent, write a similar account of one of your children's growing up, trying to pinpoint moments of significant insight into the child's personality.
2. As a young person, write an account of what you remember of your parents as you grew up, again trying to select specific moments to illuminate your discussion.

3. Choose an issue related to children: day care, health care, education. Discuss ways to make the service more effective.

The Neighborhood Mom
Ellen Goodman

Preview: Thinking Ahead

In the previous story, Tillie Olsen vividly describes what can happen to a family when there are no "safety nets" in times of economic hardship. But even suburban middle-class mothers face the balancing act of work and raising children. Some are able to stay at home out of the work force when their children are small, but even these women face questions of identity and the assumed role of the "neighborhood mom." As you read syndicated columnist Ellen Goodman's 1987 essay, try to determine just what bothers the woman who takes in the kids on snow days.

It was the fourth no-school day of the year. The Neighborhood Mother had just heard from two of those she refers to privately as her "clients."

One of these clients was the mother of Jason. The other was the mother of Andrew. The boys were friends of her own 6-year-old son, Matthew, and the mothers all knew each other through that chain that connects the parents of classmates by a Xeroxed telephone list. The Neighborhood Mother was familiar with that school list because she had typed it.

The first of her clients was a single working mother, the second was half of a two-working-parent family. Both these work lives were inflexible enough that the very first flake threatened them with disaster. But because there is no Red Cross for working parents faced with a no-school day, they called The Neighborhood Mother.

So it was that by 9 A.M., the N.M. had the boots, snowsuits and energy level of five children, including Jason's brother, under her roof for the entire day. At times like this the woman, who had not worked outside her home since her second child was born, nostalgically remembered mornings when she took a cup of coffee to her desk and worried about the sales campaign for a line of natural shampoos.

The N.M. didn't mind taking on her small extras. She understood the lives of her neighbor-clients. She knew that some longed for her option. Certainly she knew the alternative for her young visitors was to spend the day alone.

Yet there was something bothering her when we talked. Maybe it was the way Jason's mother had anxiously said, "since you're home anyway." Maybe it was the way a man at the last PTA meeting had asked her the classic question, "Are you working?" Or was it because even her clients regarded her as a volunteer?

It occurred to the N.M. that as fewer women could or did make the choice to stay home with their own children, more and more was expected of them. In the past year, she had been room mother, PTA representative, had gone on three school trips as bus monitor, and brought cookies and juice for as many birthdays. Because she was home. Anyway.

The N.M.'s name was listed under "In Case of Emergency" for no fewer than half-a-dozen kids, including her own nieces, who had spent two sick days on her daybed. Two or three times, when the baby sitter hadn't shown up at a friend's, she had done after-school care for two or three more.

It wasn't just child care, mind you. In the weeks before Christmas, the United Parcel delivery man had been at her door often enough to start a rumor, if there had been any neighbors around to gossip. He left a streetful of packages for pickup by their owners. She also held keys to the houses next door, and at one time or another had let in a repairer or deliverer to each of them.

The woman was not oppressed by this. She could and did say no. But she wondered sometimes whether anyone knew about her multi-service center. Knew how many depended on the few women who were home. Anyway.

The N.M. thought about all this especially hard because next year she would in all probability be closing down her center and reentering the work world. This endangered species would lose another member due to the environmental pressures on a single paycheck. How would she replace herself?

Was it possible, she wondered, to create a semi-professional network of Neighborhood Mothers and Fathers each on a retainer for school trips and no-school days, with a fee schedule that might include sick days? Was that too mercenary?

What about swapping, or compensatory time off, as they say in the business world? For every car pool and after-school project, every sick or snow day, each client could return the favor with equal hours of child care or maybe even—this is her fantasy—an occasional housecleaning. And what about a work place that accommodates in snow, not to mention a place that accommodates children?

Her point is that we are running the 1980s world along the 1950s model. Once, almost every family had its wife and mother. Now there is, at most, one per neighborhood. Yet the same rules, the same expectations, the same needs exist. There has been no real replacement.

So, she says, as the five snowed-in children play in the background, that next year she will be part of the problem and cannot figure out a proper solution. All she knows for sure is one thing. If she calls for help, she swears, she will never, ever, say to another N.M., "because you are home, anyway."

Respond: Thinking Independently

1. Record your reactions to Ellen Goodman's essay in your journal.
2. Write a response statement: I think that the biggest problem for the Neighborhood Mom was _____.

Reconsider: Thinking Collaboratively

1. What does the Neighborhood Mom resent about her role in the neighborhood? Discuss whether your classmates feel that her resentment is warranted. What do students think of her suggestions for compensation?
2. What solutions to the problem of working mothers and child care are there? What does it mean that "we are running the 1980s world along the 1950s model"? Have things changed since 1987 when this essay was written?
3. Is the Neighborhood Mom bothered just by the extra work, the missed cup of coffee, or is there something else bothering her about the role? Explain.

Review: Thinking Critically

1. Goodman repeats the word "Anyway" throughout the essay, echoing the comment by Jason's mother "since you are home anyway." Why does she do this? What effect does it have on the reader? What does the way this word sticks in the mind of the Neighborhood Mom show about her feelings?
2. Why does the Neighborhood Mom refer to her neighbors as "clients"? And why does she only use this word privately?
3. Why does the woman refer to herself as having a "multi-service center"? And what does this show about her need for identity?

READING TO WRITE

Understanding Causal Analysis: Analyzing Causes

Sometimes an essay involves causes and effects in a subtle way. For example, in this essay, an immediate cause of the Neighborhood Mom's problem role is the snowstorm that causes school to be called off. The effect of the snowstorm is that the working parents have to arrange care for their children very quickly, which causes them to call the Neighborhood Mom who then ends up with five youngsters to take care of. However, what causes the Neighborhood Mom to be in her position of lone mother at home? What causes the other parents not to be home? What causes the Neighborhood Mom to feel upset at her role? What is the role of society in any of these causes or the resultant effects?

Writing Applications: Causal Analysis

1. Construct the ideal child care arrangement for American society in the 1990s.
2. Discuss the changing attitudes toward women and working "outside the home" from your grandmother's and your mother's day to your own. Perhaps interview women from earlier generations. What are the advantages and disadvantages of these changes?

3. Fathers are not mentioned in "The Neighborhood Mom." Should they be? What is a father's role in child care?

Why Young Women Are More Conservative
GLORIA STEINEM

Preview: Thinking Ahead

Gloria Steinem challenges the assumption that people are liberals when they are young and grow more conservative with age—at least when the people are female. In this provocative 1979 essay, Steinem, a journalist, feminist, and founder of Ms. Magazine, *looks at the forces pressuring young women to remain conventional and the experiences of older women which may radicalize them and make them activists. As you read, highlight sentences that you agree with and those you question. Carry on a dialogue with Steinem in the margins.*

If you had asked me a decade or more ago, I certainly would have said the campus was the first place to look for the feminist or any other revolution. I also would have assumed that student-age women, like student-age men, were much more likely to be activist and open to change than their parents. After all, campus revolts have a long and well-publicized tradition, from the students of medieval France, whose "heresy" was suggesting that the university be separate from the church, through the anticolonial student riots of British India; from students who led the cultural revolution of the People's Republic of China, to campus demonstrations against the Shah of Iran. Even in this country, with far less tradition of student activism, the populist movement to end the war in Vietnam was symbolized by campus protests and mistrust of anyone over thirty.

It has taken me many years of traveling as a feminist speaker and organizer to understand that I was wrong about women; at least, about women acting on their own behalf. In activism, as in so many other things, I had been educated to assume that men's cultural pattern was the natural or the only one. If student years were the peak time of rebellion and openness to change for men, then the same must be true for women. In fact, a decade of listening to every kind of women's group—from brown-bag lunchtime lectures organized by office workers to all-night rap sessions at campus women's centers; from housewives' self-help groups to campus rallies—has convinced me that the reverse is more often true. Women may be the one group that grows more radical with age. Though some students are big exceptions to this rule, women in general don't begin to challenge the politics of our own lives until later.

Looking back, I realize that this pattern has been true for my life, too. My college years were full of uncertainties and the personal conservatism that comes from trying to win approval and fit into the proper grown-up and womanly role, whether that means finding a well-to-do man to be supported by or a male radical to support. Nonetheless, I went right on assuming that brave exploring youth and cowardly conservative old age were the norms for everybody, and that I must be just an isolated and guilty accident. Though every generalization based on female culture has many exceptions, and should never be used as a crutch or excuse, I think we might be less hard on ourselves and each other as students, feel better about our potential for change as we grow older—and educate reporters who announce feminism's demise because its red-hot center is not on campus—if we figured out that for most of us as women, the traditional college period is an unrealistic and cautious time. Consider a few of the reasons.

As students, women are probably treated with more equality than we ever will be again. For one thing, we're consumers. The school is only too glad to get the tuitions we pay, or that our families or government grants pay on our behalf. With population rates declining because of women's increased power over childbearing, that money is even more vital to a school's existence. Yet more than most consumers, we're too transient to have much power as a group. If our families are paying our tuition, we may have even less power.

As young women, whether students or not, we're still in the stage most valued by male-dominant cultures: we have our full potential as workers, wives, sex partners, and childbearers.

That means we haven't yet experienced the life events that are most radicalizing for women: entering the paid-labor force and discovering how women are treated there; marrying and find out out that it is not yet an equal partnership; having children and discovering who is responsible for them and who is not; and aging, still a greater penalty for women than for men.

Furthermore, new ambitions nourished by the rebirth of feminism may make young women feel and behave a little like a classical immigrant group. We are determined to prove ourselves, to achieve academic excellence, and to prepare for interesting and successful careers. More noses are kept to more grindstones in an effort to demonstrate newfound abilities, and perhaps to allay suspicions that women still have to have more and better credentials than men. This doesn't leave much time for activism. Indeed, we may not yet know that it is necessary.

In addition, the very progress into previously all-male careers that may be revolutionary for women is seen as conservative and conformist by outside critics. Assuming male radicalism to be the measure of change, they interpret any concern with careers as evidence of "campus conservatism." In fact, "dropping out" may be a departure for men, but "dropping in" is a new thing for women. Progress lies in the direction we have not been.

Like most groups of the newly arrived or awakened, our faith in education and paper degrees also has yet to be shaken. For instance, the percentage of women enrolled in colleges and universities has been increasing at the same time that the percentage of men has been decreasing. Among students entering college in 1978, women *outnumbered* men for the first time. This hope of excelling at the existing game is probably reinforced by the greater cultural pressure on females to be "good girls" and observe somebody else's rules.

Though we may know intellectually that we need to have new games with new rules, we probably haven't quite absorbed such facts as the high unemployment rate among female Ph.D.s; the lower average salary among women college graduates of all races than among counterpart males who graduated from high school or less; the middle-management ceiling against which even those eagerly hired new business-school graduates seem to bump their heads after five or ten years; and the barrier-breaking women in nontraditional fields who become the first fired when recession hits. Sadly enough, we may have to personally experience some of these reality checks before we accept the idea that lawsuits, activism, and group pressure will have to accompany our individual excellence and crisp new degrees.

Then there is the female guilt trip, student edition. If we're not sailing along as planned, it must be *our* fault. If our mothers didn't "do anything" with their educations, it must have been *their* fault. If we can't study as hard as we think we must (because women still have to be better prepared than men), and have a substantial personal and sexual life at the same time (because women are supposed to care more about relationships than men do), then we feel inadequate, as if each of us were individually at fault for a problem that is actually culture-wide.

I've yet to be on a campus where most women weren't worrying about some aspect of combining marriage, children, and a career. I've yet to find one where many men were worrying about the same thing. Yet women will go right on suffering from the double-role problem and terminal guilt until men are encouraged, pressured, or otherwise forced, individually and collectively, to integrate themselves into the "women's work" of raising children and homemaking. Until then, and until there are changed job patterns to allow equal parenthood, children will go right on growing up with the belief that only women can be loving and nurturing, and only men can be intellectual or active outside the home. Each half of the world will go on limiting the full range of its human talent.

Finally, there is the intimate political training that hits women in the teens and early twenties: the countless ways we are still brainwashed into assuming that women are dependent on men for our basic identities, both in our work and our personal lives, much more than vice versa. After all, if we're going to enter a marriage system that's still legally designed for a person and a half, submit to an economy in which women still average about fifty-nine cents on the dollar earned by men, and work mainly as support staff and assistants, or *co*-directors and *vice*-presidents at best, then we have to be convinced that we are not whole people on our own.

In order to make sure that we will see ourselves as half-people, and thus be addicted to getting our identity from serving others, society tries hard to convert us as young women into "man junkies"; that is, into people who are

addicted to regular shots of male-approval and presence, both professionally and personally. We need a man standing next to us, actually and figuratively, whether it's at work, on Saturday night, or throughout life. (If only
men realized how little it matters *which* man is standing there, they would
understand that this addiction depersonalizes them, too.) Given the danger
to a male-dominant system if young women stop internalizing this political
message of derived identity, it's no wonder that those who try to kick the
addiction—and, worse yet, to help other women do the same—are likely to
be regarded as odd or dangerous by everyone from parents to peers.

With all that pressure combined with little experience, it's no wonder
that younger women are often less able to support each other. Even young
women who espouse feminist goals as individuals may refrain from identi-
fying themselves as "feminist": it's okay to want equal pay for yourself (just
one small reform) but it's not okay to want equal pay for women as a group
(an economic revolution). Some retreat into individualized career obses-
sions as a way of avoiding this dangerous discovery of shared experience
with women as a group. Others retreat into the safe middle ground of "I'm
not a feminist but. . . ." Still others become politically active, but only on issues that are taken seriously by their male counterparts.

The same lesson about the personal conservatism of younger women is
taught by the history of feminism. If I hadn't been conned into believing the
masculine stereotype of youth as the "natural" time for freedom and rebellion, a time of "sowing wild oats" that actually is made possible by the as-
surance of power and security later on, I could have figured out the female
pattern of activism by looking at women's movements of the past.

In this country, for instance, the nineteenth-century wave of feminism
was started by older women who had been through the radicalizing experience of getting married and becoming the legal chattel of their husbands (or
the equally radicalizing experience of *not* getting married and being treated
as spinsters). Most of them had also worked in the antislavery movement
and learned from the political parallels between race and sex. In other countries, that wave was also led by women who were past the point of maxi-
mum pressure toward marriageability and conservatism.

Looking at the first decade of this second wave, it's clear that the early
feminist activist and consciousness-raising groups of the 1960s were organized by women who had experienced the civil rights movement, or home-
makers who had discovered that raising kids and cooking didn't occupy all
their talents. While most campuses of the late sixties were still circulating the
names of illegal abortionists privately (after all, abortion could damage our
marriage value), slightly older women were holding press conferences and
speak-outs about the reality of abortions (including their own, even though
that often meant confessing to an illegal act) and demanding reform or re-
peal of antichoice laws. Though rape had been a quiet epidemic on campus
for generations, younger women victims were still understandably fearful of
speaking up, and campuses encouraged silence in order to retain their reputation for safety with tuition-paying parents. It took many off-campus
speak-outs, demonstrations against laws of evidence and police procedures,

and testimonies in state legislatures before most student groups began to make demands on campus and local cops for greater rape protection. In fact, "date rape"—the common campus phenomenon of a young woman being raped by someone she knows, perhaps even by several students in a fraternity house—is just now being exposed. Marital rape, a more difficult legal issue, was taken up several years ago. As for battered women and the attendant exposé of husbands and lovers as more statistically dangerous than unknown muggers in the street, that issue still seems to be thought of as largely noncampus concern, yet at many of the colleges and universities where I've spoken, there has been at least one case within current student memory of a young woman beaten or murdered by a jealous lover.

This cultural pattern of youthful conservatism makes the growing number of older women going back to school very important. They are life examples and pragmatic activists who radicalize women young enough to be their daughters. Now that the median female undergraduate age in this country is twenty-seven because so many older women have returned, the campus is becoming a major place for cross-generational connections.

None of this should denigrate the courageous efforts of young women, especially women on campus, and the many changes they've pioneered. On the contrary, they should be seen as even more remarkable for surviving the conservative pressures, recognizing societal problems they haven't yet fully experienced, and organizing successfully in the midst of a transient student population. Every women's history course, rape hot line, or campus newspaper that is finally covering *all* the news; every feminist professor whose job has been created or tenure saved by student pressure, or male administrator whose consciousness has been permanently changed; every counselor who's stopped guiding women one way and men another; every lawsuit that's been fueled by student energies against unequal athletic funds or graduate school requirements: all those accomplishments are even more impressive when seen against the backdrop of the female pattern of activism.

Finally, it would help to remember that a feminist revolution rarely resembles a masculine-style one—just as a young woman's most radical act toward her mother (that is, connecting as women in order to help each other get some power) doesn't look much like a young man's most radical act toward his father (that is, breaking the father-son connection in order to separate identities or take over existing power).

It's those father-son conflicts at a generational, national level that have often provided the conventional definition of revolution; yet they've gone on for centuries without basically changing the role of the female half of the world. They have also failed to reduce the level of violence in society, since both fathers and sons have included some degree of aggressiveness and superiority to women in their definition of masculinity, thus preserving the anthropological model of dominance.

Furthermore, what current leaders and theoreticians define as revolution is usually little more than taking over the army and the radio stations. Women have much more in mind than that. We have to uproot the sexual caste system that is the most pervasive power structure in society, and that means transforming the patriarchal values of those who run the institutions, whether they are politically the "right" or the "left," the fathers or the sons. This cultural part of the change goes very deep, and is often seen as too intimate, and perhaps too threatening, to be considered as either serious or possible. Only conflicts among men are "serious." Only a takeover of existing institutions is "possible."

That's why the definition of "political," on campus as elsewhere, tends to be limited to who's running for president, who's demonstrating against corporate investments in South Africa, or which is the "moral" side of some conventional revolution, preferably one that is thousands of miles away.

As important as such activities are, they are also the most comfortable ones when we're young. They provide a sense of virtue without much disruption in the power structure of our daily lives. Even when the most consistent energies on campus are actually concentrated around feminist issues, they may be treated as apolitical and invisible. Asked "What's happening on campus?" a student may reply, "The antinuke movement," even though that resulted in one demonstration of two hours, while student antirape squads have been patrolling the campus every night for two years and women's studies have begun to transform the very textbooks we read.

No wonder reporters and sociologists looking for revolution on campus often miss the depth of feminist change and activity that is really there. Women students themselves may dismiss it as not political and not serious. Certainly, it rarely comes in the masculine sixties style of bombing buildings or burning draft cards. In fact, it goes much deeper than protesting a temporary symptom—say, the draft—and challenges the right of one group to dominate another, which is the disease itself.

Young women have a big task of resisting pressures and challenging definitions. Their increasing success is a miracle of foresight and courage that should make us all proud. But they should know that they, too, may grow more radical with age.

One day, an army of gray-haired women may quietly take over the earth.

Respond: Thinking Independently

1. Choose two of your highlighted sentences and write a paragraph on each in your journal explaining why you agree or disagree with them.
2. Write a response sentence: The truest/most untrue/most disturbing/most _____ idea in this essay is _____ because _____.

Reconsider: Thinking Collaboratively

1. Compare classmates' reactions to the essay. Do they divide along gender lines?
2. Discuss the following sentences from Steinem's essay or ones you and your classmates chose for your response statements:

   a. "Though some students are big exceptions to this rule, women in general don't begin to challenge the politics of our own lives until later."

   b. "We are still brainwashed into assuming that women are dependent on men for our basic identities. . . ."

3. What explanation does Steinem offer for female college students being conventional?

4. What are the life experiences that radicalize older women? What effect do older women returning to college have on younger women?

5. In what ways are men's political activities different from women's, according to Steinem?

6. What lesson from the history of feminism does Steinem cite?

Review: Thinking Critically

1. Look at the kinds of support Steinem offers for her assertions. Go through the essay and write down "Fact," for an objective fact such as a statistic, or a historical event; "Examples" based on experiences; or "Opinion" for ideas offered without other support. What does your survey show? How does the survey affect your reading of the essay?

2. What do you think Steinem's purpose was in writing the essay? Explain.

3. Judge whether Steinem is serious in the last sentence in this essay. If not, why does she end the essay this way?

READING TO WRITE

Understanding Comparison and Contrast: Organizing Two Pairs of Contrasts

Gloria Steinem's essay involves two pairs of contrasting elements: How and why young women are not like young men in their peak time of rebellion and how and why older women are different from younger women in their readiness to rebel. Make a brief list of the points raised under each of these two pairs to give yourself a sense of Steinem's organization. How does she keep the two ideas from becoming confusing? Look at the beginnings of Steinem's paragraphs: How often does she use the words "younger women" or "older women" or their equivalents ("women in their teens")? How does this repetition help the reader follow her ideas?

Writing Applications: Comparison and Contrast

1. Americans have been accustomed to seeing youth as the best time in life. Certainly, one can point to many advantages in being young. However, what advantages does age bring?

2. Choose one of the statements you responded to above and write a fuller explanation of your opinion, drawing on examples from your own experiences.

Richard Cory

Edwin Arlington Robinson

Preview: Thinking Ahead

This 1937 poem with its dramatic last line has inspired many discussions of success in America, the loneliness of the celebrity, how anguish can be hidden from view, and at least one popular song (by Simon and Garfunkel). It may not come as a surprise that Robinson, also a New Englander, was one of Robert Frost's favorite poets. Certainly, this three-time Pulitzer Prize winner has been remembered by many readers for his memorable characters such as Richard Cory, Miniver Cheevy, and Bewick Finzer.

Whenever Richard Cory went downtown,
  We people on the pavement looked at him:
He was a gentleman from sole to crown,
  Clean favored, and imperially slim.

And he was always quietly arrayed,
  And he was always human when he talked;
But still he fluttered pulses when he said,
  "Good morning," and he glittered when he walked.

And he was rich—yes, richer than a king,
  And admirably schooled in every grace:
In fine, we thought that he was everything
  To make us wish that we were in his place.

So on we worked, and waited for the light,
  And went without the meat, and cursed the bread;
And Richard Cory, one calm summer night,
  Went home and put a bullet through his head.

Respond: Thinking Independently

1. Record your reactions to the poem in your journal.
2. Write a response statement: Richard Cory shows that _____.
3. In your opinion, how do most Americans react to wealthy people: With envy, suspicion, respect, disrespect? Why?

Reconsider: Thinking Collaboratively

1. What is the townspeople's opinion of Richard Cory?
2. How does the economic status of the townspeople compare with that of Richard Cory? Why is that disparity important to the poem?
3. Why is the reader given no reasons for Richard Cory's suicide?

Review: Thinking Critically

1. What words does Robinson choose to describe Richard Cory? The townspeople?
2. What does "he fluttered pulses" mean? Whose pulses?
3. How can Cory "glitter" when he walks?
4. Does the ending of the poem constitute a "lesson" about wealth, success, or anything else?

READING TO WRITE

Understanding Poetry: Cosmic Irony

In Hemingway's "Hills Like White Elephants," you were introduced to the irony created when a character says something that she really doesn't mean. In "Richard Cory" a different kind of irony is created by the disparity between the townspeople's regard for Richard Cory as an enviable success and his own despair leading to suicide. In fact, it is this disparity that provokes the reader to consider the differences between public celebrity and private character, to define success in American society, and to explore the difference between appearance and reality. Such irony is larger than the verbal irony displayed in the Hemingway story and has been termed "cosmic irony." Irony of all kinds is a powerful way for writers of fiction or poetry to make readers think.

Writing Applications

1. Richard Cory had a side the townspeople did not see. Write about someone you know who has an aspect of his or her personality hidden from most people.
2. Define success the way you think of it and compare your definition with the definition that you think most Americans believe. Are they the same?
3. Write a poem or paragraph from Richard Cory's point of view.

Real Trouble Ahead

JACK McCLINTOCK

Preview: Thinking Ahead

What the future will bring, none of us knows, but sometimes an event occurs which gets us to think about what's ahead. Jack McClintock's backyard mishap gets him thinking about growing older, living alone, and the anxiety of what "real trouble" may lie ahead. As you read, think about growing older in our society. How well do any of us handle aging?

Hitting myself on the head with a pickax changed a pleasant afternoon of puttering in the yard into a revelation. Or perhaps I should say half a revelation. The blow knocked my glasses off; they haven't turned up yet, and my view of the event—and its meaning—is still unclear.

It began with the lawn. I regard the lawn as the enemy. I've hated lawns since boyhood, when it was my chore to mow ours, and the only way to earn pocket money was to mow the neighbors' too. I would spend the next week resentfully watching the grass grow. Lawns make no sense.

When I bought this house nine months ago, I decided to do away with nearly all the lawn. Almost every day I take out grass and install something else: trees, shrubs, ferns, deck, ground cover, flowers, pathways of cypress chips—anything but grass.

The mango tree I had ordered had not arrived that afternoon, but I decided to get a head start and begin digging. Where I live in south Florida, a head start is a good idea. There is solid limestone six inches down.

It was hot. I had on shorts and a T-shirt. I wore a sun hat and an old pair of glasses. I got the necessary tool from the garage. I think it is accurately called a pick mattock. The pick end of the blade—the end you use for rock—is a 10-inch spike of steel. The mattock end is wide and flattened, almost like a curved hoe.

You have to take a big swing to penetrate the turf with the mattock. You grip the too with both hands like an ax, raise it high over your shoulder and then bring it down with all your might. *Chop,* it goes into the detested sod. I have found this very satisfying.

I picked up the mattock and brought it down as hard as I could. But it never struck the ground. What hit the ground was me. I was lying on my back on the lawn, my hat in the grass beside my right foot, the mattock by my left. I looked up groggily. A mockingbird chirped merrily in the mahogany tree above me.

I felt blank, then dizzy, then confused; I touched my face. I was sweating a lot. I looked at my palm. No, I was bleeding a lot. I stumbled, trying to rise and my vision seemed unclear.

It took a few seconds to figure out what had happened. I had brought the mattock down on the clothesline. This was a well-built clothesline: steel pipes solidly set in concrete and heavy wire. I had hit the wire on the downswing and, like the string of a bow, it had flung the mattock straight back into my face, point first.

I yanked off my blood-soaked T-shirt and wadded it against my face, covering the right eye, and stumbled into the house to inspect the damage. I looked into the hall mirror and hesitantly moved the shirt aside. The eye was full of blood. I couldn't remember pulling the mattock point out of the eye, but knew that I must have.

I decided not to try to drive. And it struck me just then, trying to think what to do, staring into a bloody face that mirrored horror, that one of my worst fears had been realized.

I don't know how to phrase this fear exactly, because it is not entirely clear, but it goes something like this: I live alone and something happens—I get sick or hurt or poor or old—and nobody is *there*.

And it had just happened! And my first thought was, "It isn't so bad."

I called a friend, who said, "I'll be right there."

She arrived, took over, calmly said that she could see the skull in the bloody gap and we'd better get rolling.

"You're going to have a dashing scar on your brow," she said, glancing over but keeping both hands on the wheel. The sight of blood makes careful drivers.

Things went smoothly at the doctor's office. His quick inspection showed that, under the blood, the eye was fine; I had missed it by an inch. My vision was still bleary, but now I could see clearly enough to know why—my glasses were missing. The gash was perfectly straight and closed up neatly with only five stitches. The skull was whole.

The doctor gave me a tetanus shot. The nurse gave me a bill for "Laceration Repair Face etc.," and I wrote a check. The dizziness went away in a few hours, though I had a terrific headache that night and a queasy stomach the next day.

What seems remarkable now are the gaps in this adventure. There was the gap of consciousness—before I found myself on my back on the lawn. There was a mundane insurance coverage gap: I had left a job and the health insurance it provided and had not yet established my own coverage. I suspect the doctor gave me a break on the bill.

There was a gap between the idiotic Dagwood Bumstead comedy of incompetence I had created and the serious damage it could have caused and didn't—the gap between what happened to me and real trouble; I knew this was not real trouble.

And there was the gap between the daily necessary illusion of safety and the truth: that sweet life can turn sour in a second.

There is, too, that matter of what I had feared. My father died six months ago; my mother had been with him 24 hours a day for all the years of heart attacks, bone cancer, kidney failure, Alzheimer's disease. It was terrible for her, and she was enormously brave. Perhaps everyone who has witnessed the aging of loyal parents knows the anxiety I felt: When things get really bad, will someone be there for me? Our times are not like theirs.

Home from the doctor's, I wandered into the backyard. The mattock and my hat were lying where I'd left them on the lawn. I touched the bristling stitches over my eye, smiled and said thanks again.

Over the next few days my friend was generous and kind, sometimes there and sometimes not. Sometimes it was good to be alone, unsmothered. Others called and stopped by. I got to tell my comical Dagwood story lots of times and began to see it as a short movie about this ridiculous character in a funny hat who wakes up to the mockingbird's chirp. The audience always laughed.

The problem is that real trouble exists. I didn't have to face it this time; even without health insurance or a loving partner, I didn't need anything more than was there. The scar will be insignificant; not dashing at all.

But real trouble exists, and how many of us are equipped to endure it alone? I still don't know how to think about this. And every time I go into the backyard I search for my glasses. But they're still missing.

Respond: Thinking Independently

1. Write your reaction to McClintock's "adventure" in your journal.
2. What is your greatest concern about getting older? If you know people 20 or more years older than you, what are their concerns?

Reconsider: Thinking Collaboratively

1. McClintock says that this event was not "real trouble." Why not? Do you agree with him?
2. What does the writer mean by the "daily necessary illusion of safety"? Why "necessary"? What is the truth, as he sees it?
3. Why does McClintock mention his father's illnesses and his mother's care of his father? What does he mean by "our times are not like theirs"?

Review: Thinking Critically

1. Why does McClintock tell us in the first sentence what happened to him?
2. Why does he mention his missing glasses several times? Do they take on any significance beyond the physical fact of their loss?
3. Why does McClintock tell the event to his friends as a comical story?
4. What impact does this event have on the writer's identity?

READING TO WRITE

Understanding Examples/Illustration: Using an Extended Illustration

An extended illustration acts much like a narrative. As in this essay, both may proceed in chronological order, as McClintock does in the telling of his accident with the mattock. However, the extended illustration usually breaks away from the chronology to allow the writer a chance to discuss the meaning of the event to him or her and to examine its possible implications for all of us. For example, departing from the chronological illustration, we readers are told in paragraph 11 that one of McClintock's "worst fears had been realized." Later in the essay the writer again leaves the incident and discusses the "gaps" he discovered and his anxiety over growing older alone. As we have seen, narratives are used in expository writing to make a point, but usually the focus of such an essay is on the story such as in

Langston Hughes's "Salvation." In this essay the incident becomes the occasion for McClintock to focus his previously vague thoughts on aging and loneliness.

Writing Applications: Examples/Illustration

1. Using examples of older people you know or perhaps after interviewing some older people, discuss aging in our society. How does it affect the people you know? What changes in identity if any do they experience?
2. Although this essay does not focus extensively on health care, McClintock does mention the "gap" in coverage because he had left a job that offered benefits and had not yet arranged for his own insurance. Using examples of people you know or by again interviewing people, discuss the current state of health care insurance and people's sense of security.

The Doctor
ANDRE DUBUS

Preview: Thinking Independently

While our inability to help someone in trouble might upset any of us, it might make a doctor, the main character in this story, feel even worse, since he is trained to help people. In this case the event shakes his sense of competency and identity. As you read the story published in 1975, think about how you would react.

In late March, the snow began to melt. First it ran off the slopes and roads, and the brooks started flowing. Finally there were only low, shaded patches in the woods. In April, there were four days of warm sun, and on the first day Art Castagnetto told Maxine she could put away his pajamas until next year. That night he slept in a T-shirt, and next morning, when he noticed the pots on the radiators were dry, he left them empty.

Maxine didn't believe in the first day, or the second, either. But on the third afternoon, wearing shorts and a sweat shirt, she got the charcoal grill from the garage, put it in the backyard, and broiled steaks. She even told Art to get some tonic and limes for the gin. It was a Saturday afternoon; they sat outside in canvas lawn chairs and told Tina, their four-year-old girl, that it was all right to watch the charcoal but she mustn't touch it, because it was burning even if it didn't look like it. When the steaks were ready, the sun was behind the woods in the back of the house; Maxine brought sweaters to Art and the four children so they could eat outside.

Monday it snowed. The snow was damp at first, melting on the dead grass, but the flakes got heavier and fell as slowly as tiny leaves and covered the ground. In another two days the snow melted, and each gray, cool day was warmer than the one before. Saturday afternoon the sky started clearing; there was a sunset, and before going to bed Art went outside and looked up at the stars. In the morning, he woke to a bedroom of sunlight. He left Maxine sleeping, put on a T-shirt, trunks, and running shoes, and carrying his sweat suit he went downstairs, tiptoeing because the children slept so lightly on weekends. He dropped his sweat suit into the basket for dirty clothes; he was finished with it until next fall.

He did side-straddle hops on the front lawn and then ran on the shoulder of the road, which for the first half mile was bordered by woods, so that he breathed the scent of pines and, he believed, the sunlight in the air. Then he passed the Whitfords' house. He had never seen the man and woman but had read their name on the mailbox and connected it with the children who usually played in the road in front of the small graying house set back in the trees. Its dirt yard was just large enough to contain it and a rusting Ford and an elm tree with a tire-and-rope swing hanging from one of its branches. The house now was still and dark, as though asleep. He went around the bend and, looking ahead, saw three of the Whitford boys standing by the brook.

It was a shallow brook, which had its prettiest days in winter when it was frozen; in the first weeks of spring, it ran clearly, but after that it became stagnant and around July it dried. This brook was a landmark he used when he directed friends to his house. "You get to a brook with a stone bridge," he'd say. The bridge wasn't really stone; its guard walls were made of rectangular concrete slabs, stacked about three feet high, but he liked stone fences and stone bridges and he called it one. On a slope above the brook, there was a red house. A young childless couple lived there, and now the man, who sold life insurance in Boston, was driving off with a boat and trailer hitched to his car. His wife waved goodbye from the driveway, and the Whitford boys stopped throwing rocks into the brook long enough to wave too. They heard Art's feet on the blacktop and turned to watch him. When he reached the bridge, one of them said, "Hi, Doctor," and Art smiled and said "Hello" to them as he passed. Crossing the bridge, he looked down at the brook. It was moving, slow and shallow, into the dark shade of the woods.

About a mile past the brook, there were several houses, with short stretches of woods between them. At the first house, a family was sitting at a picnic table in the side yard, reading the Sunday paper. They did not hear him, and he felt like a spy as he passed. The next family, about a hundred yards up the road, was working. Two little girls were picking up trash, and the man and woman were digging a flower bed. The parents turned and waved, and the man called, "It's a good day for it!" At the next house, a young couple were washing their Volkswagen, the girl using the hose, the man scrubbing away the dirt of winter. They looked up and waved. By now Art's T-shirt was damp and cool, and he had his second wind.

All up the road it was like that: people cleaning their lawns, washing cars, some just sitting under the bright sky; one large bald man lifted a beer can and grinned. In front of one house, two teenage boys were throwing a Frisbee; farther up the road, a man was gently pitching a softball to his small son, who wore a baseball cap and choked up high on the bat. A boy and girl passed Art in a polished green M.G., the top down, the girl's unscarfed hair blowing across her cheeks as she leaned over and quickly kissed the boy's ear. All the lawn people waved at Art, though none of them knew him; they only knew he was the obstetrician who lived in the big house in the woods. When he turned and jogged back down the road, they waved or spoke again; this time they were not as spontaneous but more casual, more familiar. He rounded a curve a quarter of a mile from the brook; the woman was back in her house and the Whitford boys were gone too. On this length of road he was alone, and ahead of him squirrels and chipmunks fled into the woods.

Then something was wrong—he felt it before he knew it. When the two boys ran up from the brook into his vision, he started sprinting and had a grateful instant when he felt the strength left in his legs, though still he did-n't know if there was any reason for strength and speed. He pounded over the blacktop as the boys scrambled up the lawn, toward the red house, and as he reached the bridge he shouted.

They didn't stop until he shouted again, and now they turned, their faces pale and open-mouthed, and pointed at the brook and then ran back toward it. Art pivoted off the road, leaning backward as he descended the short rocky bank, around the end of the bridge, seeing first the white rectangle of concrete lying in the slow water. And again he felt before he knew: he was in the water up to his knees, bent over the slab and getting his fingers into the sand beneath it before he looked down at the face and shoulders and chest. Then he saw the arms, too, thrashing under water as though digging out of caved-in snow. The boy's pale hands did not quite reach the surface.

In perhaps five seconds, Art realized he could not lift the slab. Then he was running up the lawn to the red house, up the steps and shoving open the side door and yelling as he bumped into the kitchen table, pointing one hand at the phone on the wall and the other at the woman in a bright yellow halter as she backed away, her arms raised before her face.

"Fire Department! A boy's drowning!" Pointing behind him now, to-ward the brook.

She was fast; her face changed fears and she moved toward the phone, and that was enough. He was outside again, sprinting out of a stumble as he left the steps, darting between the two boys, who stood mute at the brook's edge. He refused to believe it was this simple and this impossible. He thrust his hands under the slab, lifting with legs and arms, and now he heard one of the boys moaning behind him, "It fell on Terry, it fell on Terry." Squatting in the water, he held a hand over the Whitford boy's mouth and pinched his nostrils together; then he groaned, for now his own hand was killing the child. He took his hand away. The boy's arms had stopped moving—they seemed to be resting at his sides—and Art reached down and felt the right one and then jerked his own hand out of the water. The small arm was hard and tight and quivering. Art touched the left one, running his hand the length of it, and felt the boy's fingers against the slab, pushing.

The sky changed, was shattered by a smoke-gray sound of winter nights —the fire horn—and in the quiet that followed he heard a woman's voice, speaking to children. He turned and looked at her standing beside him in the water, and he suddenly wanted to be held, his breast against hers, but her eyes shrieked at him to do something, and he bent over and tried again to lift the slab. Then she was beside him, and they kept trying until ten minutes later, when four volunteer firemen descended out of the dying groan of the siren and splashed into the brook.

No one knew why the slab had fallen. Throughout the afternoon, whenever Art tried to understand it, he felt his brain go taut and he tried to stop but couldn't. After three drinks, he thought of the slab as he always thought of cancer: that it had the volition of a killer. And he spoke of it like that until Maxine said, "There was nothing you could do. It took five men and a woman to lift it."

They were sitting in the backyard, their lawn chairs touching, and Maxine was holding his hand. The children were playing in front of the house, because Maxine had told them what happened, told them Daddy had been through the worst day of his life, and they must leave him alone for a while. She kept his glass filled with gin and tonic and once, when Tina started screaming in the front yard, he jumped out of the chair, but she grabbed his wrist and held it tightly and said, "It's nothing, I'll take care of it." She went around the house, and soon Tina stopped crying, and Maxine came back and said she'd fallen down in the driveway and skinned her elbow. Art was trembling.

"Shouldn't you get some sedatives?" she said.

He shook his head, then started to cry.

Monday morning an answer—or at least a possibility—was waiting for him, as though it had actually chosen to enter his mind now, with the buzzing of the alarm clock. He got up quickly and stood in a shaft of sunlight on the floor. Maxine had rolled away from the clock and was still asleep.

He put on trousers and moccasins and went downstairs and then outside and down the road toward the brook. He wanted to run but he kept walking. Before reaching the Whitfords' house, he crossed to the opposite side of the road. Back in the trees, their house was shadowed and quiet. He walked all the way to the bridge before he stopped and looked up at the red house. Then he saw it, and he didn't know (and would never know) whether he had seen it yesterday, too, as he ran to the door or if he just thought he had seen it. But it was there: a bright green garden hose, coiled in the sunlight beside the house.

He walked home. He went to the side yard where his own hose had lain all winter, screwed to the faucet. He stood looking at it, and then he went inside and quietly climbed the stairs, into the sounds of breathing, and got his pocketknife. Now he moved faster, down the stairs and outside, and he picked up the nozzle end of the hose and cut it off. Farther down, he cut the hose again. He put his knife away and then struck one end of the short piece of hose into his mouth, pressed his nostrils between two fingers, and breathed.

He looked up through a bare maple tree at the sky. Then he walked around the house to the Buick and opened the trunk. His fingers were trembling as he lowered the piece of hose and placed it beside his first-aid kit, in front of a bucket of sand and a small snow shovel he had carried all through the winter.

Respond: Thinking Independently

1. Write your response to the story in your journal. If you have ever been called upon to help someone in trouble, write about that experience and your part in it.
2. Write a response statement: I was surprised/upset/angered/saddened by _____ because _____
_____.

Reconsider: Thinking Collaboratively

1. Compare the experiences of Jack McClintock and the doctor in this story. What lessons about life and their own identities might they have shared?
2. The first half of this story portrays a normal, routine, even conventionally dull scene. What purpose of the author is served by beginning the story this way?
3. How does Dubus convey the doctor's frustration in his attempts to free the boy?
4. How does the solution to the problem occur to him? Why didn't it occur in time to save the boy? What blinds us sometimes in our attempts to solve the problems?

Review: Thinking Critically

1. Upon rereading the story, do you notice mention of a hose? Where? Is it connected with the red house?
2. Twice, Dubus says that Art "felt before he knew it." What does he mean?
3. The doctor says about the slab holding down the boy, "He refused to believe it was this simple and this impossible." What does he mean? How does he compare the slab to cancer?
4. What is ironic about Maxine's telling him, "There was nothing you could do. It took five men and a woman to lift it"?

READING TO WRITE

Understanding Fiction: Descriptive Details

In other selections in the text, the power of specific, descriptive details to provide evidence supporting a writer's ideas has been noted. You have also seen the importance of details in helping poets convey their messages. In this short story an overlooked detail, the hose, literally provides the solution, though belated, to the "impossible problem." Dubus prepares readers for this ending by making the doctor highly observant as he jogs in the neighborhood. Details of the brook and the bridge with its concrete slabs, the activities of the neighbors washing their cars, playing Frisbee, and the boys throwing stones in the brook create an atmosphere of comfort and routine, soon to be shattered. However, the details also underscore the irony of the doctor's probably having seen the hose but not connecting it as a solution to the boy's drowning until the next day.

Writing Applications

1. What other "simple but impossible" problems can you think of? Is there a solution that might have been overlooked in one of these cases too?
2. Based on your collaborative discussion above and your own reading, compare the experiences of Jack McClintock and the doctor in this story. What lessons about life and their own identities might they have shared?

FIVE

What Do I Believe? Defining a National Identity

Our individual identity is only a part of who we are because we are also a part of a society. While a society is complex and composed of many elements not experienced the same way by all of a society's members, there, nevertheless, may be a kind of societal identity. For example, many Americans of African American descent have said that while they have experienced prejudice against them in America, when they traveled to other countries they felt keenly American. Many Americans abroad tell of their feelings when they happened to see an American flag.

Whether or not we identify ourselves with and maintain the cultural heritage of the country or ethnic group of our background (for example, Irish American, Mexican American, Japanese American), we may share the dreams of all Americans. In this chapter Thomas Jefferson and Martin Luther King, Jr., articulate some of the American dreams that form the basis of an American philosophy. Maya Angelou links these dreams to our realistic past and our hopeful future. Other writers here explore some concerns such as the environment and homelessness that face contemporary Americans.

The Pretty Colored Snake
A CHEROKEE STORY

Preview: Thinking Ahead

Many Native Americans have stories about the coming of Europeans to North America. If you have read or seen Dances with Wolves, *you may recall the stunned reaction of the Native Americans to the realization that the numbers of Europeans were as many "as the stars in the sky." This modern Cherokee story takes the form of a fable which uses humans interacting with animals to comment on the impact of Europeans on Native American life. Think about why the storyteller uses the hunter and the snake in this story.*

A long time ago there was a famous hunter who used to go all around hunting and always brought something good to eat when he came home. One day he was going home with some birds that he had shot, and he saw a little

221

snake by the side of the trail. It was a beautifully colored snake with all pretty colors all over it, and it looked friendly too. The hunter stopped and watched it for a while. He thought it might be hungry, so he threw it one of the birds before he went on home.

A few weeks later he was coming by the same place with some rabbits he had shot, and saw the snake again. It was still very beautiful and seemed friendly, but it had grown quite a bit. He threw it a rabbit and said "Hello" as he went on home.

Some time after that, the hunter saw the snake again. It had grown very big, but it was still friendly and seemed to be hungry. The hunter was taking some turkeys home with him, so he stopped and gave the snake a turkey gobbler.

Then, one time, the hunter was going home that way with two buck deer on his back. By this time, that pretty colored snake was very big and looked so hungry that the hunter felt sorry for him and gave him a whole buck to eat. When he got home, he heard that the people were going to have a stomp-dance. All the Nighthawks came, and that night they were going around the fire, dancing and singing the old songs, when the snake came and started going around too, outside of where the people were dancing. That snake was so big and long that he stretched all around the people and the people were penned up. The snake was covered all over with all pretty colors and he seemed friendly; but he looked hungry, too, and the people began to be afraid. They told some boys to get their bows and arrows and shoot the snake. Then the boys got their bows. They all shot together and they hit the snake all right. That snake was hurt. He thrashed his tail all around and killed a lot of the people.

They say that snake was just like the white man.

Respond: Thinking Independently

1. In your journal, write your reactions to this Cherokee story. Why do you think the snake was described as colorful and friendly? What caused the conflict between the snake and the people?
2. Write a response statement: I was surprised at/puzzled about/angered by _____ because _____.

Reconsider: Thinking Collaboratively

1. Discuss what happens each time the hunter meets the snake.
2. What do the hunter's actions tell us about the hunter?
3. Why do the people become afraid of the snake? Were they justified in becoming afraid? Explain.
4. Why did they shoot the snake? Was that action justified? Explain.

Review: Thinking Critically

1. The last line of the story clearly connects the snake to the "white man." But the reader must decide exactly in what ways the two are alike. Based on your interpretation, how are the snake and the "white man" alike?

READING TO WRITE

Understanding Fiction: Metaphors

One type of figurative language is the metaphor which is a direct comparison not using the word "like" or "as." For example, if a person says, "He's a rat," that's a metaphor (unless, of course, the male is literally a rodent). Metaphors may be simple phrases like "she's a pig," or "the wind's a knife in my back," or "life is a circus," or they can be longer, extending through a whole piece of writing. The latter is the case in "The Pretty Colored Snake." In this fable, as you have seen, the snake is a metaphor for the white Europeans who came to North America and grew dangerous to the Native American population. The end of the fable makes that point explicitly, but most readers quickly spot the comparison.

Writing Applications

1. One interpretation of this story might be that things are not always the way they appear to be.
   a. Write about the reasons the people in the story feared the snake.
   b. If you or someone you know came from another country to live in the United States, write about what the person expected from America and what he or she found.

The Declaration of Independence

THOMAS JEFFERSON

Preview: Thinking Ahead

This is a document that almost everyone in America knows but probably has not read. What surprises some people is the long middle section listing all of King George's offenses against the colonies. Ask yourself why Jefferson and the committee that helped him write this decided to include that long list. Why didn't Jefferson just declare the colonies independent and be done with it? What purpose does the list serve? Note which ideas in the Declaration became a part of our government and laws and hence, a part of our culture.

When in the Course of human events it becomes necessary for one people to dissolve the political bands which have connected them with another, and to assume among the powers of the earth, the separate and equal station to which the Laws of Nature and of Nature's God entitle them, a decent respect to the opinions of mankind requires that they should declare the causes which impel them to the separation.

We hold these truths to be self-evident, that all men are created equal, that they are endowed by their Creator with certain unalienable Rights, that among these are Life, Liberty and the pursuit of Happiness. That to secure these rights, Governments are instituted among Men, deriving their just powers from the consent of the governed. That whenever any Form of Government becomes destructive of these ends, it is the Right of the People to alter or to abolish it, and to institute new Government, laying its foundation on such principles and organizing its powers in such form, as to them shall seem most likely to affect their Safety and Happiness. Prudence, indeed, will dictate that Governments long established should not be changed for light and transient causes; and accordingly all experience hath shewn that mankind are more disposed to suffer, while evils are sufferable, than to right themselves by abolishing the forms to which they are accustomed. But when a long train of abuses and usurpations, pursuing invariably the same Object evinces a design to reduce them under absolute Despotism, it is their right, it is their duty, to throw off such Government, and to provide new Guards for their future security. Such has been the patient sufferance of these Colonies; and such is now the necessity which constrains them to alter their former Systems of Government. The history of the present King of Great Britain is a history of repeated injuries and usurpations, all having in direct object the establishment of an absolute Tyranny over these States. To prove this, let Facts be submitted to a candid world.

He has refused his Assent to Laws, the most wholesome and necessary for the public good.

He has forbidden his Governors to pass laws of immediate and pressing importance, unless suspended in their operation till his Assent should be obtained; and when so suspended, he has utterly neglected to attend to them.

He has refused to pass other Laws for the accommodation of large districts of people, unless those people would relinquish the right of Representation in the Legislature, a right inestimable to them and formidable to tyrants only.

He has called together legislative bodies at places unusual, uncomfortable, and distant from the depository of their Public Records, for the sole purpose of fatiguing them into compliance with his measures.

He has dissolved Representative Houses repeatedly, for opposing with manly firmness his invasions on the rights of the people.

He has refused for a long time, after such dissolutions, to cause others to be elected; whereby the Legislative Powers, incapable of Annihilation, have returned to the People at large for their exercise; the State remaining in the mean time exposed to all the dangers of invasion from without, and convulsions within.

He has endeavored to prevent the population of these States; for that purpose obstructing the Laws for Naturalization of Foreigners; refusing to pass others to encourage their migration hither, and raising the conditions of new Appropriations of Lands.

He has obstructed the Administration of Justice, by refusing his Assent to Laws for establishing Judiciary Powers.

He has made Judges dependent on his Will alone, for the tenure of their offices, and the amount and payment of their salaries.

He has erected a multitude of New Offices, and sent hither swarms of Officers to harass our people, and eat out their substance.

He has kept among us, in times of peace, Standing Armies without the Consent of our legislatures.

He has affected to render the Military independent of and superior to the Civil Power.

He has combined with others to subject us to a jurisdiction foreign to our constitution, and unacknowledged by our laws; giving his Assent to their Acts of pretended Legislation; For quartering large bodies of armed troops among us; For protecting them, by a mock Trial, from punishment for any Murders which they should commit on the Inhabitants of these States; For cutting off our Trade with all parts of the world; For imposing Taxes on us without our Consent; For depriving us in many cases, of the benefits of Trial by Jury; For transporting us beyond Seas to be tried for pretended offenses; For abolishing the free System of English Laws in a neighboring Province, establishing therein an Arbitrary government, and enlarging its Boundaries so as to render it at once an example and fit instrument for introducing the same absolute rule into these Colonies; For taking away our Charters, abolishing our most valuable Laws and altering fundamentally the Forms of our Governments; For suspending our own Legislatures, and declaring themselves invested with power to legislate for us in all cases whatsoever.

He has abdicated Government here, by declaring us out of his Protection and waging War against us.

He has plundered our seas, ravaged our Coasts, burnt our towns, and destroyed the lives of our people.

He is at this time transporting large Armies of foreign Mercenaries to complete the works of death, desolation and tyranny, already begun with circumstances of Cruelty & Perfidy scarcely paralleled in the most barbarous ages, and totally unworthy the Head of a civilized nation.

He has constrained our fellow Citizens taken Captive on the high Seas to bear Arms against their Country, to become the executioners of their friends and Brethren, or to fall themselves by their Hands.

He has excited domestic insurrections amongst us, and has endeavored to bring on the inhabitants of our frontiers, the merciless Indian Savages, whose known rule of warfare, is an undistinguished destruction of all ages, sexes, and conditions.

In every stage of these Oppressions We have Petitioned for Redress in the most humble terms; Our repeated Petitions have been answered only by repeated injury. A Prince, whose character is thus marked by every act which may define a Tyrant, is unfit to be the ruler of a free people.

Nor have We been wanting in attention to our British brethren. We have warned them from time to time of attempts by their legislature to extend an unwarrantable jurisdiction over us. We have reminded them of the circumstances of our emigration and settlement here. We have appealed to their native justice and magnanimity, and we have conjured them by the ties of our common kindred to disavow these usurpations, which would inevitably interrupt our connections and correspondence. They too have been deaf to the voice of justice and of consanguinity. We must, therefore, acquiesce in the necessity, which denounces our Separation, and hold them, as we hold the rest of mankind, Enemies in War, in Peace Friends.

WE, THEREFORE, the Representatives of the UNITED STATES OF AMERICA, in General Congress, Assembled, appealing to the Supreme Judge of the world for the rectitude of our intentions, do, in the Name, and by authority of the good People of these Colonies, solemnly publish and declare, That these United Colonies are, and of Right ought to be FREE AND INDEPENDENT STATES; that they are Absolved from all Allegiance to the British Crown, and that all political connection between them and the State of Great Britain, is and ought to be totally dissolved; and that as Free and Independent States, they have full Power to levy War, conclude Peace, contract Alliances, establish Commerce, and to do all other Acts and Things which Independent States may of right do. And for the support of this Declaration, with a firm reliance on the protection of Divine Providence, we mutually pledge to each other our Lives, our Fortunes, and our sacred Honor.

Respond: Thinking Independently

1. In your journal, record your thoughts about the document.
2. Choose two sentences or parts of sentences from the Declaration and discuss their impact on American ideas.
3. What items in the document might cause controversy even today?

Reconsider: Thinking Collaboratively

1. Discuss the sentences which members of the class singled out for their impact on American ideas.
2. Discuss the ideas that class members thought might be controversial.
3. What are the "self-evident" truths that Jefferson says the colonists hold about the nature of people and governments?
4. In the second paragraph, what does Jefferson say gives people the right to "alter or abolish" a government?
5. What are the "injuries and usurpations" that the king committed against the colonies?

Review: Thinking Critically

1. What evidence is there in the document that Jefferson was writing both for the colonists themselves and to the powers in Great Britain? If he had had just one audience in mind, how would the document be changed?
2. What is the tone or attitude of the first paragraph? Why didn't Jefferson begin with an angrier tone?
3. Why does the document repeat "he" at the beginning of several paragraphs explaining the wrongs done to the colonies?
4. The Declaration follows the pattern of a classic deductive argument. See if you can find these elements:

a. A major premise on which all readers can agree.
b. A minor premise that needs to be proved by providing evidence.
c. A conclusion that follows logically from the major and minor premises.

(See following for more discussion of deductive arguments.)

READING TO WRITE

Understanding Argument: Inductive and Deductive Arguments

Classic arguments are said to follow two main patterns: induction and deduction. Induction follows the pattern of testing, experimenting, or observing a number of instances before arriving at a generalization or conclusion. For example, if you start sneezing and your eyes itch and water each August when the ragweed pollen is high, you may conclude that you are allergic to ragweed. If scientists observe that a certain substance kills bacteria on a petri dish, kills the same bacteria infecting the blood of animals, and also kills bacteria in the blood of human volunteers, they may conclude that they have found an effective antibiotic against that bacteria.

We also use inductive reasoning in everyday interactions with people. For example, if you have a delicious meal everytime you eat at a neighbor's house, you might draw the conclusion that your neighbor is a good cook. The conclusion grows stronger with each instance. Twenty good meals in a row would make you more certain than just two. However, such conclusions do not constitute absolute proof, just a logical conclusion drawn from available evidence.

Deductive reasoning sometimes is used with inductive reasoning to persuade a reader, as it is here in the Declaration of Independence. A deductive argument follows a three-part logical "proof" known as a syllogism. The first part is a major premise, which is usually phrased as an assumption that a reader accepts as true. Note that in the Declaration, Jefferson begins the second paragraph with "we hold these truths to be self-evident." It is doubtful that the king of England would agree that "all men are created equal" and that they are "endowed by their Creator with certain unalienable rights," or that "it is the right of the people to alter or abolish" a destructive form of government, but Jefferson and the other colonial leaders believed this major premise.

The minor premise of a deductive argument is one that generally needs to be demonstrated or substantiated. The minor premise of the Declaration is that the king of England has violated the rights of the people with "repeated injuries and usurpations." The list of the king's crimes that follows this statement at the end of the second paragraph constitutes the evidence that the minor premise is valid.

The conclusion of the syllogism should follow logically from these two premises. The last paragraph of the Declaration begins "WE, THEREFORE, . . . declare, That these United Colonies are, and of right ought to be FREE

AND INDEPENDENT STATES." If we reconstruct the syllogism in a simplified form we can see that the conclusion follows:

Major Premise:	People have certain rights, and can change a government that violates these rights.
Minor Premise:	The king and his government have violated the people's rights.
Conclusion:	Therefore, the people have the right to change the government.

A deductive argument is only as good as its premises are. If a major premise is faulty, the argument will be faulty. For example, in the statement "you broke a mirror so you will have seven years of bad luck," the premise is that breaking a mirror causes seven years of bad luck which is an assumption based on superstition. Many other superstitions are based on faulty major premises. Moreover, people often draw incorrect conclusions about others based on faulty assumptions. For example, "the worker won't look me in the eye, he must be the thief" is based on the premise that thieves won't make eye contact, when brazen thieves and shy, honest workers may be just as common.

Writing Applications: Argument

1. Construct a "Declaration of Independence" for another group of people following Jefferson's pattern. It could be whimsical (freeing students from parental rules) or serious (liberating a country like Cuba or Iraq from its ruler).
2. Investigate a crime (from published accounts) and present the evidence that you think warrants a verdict of guilty or not guilty.

Indian Singing in 20th Century America
GAIL TREMBLAY

Preview: Thinking Ahead

Gail Tremblay is an artist and poet of Iroquois, French, and English ancestry. In addition to international exhibitions of her art, she has published two collections of poetry and contributed to journals and anthologies. In this poem she tries to make readers see the split between Native American perceptions and those of the majority culture. Could she be speaking for any other minority culture also?

We wake; we wake the day,
the light rising in us like sun—
our breath a prayer brushing

against the feathers in our hands.
We stumble out into streets;
patterns of wires invented by strangers
are strung between eye and sky,
and we dance in two worlds,
inevitable as seasons in one,
exotic curiosities in the other
which rushes headlong down highways,
watches us from car windows, explains
us to its children in words
that no one could ever make
sense of. The images obscures
the vision, and we wonder
whether anyone will ever hear
our own names for the things
we do. Light dances in the body,
surrounds all living things—
even the stones sing
although their songs are infinitely
slower than the ones we learn
from trees. No human voice lasts
long enough to make such music sound.
Earth breath eddies between factories
and office buildings, caresses the surface
of our skin; we go to jobs, the boss
always watching the clock to see
that we're on time. He tries to shut
out magic and hopes we'll make
mistakes or disappear. We work
fast and steady and remember
each breath alters the composition
of the air. Change moves relentless,
the pattern unfolding despite their planning—
we're always there—singing round dance
songs, remembering what supports
our life—impossible to ignore.

Respond: Thinking Independently

1. In your journal write a brief summary of what the speakers in the poem,
   the "We," think as they wake and go to work.
2. Choose a line in the poem you thought was important, that you could
   identify with, or that you disagreed with. Explain your choice. _____

3. What difficulties do people from different cultures have living in majority American culture? Respond from your experience, the experiences of
   others you know, or from things you have read or observed.

Reconsider: Thinking Collaboratively

1. Discuss your summaries with each other and try to create a class or group summary for the poem.
2. Discuss the lines each of you chose and your reasons for choosing these lines.
3. Discuss the difficulties people from different cultures have living in majority American culture and how Gail Tremblay expresses that difficulty in this poem. How much of the difficulty is caused by prejudice and how much is caused by the differences in the way people perceive?

Review: Thinking Critically

1. The poet mentions "breath" three times. What is meant in each instance? Of what importance are the three taken together?
2. What attitude do the people in their cars and the boss have toward the speakers?
3. What gives the speakers some comfort and support?
4. What point do the speakers make about light? What do they mean by "The images obscures the vision"?

READING TO WRITE

Understanding Poetry: A Song or Chant

Gail Tremblay's poem may be appreciated for its sound if read aloud. The title suggests a song and the rhythm of the lines reinforces that idea. Note that frequently there are two strong beats at the beginning of each of the lines that may suggest a drum beat. Other Native American poets use rhythms of their traditional music in their poetry.

Writing Application

1. Building on your journal writing, write an essay examining the cultural perceptions of a person representing a minority culture in majority American society. You may wish to add to your store of knowledge by interviewing a person or by reading more essays, or in some other way.

I Have a Dream

MARTIN LUTHER KING, JR.

Preview: Thinking Ahead

Scholar Garry Wills calls Martin Luther King, Jr. "the greatest orator of modern times," whose greatest speech is this one, delivered on August 28, 1963, in

*front of the Lincoln Memorial to over 200,000 people gathered for the March
on Washington for Jobs and Freedom. He was awarded the Nobel Peace Prize
in 1964. King led the civil rights movement in his role as president of the
Southern Christian Leadership Conference until his assassination in 1968.
As you read the speech from the perspective of over 30 years later, reflect on
what you think has changed and what has not changed. To what elements of
national identity does King link his call for freedom?*

Five score years ago, a great American, in whose symbolic shadow we
stand signed the Emancipation Proclamation. This momentous decree came
as a great beacon light of hope to millions of Negro slaves who had been
seared in the flames of withering injustice. It came as a joyous daybreak to
end the long night of captivity.

But one hundred years later, we must face the tragic fact that the Negro
is still not free. One hundred years later, the life of the Negro is still sadly
crippled by the manacles of segregation and the chains of discrimination.
One hundred years later, the Negro lives on a lonely island of poverty in the
midst of a vast ocean of material prosperity. One hundred years later, the
Negro is still languishing in the corners of American society and finds himself an exile in his own land. So we have come here today to dramatize an
appalling condition.

In a sense we have come to our nation's capital to cash a check. When
the architects of our republic wrote the magnificent words of the Constitution and the Declaration of Independence, they were signing a promissory
note to which every American was to fall heir. This note was a promise that
all men would be guaranteed the unalienable rights of life, liberty, and the
pursuit of happiness.

It is obvious today that America has defaulted on this promissory note
insofar as her citizens of color are concerned. Instead of honoring this sacred
obligation, America has given the Negro people a bad check; a check which
has come back marked "insufficient funds." But we refuse to believe that the
bank of justice is bankrupt. We refuse to believe that there are insufficient
funds in the great vaults of opportunity of this nation. So we have come to
cash this check—a check that will give us upon demand the riches of freedom and the security of justice. We have also come to this hallowed spot to
remind America of the fierce urgency of *now*. This is no time to engage in the
luxury of cooling off or to take the tranquilizing drugs of gradualism. *Now* is
the time to make real the promises of Democracy. *Now* is the time to rise
from the dark and desolate valley of segregation to the sunlit path of racial
justice. *Now* is the time to open the doors of opportunity to all of God's children. *Now* is the time to lift our nation from the quicksands of racial injustice
to the solid rock of brotherhood.

It would be fatal for the nation to overlook the urgency of the moment
and to underestimate the determination of the Negro. This sweltering summer of the Negro's legitimate discontent will not pass until there is an invig-
orating autumn of freedom and equality. 1963 is not an end, but a beginning.
Those who hope that the Negro needed to blow off steam and will now be

content will have a rude awakening if the nation returns to business as usual. There will be neither rest nor tranquillity in America until the Negro is granted his citizenship rights. The whirlwinds of revolt will continue to shake the foundations of our nation until the bright day of justice emerges.

But there is something that I must say to my people who stand on the warm threshold which leads into the palace of justice. In the process of gaining our rightful place we must not be guilty of wrongful deeds. Let us not seek to satisfy our thirst for freedom by drinking from the cup of bitterness and hatred. We must forever conduct our struggle on the high plane of dignity and discipline. We must not allow our creative protest to degenerate into physical violence. Again and again we must rise to the majestic heights of meeting physical force with soul force. The marvelous new militancy which has engulfed the Negro community must not lead us to a distrust of all white people, for many of our white brothers, as evidenced by their presence here today, have come to realize that their destiny is tied up with our destiny and their freedom is inextricably bound to our freedom. We cannot walk alone.

And as we talk, we must make the pledge that we shall march ahead. We cannot turn back. There are those who are asking the devotees of civil rights, "When will you be satisfied?" We can never be satisfied as long as the Negro is the victim of the unspeakable horrors of police brutality. We can never be satisfied as long as our bodies, heavy with the fatigue of travel, cannot gain lodging in the motels of the highways and the hotels of the cities. We cannot be satisfied as long as the Negro's basic mobility is from a smaller ghetto to a larger one. We can never be satisfied as long as a Negro in Mississippi cannot vote and a Negro in New York believes he has nothing for which to vote. No, no, we are not satisfied, and we will not be satisfied until justice rolls down like waters and righteousness like a mighty stream.

I am not unmindful that some of you have come here out of great trials and tribulations. Some of you have come fresh from narrow jail cells. Some of you have come from areas where your quest for freedom left you battered by the storms of persecution and staggered by the winds of police brutality. You have been the veterans of creative suffering. Continue to work with the faith that unearned suffering is redemptive.

Go back to Mississippi, go back to Alabama, go back to South Carolina, go back to Georgia, go back to Louisiana, go back to the slums and ghettos of our northern cities, knowing that somehow this situation can and will be changed. Let us not wallow in the valley of despair.

I say to you today, my friends, that in spite of the difficulties and frustrations of the moment I still have a dream. It is a dream deeply rooted in the American dream.

I have a dream that one day this nation will rise up and live out the true meaning of its creed: "We hold these truths to be self-evident; that all men are created equal."

I have a dream that one day on the red hills of Georgia the sons of former slaves and the sons of former slaveowners will be able to sit down together at the table of brotherhood.

I have a dream that one day even the state of Mississippi, a desert state sweltering with the heat of injustice and oppression, will be transformed into an oasis of freedom and justice.

I have a dream that my four little children will one day live in a nation where they will not be judged by the color of their skin but by the content of their character.

I have a dream today.

I have a dream that one day the state of Alabama, whose governor's lips are presently dripping with the words of interposition and nullification, will be transformed into a situation where little black boys and black girls will be able to join hands with little white boys and white girls and walk together as sisters and brothers.

I have a dream today.

I have a dream that one day every valley shall be exalted, every hill and mountain shall be made low, the rough places will be made plain, and the crooked places will be made straight, and the glory of the Lord shall be revealed, and all flesh shall see it together.

This is our hope. This is the faith with which I return to the South. With this faith we will be able to hew out of the mountain of despair a stone of hope. With this faith we will be able to transform the jangling discords of our nation into a beautiful symphony of brotherhood. With this faith we will be able to work together, to pray together, to struggle together, to go to jail together, to stand up for freedom together, knowing that we will be free one day.

This will be the day when all of God's children will be able to sing with new meaning

My country, 'tis of thee,
Sweet land of liberty,
   Of thee I sing:
Land where my fathers died,
Land of the pilgrims' pride,
From every mountain-side
   Let freedom ring.

And if America is to be a great nation this must become true. So let freedom ring from the prodigious hilltops of New Hampshire. Let freedom ring from the mighty mountains of New York. Let freedom ring from the heightening Alleghenies of Pennsylvania!

Let freedom ring from the snowcapped Rockies of Colorado!

Let freedom ring from the curvaceous peaks of California!

But not only that; let freedom ring from Stone Mountain of Georgia!

Let freedom ring from Lookout Mountain of Tennessee!

Let freedom ring from every hill and molehill of Mississippi. From every mountainside, let freedom ring.

When we let freedom ring, when we let it ring from every village and every hamlet, from every state and every city, we will be able to speed up that day when all of God's children, black men and white men, Jews and Gentiles, Protestants and Catholics, will be able to join hands and sing in the words of the old Negro spiritual. "Free at last! free at last! thank God almighty, we are free at last!"

Respond: Thinking Independently

1. Record your thoughts about this speech in your journal.
2. Choose a sentence or phrase from King's speech that you admire, you disagree with, or you have a question about: _____
3. What has changed in civil rights since King delivered this speech in 1963?

Reconsider: Thinking Collaboratively

1. Discuss the sentences or phrases chosen by the class to admire, to disagree with, or to explain.
2. What references to American history or American philosophy does King use in his speech? Why?
3. What references to religion does King use in his speech? Why?
4. What is King's opinion of moving gradually toward civil rights? Of violent behavior to secure civil rights? Of what will "satisfy" those asking for civil rights?

Review: Thinking Critically

1. When a person gives a speech, he or she must help listeners to follow the train of thought even though they don't have a text of the speech in front of them to read. One way to do this is to repeat certain phrases to connect one idea with another. Notice how King repeats the phrase "one hundred years later" to link the action he desires toward civil rights with Abraham Lincoln's Emancipation Proclamation. Find other examples of repetition and try to explain why they are used.
2. Another way a speaker can help listeners to follow ideas is to use analogies—comparisons between more familiar ideas and less familiar ideas. In this speech King uses the idea of cashing a check. What does he say is the "check" the marchers have come to cash? Why does he say that "America has given the Negro people a bad check"?
3. Find other examples of King's use of comparisons (there are many like "justice rolls down like waters").
4. What connections does King make with the song "America" and the search for civil rights?
5. King was speaking to the 200,000 marchers directly, but he was also speaking to the millions of Americans watching on TV. What parts of his speech do you think were persuasive to his larger audience?

READING TO WRITE

Understanding Argument: Persuasive Use of Images

The use of words that create pictures or the pictures themselves can be powerful persuaders. In this speech, King links freedom ringing from a mountainside in the patriotic song "America" to freedom ringing from individual mountain ranges north and south, east and west. When Bill Clinton and Al Gore ran for office in 1992, they set out from the Democratic National Convention in New York in a bus caravan, thus bringing their message in a more humble, low-tech way. Advertisers of tires put adorable babies in their commercials to make buying tires a mark of love, responsibility, and good parenthood ("because so much is riding on your tires"). What other examples of persuasive images can you name?

Writing Applications: Argument

1. Garry Wills has said, "Dr. King's genius was his ability to evoke the best in us, to remind us what America means." Based on your reading and discussion of the speech agree or disagree with Wills, citing examples from the text of the speech.
2. Analyze another persuasive message—it could be a speech, an advertisement, or even a video that you think has a persuasive purpose. How does the creator of the message persuade the audience?
3. a. How is your own identity affected by being an American (if you are an American citizen)?
   b. If you are not an American citizen, do you wish to become one? How do you think changing your nationality will affect your sense of your identity?
   c. If you do not wish to become an American citizen but want to retain your present country status, discuss your reasons and how identity plays a part in your reasons.

Beyond the Melting Pot
WILLIAM A. HENRY III

Preview: Thinking Ahead

This article, originally appearing in Time *magazine in 1990, looks at America's ethnic and racial present and future and the challenges that a multicultural society brings. Given the difficulties in many places in the world (Bosnia,*

Rwanda) of dealing with differences among people, how will the United States handle this diversity of cultures?

Someday soon, surely much sooner than most people who filled out their Census forms last week realize, white Americans will become a minority group. Long before that day arrives, the presumption that the "typical" U.S. citizen is someone who traces his or her descent in a direct line to Europe will be part of the past. By the time these elementary students at Brentwood Science Magnet School in Brentwood, California, reach mid-life, their diverse ethnic experience in the classroom will be echoed in neighborhoods and workplaces throughout the U.S.

Already 1 American in 4 defines himself or herself as Hispanic or nonwhite. If current trends in immigration and birth rates persist, the Hispanic population will have further increased an estimated 21%, the Asian presence about 22%, blacks almost 12% and whites a little more than 2% when the 20th century ends. By 2020, a date no further into the future than John F. Kennedy's election is in the past, the number of U.S. residents who are Hispanic or nonwhite will have more than doubled, to nearly 115 million, while the white population will not be increasing at all. By 2056, when someone born today will be 66 years old, the "average" U.S. resident, as defined by Census statistics, will trace his or her descent to Africa, Asia, the Hispanic world, the Pacific Islands, Arabia—almost anywhere but white Europe.

While there may remain towns or outposts where even a black family will be something of an oddity, where English and Irish and German surnames will predominate, where a traditional (some will wistfully say "real") America will still be seen on almost every street corner, they will be only the vestiges of an earlier nation. The former majority will learn, as a normal part of everyday life, the meaning of the Latin slogan engraved on U.S. coins—E PLURIBUS UNUM, one formed from many.

Among the younger populations that go to school and provide new entrants to the work force, the change will happen sooner. In some places an America beyond the melting pot has already arrived. In New York State some 40% of elementary- and secondary-school children belong to an ethnic minority. Within a decade, the proportion is expected to approach 50%. In California white pupils are already a minority. Hispanics (who, regardless of their complexion, generally distinguish themselves from both blacks and whites) account for 31.4% of public school enrollment, blacks add 8.9%, and Asians and others amount to 11%—for a nonwhite total of 51.3%. This finding is not only a reflection of white flight from desegregated public schools. Whites of all ages account for just 58% of California's population. In San Jose bearers of the Vietnamese surname Nguyen outnumber the Joneses in the telephone directory 14 columns to eight.

Nor is change confined to the coasts. Some 12,000 Hmong refugees from Laos have settled in St. Paul. At some Atlanta low-rent apartment complexes that used to be virtually all black, social workers today need to speak Spanish. At the Sesame Hut restaurant in Houston, a Korean immigrant owner trains Hispanic immigrant workers to prepare Chinese-style food for a largely black clientele. The Detroit area has 200,000 people of Middle Eastern descent; some 1,500 small grocery and convenience stores in the vicinity are owned by a whole subculture of Chaldean Christians with roots in Iraq. "Once America was a microcosm of European nationalities," says Molefi Asante, chairman of the department of African-American studies at Temple University in Philadelphia. "Today America is a microcosm of the world."

History suggests that sustaining a truly multiracial society is difficult, or at least unusual. Only a handful of great powers of the distant past—Pharaonic Egypt and Imperial Rome, most notably—managed to maintain a distinct national identity while embracing, and being ruled by, an ethnic mélange. The most ethnically diverse contemporary power, the Soviet Union, is beset with secessionist demands and near tribal conflicts. But such comparisons are flawed, because those empires were launched by conquest and maintained through an aggressive military presence. The U.S. was created, and continues to be redefined, primarily by voluntary immigration. This process has been one of the country's great strengths, infusing it with talent and energy. The "browning of America" offers tremendous opportunity for capitalizing anew on the merits of many peoples from many lands. Yet this fundamental change in the ethnic makeup of the U.S. also poses risks. The American character is resilient and thrives on change. But past periods of rapid evolution have also, alas, brought out deeper, more fearful aspects of the national soul.

A truly multiracial society will undoubtedly prove much harder to govern. Even seemingly race-free conflicts will be increasingly complicated by an overlay of ethnic tension. For example, the expected showdown in the early 21st century between the rising number of retiree's and the dwindling number of workers who must be taxed to pay for the elders' Social Security benefits will probably be compounded by the fact that a large majority of recipients will be white, whereas a majority of workers paying for them will be nonwhite.

While prior generations of immigrants believed they had to learn English quickly to survive, many Hispanics now maintain that the Spanish language is inseparable from their ethnic and cultural identity, and seek to remain bilingual, if not primarily Spanish-speaking, for life. They see legislative drives to make English the sole official language, which have prevailed in some fashion in at least 16 states, as a political backlash. Says Arturo Vargas of the Mexican American Legal Defense and Educational Fund: "That's what English-only has been all about—a reaction to the growing population and influence of Hispanics. It's human nature to be uncomfortable with change. That's what the Census is all about, documenting changes and making sure the country keeps up."

Racial and ethnic conflict remains an ugly fact of American life everywhere, from working-class ghettos to college campuses, and those who do not raise their fists often raise their voices over affirmative action and other power sharing. When Florida Atlantic University, a state-funded institution under pressure to increase its low black enrollment, offered last month to give free tuition to every qualified black freshman who enrolled, the school was flooded with calls of complaint, some protesting that nothing was being done for "real" Americans. As the numbers of minorities increase, their demands for a share of the national bounty are bound to intensify, while whites are certain to feel ever more embattled. Businesses often feel whipsawed between immigration laws that punish them for hiring illegal aliens and antidiscrimination laws that penalize them for demanding excessive documentation from foreign-seeming job applicants. Even companies that consistently seek to do the right thing may be overwhelmed by the problems of diversifying a primarily white managerial corps fast enough to direct a work force that will be increasingly nonwhite and, potentially, resentful.

Nor will tensions be limited to the polar simplicity of white vs. nonwhite. For all Jesse Jackson's rallying cries about shared goals, minority groups often feel keenly competitive. Chicago's Hispanic leaders have leapfrogged between white and black factions, offering support wherever there seemed to be the most to gain for their own community. Says Dan Solis of the Hispanic-oriented United Neighborhood Organization: "If you're thinking power, you don't put your eggs in one basket."

Blacks, who feel they waited longest and endured most in the fight for equal opportunity, are uneasy about being supplanted by Hispanics or, in some areas, by Asians as the numerically largest and most influential minority—and even more, about being outstripped in wealth and status by these newer groups. Because Hispanics are so numerous and Asians such a fast-growing group, they have become the "hot" minorities, and blacks feel their needs are getting lower priority. As affirmative action has broadened to include other groups—and to benefit white women perhaps most of all—blacks perceive it as having waned in value for them.

Political pressure has already brought about sweeping change in public school textbooks over the past couple of decades and has begun to affect the core humanities curriculum at such élite universities as Stanford. At stake at the college level is whether the traditional "canon" of Greek, Latin and West European humanities study should be expanded to reflect the cultures of Africa, Asia and other parts of the world. Many books treasured as classics by prior generations are now seen as tools of cultural imperialism. In the extreme form, this thinking rises to a value-deprived neutralism that views all cultures, regardless of the grandeur or paucity of their attainments, as essentially equal.

Even more troubling is a revisionist approach to history in which groups that have gained power in the present turn to remaking the past in the image of their desires. If 18th, 19th, and earlier 20th century society should not have been so dominated by white Christian men of West European ancestry, they reason, then that past society should be reinvented as pluralist and democratic. Alternatively, the racism and sexism of the past are treated as inextricable from—and therefore irremediably tainting—traditional learning and values.

While debates over college curriculum get the most attention, professors generally can resist or subvert the most wrong-headed changes and students generally have mature enough judgment to sort out the arguments. Elementary- and secondary-school curriculums reach a far broader segment at a far more impressionable age, and political expediency more often wins over intellectual honesty. Exchanges have been vituperative in New York, where a state task force concluded that "African-Americans, Asian-Americans, Puerto Ricans and Native Americans have all been victims of an intellectual and educational oppression. . . . Negative characterizations, or the absence of positive references, have had a terribly damaging effect on the psyche of young people." In urging a revised syllabus, the task force argued, "Children from European culture will have a less arrogant perspective of being part of a group that has 'done it all.' " Many intellectuals are outraged. Political scientist Andrew Hacker of Queens College lambastes a taskforce suggestion that children be taught how "Native Americans were here to welcome new settlers from Holland, Senegal, England, Indonesia, France, the Congo, Italy, China, Iberia." Asks Hacker: "Did the Indians really welcome all those groups? Were they at Ellis Island when the Italians started to arrive? This is not history but a myth intended to bolster the self-esteem of certain children and, just possibly, a platform for advocates of various ethnic interests."

Values: Something in Common

Economic and political issues, however much emotion they arouse, are fundamentally open to practical solution. The deeper significance of America's becoming a majority nonwhite society is what it means to the national psyche, to individuals' sense of themselves and their nation—their idea of what it is to be American. People of color have often felt that whites treated equality as a benevolence granted to minorities rather than as an inherent natural right. Surely that condescension will wither.

Rather than accepting U.S. history and its meaning as settled, citizens will feel ever more free to debate where the nation's successes sprang from and what its unalterable beliefs are. They will clash over which myths and icons to invoke in education, in popular culture, in ceremonial speechmaking from political campaigns to the State of the Union address. Which is the more admirable heroism: the courageous holdout by a few conquest-minded whites over Hispanics at the Alamo, or the anonymous expression of hope by millions who filed through Ellis Island? Was the subduing of the West a daring feat of bravery and ingenuity, or a wretched example of white imperialism? Symbols deeply meaningful to one group can be a matter of indifference to another. Says University of Wisconsin chancellor Donna Shalala: "My grandparents came from Lebanon. I don't identify with the Pilgrims on a personal level." Christopher Jencks, professor of sociology at Northwestern, asks, "Is anything more basic about turkeys and Pilgrims than about Martin Luther King and Selma? To me, it's six of one and half a dozen of the other, if children understand what it's like to be a dissident minority. Because the civil rights struggle is closer chronologically, it's likelier to be taught by someone who really cares."

Traditionalists increasingly distinguish between a "multiracial" society, which they say would be fine, and a "multicultural" society, which they deplore. They argue that every society needs a universally accepted set of values and that new arrivals should therefore be pressured to conform to the mentality on which U.S. prosperity and freedom were built. Says Allan Bloom, author of the best-selling *The Closing of the American Mind:* "Obviously, the future of America can't be sustained if people keep only to their own ways and remain perpetual outsiders. The society has got to turn them into Americans. There are natural fears that today's immigrants may be too much of a cultural stretch for a nation based on Western values."

The counterargument, made by such scholars as historian Thomas Bender of New York University, is that if the center cannot hold, then one must redefine the center. It should be, he says, "the ever changing outcome of a continuing contest among social groups and ideas for the power to define public culture." Besides, he adds, many immigrants arrive committed to U.S. values; that is part of what attracted them. Says Julian Simon, professor of business administration at the University of Maryland: "The life and institutions here shape immigrants and not vice versa. This business about immigrants changing our institutions and our basic ways of life is hogwash. It's nativist scare talk."

Historians note that Americans have felt before that their historical culture was being overwhelmed by immigrants, but conflicts between earlier-arriving English, Germans and Irish and later-arriving Italians and Jews did not have the obvious and enduring element of racial skin color. And there was never a time when the nonmainstream elements could claim, through sheer numbers, the potential to unite and exert political dominance. Says Bender: "The real question is whether or not our notion of diversity can successfully negotiate the color line."

For whites, especially those who trace their ancestry back to the early years of the Republic, the American heritage is a source of pride. For people of color, it is more likely to evoke anger and sometimes shame. The place where hope is shared is in the future. Demographer Ben Wattenberg, formerly perceived as a resister to social change, says, "There's a nice chance that the American myth in the 1990s and beyond is going to ratchet another step toward this idea that we are the universal nation. That rings the bell of manifest destiny. We're a people with a mission and a sense of purpose, and we believe we have something to offer the world."

Not every erstwhile alarmist can bring himself to such optimism. Says Norman Podhoretz, editor of *Commentary:* "A lot of people are trying to undermine the foundations of the American experience and are pushing toward a more Balkanized society. I think that would be a disaster, not only because it would destroy a precious social inheritance but also because it would lead to enormous unrest, even violence."

While know-nothingism is generally confined to the more dismal corners of the American psyche, it seems all too predictable that during the next decades many more mainstream white Americans will begin to speak openly about the nation they feel they are losing. There are not, after all, many non-white faces depicted in Norman Rockwell's paintings. White Americans are accustomed to thinking of themselves as the very picture of their nation. Inspiring as it may be to the rest of the world, significant as it may be to the U.S. role in global politics, world trade and the pursuit of peace, becoming a conspicuously multiracial society is bound to be a somewhat bumpy experience for many ordinary citizens. For older Americans, raised in a world where the numbers of whites were greater and the visibility of nonwhites was carefully restrained, the new world will seem ever stranger. But as the children at Brentwood Science Magnet School, and their counterparts in classrooms across the nation, are coming to realize, the new world is here. It is now. And it is irreversibly the America to come.

Respond: Thinking Independently

1. Write your reactions to the writer's predictions.
2. Choose a quote from the essay that you think is most important to consider.
3. What tensions among ethnic or immigrant groups are you aware of at home? On campus? Why do you think these tensions have arisen? Can you think of any way to ease the tensions?

Reconsider: Thinking Collaboratively

1. Summarize the arguments made in Henry's essay:
   a. for and against people retaining their ethnic culture and separate language
   b. for and against changing texts and curricula to reflect different cultures
   c. for and against debating interpretations of U.S. history
2. Compare the quotes classmates chose as important and discuss why these quotes were chosen.

Review: Thinking Critically

1. Discuss the possibly differing views of older and younger Americans about multiculturalism. Do you think it is true, as Henry asserts, that older people are more troubled by these changes?
2. What advantages do you see to the changing population of the United States?

READING TO WRITE

Understanding Causal Analysis: Emphasizing Effects

Most of this essay traces the effects of the changing diversity of America's population. Thus, the writer establishes the cause in the first few paragraphs, coupled with statistics and examples that are evidence that what he says is really true. Examine the first five paragraphs and make a list of his evidence. Is it convincing to you?

The rest of the essay examines effects—present and future. What kinds of evidence does he use to show that these effects are likely to occur? Why is he careful to point out opposing viewpoints? How does his evidence affect your opinion as a reader? Do you agree with his conclusion?

Writing Application: Causal Analysis

1. Write an essay based on your answer to question 3 in Respond: Thinking Independently. Analyze the causes of tensions among ethnic or immigrant groups at home or on campus.
2. Write an essay analyzing the effects you see of America's increasing diversity of population.

The Stream: Leonel I. Castillo
STUDS TERKEL

Preview: Thinking Ahead

The former director of the U.S. Immigration and Naturalization Service was himself descended from Mexican immigrants who came to Texas in 1880. In his interview with Studs Terkel, he gives us a perspective on why people continue to immigrate to the United States and what extreme hardships they suffer to come here and to stay here. As you read, ask yourself how you would define the American dream.

New immigrants are trying all over again to integrate themselves into the system. They have the same hunger. On any given day, there are about three million throughout the world who are applying to come to the United States and share the American Dream. The same battles. I still read old newspaper clips: 1886. Housemaid wanted. We'll accept any person, any color, any nationality, any religion, except Irish. (Laughs.) Rough ads: No Irish need apply.

Most of the undocumented here without papers, without legal permission, think they're gonna go back home in six months. Relatively few go back. Some old Italians are going back to *pensionares*, and some old Eastern Europeans are going back home. But, by and large, immigrants, old and new, stay. They don't feel they know anyone in the old village. Their children don't speak Polish or Italian or Greek. Their children are used to air conditioning, McDonald's.

The Vietnamese boat people express it as well as anyone. They don't know if they're gonna land, if the boat's gonna sink. They don't know what's gonna happen to 'em, but they've a hunch they might make it to the U.S. as the "freedom place."

There is the plain hard fact of hunger. In order to eat, a person will endure tremendous hardship. Mexican people who come here usually are not the most destitute. Someone who's too poor can't afford the trip. You've got to buy *coyotes*. A *coyote* is a smuggler of people. He's also called a *pollero*. *Pollo* is chicken. He's the one who guides chickens through the border.

Sometimes the whole family saves up and gives the bright young man or the bright young woman the family savings. It even goes in hock for a year or two. They pin all their hopes on this one kid, put him on a bus, let him go a thousand miles. He doesn't speak a word of English. He's only seventeen, eighteen years old, but he's gonna save that family. A lot rides on that kid who's a bus boy in some hotel.

We've had some as young as eleven who have come a thousand miles. You have this young kid, all his family savings, everything is on him. There are a lot of songs and stories about mother and child, the son leaving who may never return. We end up deporting him. It's heartrending.

He's the bright kid in the family. The slow one might not make it, might get killed. The one who's sickly can't make the trip. He couldn't walk through the desert. He's not gonna be too old, too young, too destitute, or too slow. He's the brightest and the best.

He's gonna be the first hook, the first pioneer coming into an alien society, the United States. He might be here in Chicago. He works as a busboy all night long. They pay him minimum or less, and work him hard. He'll never complain. He might even thank his boss. He'll say as little as possible because he doesn't want anyone to know what his status is. He will often live in his apartment, except for the time he goes to work or to church or to a dance. He will stay in and watch TV. If he makes a hundred a week, he will manage to send back twenty-five. All over the country, if you go to a Western Union office on the weekend, you'll find a lot of people there sending money orders. In a southwest office, like Dallas, Western Union will tell you seventy-five percent of their business is money orders to Mexico.

After the kid learns a bit, because he's healthy and young and energetic, he'll probably get another job as a busboy. He'll work at another place as soon as the shift is over. He'll try to work his way up to be a waiter. He'll work incredible hours. He doesn't care about union scale, he doesn't care about conditions, about humiliations. He accepts all this as his fate.

He's burning underneath with this energy and ambition. He outworks the U.S. busboys and eventually becomes the waiter. Where he can maneuver, he tries to become the owner and gives a lot of competition to the locals. Restaurant owners tell me, if they have a choice, they'll always hire foreign nationals first. They're so eager and grateful. There's a little greed here, too. (Laughs.) They pay 'em so little.

We've got horrible cases of exploitation. In San Diego and in Arizona, we discovered people who live in holes in the ground, live under trees, no sanitation, no housing, nothing. A lot of them live in chicken coops.

They suffer from *coyotes,* too, who exploit them and sometimes beat 'em. *Coyotes* advertise. If the immigrant arrives in San Diego, the word is very quick: where to go and who's looking. He'll even be approached. If he's got a lot of money, the *coyote* will manage to bring him from Tijuana all the way to Chicago and guarantee him a job. He'll get all the papers: Social Security, birth certificate, driver's license. The *coyote* reads the papers and finds which U.S. citizens have died and gets copies of all their vital statistics. In effect, the immigrant carries the identity of a dead person.

Often the employer says he doesn't know anything about it. He plays hands off. He makes his bucks hiring cheap labor. The *coyote* makes his off the workers.

Coyotes come from the border with these pickup trucks full of people. They may put twenty in a truck. They bring 'em in all sorts of bad weather, when they're less likely to be stopped. They might be going twenty, twenty-eight hours, with one or two pit stops. They don't let the people out. There's no urinal, no bathroom. They sit or they stand there in this little cramped space for the whole trip.

A truck broke down outside Chicago. It was a snowstorm. The driver left. People were frostbitten, lost their toes. In Laredo, the truck was in an accident. Everybody ran off because the police were coming. The truck caught fire. No one remembered the two fellows in the trunk. It was locked and no keys. Of course, they burned to death. The border patrol found thirty-three people dying in the deserts of Arizona. They were saved at the last minute and deported. I'll bet you a dollar every one of them, as soon as they are well enough, will try again.

At least a quarter of a million apprehensions were made last year. If we apprehend them at the border, we turn 'em around and ask them to depart voluntarily. They turn around and go back to Mexico. A few hours later, they try again. In El Paso, we deported one fellow six times in one day. There's a restaurant in Hollywood run by a fellow we deported thirty-seven times. We've deported some people more than a hundred times. They always want to come back. There's a job and there's desperation.

In World War Two, we recruited Mexicans to work here. As soon as the war ended and our young men came back, we deported them. In 1954, the deportation problem was so big that the general in charge of immigration ordered Operation Wetback. That one year, we had a million apprehensions. It was similar to what we did during the depression. We rounded everybody up, put 'em on buses, and sent them back to Mexico. Sometimes they were people who merely looked Mexican. The violations of civil liberties were terrible.

Half the people here without papers are not Mexicans. They're from all over the world. They came legally, with papers, as tourists ten years ago. They're much harder to deal with. We're discussing a program that would allow people to have permanent residence, who have been here seven years or more, have not broken any laws, have paid taxes and not been on welfare. You can't be here and become a public charge. All too often, the public gets the impression that all immigrants are on welfare. It's the exact opposite. Very few go on welfare.

A lot of people who are humanitarian, who believe they should be hospitable toward the stranger, are very restrictive when it comes to their jobs. (Laughs.) We've had protests from *mariachis* and soccer players. The *mariachis* are upset because the Mexicans were coming in and playing for less. The manager of soccer teams would rather hire the foreign nationals because often they're better players.

We get people coming in from Haiti, the poorest country in the western hemisphere. They come over by boat and land in Florida. The Floridians raised hell about this. I've even had Cuban-Americans tell me that Haitians were going to destroy their culture. There's a weird pecking order now.

We make three thousand apprehensions at the border every weekend. It's just a little fourteen-mile stretch. Our border patrol knows this little fellow comin' across is hungry. He just wants to work. They know he's no security threat. They say: "It's my job." Many of them come to have a great deal of respect for the people they're deporting. What do you think of a person you deport three, four times, who just keeps coming back? You would never want to get in the same ring with that person.

I'm torn. I saw it in the Peace Corps, when I was in the Philippines. A mother offered you her infant. You're just a twenty-one-year-old kid and she says: "Take my child, take him with you to the States." When you see this multiplied by thousands, it tears you up.

It's clear to me that the undocumented, even more than the immigrant, is a contributor to our society and to our standard of living. It's one of the few groups that has no parasites. They walk the tightrope and try not to fall off. If you're a citizen and you fall, we have a net that catches you: welfare, food stamps, unemployment, social services. If you're undocumented and fall off that tightrope, you can't go to any of the agencies because you may end up bein' deported. He can't draw welfare, he can't use public services. He's not gonna call a policeman even when he's beat up. If he's in a street fight and somebody whips him bad, assaults him, robs him, rapes her, there's no complaint. In Baltimore, an employer raped two girls. The person who complained wouldn't give us the names of the victims because she was afraid we'd deport 'em. We end up in this country with enormous abuse against four million people.

The only thing that helps me is remembering the history of this country. We've always managed, despite our worst, unbelievably nativist actions to rejuvenate ourselves, to bring in new people. Every new group comes in believing more firmly in the American Dream than the one that came a few years before. Every new group is scared of being in the welfare line or in the unemployment office. They go to night school, they learn about America. We'd be lost without them.

The old dream is still dreamt. The old neighborhood Ma-Pa stores are still around. They are not Italian or Jewish or Eastern European any more. Ma and Pa are now Korean, Vietnamese, Iraqi, Jordanian, Latin American.

They live in the store. They work seven days a week. Their kids are doing well in school. They're making it. Sound familiar?

Near our office in Los Angeles is a little café with a sign: KOSHER BUR-RITOS. (Laughs.) A *burrito* is a Mexican tortilla with meat inside. Most of the customers are black. The owner is Korean. (Laughs.) The banker, I imagine, is WASP. (Laughs.) This is what's happening in the United States today. It is not a melting pot, but in one way or another, there is a melding of cultures.

I see all kinds of new immigrants starting out all over again, trying to work their way into the system. They're going through new battles, yet they're old battles. They want to share in the American Dream. The stream never ends.

Respond: Thinking Independently

1. In your journal write your responses to Castillo's interview. If you wish, compare the article with Henry's essay.
2. Write a response statement: I was surprised/confused/upset by _____ _____ because _____.

Reconsider: Thinking Collaboratively

1. Discuss your classmates' responses to Castillo's interview.
2. In what ways are immigrants exploited? In what ways do immigrants contribute or detract from society?
3. What mixed feelings does Castillo have toward enforcing the immigration laws? What do you think American policy should be?

Review: Thinking Critically

1. What historical information does Castillo mention in his interview? Why does he refer to earlier waves of immigration?
2. What point is Castillo making when he mentions the sign "KOSHER BURRITOS"?

READING TO WRITE

Understanding Examples/Illustration: Historical Examples

Leonel Castillo supports his points about the American dream of opportunity and the motives of immigrants with many references to American history. He wishes to give readers a perspective which is broader than just today's headlines. So, for example, he mentions an 1886 news clipping, the situation of allowing Mexican immigration in World War II and deporting Mexicans afterward, and the more recent Vietnamese, Cuban, and Haitian immigrations. Castillo also includes examples from cases the Immigration Service has investigated to allow readers the opportunity to understand the magnitude of the immigration problem.

Writing Applications: Examples/Illustrations

1. What examples in your own community can you find of jobs immigrants are likely to fill? After some investigation, write an essay explaining what you find.

Other Writing Applications

1. After reading Castillo's interview, write an essay in which you argue for or against a change in U.S. immigration policy or enforcement of that policy.
2. Define the American dream as you see it, perhaps drawing on the writings of Martin Luther King, Jr. and the interview of Leonel Castillo.

I Just Wanna Be Average
MIKE ROSE

Preview: Thinking Ahead

Mike Rose is an English professor who has tried to find the best ways to teach writing to many students who are just like he was, what he calls "underprepared." In his award-winning 1989 book, Lives on the Boundary: The Struggles and Achievements of America's Underprepared, *Rose explains his own background as the son of Italian immigrants and his experience as a first-generation college student. In this excerpt, Rose describes his parents' way of life as he is growing up.*

Between 1880 and 1920, well over four million Southern Italian peasants immigrated to America. their poverty was extreme and hopeless—twelve hours of farm labor would get you one lira, about twenty cents—so increasing numbers of desperate people booked passage for the United States, the country where, the steamship companies claimed, prosperity was a way of life. My father left Naples before the turn of the century; my mother came with her mother from Calabria in 1921. They met in Altoona, Pennsylvania at the lunch counter of Tom and Joe's, a steamy diner with twangy-voiced waitresses and graveyard stew.

For my mother, life in America was not what the promoters had told her father it would be. She grew up very poor. She slept with her parents and brothers and sisters in one room. She had to quit school in the seventh grade to care for her sickly younger brothers. When her father lost his leg in a railroad accident, she began working in a garment factory where women sat crowded at their stations, solitary as penitents in a cloister. She stayed there until her marriage. My father had found a freer route. He was closemouthed about his past, but I know that he had been a salesman, a tailor, and a gambler; he knew people in the mob and had, my uncles whisper, done time in Chicago. He went through a year or two of Italian elementary school and could write a few words—those necessary to scribble measurements for a suit—and over the years developed a quiet urbanity, a persistence, and a slowly debilitating arteriosclerosis.

When my father proposed to my mother, he decided to open a spaghetti house, a venture that lasted through the war and my early years. The restaurant collapsed in bankruptcy in 1951 when Altoona's major industry, the Pennsylvania Railroad, had to shut down its shops. My parents managed to salvage seven hundred dollars and, on the advice of the family doctor, headed to California, where the winters would be mild and where I, their seven-year-old son, would have the possibility of a brighter future.

At first we lived in a seedy hotel on Spring Street in downtown Los Angeles, but my mother soon found an ad in the *Times* for cheap property on the south side of town. My parents contacted a woman named Mrs. Jolly, used my mother's engagement ring as a down payment, and moved to 9116 South Vermont Avenue, a house about one and one-half miles northwest of Watts. The neighborhood was poor, and it was in transition. Some old white folks had lived there for decades and were retired. Younger black families were moving up from Watts and settling by working-class white families newly arrived from the South and the Midwest. Immigrant Mexican families were coming in from Baja. Any such demographic mix is potentially volatile, and as the fifties wore on, the neighborhood would be marked by outbursts of violence.

I have many particular memories of this time, but in general these early years seem a peculiar mix of physical warmth and barrenness: a gnarled lemon tree, thin rugs, a dirt alley, concrete in the sun. My uncles visited a few times, and we went to the beach or to orange groves. The return home, however, left the waves and spray, the thick leaves and pulp far in the distance. I was aware of my parents watching their money and got the sense from their conversations that things could quickly take a turn for the worse. I started taping pennies to the bottom of a shelf in the kitchen.

My father's health was bad, and he had few readily marketable skills. Poker and pinochle brought in a little money, and he tried out an idea that had worked in Altoona during the war: He started a "suit club." The few customers he could scare up would pay two dollars a week on a tailor-made suit. He would take the measurements and send them to a shop back East and hope for the best. My mother took a job at a café in downtown Los Angeles, a split shift 9:00 to 12:00 and 5:00 to 9:00, but her tips were totaling sixty cents a day, so she quit for a night shift at Coffee Dan's. This got her to the bus stop at one in the morning, waiting on the same street where drunks were urinating and hookers were catching the last of the bar crowd. She made friends with a Filipino cook who would scare off the advances of old men aflame with the closeness of taxi dancers. In a couple of years, Coffee Dan's would award her a day job at the counter. Once every few weeks my father and I would take a bus downtown and visit with her, sitting at stools by the window, watching the animated but silent mix of faces beyond the glass.

My father had moved to California with faint hopes about health and a belief in his child's future, drawn by that far edge of America where the sun descends into green water. What he found was a city that was warm, verdant, vast, and indifferent as a starlet in a sports car. Altoona receded quickly, and my parents must have felt isolated and deceived. They had fallen into the abyss of paradise—two more poor settlers trying to make a go of it in the City of the Angels.

Respond: Thinking Independently

1. Write your responses to Rose's description of his parents' life in your journal. To what extent can you identify with Rose or his parents?
2. Write a response statement: When I read an account of peoples' lives like this I feel/think _____.

Reconsider: Thinking Collaboratively

1. Discuss the strengths and weaknesses of Rose's parents. What outside events affected their lives?
2. Rose says that his memories of his early years in California were "a peculiar mix of physical warmth and barrenness." Discuss what he means.
3. What hopes and disappointments did Rose's parents experience?

Review: Thinking Critically

1. Choose two sentences that you find particularly vivid or memorable. Write them here and explain why you chose them.
2. A writer's tone is the attitude he or she takes toward the subject. What is Rose's tone in this excerpt? Is he indifferent, angry, self-pitying, sympathetic, or something else? What creates the tone? That is, what does he say that makes you feel his attitude?

READING TO WRITE

Understanding Description: Using Descriptive Adjectives

When a writer wants people to picture a scene or way of life, he or she may use a well-chosen adjective to create the picture in the reader's mind. Adjectives such as good, nice, awesome, and fabulous are so overused that they really don't bring any pictures to mind, so writers are constantly searching for a specific word that will carry the meaning they intend. In his book Mike Rose tries to choose specific words that will create pictures in readers' minds. For example, his parents met at Tom and Joe's, a "steamy diner," with "twangy-voiced waitresses and graveyard stew." Find other examples in the essay of such specific adjectives.

Writing Applications: Description

1. As objectively as you can, describe your parents' early life from child-hood to when they met and married.
2. Describe your early memories of your house, neighborhood, school, or journeys away from home.

Homeless

Anna Quindlen

Preview: Thinking Ahead

For several years, Anna Quindlen wrote a column for The New York Times *about life in the eighties. Her observations about working, raising children, and understanding life in an urban environment appealed to many readers. She collected many of her essays in books and recently has turned to writing novels. In this 1987 essay she examines the subject of the homeless from a very personal perspective. How does your sense of "rootedness" compare with hers? Does she help you see the plight of the homeless in a different way?*

Her name was Ann, and we met in the Port Authority Bus Terminal several Januarys ago. I was doing a story on homeless people. She said I was wast-ing my time talking to her; she was just passing through, although she'd been passing through for more than two weeks. To prove to me that this was true, she rummaged through a tote bag and a manila envelope and finally unfolded a sheet of typing paper and brought out her photographs.

They were not pictures of family, or friends, or even a dog or cat, its eyes brown-red in the flashbulb's light. They were pictures of a house. It was like a thousand houses in a hundred towns, not suburb, not city, but somewhere in between, with aluminum siding and a chain-link fence, a narrow drive-way running up to a one-car garage and a patch of backyard. The house was yellow. I looked on the back for a date or a name, but neither was there. There was no need for discussion. I knew what she was trying to tell me, for it was something I had often felt. She was not adrift, alone, anonymous, al-though her bags and her raincoat with the grime shadowing its creases had made me believe she was. She had a house, or at least once upon a a time had had one. Inside were curtains, a couch, a stove, potholders. You are where you live. She was somebody.

I've never been very good at looking at the big picture, taking the global view, and I've always been a person with an overactive sense of place, the legacy of an Irish grandfather. So it is natural that the thing that seems most wrong with the world to me right now is that there are so many people with no homes. I'm not simply talking about shelter from the elements, or three square meals a day or a mailing address to which the welfare people can send the check—although I know that all these are important for survival. I'm talking about a home, about precisely those kinds of feelings that have wound up in cross-stitch and French knots on samplers over the years.

Home is where the heart is. There's no place like it. I love my home with a ferocity totally out of proportion to its appearance or location. I love dumb things about: the hot-water heater, the plastic rack you drain dishes in, the roof over my head, which occasionally leaks. And yet it is precisely those dumb things that make it what it is—a place of certainty, stability, predictability, privacy, for me and for my family. It is where I live. What more can you say about a place than that? That is everything.

Yet it is something that we have been edging away from gradually during my lifetime and the lifetimes of my parents and grandparents. There was a time when where you lived often was where you worked and where you grew the food you ate and even where you were buried. When that era passed, where you lived at least was where your parents had lived and where you would live with your children when you became enfeebled. Then, suddenly where you lived was where you lived for three years, until you could move on to something else and something else again.

And so we have come to something else again, to children who do not understand what it means to go to their rooms because they have never had a room, to men and women whose fantasy is a wall they can paint a color of their own choosing, to old people reduced to sitting on molded plastic chairs, their skin blue-white in the lights of a bus station, who pull pictures of houses out of their bags. Homes have stopped being homes. Now they are real estate.

People find it curious that those without homes would rather sleep sitting up on benches or huddled in doorways than go to shelters. Certainly some prefer to do so because they are emotionally ill, because they have been locked in before and they are damned if they will be locked in again. Others are afraid of the violence and trouble they may find there. But some seem to want something that is not available in shelters, and they will not compromise, not for a cot, or oatmeal, or a shower with special soap that kills the bugs. "One room," a woman with a baby who was sleeping on her sister's floor, once told me, "painted blue." That was the crux of it; not size or location, but pride of ownership. Painted blue.

This is a difficult problem, and some wise and compassionate people are working hard at it. But in the main I think we work around it, just as we walk around it when it is lying on the sidewalk or sitting in the bus terminal—the problem, that is. It has been customary to take people's pain and lessen our own participation in it by turning it into an issue, not a collection of human beings. We turn an adjective into a noun: the poor, not poor people; the homeless, not Ann or the man who lives in the box or the woman who sleeps on the subway grate.

Sometimes I think we would be better off if we forgot about the broad strokes and concentrated on the details. Here is a woman without a bureau.

There is a man with no mirror, no wall to hang it on. They are not the homeless. They are people who have no homes. No drawer that holds the spoons. No window to look out upon the world. My God. That is everything.

Respond: Thinking Independently

1. How do you react to Quindlen's definition of homeless? Of a home? Would you replace it with another?
2. Write a response statement: One of Quindlen's points that really struck me was _____ because _____.
3. Write about what having or not having a home means to you.

Reconsider: Thinking Collaboratively

1. In groups or as a class discuss what Anna Quindlen means by "homes have stopped being homes. Now they are real estate."
2. Discuss the effect of the homeless on society, on the American identity. What solutions can classmates offer?

Review: Thinking Critically

1. Explain what you think Quindlen means by "it has been customary to take people's pain and lessen our own participation in it by turning it into an issue, not a collection of human beings."
2. In a recent John Grisham novel, *The Client*, a character longs for a house with a "walk-in closet." What does Quindlen say about the desires of some homeless people she has talked to for some very specific types of rooms or homes? What is her explanation for why some homeless people reject shelters?
3. How does individual identity or a sense of pride enter into a discussion of the homeless?

READING TO WRITE

Understanding Definition: Using the First Person

Some readers may be surprised by the very personal observations made in this essay by Anna Quindlen, particularly her use of "I" in an essay defining the homeless. Some readers may have been taught in school to avoid "I" and "you" in writing essays and concentrate on the objective third person, "he, she, it, or they." While it is true that academic writing in term papers or journal articles strives to be evidence-based and very objective, many essays get their power from personal observation and personal involvement.

The key here is to understand the purpose of the piece of writing and the audience who will read the essay. Certainly an essay on Abraham Lincoln's views of slavery and the emancipation of slaves written for a history professor or historical journal should rely on historical documents objectively presented. Generally, a writer should not involve him- or herself in the presentation by saying "I," unless a personal opinion in the form of a conclusion drawn from the evidence is warranted.

However, not all nonfiction essays need to follow that model. When a writer is recording observations made first hand and is also reflecting on what some events mean to him or her, the use of "I" is not only acceptable but necessary. Students receiving writing assignments should ask their instructors for guidance about the particular type of writing called for by the assignment.

Writing Applications: Definition

1. Writing in a personal style, define your own view of what a home is. How does your definition involve your sense of identity, of who you are?
2. Read other essays on the problem of the homeless and write a brief objective description of the problem as it faces Americans today.
3. In your opinion, is homelessness an individual problem or a societal problem? Find evidence to support what you say.

King Death

TESS GALLAGHER

Preview: Thinking Ahead

Among contemporary American writers interested in portraying life in America as it appears at the end of the twentieth century is the poet and short story writer Tess Gallagher. Her work has appeared in journals like The North American Review *and in more widely read magazines like* The New Yorker, *where this 1982 story first appeared under the title "A Figure of Speech." Gallagher has won awards for her fiction including the PEN syndicated Fiction Award in 1985. As you read this story, think about the character, her sense of home, and her changing reactions to the homeless man in her alley.*

It was five-thirty and the sun was just coming up when I heard Dan brace his ladder outside the bedroom wall. His paint bucket clanged against the rungs. I'd been dreaming. Something about dressing myself, then finding later that I hadn't dressed myself. Nobody in the dream minded that I was half-dressed, but I minded. Leonard was on his side, with his hands up near his chest. He was grinding his teeth. I gave him a little nudge with my knee and he stopped.

I got up, put my robe on, and went to make the coffee. Dan passed the kitchen window on his way to get something from his truck. We waved good morning and smiled at each other. I liked having him around the house. He was a hard worker; he had just gotten married and was doing odd jobs in addition to his regular one with the city parks department.

I let Leonard sleep. I knew the light falling across the bed would wake him soon enough. I took a glass of juice out to Dan.

"Going to get hot," he said. "I should start at midnight and work till daylight."

"Then you'd have to fight the bugs," I said. "If it's not one thing, it's two dozen others."

"I don't mind bugs," he said. "You can kill a few bugs and feel better, but you can't kill sun. It's going to get hot as Hades pretty soon." Dan was a Mormon, so he was always careful about what he said. He used the words "darn" and "shucks" a lot.

Dan was helping me get the house ready to sell. Leonard designed heating and air-conditioning systems for industrial buildings, and he was due to be transferred to Dallas in the next couple of months. The transfer meant a promotion for him, so he was glad about it. If every move we'd made had meant a promotion, Leonard would have been president of the company. But most of the time the bosses were just shifting personnel here and there to cover themselves.

I met Dan a year ago, when we first moved to Tucson. Leonard and I had closed on the house deal and then driven back to Sacramento to pack things up for the move. But before the movers could get our things to Tucson, the house was vandalized—the living room carpet slashed, light fixtures broken, cabinet doors yanked off, handprints smeared on the walls. The neighbors said it must have been the gang of young men who'd rented the house before we bought it. They'd had wild parties. Sometimes as many as fifty cars and motorcycles would be parked along the street.

"We weren't about to mess with them," the man across the street told me. "We saw all kinds of things. Thugs like that run in a pack. They wouldn't think twice about cutting your throat. I got kids and a wife and a home to think about. No, they made their music day and night, and we put up with it."

Leonard wanted to sell the house immediately. He was spooked by the fact that it had been broken into. But I didn't want to be run out of a house before I'd even lived in it. I said I'd take charge of fixing the place up again. It was going to be a nice place, I told him. I got Dan's name from a man at the hardware store, and Dan came to paint the inside of the house. Leonard and I stayed in a motel for two weeks, eating restaurant food and watching TV in bed at night. It wasn't so bad. Now, a year later, Dan was painting the outside. The house was starting to look so good I wanted to forget about having to move again.

"You got yourself a new neighbor," Dan said to me. He was resting his glass on a rung of the ladder.

"What do you mean?" I asked.

"There's somebody in the alleyway between your house and the next one," Dan said. "I saw him from the ladder while I was painting."

There was a high board fence around the house. It was over my head and nearly over Dan's head, too. The property had been fenced to leave a wide fire lane between our house and the house of a neighbor who called himself the Mad Hatter. He was a middle-aged disc jockey. He probably had a real name, but on the radio he called himself the Mad Hatter and that's all we ever knew him by. His mailbox had recently been vandalized, and he told me he was going to shoot the next kids he caught messing with it. He didn't care if they were in diapers, he said; he was going to plug them.

Dan motioned toward the fence and shook his head. "He's as comfortable as a king," he said. "He's laying over there sleeping on his back, this old guy."

"On the ground?" I said. "With no covers?"

"Just his clothes," Dan said. "It's nobody I know," he added, and laughed. He drank down the last of his juice.

"You hold the ladder," I said. I cinched my robe around my waist and went up the ladder just far enough to see over the fence. There in the tall grass was a man lying face up with his eyes closed. One big-knuckled hand was stretched out in the grass. The other lay across his chest. He was using a flattened-out cardboard box for a bed. Paper wrappers and some wine bottles lay near him. I looked down at Dan and lowered my voice. "Maybe he's dead," I said.

"No, he moved," Dan said. "I just saw him move."

"He could die over there and not be found for days," I said. "He's probably been smoking in that high grass." I remembered how when I was a child the railroad bums had come up to our back fence and my mother had gone into the house and gotten slices of bread for them. She was superstitious about beggars. She believed that if you turned them away they'd put a curse on you. But instead my father cursed at her, and said he didn't buy bread so she could hand it away to every down-and-outer who passed the fence.

I went inside and woke Leonard. It was time for him to get ready for work anyway. I followed him into the bathroom and talked to him while he splashed water on his face. "There's a bum sleeping on the other side of our fence," I said. "I want you to go out there before you leave for work and tell him he can't sleep there. He can't make a bedroom out of our yard."

"Maybe he's just passing through," Leonard said. "I need a clean towel." He turned to me with his eyes squinted shut and water dripping onto his chest.

I handed him a towel from the cupboard near the medicine cabinet. "He'll tell his bum pals about this place," I said. "I don't want him out there. We'll never sell the house. Can you imagine me showing people around and saying, 'Oh and the fellow right here over the fence—that's our resident bum'?"

"I'll take care of it," Leonard said.

I went back into the kitchen to fix some eggs and toast. Leonard came in, smelling of shaving lotion. "Some neighborhood we landed in," he said. He pulled out his chair and sat down at the table. "We should never have moved into this house. You'll listen to me now."

"It's like this all over," I said. "Jeana, right next to the university, she told me that little nurse next door to her woke up with a man standing over her bed. It was the middle of the night. The nurse asked him what he wanted. She stayed calm the whole time. He said he was looking for his friend John. 'John doesn't live here,' the nurse told him. 'I think you better leave,' she said. So the man left, all right—with her stereo, her hair dryer, some eggs, and a pair of fingernail clippers. She was lucky she wasn't killed. He'd cut a hole in a screen on one of the living room windows and crawled in."

"We may as well live in Alaska," Leonard said. "It's worse than Alaska. It's lawless here. It's like the Old West. Like the Gold Rush all over again. Two thousand people a month moving into this place. It's a wonder they don't put tents on our lawn."

"Some of them don't even have tents," I said. I pointed my spatula toward the alley.

"I know, I know. I'll take care of it," he said.

In a little while he picked his car keys off the counter, gave me a kiss on the cheek, and headed outside. I went into the bedroom and opened the blinds. Leonard was at the fence. He'd taken a cigarette out and was lighting it. Then a head came up on the other side of the fence.

The bum had short white hair, and his face was tanned and wrinkled. I could see a white stubble of beard. The bum was squinting at Leonard. Then one of his hands came up over the fence and he took a cigarette from the pack Leonard held out to him. Leonard steadied the bum's hand until he could get the cigarette lit. The window was up, so I could hear through the screen some of what they were saying. Something about the V.A. hospital. The bum was saying he was going to have to go there. Leonard was smoking and listening. Then he nodded and said yes, he knew what it was to be hooked on booze.

"I was a practicing alcoholic for fifteen years," I heard my husband say. It was a history he gave every now and then—mostly when he heard somebody was having trouble with drinking. It made me mad sometimes to hear him say he was an alcoholic, as if it were a kind of reverse status. But I knew it was serious business—that he's got out of the drinking and managed to stay out. His recovery happened a few years before we met, and this made it hard for me to appreciate how much he's changed. I believed it, but only because he told me he'd been another person then. If he hadn't kept telling me about it—what an awful drunk he used to be—I would have forgotten. I guess that's what I wanted.

"I'd do anything for a drink," the bum said. "Oh, it's the Devil's juice, don't I know it. But I tell you, I'd kill for a drink. There's times I want it that bad," he said.

"Well, you get yourself in there to the hospital and let them help you," Leonard said. Then he took some money out of his billfold and gave it to the bum, along with the pack of cigarettes.

"What's your name?" the bum asked.

"Leonard."

"Put her there, Leonard," he said. Leonard took his hand. "I won't forget this," the bum said. "I used to be somebody myself once," he said. "I might pull out of this yet. You know what it is, don't you, to be drowned alive like this? I can tell you do. It's in your eyes. You know about it. I thank you," he said. "I thank you."

About noon Dan came into the house. He'd been painting the trim on the shady side of the house.

"Is he gone?" I asked.

"Yes," Dan said. "He went off toward the boulevard. But he'll be back."

"How do you know?" I said.

"If you give them money they always come back," he said. "Give them anything but money." He went over to the sink and drew himself a glass of water. When he got ready to go back to work I walked outside with him and went over to the fence. I lined up my eye with a knothole. In the fire lane I could see the flattened cardboard box. The grass was crushed down, and I counted four empty wine bottles.

"You know that doughnut stand over by the park?" Dan asked. "Well, it's open twenty-four hours. That's where these transients—we call them blanket people—that's where they go to stay warm in the winter. They must be feeding them doughnut holes over there," he said. He laughed, and pulled the bill of his blue work cap.

When Leonard came home from work, I asked him what the bum had said.

"I told him he'd have to move on," Leonard said. "I told him he should get some help for his drinking. He said he was a vet, was in Korea. He's only fifty-five, but he looks like King Death himself. I'd say seventy if I had to guess."

"Did he say anything else?" I asked. I was at the kitchen table shelling fresh peas into an aluminum bowl.

"Just that he used to have a house, kids, a wife—the whole works."

"I heard him say he'd kill for a drink," I said. I tossed an empty pod onto a newspaper on the floor.

"That was a figure of speech," Leonard said. "I don't think he'd hurt anybody. He just wants enough to drink, and maybe some cigarettes."

"Dan says he'll be back. He says if you give them money they come back."

"I could be where he is, but for the grace of God," Leonard said.

"You were never that bad," I said.

"In a way, I was worse," he said. "I blamed it all on somebody else. I made somebody who loved me pay and pay hard."

"I'm glad I didn't know you then," I said.

"I'm glad, too," he said.

I bundled up the empty pods in the newspaper and stuffed them into a garbage bag near the back door. I was thinking that I wouldn't have stuck it with Leonard in those days. I would have let him down and I was ashamed, knowing that. But it was true.

I was drying my hands on the towel near the sink. Leonard came over to me at the sink and turned me toward him. He put his arms around me and held me in close under his chin. I kept my eyes closed. We stood still and hugged each other.

One morning we'd just finished breakfast and Leonard was on the phone talking long-distance when someone knocked on the door. I pulled the curtain back and saw the bum. He hadn't been around for at least a week. I'd kept checking the fire lane to make sure. I opened the door a crack.

"Is Leonard here?" the bum asked. His eyes were the bluest blue I'd ever seen—two caves of blue. I shut the door and went into the kitchen.

"Leonard," I said. "It's him. King Death."

Leonard put his hand on the receiver. "Tell him just a minute," he said.

I went back to the door and opened it. "Just a minute," I said. Then I shut the door and sat down near the window, where I could see him standing on the porch. He looked like one of those dogs you see tied to parking meters, waiting for somebody to come back.

Leonard came out of the kitchen. He opened the door and stepped onto the porch. "Here," Leonard said. He handed the bum some money. "Take this and don't come back," he said.

"You're God's own," the bum said.

"Don't come back, now," Leonard said. "You understand me?"

"I got you, friend. Don't you worry," the bum said. I stood up, so I could see through the open door. The bum was walking backwards toward the street. "You touched my heart," he called out to Leonard. "Yes, you did."

Leonard came back inside. He shook his head and reached for a cigarette from a pack on the counter. "It's like being hunted," he said. "He's like a piece of the past that nearly happened. It hunts you down and tries to move in."

"Don't give him more money," I said. "I like your goodness. I admire it. But you can't really do anything for him. Not in the long run."

"No, nothing that lasts," Leonard said. "He'll cash it in out there. He'll just lie down with his bottle, and some morning he won't wake up."

Leonard's company needed him a month early, so the transfer went through before I'd sold the house. Leonard drove to Dallas and I stayed behind to supervise the last of the repairs. Dan was doing the work. With Leonard gone, it was good to have him around. I told him he should bring his new wife over for me to meet, and he joked with me, saying he didn't want to do that. She'd be too jealous. He'd never get in a day's work for me again.

One day I asked Dan to help me pick up all the papers and bottles in the fire lane. It was a mess.

"Shameful for any human being to live like this," Dan said. "You'd think salvation cost a million dollars, when it's free." That was the one thing about Dan that made me uncomfortable—how absolutely convinced he was about his salvation and about salvation being within everybody's reach. I'd given up talking to him about anything resembling religious matters. But once in a while I couldn't resist saying what I thought.

"It's a shame, all right," I said. "But maybe he's got to pay for his salvation in ways we can't even imagine. Or maybe he asked to be quits with drink but God turned him down."

"God's not like that," Dan said. "Ask, and ye shall receive."

"But he doesn't say *what* ye shall receive," I said. I'd carried a rake along and I was using it to scrape some broken glass into a little pile. I noticed how even the smallest pieces of glass glittered in the bright sunlight. "You might have to earn your salvation," I said. "You might have to go through some things before God would even turn his face in your direction."

"If he can save little children, he can save anybody anytime," Dan said. He was pulling a large cardboard box full of trash along the fence. He stopped and folded up the bum's cardboard bed and stuffed it into the box. Then he climbed into the box and jumped. He raised each foot up and brought it down hard.

"I don't believe salvation is something you get once when you're a kid, like the chicken pox, and then you're bound for Heaven," I said. "There are times you fail. Times nobody may know about. You've got to set yourself straight again and again." I looked up and saw that the Mad Hatter had come out of his house and was pacing along a row of pineapple palms he'd planted to let us know where his property line was. He walked over to the fire lane and stood with his hands on his hips, looking at the trash we were piling up.

"I'm going to get this grass mowed," I told him.

"Those hoodlum kids use this fire lane as a footpath," he said. "I've warned them. I told them I'll pull the trigger on them without batting an eye if they so much as set their big toe on my property." His face was puffy and he didn't stand still when he talked; he moved sideways, as if he were working up to something.

"You can't shoot to maim anymore," the Mad Hatter said. "You got to shoot to kill. Then you're O.K. If you just maim, they'll sue you for everything you've got. You have to kill them outright to stay within the law." Then he recited the findings of some court case he'd read about in the newspaper. Somebody who'd shot a robber in the arm and had to pay the hospital bill.

I never said anything when I heard him go into his tirades. I just nodded and got away from him as fast as I could. His wife locked him out of the house sometimes. I'd been woken up more than once when he was drunk and pouncing on his own door to get in. One time I heard glass breaking over there.

Dan and I carried the trash to the front of the lot. The Mad Hatter was striding along the fire lane with his eyes on the ground. I watched him cross onto his property and make the rounds of his palms, checking with the toe of his shoe to see if they were still tamped into the ground firmly.

I felt better once the fire lane had been cleared. Dan had a friend with a big mower, and I hired him to cut the grass. Then I had Dan stretch a length of barbed-wire fencing along the back of the property. Several people came to look at the house, and one young couple seemed particularly interested. Leonard and I talked on the phone, making plans for me to pack and call the movers as soon as the house was sold. I began sorting clothes, getting rid of a lot of winter things we'd kept in case we should ever get sent back to up-state New York. I packed the clothes in paper sacks—Leonard's wool trousers, neck scarves, several hand-knitted vests, odds and ends of things—and I was planning to take them to Goodwill.

Dan had just one more job to do on the house. He was going to repair some bathroom tiles. I was making jam on the morning he was supposed to come, when I heard a knock at the front door. I turned the burner off and went into the front room. I opened the door and there he was—King Death himself. But he was clean-shaven now, and he had on a white shirt with a spangled vest over it. He looked like a rich gypsy. His eyes hadn't changed, though. They were the only young thing about him. They sizzled with en-ergy. I took a step back and pulled the door closed to a narrow opening for my eyes and mouth.

"Your husband, Leonard," he said. "Is he here?"

Before I could think, I'd said it—that Leonard didn't live here anymore. "He's moved away," I said. "He won't be back."

The man looked down at this feet as though he were embarrassed. I was panicky, thinking now he'd know that I was alone. I tried to figure how to put Leonard back in the picture.

"Tell him for me—tell Leonard when you see him—that I didn't want anything," he said. "Tell him I just stopped by to see him."

"Just a minute," I said. I closed the door and locked it. Then I went into the bedroom and got one of the sacks of clothes. There were some of my things in it and some of Leonard's, but I didn't take time to sort out anything. I went back to the door, unlocked it, and pushed the sack through until I felt the man take it. "You might get some use out of these," I said. I was afraid and glad at the same time, but I was trying to keep from showing how I felt.

The man made a little bow with the sack in one arm. His eyes snapped down. "Thank you, ma'am. I thank you."

Then he turned and started down the walk. I watched him pass along the street a little way, then I shut the door and went to heat the jam again. I sat down at the kitchen table. The house seemed very quiet. Soon there was the soft burbling of the jam beginning to boil, but that was all. I thought of the man going somewhere behind a building or into the park and taking our clothes out of the sack, holding them up to himself, trying them on but hav-ing no mirror to look into. If Leonard had been there, I'd never have given the man anything.

The young couple finally decided to buy the house. The man was about twenty-five. He climbed onto the roof and said he thought the house should have a new roof. I said if he wanted a new roof he could put it on himself. "This house is for sale *as is*," I said. When he saw he couldn't bully me, he went ahead and offered what we were asking.

I'd backed the car to the end of the driveway and was about to head for the real-estate office to sign the papers when I spotted the bum again. He was knocking at the Mad Hatter's door, gazing across to our oleander bushes while he waited. He had on Leonard's wool slacks. It was ninety-degree weather. The slacks were drawn up around his waist with a length of white cord. He was wearing my black knit vest over Leonard's blue shirt.

I scooted over to the passenger side and rolled the window down. I sat there a minute waiting to see if anyone would answer the Mad Hatter's door. I hoped no one was home. I could hear the dogs barking inside the house, and then the door opened and the Mad Hatter appeared. "You want to get shot?" he said. "You know where you're standing?"

"I need a little help," the bum said.

"Just a minute," the Mad Hatter said. He shut the door. I heard the dogs start up again.

The bum looked up at the sky. Then he clasped his hands behind his back and waited. His having our clothes on made him seem somehow familiar, as if I ought to know his name and be able to call out to him. I thought of Leonard, the Leonard I had never known.

The Mad Hatter opened the door again. "You see this?" he said. "This is a Smith and Wesson .38. It's loaded. I'm going to count to ten and on the count of ten I'm going to fire it directly at you."

The bum did not move. He did not say anything, either. I couldn't see his face, but I could see the Mad Hatter's mouth counting. I got out of the car when he reached six. I walked into my driveway on seven and eight. I could see both their faces then. I knew there wasn't time to make it to the phone. I kept remembering what the Mad Hatter had said earlier about not maiming but shooting to kill. I could see the gun pointing at the bum's chest. He was looking straight at the Mad Hatter. The Mad Hatter had said *nine* some time ago.

"Ten," said King Death.

Then he held there a minute, looking past the Mad Hatter. It was as if he were looking right through the house and out the back. Finally, he turned and began to walk toward the street. The Mad Hatter stood in the doorway holding the gun. He took a step forward onto the porch. The gun was aimed at the man's back. I thought of the bullet going through my vest and through Leonard's blue shirt, knocking the man down. Then the Mad Hatter turned and the gun began to drift slowly toward me. I stood still. I could feel my strength slipping from me. It was as though I were there and not there at the same time. The gun was trained on me. I had nothing, was nothing. I wanted to call out, "It's me, your neighbor." But I couldn't make any words. The Mad Hatter raised the gun over his head. A bullet cracked out of it. I looked up into the sky where the bullet must have gone. There were no clouds. There was nothing to see.

"It's loaded!" he called. "You better believe it's loaded. All of you!"

I was still looking up at the sky. I heard the door close and it was quiet a minute. Then I heard the yipping and whining of the dogs.

I stood a moment in the driveway, trying to think what to do with myself. I saw my car sitting near the street, where I'd left it. I made my way slowly toward it. I got inside and sat behind the wheel. The seat was hot. I closed my eyes. I put my hands on the wheel and turned it as I sat there. I felt like I'd died and come to life in the front seat of a car in a strange city. I opened my eyes and looked up at my house. It seemed far away and nowhere I'd ever lived.

Respond: Thinking Independently

1. Write your response to the woman, her husband, and the homeless man, King Death.
2. Ask a question about one of the characters or some other aspect of the story: _____.

Reconsider: Thinking Collaboratively

1. Compare your responses to the woman, her husband, and the homeless man with your group or your class as a whole.
2. Read each other's questions and try to answer them in your groups or in class.
3. How does the woman view her home? How does it affect her reactions to the homeless man?
4. How does Leonard, the husband, react to the homeless man at first? Why?
5. What part in the story does Dan play? The Mad Hatter?

Review: Thinking Critically

1. Why does the wife give King Death some clothes? What effect does his wearing the clothes have on her as she sees him on the Mad Hatter's porch?
2. Explain the confrontation between the Mad Hatter and King Death. Why does King Death finish the count, saying "ten"?
3. What is the woman's reaction to Mad Hatter's pointing a gun at her? Why does she feel that she never lived in her house?
4. What general conditions of contemporary America are mentioned in the story? Why do you think that Gallagher included them?

READING TO WRITE

Understanding Fiction: Characterization

Creating believable characters is a major challenge to the writer of fiction. Often the strength or weakness of a story hinges on whether readers accept the characters as credible human beings. How do writers create characters? One way is to tell readers about a character directly. For example, in this story readers are told that, "Dan was a Mormon, so he was always careful about what he said." Are there explicit statements about Leonard and the Mad Hatter? Another way is to show characters in action. For example, although Leonard tells his wife that he'll "take care" of the homeless man, we see him giving money and cigarettes to the man after advising him to seek treatment for his alcoholism. What other actions show character? A third way writers create character is to allow readers a chance to learn their innermost thoughts. In this story readers learn how the wife feels when the Mad Hatter's gun is pointed at her, "I could feel my strength slipping from me." What other instances of inner feelings being expressed do you see in this story? Which characters in this story are the most fully realized in your opinion? Why?

Writing Applications

1. In what ways does the woman in Gallagher's story bear out the observations that Quindlen makes in her essay about rootedness and the changing sense of home in American society?
2. Write about the instances of random violence mentioned in this story and what they show about contemporary America.

Longing to Die of Old Age
ALICE WALKER

Preview: Thinking Ahead

Millions of people have read Alice Walker's novel The Color Purple *or have seen the film of the same name, but fewer know her work as an essay writer. In this 1988 essay from her collection* Living by the Word, *Walker draws on her experience and her relatives' experiences to bring us a warning about the harm people are causing the environment and themselves.*

Mrs. Mary Poole, my "4-greats" grandmother, lived the entire nineteenth century, from around 1800 to 1921, and enjoyed exceptional health. The key to good health, she taught (this woman who as an enslaved person was forced to carry two young children, on foot, from Virginia to Georgia), was never to cover up the pulse at the throat. But, with the benefit of hindsight, one must believe that for her, as for generations of people after her, in our small farming community, diet played as large a role in her longevity and her health as loose clothing and fresh air.

For what did the old ones eat?

Well, first of all, almost nothing that came from a store. As late as my own childhood, in the fifties, at Christmas we had only raisins and perhaps bananas, oranges, and a peppermint stick, broken into many pieces, a sliver for each child; and during the year, perhaps, a half-dozen apples, nuts, and a bunch of grapes. All extravagantly expensive and considered rare. You ate *all* of the apple, sometimes, even, the seeds. Everyone had a vegetable garden; a garden as large as there was energy to work it. In these gardens people raised an abundance of food: corn, tomatoes, okra, peas and beans, squash, peppers, which they ate in summer and canned for winter. There was no chemical fertilizer. No one could have afforded it, had it existed, and there was no need for it. From the cows and pigs and goats, horses, mules, and fowl that people also raised, there was always ample organic manure.

Until I was grown I never heard of anyone having cancer.

In fact, at first cancer seemed to be coming from far off. For a long time if the subject of cancer came up, you could be sure cancer itself wasn't coming any nearer than to some congested place in the North, then to Atlanta, seventy-odd miles away, then to Macon, forty miles away, then to Monticello, twenty miles away. . . . The first inhabitants of our community to die of acknowledged cancer were almost celebrities, because of this "foreign" disease. But now, twenty-odd years later, cancer has ceased to be viewed as a visitor and is feared instead as a resident. Even the children die of cancer now, which at least in the beginning, seemed a disease of the old.

Most of the people I knew as farmers left the farms (they did not own the land and were unable to make a living working for the white people who did) to rent small apartments in the towns and cities. They ceased to have gardens, and when they did manage to grow a few things they used fertilizer from boxes and bottles, sometimes in improbable colors and consistencies, which they rightly suspected, but had no choice but to use. Gone were their chickens, cows, and pigs. Gone their organic manure.

To their credit, they questioned all that happened to them. Why must we leave the land? Why must we live in boxes with hardly enough space to breathe? (Of course, indoor plumbing seduced many a one.) Why must we buy all our food from the store? Why is the price of food so high—and it so tasteless? The collard greens bought in the supermarket, they said, "tasted like water."

The United States should have closed down and examined its every intention, institution, and law on the very first day a black woman observed that the collard greens tasted like water. Or when the first person of any color observed that store-bought tomatoes tasted more like unripened avocados than tomatoes.

The flavor of food is one of the clearest messages the Universe ever sends to human beings; and we have by now eaten poisoned warnings by the ton.

When I was a child growing up in middle Georgia in the forties and fifties, people still died of old age. Old age was actually a common cause of death. My parents inevitably visited dying persons over the long or short period of their decline; sometimes I went with them. Some years ago, as an adult, I accompanied my mother to visit a very old neighbor who was dying a few doors down the street, and though she was no longer living in the country, the country style lingered. People like my mother were visiting her constantly, bringing food, picking up and returning laundry, or simply stopping by to inquire how she was feeling and to chat. Her house, her linen, her skin all glowed with cleanliness. She lay propped against pillows so that by merely turning her head she could watch the postman approaching, friends and relatives arriving, and, most of all, the small children playing beside the street, often in her yard, the sound of their play a lively music.

Sitting in the dimly lit, spotless room, listening to the lengthy but warm-with-shared-memories silences between my mother and Mrs. Davis was extraordinarily pleasant. Her white hair gleamed against her kissable black skin, and her bed was covered with one of the most intricately patterned quilts I'd ever seen—a comparison to the dozen or more she'd stored in a closet, which, when I expressed interest, she invited me to see.

I thought her dying one of the most reassuring events I'd ever witnessed. She was calm, she seemed ready, her affairs were in order. She was respected and loved. In short, Mrs. Davis was having an excellent death. A week later, when she had actually died, I felt this all the more because she had left, in me, the indelible knowledge that such a death is possible. And that cancer and nuclear annihilation are truly obscene alternatives. And surely, teaching this very vividly is one of the things an excellent death is supposed to do.

To die miserably of self-induced sickness is an aberration we take as normal; but it is crucial that we remember and teach our children that there are other ways.

For myself, for all of us, I want a death like Mrs. Davis's. One in which we will ripen and ripen further, as richly as fruit, and then fall slowly into the caring arms of our friends and other people we know. People who will remember the good days and the bad, the names of lovers and grandchildren, the time sorrow almost broke, the time loving friendship healed.

It must become a right of every person to die of old age. And if we secure this right for ourselves, we can, coincidentally, assure it for the planet. And that, as they say, will be excellence, which is, perhaps, only another name for health.

Respond: Thinking Independently

1. In your journal react to Walker's essay.
2. Write a response statement: I was particularly interested in Walker's statement about _____ because _____.
3. What did you think of Walker's description of Mrs. Davis's death?

Reconsider: Thinking Collaboratively

1. Compare response statements with groups or the class.
2. Discuss Walker's description of the way her older relatives lived on the farm. What was different when people moved from the farm to the city?

What effects does Walker think were caused? How does she convey the threat of cancer?

3. Why does Walker describe the death of Mrs. Davis? How does it fit into the essay? What point is she making?

Review: Thinking Critically

1. Many people are uncomfortable with the subject of death. How does Walker make Mrs. Davis's death seem less frightening?
2. What distinction does Walker make between dying of "old age" and dying from "self-induced" causes?
3. What does Walker mean by "the flavor of food is one of the clearest messages the Universe ever sends to human beings"?
4. Is the issue of environmental dangers connected to modern American identity? Can we say in a national sense, "We are what we eat"?

READING TO WRITE

Understanding Argument: Using Many Organizational Patterns

As you have seen in previous selections, writers call upon many strategies to make their points, frequently using several different methods of organization even within one essay. Rarely is an essay all description, all comparison or contrast, all illustration, or all any one pattern. Rather, the writer weaves together an effective pattern of his or her own, calling upon all the individual patterns of organization he or she has learned. In "Longing to Die of Old Age," Alice Walker uses a short example, a contrast, and a longer narrative example to help her make her argument. See if you can identify these elements in her essay.

Writing Application: Argument

1. Explain what an environmental issue means to you, both in personal terms and as a national concern.
2. Choose another issue such as public education, violence, health care, or the like and write what it means to you both personally and for America.

On the Pulse of Morning

MAYA ANGELOU

Preview: Thinking Ahead

At President Clinton's inauguration, the nation heard this poem for the first time, read by the poet herself, and was moved at the images of unity and change. Angelou, born Marguerite Johnson in St. Louis, Missouri, in 1928, is

well-known to Americans as the author of I Know Why a Caged Bird Sings
and other volumes of her autobiography, and as an actor in "Roots," the tele-
vised version of Alex Haley's biography. She also danced in Porgy *and* Bess,
appeared on PBS, wrote five books of poetry, and many songs, scores, plays,
and screenplays. As you read the poem, think of all the identity issues she
raises, both individual and national. What view does Maya Angelou have of
the future of America?

A Rock, A River, A Tree
Hosts to species long since departed,
Marked the mastodon,
The dinosaur, who left dried tokens
Of their sojourn here
On our planet floor,
Any broad alarm of their hastening doom
Is lost in the gloom of dust and ages.

But today, the Rock cries out to us, clearly, forcefully,
Come, you may stand upon my
Back and face your distant destiny,
But seek no haven in my shadow.
I will give you no hiding place down here.

You, created only a little lower than
The angels, have crouched too long in
The bruising darkness
Have lain too long
Face down in ignorance.
Your mouths spilling words

Armed for slaughter.
The Rock cries out to us today, you may stand upon me,
But do not hide your face.

Across the wall of the world,
A River sings a beautiful song. It says,
Come, rest here by my side.

Each of you, a bordered country,
Delicate and strangely made proud,
Yet thrusting perpetually under siege.
Your armed struggles for profit
Have left collars of waste upon
My shore, currents of debris upon my breast.
Yet today I call you to my riverside,
If you will study war no more. Come,
Clad in peace, and I will sing the songs
The Creator gave to me when I and the
Tree and the rock were one.

Before cynicism was a bloody sear across your
Brow and when you yet knew you still knew nothing.
The River sang and sings on.

There is a true yearning to respond to
The singing River and the wise Rock.
So say the Asian, the Hispanic, the Jew
The African, the Native American, the Sioux,
The Catholic, the Muslim, the French, the Greek
The Irish, the Rabbi, the Priest, the Sheik,
The Gay, the Straight, the Preacher,
The privileged, the homeless, the Teacher.
They hear. They all hear.
The speaking of the Tree.

They hear the first and last of every Tree
Speak to humankind today. Come to me,
here beside the River.
Plant yourself beside the River.

Each of you, descendant of some passed
On traveller, has been paid for.
You, who gave me my first name, you
Pawnee, Apache, Seneca, you
Cherokee Nation, who rested with me, then
Forced on bloody feet, left me to the employment of
Other seekers—desperate for gain, starving for gold.
You, the Turk, the Arab, the Swede, the German, the Eskimo, the Scot,
You the Ashanti, the Yoruba, the Kru, bought,
Sold, stolen, arriving on a nightmare
Praying for a dream.
Here, root yourselves beside me.
I am that Tree planted by the River,
Which will not be moved.
I, the Rock, I, the River, I, the Tree
I am yours—your passages have been paid.
Lift up your faces, you have a piercing need
For this bright morning dawning for you.
History, despite its wrenching pain,
Cannot be unlived, but if faced
with courage, need not be lived again.

Lift up your eyes upon
This day breaking for you.
Give birth again
To the dream.

Women, children, men,

Take it into the palms of your hands,
Mold it into the shape of your most
Private need. Sculpt it into
The image of your most public self.
Lift up your hearts
Each new hour holds new chances
For a new beginning.
Do not be wedded forever
To fear, yoked eternally
To brutishness.

The horizon leans forward,
Offering you space to place new steps of change.
Here, on the pulse of this fine day
You may have the courage
To look up and out and upon me, the
Rock, the River, the Tree, your country.
No less to Midas than the mendicant.
No less to you now than the mastodon then.

Here, on the pulse of this new day
You may have the grace to look up and out
And into your sister's eyes, and into
Your brother's face, your country
And say simply
Very simply
with hope—
Good morning.

Respond: Thinking Independently

1. Write your reactions to Angelou's images of the Rock, River, and the Tree.
2. Choose a line from the poem that seems important to you personally, or to a sense of American identity, and explain why you chose it.

Reconsider: Thinking Collaboratively

1. Discuss the views of the Rock, River, and Tree in groups or in class. What does each object seem to mean to America in Angelou's poem?
2. Discuss the lines chosen from the second question of Thinking Independently with those in your group or class.
3. What harm does the River say has been done to it? Why?
4. What does the poet mean that "Each of you . . . has been paid for?"
5. What point about history does Angelou make on page 268?

Review: Thinking Critically

1. What image of America's future does Angelou give? Explain.
2. What dangers are there that the nation will not realize this future? That is, what does Angelou say the people will have to do for it to be a reality?

READING TO WRITE

Understanding Poetry: Allusions

The fact that poetry is compressed and must convey complex thoughts in few words has been emphasized throughout the text. Another technique that enables poets to accomplish this compression is the use of allusions. Do not confuse "allusion" with "illusion." Allusion is a reference to a previous event in history or to another piece of literature, such as the Bible. When Angelou says, "You, created only a little lower / than the angels," she is referring to the Biblical idea of the creation of human beings. When Angelou says, "you / Cherokee Nation, who rested with me, then / Forced on bloody feet," she is referring to the Trail of Tears, a forced march of the Cherokee Indians from North Carolina to Oklahoma in 1838 in which many thousands died. If a reader does not understand an allusion, he or she may still appreciate a poem but perhaps not in all its complexity. Allusions help a poet "bring in" other events and literary works without using the words it would take to explain those ideas. Allusions put the burden on the reader to explore the poet's ideas fully.

Writing Applications

1. Take the Rock, River, or Tree and explore the ideas that the poet attaches to one of these.
2. Write an essay about Angelou's vision of America's future based on your reading of the poem and class discussion.

APPENDIX

Understanding Grammar and Usage

Applying the basic principles of Standard English in your writing will enable you to communicate more effectively with instructors at school and employers and colleagues on the job. Writing effectively, which includes writing correct standard forms, is often cited as a requirement for success in college and in a career. Fortunately, you probably know more about grammar than you realize. If you are a native speaker of English, you already know the basic structure of English. If you are learning English as a second language, your study and everyday practice are helping you to understand the principles of English grammar.

However, the demands of written English are very different from those of spoken English. When we talk to people directly, we can use body language to help express our ideas and feelings. We can wave our arms, point, shrug our shoulders, smile, or frown to illustrate our points. We can raise or lower our voices or pause frequently to clarify an idea. And we can adjust our explanation to our listeners' feedback. We are able to respond immediately to questions, blank stares, or shrugs. Writers rarely have the same opportunity to supplement, correct, or clarify their material after it has been given to their readers. Your written work must do the job the first time, and it must do it effectively on its own.

In order to talk about language, you may need to know specific terms to refer to parts of sentences or to word choices. Sometimes you may feel that the study of English gets bogged down with such terms. While it is true that most writers may not know or think of all the terms as they write; nevertheless, knowing some of the terms will make it easier for your instructor to talk with you and your classmates about revising your writing. Also, knowing what options you have in constructing effective sentences may help you revise your written work. If you have ever fumbled over terms for the parts of your car's engine when you were describing some problem to a garage mechanic, you have an idea of the importance of a specific vocabulary. More than one of us has wished we had known a carburetor or an intake manifold or an alternator instead of a whatchamacallit.

Although past experience in speaking and writing will help you make many correct grammatical choices, learning some rules of standard written English and applying them may help you improve your writing skill.

271

A1

Defining Key Terms

Parts of Speech

Noun

A noun is the name of a person, a place, an object, or an idea. A noun can be one word, a verbal ending in *-ing* or *to* + verb, or a clause. Examples are italicized in the following sentences.

Mary and *George* live in *Chicago*.

A *democracy* requires educated *citizens*.

The *windows* needed to be cleaned.

Pitching is a special *skill*.

To be a quarterback takes practice.

He waited for *whoever was in charge*.

Pronoun

A pronoun is a word used in place of a noun. Pronouns include: *I, you, he, she, it, we, they, me, him, her, us, them, mine, your, ours, its, theirs, who, whom, one, everyone, someone, anyone, no one, everybody, somebody, anybody, nobody, this, these, that, those, which, each, either, neither, what*. Examples are italicized in the following sentences.

They live in Chicago.

It requires educated citizens.

Those needed to be cleaned.

Verb

A verb expresses an action or a state of being and can be tested by putting a noun or pronoun before it to make a small sentence ("She swims." "Mary has gone." "He runs."). Examples are italicized in the following examples.

The students *work* at several jobs.

The club *raised* money through a volleyball marathon.

Hard work *is* necessary for success.

The store manager *had been* a football player in college.

Adjective

An adjective describes a noun or pronoun by answering the questions "Which," "What kind of," or "How many." Sometimes a verb form ending in *-ed* or *-ing* is used as an adjective, and sometimes a clause is an adjective. Examples follow.

That dress will be put in a museum. (Which dress?)

The *helium* balloon burst. (What kind of balloon?)

The *frightened* children fled the *swimming* snake. (What kind of children? What kind of snake?)

The children *who were frightened* fled the lake. (Which?)

Four students head the *student* government. (How many students? What kind of government?)

Note: As in the preceding sentence, *students* is a noun when it names something but can become an adjective when it describes a word like *government*. Words may change their part of speech as they take on different functions.

Adverb

An adverb describes a verb, an adjective, or another adverb by answering the questions "When," "Where," "Why," "How," "How much," or "How often." Adverbs may be one or more words, including clauses. Here are some examples.

George draws *well*. (Draws how?)

George *frequently* draws *well*. (Draws how and how often?)

Put the paper *there*. (Put where?)

Put the paper *where it can dry out*. (Put where?)

Recently, Juan received a raise. (Received when?)

The monster raised its arm *quite threateningly*. (How raised, how much threateningly?)

The children were *very* happy. (How much happy?)

Note: Adverbs are more movable than many other parts of speech. You may find them next to the word they describe or at the beginning or the end of a sentence. Ask yourself what word they are describing. If it's a verb, an adjective, or an adverb, then you know the word itself is an adverb.

Preposition

A preposition is a word that expresses a relationship and is always followed by a noun or pronoun in what is called a *prepositional phrase*. The following examples of prepositional phrases have their prepositions italicized.

under the house	*during* the storm
over the house	*after* the storm
through the house	*before* the storm
into the house	*of* the court

Note: Prepositional phrases are used in sentences to describe nouns or pronouns (therefore acting as adjectives) and to describe verbs (therefore acting as adverbs).

Conjunction

A conjunction joins two words, two clauses, or two sentences. Most common are the coordinating conjunctions *and, but, or, nor, for, so,* and *yet.*

Certain words that sometimes serve as other parts of speech may also serve as subordinating conjunctions that introduce dependent clauses. In the following sentences, each italicized word is a conjunction introducing a dependent clause.

Because there had been so much rain, crops rotted in the field.

He walked to the corner, *where* he caught a bus.

Susan agreed to join her friends *unless* she found out that she had to work.

Parts of the Sentence

Verb

The verb in a sentence expresses an action or a state of being. It may be one word, two or more verbs connected by *and*, or a main word together with auxiliaries such as *may, can, has, have, is,* and *are*. An *-ing* word must have an auxiliary with it to be a verb. Here are some examples.

The dog *buried* the bone.

The dog *chased* and *caught* a rabbit.

The dog *is being chased* by the neighbor's cat.

The cat *may have* some wildcat ancestors.

The cat *is winning* the race.

Subject

The subject of a sentence is the noun or pronoun that performs the action of the sentence or is spoken about in the sentence. It may be one word, two or more words linked by *and*, a verbal like *swimming*, or a clause.

The *telephone* revolutionized communication.

Hurricanes and *tornadoes* are still highly unpredictable.

Hurrying along an icy sidewalk is dangerous.

Whoever is next may use the computer.

Direct Object

The direct object in a sentence is the noun or pronoun that receives the action of the verb. It can be one word, two or more words connected by *and*, a verbal ending in *-ing*, or a clause. The best way to find it is to repeat the subject and verb and ask the question "what?". Examples:

The dog buried the bone. (The dog buried what? *bone*)

The dog chased and caught a rabbit. (The dog chased and caught what? *rabbit*)

The dog bit him. (The dog bit what? *him*)

The dog dodged whatever was in her way. (The dog dodged what? *whatever was in her way*)

The dog hates bathing. (The dog hates what? *bathing*)

Indirect Object

Sometimes a sentence with a direct object has an indirect object that receives the action of the direct object, such as:

I gave my friend some money. (I gave what? *some money* [direct object] to whom? *my friend* [indirect object].)

The indirect object is almost always a person or group of people. More examples:

The quarterback threw the *receiver* (indirect object) the ball.

The boss paid *me* (indirect object) my wages.

I made my *mother* (indirect object) a sweater.

We gave the *Boy Scouts* (indirect object) a donation.

Predicate Noun and Predicate Adjective

In sentences with state-of-being verbs (*is, am, are, was, were*), words following the verb rename or describe the subject of the sentence. The verb can be thought to act as an equal sign:

The doctor is Lynn Smith.   The doctor = Lynn Smith

The doctor is young.   The doctor = young.

In these two sentences, *Lynn Smith* is a predicate noun and *young* is a predicate adjective. Examples follow.

Herbert Morris is the star *scholar* (predicate noun).

The cat was *black* (predicate adjective) and *white* (predicate adjective).

The winner is *whoever claims the prize first* (predicate noun).

This season's sport is *swimming* (predicate noun).

Writing Complete Sentences

When people speak to others, they rarely pay attention to the way their sentences are put together. It isn't necessary. If they give their listeners too little information, listeners can stop them to ask for more detail. If they give their listeners too much information without pausing enough, those listening can say "Slow down," or "What was that again?" Writers don't get that kind of feedback most of the time. Their readers have only the words on the printed page to communicate the writers' ideas. If writers want their ideas understood and taken seriously by readers, they must use complete, grammatically correct sentences to express their thoughts.

Let's briefly review some points about sentences:

1. A sentence expresses a complete thought.

2. A sentence usually makes sense when it is standing alone.

3. A sentence usually contains a complete subject-verb combination.

4. A sentence begins with a capital letter and ends with a period, an exclamation point, or a question mark.

Finding Subjects and Verbs

Test 1.   It is usually easier to find the verb in a sentence before locating the subject. Ask yourself the following questions about the sentence.

What word is the action word?

What word shows that something exists?

The answer to each question will be a verb.

Examples
Dogs bark.

What word is the action word? *bark. Bark* is the verb.

John ate pizza.

What word is the action word? *ate. Ate* is the verb.

Quick Reference Chart
Avoiding Sentence Errors

Type of Error	Example	Correction
Fragment		
Missing verb	the horse with a long mane	The horse with the long mane runs swiftly.
Incomplete verb	the horse running in the third race	The horse is running in the third race.
Missing subject	runs every day	The horse runs every day.
Missing subject and verb	in all kinds of weather	The horse runs in all kinds of weather.
Dependent clause	because the horse likes exercise	Because the horse likes exercise, the trainer takes it out every day.
	who rides the horse	The groom who rides the horse enjoys the work.
Run-on	Horses are expensive to feed and groom they also run up huge veterinary bills.	Horses are expensive to feed and groom, and they also run up huge veterinary bills.
Comma splice	Some people will always enjoy watching horses, they are such graceful runners.	Some people will always enjoy watching horses, for they are such graceful runners.

Susan is my neighbor.

What word shows that something exists? *is. Is* is the verb.

Test 2. Another test for a verb is to put the words *he, she,* or *they* before the word you are testing to see if it makes a sentence (no matter how short!).

Examples
They bark.   He ate.   She is.

Once you have found the verb, ask, "Who or what is doing the action or existing?" The answer will be the subject of the sentence.

Examples
The horses ran swiftly toward the finish line.

What word is the action word? *ran.* Test: They ran. *Ran* is the verb. Who or what ran? *horses. Horses* is the subject.

My sister is an expert skier.

What word is the action word or shows something that exists? *is.* Test: She is. *Is* is the verb. Who or what is? *sister. Sister* is the subject. (Note: "Skier" doesn't pass the test as an action word: She skier?)

Sometimes a verb will need more than one word to be complete and pass the test. An *-ing* word such as *swimming* will not pass the test alone. "They swimming" is not complete in Standard English usage. However, if you add *are* ("They are swimming"), it does pass. The word *are* is a helper, or auxiliary, which makes an *-ing* verb form such as *swimming* complete. Another example of the need for a helper is a word ending in *-en*, such as *stolen* or *spoken*. Let's apply the test: "He spoken" doesn't pass. But if you add a helper to the verb, "He *has* spoken," it does.

Other helpers are *is, am, was, were, has been, have been*, and *will be*. When you are asked to "find the verb," that means find any helpers too.

Another tricky form is the word *to* plus the verb, as in *to swim* or *to run*. This form is called an *infinitive* and can't serve as the verb. Try the test: "They to swim." It doesn't pass. You need to add a verb, such as *like* or *hate*, or *prefer*: "They hate to swim."

Try your hand at completing sentences by filling in the missing word in the following word groups so that each makes a sentence. Then indicate if the word you filled in is a subject or a verb.

EXERCISE 1

1. Movies _____ one of my favorite things. (subject or verb)

2. As a child, I _____ to the movies every Saturday afternoon. (subject or verb)

3. Sometimes the _____ included five cartoons, a continuing story called a serial, and the main feature. (subject or verb)

4. Even as an adult, I _____ to see movies frequently. (subject or verb)

5. _____ is the kind of movie I like best. (subject or verb)

EXERCISE 2

Underline the verb twice and the subject once in each of the following sentences.

1. David rode his motorcycle across the country.

2. Shana is my roommate and my best friend.

3. Justin drove his neighbor's car to the service station.

4. The expensive speakers in his television set are broken.

5. Gary asked to borrow my history notes.

Eliminating Fragments

A *fragment* is a part of a sentence that is written and punctuated as if it were a complete sentence. A fragment cannot stand alone, because it lacks a subject, a verb, or both, *or* because it begins with a subordinating word such as *after, because, which*, or *that. Subordinating words* make an idea incomplete or dependent so that another idea has to be added to the first idea to make a complete thought. Thus, our earlier example, "The weather was warm," is complete, but "Because the weather was warm" is a fragment. You want to know what happened "Because the weather was warm"? So you could add an idea: "Because the weather was warm, we ate our lunch outside by the duck pond." Here is a partial list of subordinating words: after, although, as, because, before, if, since, than, that, though, unless, until, when, where, while.

Let's look now at some examples of different kinds of fragments and ways to correct them.

Missing Subject and Verb Fragments

Example
Whistling in the dark hallway.

This is a fragment that has a verb form "whistling" but no complete verb that passes the *he, she, they* test. "They whistling" is not a sentence.
To correct such a fragment you can add it to a complete sentence:

Correction
The guests could hear the monster whistling in the dark hallway.

Or you can make it into a complete sentence:

Correction
The monster was whistling in the dark hallway.

Correction
Whistling in the dark hallway *gave the child courage.*

Missing Verb Fragments

Example
At one point in the semester, the chemistry professor along with several of his colleagues and students.

Although this fragment is very long and looks like a sentence, it lacks a verb, so we don't know what the chemistry professor did.
To correct such a fragment, add a verb:

Correction
At one point in the semester, the chemistry professor along with several of his colleagues and students *discovered a formula for unbreakable pencil points.*

Fragment
The moon rising over the trees and shining on the lake.

Note the *-ing* verb forms do not pass the *he, she, they* test: "She rising"? We need to add a helper:

Correction
The moon *was* rising over the trees and *was* shining on the lake.

Missing Subject Fragments

Example
And invited hundreds of guests to their dormitory after the football game.

This fragment sounds like a continuation of another idea, perhaps from the previous sentence. Even if two sentences make sense when read together, each one needs a subject if it is going to stand alone with a capital letter and a period.

Correction
The dorm council got together and invited hundreds of guests to their dormitory after the football game.

Fragment
The cafeteria was noisy. Filled with the voices of impatient students.

Correction
The cafeteria was noisy, filled with the voices of impatient students.

Note that in this case the two parts could simply be joined, with the fragment now becoming part of the sentence.

Fragment
Made me promise not to tell her parents.

Correction
My roommate made me promise not to tell her parents.

Fragment
The young-looking movie star with the big eyes.

Correction
The young-looking movie star with the big eyes *is actually forty-four years old.*

Dependent Clause Fragments

Example
Because Jeffrey had forgotten two of their dates.

This word group is a fragment because of the word *because*. That word, a subordinator, makes a reader think that another idea will follow. To fix the fragment, the subordinator may be dropped, or another complete sentence (*independent clause*) may be added:

Correction
Jeffrey had forgotten two of their dates.

Correction
Because Jeffrey had forgotten two of their dates, *Charlene refused to go out with with him again.*

Fragment
Whose brother is a famous rock star.

Note that with a question mark this sentence would be complete: "Whose brother is a famous rock star?"

Correction
I am going to spend the weekend with my roommate, whose brother is a famous rock star.

EXERCISE 3

In the following word groups, put capital letters and end punctuation on those that are complete sentences. Rewrite the fragments.

1. speaking in to the microphone as clearly as possible
2. burned to a crisp and shriveled into small pieces
3. that I ordered from a catalogue that the postal courier delivered last Thursday

4. my sister watches soap operas every afternoon after school

5. the race car driver, being afraid to approach the sharp turn at high speed

Working Collaboratively

In pairs or groups, write five sentences more than eight words long. Check each one to see that it is a complete sentence. You should be able to answer "yes" to the following questions:

1. Does the word group contain a complete verb that passes the *he, she, they* test?

2. Does the word group contain a subject?

3. If the word group begins with a subordinator such as *because, since, while, when,* or *that,* is there an independent clause (a complete sentence) attached to the word group to make it a complete thought?

4. Does the word group express a complete thought?

Eliminating Run-Ons

A *run-on,* or fused, sentence occurs when two complete sentences are written as one without the proper punctuation.

Example
Arthur always sleeps late he never gets to class on time.

Note that "Arthur always sleeps late" is the first sentence and "he never gets to class on time" is the second. Even though the ideas are related, they are independent thoughts and have to be punctuated correctly.

There are several methods to correct run-ons. The method you choose depends on the way you wish the ideas to be joined.

1. Make two separate sentences by adding a period at the end of the first sentence (independent clause) and capitalizing the first word of the second sentence.

Correction
Arthur always sleeps late. He never gets to class on time.

2. Add a coordinating conjunction (*and, but, or, nor, for, so,* or *yet*) between the two sentences *and* put a comma before the conjunction unless the sentences are very short.

Correction
Arthur always sleeps late, so he never gets to class on time.

3. Join the sentences by leaving out the second subject.

Correction
Arthur always sleeps late and never gets to class on time.

We now have one subject with two verbs (a simple sentence with a compound predicate). We don't need a comma before the *and* in that case.

4. If the two sentences are closely related, put a semicolon between them. As a general rule, do not use a semicolon with *and, but, or, nor, for, so,* or *yet.*

Correction
Arthur always sleeps late; he never gets to class on time.

5. You may use a transition word after the semicolon, such as *however, moreover, therefore,* or *indeed.* If you do, use a comma after the transition word.

Correction
Arthur always sleeps late; therefore, he never gets to class on time.

Note: Sometimes we use a transition word in the middle of one sentence ("He is, however, a miser"). In order to justify using a semicolon, we need to have two independent clauses: a sentence structure of "subject-verb; subject-verb."

6. Turn one of the sentences into a dependent clause, using a subordinator like *because, since, while,* or *after.*

Correction
Because Arthur always sleeps late, he never gets to class on time.

It may seem odd to you that there are so many ways to correct run-ons, but the choices give you several ways to express your ideas and vary your sentence structure. Just as you tired of the simple sentences in your reading primer ("See Dick run. Run, Spot. Run, Jane."), your reader tires of the same sentence structures. Also, each way of connecting two sentences may change the relationship slightly between the two sentences. In the next exercise you will be experimenting with these choices. Discuss how connecting ideas in different ways changes the meaning of the sentences.

EXERCISE 4

In the following word groups, correct the run-on sentences in at least two different ways. Try to use all the options just discussed by the time you have finished the exercise. Be prepared to discuss how connecting the sentences in different ways affects meaning. Note: Some sentences are already correct.

1. Andrew tried out for the school hockey team he wanted to be the goalie.
2. Even though he tried his best, the coach was not impressed with his skating ability or with his courage.
3. Every day after school, Andrew went to the local rink to practice skating his best friend went also.
4. One afternoon, as they were chasing each other around the rink, a scout happened to wander in several other people gathered also.
5. Before the boys realized what had happened, they were putting on a show the spectators loved it.

Working Collaboratively
With other classmates, write five sentences of your own that contain two independent clauses, then connect each of them in two different ways.

Eliminating Comma Splices

Comma splices are similar to run-ons, in that two sentences are put together incorrectly. A *comma splice* occurs when two sentences are separated only by a comma.

Example
Heavy snow fell for three days, the students were trapped in their dorm.

A comma is not strong enough to separate two sentences. Use one of the methods already discussed for correcting run-ons:

1. Use a period and capital letter.
2. Use a comma *with* a coordinating conjunction: , *and*

3. Use a semicolon: ;

4. Use a semicolon with a transitional word: ; *therefore,*

5. Rewrite the sentence, making one clause subordinate:

The students were trapped in their dorm after heavy snow fell for three days.

A3

Writing Varied Sentences

Learning how to vary your sentence structure will give you more choices when you write sentences. In addition, writing that contains a variety of sentences generally is easier for a reader to understand. Short, choppy sentences make readers feel as if they are marching, rather than strolling, through your ideas. At the other extreme, long, complicated sentences make readers feel as if they are plodding, rather than walking, through your material. What you want to strive for is a balance of different types of sentences.

Four Basic Sentence Patterns

Simple Sentence

A simple sentence contains one independent (or main) clause. That is, it has a subject-verb combination that can stand alone.

Example
According to the latest survey, pizza is everyone's favorite food.

Compound Sentence

A compound sentence contains at least two independent (or main) clauses connected by *and, but, or, nor, for, so,* or *yet*.

Example
According to the latest survey, pizza is everyone's favorite food, but hamburgers are probably in second place.

Complex Sentence

A complex sentence has one independent (or main) clause *and* at least one dependent clause that could not stand alone. The dependent clause usually begins with a subordinating word such as *because, since, while, when, after,* or *until*.

Example
According to the latest survey, pizza is everyone's favorite food, which accounts for the large number of pizza restaurants.

Compound–Complex Sentence

A compound–complex sentence has at least two independent (or main) clauses connected by *and, but, or, nor, for, so,* or *yet*, plus at least one dependent clause.

Quick Reference Chart
Writing Varied Sentences

Type of Sentences	Number and Kinds of Clauses	Examples
Simple	One independent clause	David can hit home runs.
		David and Jeffrey can hit home runs.
		David can hit home runs and field fly balls.
		David and Jeffrey can hit home runs and field fly balls.
Compound	Two independent clauses —joined either by a co-ordinating conjunction (*and, but, or, nor, for, so, yet*) or by a semicolon	David can hit home runs, and Jeffrey can field fly balls.
		David can hit home runs; Jeffrey can field fly balls.
Complex	One independent and at least one dependent clause	While David can hit home runs, Jeffrey can field fly balls.
		David, who can hit home runs, can also field fly balls.
		David and Jeffrey can hit home runs exactly as the coach wants them to do.
Compound-complex	Two independent clauses and at least one dependent clause	While David can hit home runs, Jeffrey can field fly balls, but neither one can slide home head first.

Example
According to the latest survey, pizza is everyone's favorite food, but people don't eat it every day because it is very filling and often expensive.

EXERCISES: *Using Simple Sentences*

Simple sentences contain only one independent clause. They do not have any dependent clauses. Simple sentences are often short, but they do not have to be. They can be lengthened by adding phrases, such as the phrase above "According to the latest survey." Regardless of their length, simple sentences have only one noun-verb combination. Generally, no commas are used to separate the subject(s) from the verb(s) in a simple sentence.

                                    phrase

       s   v
The student jogged (to the pizza parlor).

phrase

(After studying for a test), the student jogged

s   v

(to the pizza parlor) (in the shopping mall) (near his home).

phrases

The student and his friends jogged (to the pizza parlor) (in the shopping

s   s   v   phrases

phrase

mall) (near his home).

NOTE: Two subjects and one verb but still a simple sentence.

s   s   v   phrases

The student and his friends jogged (to the pizza parlor) (in the shopping

phrases
v

mall) (near his home) and ordered six pies (with pepperoni and mushrooms).

NOTE: Even though this is a long sentence, it is still considered a simple sentence because it has the subjects together and the verbs together in one combination: s and s
v and v

Sometimes, sentences are constructed with the subject and verb in reverse order.
Don't let this confuse you. Words like *there* and or *where* are not subjects. Remember
to find the verb first in the sentence and then ask who or what is doing the action.
Then you will find the true subject.

v   s   v

There were seven swans swimming in their bathtub.

v s v

Where did I put my term paper?

EXERCISE 1

Write a simple sentence using the information given. Label each of your subjects and
verbs.

Example
a zookeeper—two duties

A zookeeper feeds the animals and keeps them healthy.

1. two friends—one action
2. one athlete—one accomplishment
3. thousands of college students—two actions
4. one subject mumbled under his/her breath

EXERCISE 2

In this exercise are some short, simple sentences for you to combine into one by joining the two subjects or the two verbs or both. An example is given first.

Debra shouted at the top of her lungs. Debra frightened the robber away.

Combined
Debra shouted at the top of her lungs and frightened the robber away.

1. George likes to sail and play tennis. Jill likes to sail and play tennis.
2. The police officer argued with the motorist about the parking ticket. The motorist argued with the police officer about the parking ticket.
3. The nervous student mumbled. The nervous student stared at the floor. The nervous student stuttered during a speech.
4. Larry, Moe, and Curly were the Three Stooges. They pretended to be plumbers, tore up a bathroom, and finally destroyed a house.

EXERCISES: *Using Compound Sentences*

Compound sentences are two or more simple sentences joined together. They can be split apart where they are joined, and both halves remain as independent sentences.

Example

s   v   s   v

Mary takes algebra, / and Joan takes calculus.

Note that a comma and a coordinating conjunction (*and, but, or, nor, for, so, yet*) join the two.

Another way to join the two sentences into one is by using a semicolon (*;*).

Example

s v v   s v v

Today we are going to have a test; / tomorrow we will start a new chapter in the text.

Sometimes after the semicolon a writer will use a transition before the next sentence. The sentence can still be split into two independent parts.

Example

s v   s v

On Wednesday it rained; / therefore, we canceled the picnic.

Other transitions include *however, moreover, nevertheless, subsequently, for example,* and *as a result.* We use a comma after the transition, before the start of the next sentence. Remember to use *either* the comma and the coordinating conjunction *or* the semicolon to join two simple sentences into a compound sentence.

EXERCISE 3

Combine the following simple sentences into *one compound* sentence. Use the conjunction or transition in parentheses at the end of the sentences to join them. Use commas with the conjunctions; use semicolons with the transitions or if there is no joining word. Label the subjects and verbs. An example is given first.

My twin sister is majoring in education. I am enrolled in liberal arts. (but)

Combined

$$\text{s} \quad \text{v} \qquad \text{v} \qquad\qquad\qquad \text{s} \quad \text{v} \qquad \text{v}$$

My twin sister is majoring in education, but I am enrolled in liberal arts.

1. I enjoyed the movie very much. The book was even better (however)
2. After the storm, the electric company repaired the power lines. The fire fighters evacuated the elderly residents from their homes. (and)
3. Agatha continued to refuse Harold's phone calls. He quit calling. (finally)
4. John could use his prize money to buy a new battery for his car. He could use it to buy a new stereo system. (or)

Exercise 4

Make each of the following sentences a compound sentence by writing another sentence and joining it to the first one. Be sure to join the two with a comma and a coordinating conjunction (*and, but, or, nor, for, so, yet*) or with a semicolon. Use transitions with the semicolons as you think necessary. An example is given first.

After dinner, Andrew took the dog for a walk.

New Compound Sentences
After dinner, Andrew took the dog for a walk; later, they both curled up in front of the fireplace.

1. The bank lowered the interest rate on home mortgage loans.
2. The prosecutor asked the judge to give the convicted robber a ten-year sentence.
3. Harold agreed to take his cousin to a school party.
4. Torrential downpours flooded the coastal regions.

EXERCISES: *Using Complex Sentences*

What we have studied so far are sentences that present ideas that are equal in rank. That is, we have written a simple sentence, or we have simply joined together two sentences that each claim equal attention from the reader. Sometimes, however, we want to present two ideas that are not equal. Perhaps some event occurred *before* another event, or perhaps something was going on *while* an event was occurring, or perhaps one thing occurred *because of* another vent. Complex sentences allow us to present ideas that are unequal in rank. Read the examples that follow:

Example

$$\text{sub.} \quad \text{s} \quad \text{v} \quad \textit{dependent clause} \qquad \text{s} \quad \text{v} \qquad \textit{independent clause}$$

(Before we could go on our trip,) we had to arrange for the cat to be fed and the mail to be brought in.

Example

$$\text{s} \quad \text{v} \qquad \textit{independent clause} \qquad\qquad \text{sub.} \quad \text{s} \quad \text{v} \quad \textit{dependent clause}$$

Mark thought of his family every day (while he was away.)

Example

s   v   independent clause   sub.   s   v   v   dependent clause

Joan decided to take an insurance course at night (because it would help her get a promotion at work.)

As you can see, each of these sentences has an independent clause and a dependent clause that begins with a subordinator like *before, while,* or *because.* Sometimes writers will leave out the subordinator *that* in speech and in writing, although it is clearer to use it:

Example

(that)

s   v   v   s   v   v

Maria couldn't believe (she had won the lottery.) OR

independent clause   dependent clause

s   v   v   sub. s   v   v

Maria couldn't believe (that she had won the lottery.)

independent clause   dependent clause

Dependent clauses may occur anywhere in a sentence, but we punctuate them differently depending on where they occur. If the dependent clause begins the sentence, we put a comma after it and before the main clause.

Example

sub.   s   v   v   s   v   v

(Although Jim had studied for the test), he was not prepared for the

dependent clause   independent clause

difficult questions.

However, if the dependent clause goes at the end of the sentence, no punctuation is used unless needed for clarity or contrast:

Example

s   v   v   sub.   s   v   v

Jim was not prepared for the difficult questions (although he had studied

independent clause   dependent clause

for the test.)

Finally, when the dependent clause comes in the middle of the sentence, we put commas around it if it interrupts the main sentence.

Example

s   sub./s   v   v   v

Jim, (who studied for the test), was not prepared for the difficult questions.

dependent clause

(NOTE: In this example, the dependent clause begins with a word that acts as a sub-ordinator AND the subject of the clause. Words like *who, whom, which,* and *that* serve these two functions.)

(For more discussion of punctuating dependent clauses, see A4.)

Working Collaboratively

Here are some dependent clauses you are to use as part of a complex sentence. You will need to write an independent clause and attach the dependent clause at the beginning, middle, or end. Try to punctuate correctly. An example is given first.

after the rain stopped.

Complex Sentence
After the rain stopped, the baseball team ran back onto the field.

1. although Jerry apologized
2. which was canceled
3. since Kate was a college freshman
4. although I felt my meal at Luigi's was tasty and well-prepared

EXERCISES: *Using Compound-Complex Sentences*

The last pattern is the most complicated, and allows writers to combine ideas in two ways. First, they can join two ideas together in a compound sentence made up of two independent clauses; and second, they can include other ideas in dependent clauses within the main sentences. Study the following example. The independent clauses are underlined and the dependent ones are in brackets:

Some of the families *[*who left the cities a few years ago*]* missed the excitement of urban life. and they began moving back to their former neighborhoods *[*where they can get a newspaper or a sandwich without driving five miles*]*.

Working Collaboratively

In the following exercise, combine the simple sentences into one compound-complex sentence. Remember to put a comma before the coordinating conjunction (*and, but, or, nor, for, so, yet*) that joins the two sentences. An example is given first.

The film became tangled. The audience began stamping its feet. One man asked for his money back.

Compound-Complex Sentences
When the film became tangled, the audience began stamping its feet, and one man asked for his money back.

1. Growing your own vegetables can save money. Growing vegetables is a relaxing hobby. The cost of vegetables in the supermarket is rising every day.

2. We admire our neighbor Mrs. Martinez. She is the school board president. She oversees the finances and curriculum of the schools. She listens patiently to parents, teachers, and students.

3. Close the door. Lock the door securely. Do this each time. You leave the house.

4. The movie had many special effects. One was a disappearing car. The car traveled through time. The car needed an enormous amount of electricity to recharge it for its return.

A4

Punctuating Sentences: Commas and Semicolons

Punctuation principles developed as an attempt to signal pauses, ends of sentences, and other marks of intonation for people reading what someone else wrote. When people speak, their voices supply the needed pauses and variations in tone. For example, if you meet a neighbor on the street, you may say, "Hello, Mrs. Jones." However, if you call the Jones' house on the telephone and a female answers, you may say, "Hello, Mrs. Jones?" with a rising tone in your voice to indicate a question as to the identity of the person you have reached. As you can see, the only way to render the difference between the two sentences in writing is with a change in the end punctuation mark.

Similar reasons exist for using commas and semicolons as ways to signal pauses that separate groups of words. What is acceptable as "correct" comma and semicolon use varies over time, but some agreed-upon, regular system of punctuation seems to be necessary so that readers will be able to understand writers' thoughts. Take, for example, a sentence like "The police officer met Tom O'Malley the block captain for Crime Watch Joseph Brown a witness and Maureen Linder the owner of the house at the site of the burglary." Without any internal punctuation, the sentence could be understood in one of several ways. For instance, the police officer could have met five different people—(a) Tom O'Malley, (b) the block captain for Crime Watch, (c) Joseph Brown, (d) a witness, and (e) Maureen Linder—as in the following sentence:

> The police officer met Tom O'Malley, the block captain for Crime Watch, Joseph Brown, a witness, and Maureen Linder, the owner of the house, at the site of the burglary.

Or the police officer could have met three people—(a) Tom O'Malley, the block captain, (b) Joseph Brown, a witness, and (c) Maureen Linder, the owner—as in this sentence:

> The police officer met Tom O'Malley, the block captain for Crime Watch; Joseph Brown, a witness; and Maureen Linder, the owner of the house, at the site of the burglary.

Can you think of other possible readings of the original sentence? For example, could Joseph Brown be the Crime Watch captain?

Using commas and semicolons correctly helps your reader understand what you are saying and avoids confusion.

Joining Sentences

1. Use a comma between two complete sentences connected by *and, but, or, nor, for, so,* or *yet.*

   Example
   Teresa waited in a long line to register, but her patience was rewarded with the course schedule she wanted.

   Exception: If the sentences are *very* short, you can leave out the comma:

   Teresa talked and Brian listened.

2. Use a semicolon between two sentences *not* connected by *and, but, or, nor, for, so,* or *yet.*

   Example
   Teresa waited in a long line to register; her patience was rewarded with the course schedule she wanted.

Quick Reference Chart

Punctuating Sentences: Commas and Semicolons

Guideline	Examples
Use a comma . . .	
1. and a conjunction (*and, but, or, nor, for, so, yet*) to join two or more sentences.	The basketball player grabbed the rebound, but the buzzer sounded before he could shoot.
2. to separate an introduction from the main sentence.	If the player had made the basket, his team would have won.
3. to separate words in a series.	The coach, the fans, and the players on the bench groaned in disappointment. The tall, lean player slumped in defeat.
4. to set off interrupters from the rest of the sentence.	The coach, though disappointed, congratulated the player on a nice try.
5. to set off dates, places, and quotations.	"The next game will be Wednesday, March 1st, in Denver, Colorado," said the coach.
Use a semicolon . . .	The basketball player grabbed the rebound; the buzzer sounded before he could shoot,
1. to join two or more sentences without *and, but, or, nor, for, so, yet.*	
	or
	The basketball player grabbed the rebound; however, the buzzer sounded before he could shoot.
2. to separate items in a series if the series also has commas.	The key players on the team were LeRoy Grooms, guard; Kevin White, center; and Joseph Dorsey, forward.

Note: After a semicolon, you may use a transition such as *however, moreover, therefore, in addition,* or *for example.* If you do, remember to use a comma after the transition:

Teresa waited in a long line to register; however, her patience was rewarded with the course schedule she wanted.

Separating an Introduction from a Main Sentence

Use a comma to separate any type of introduction from the rest of the sentence.

Examples
When I fall in love, it will be forever.
Yes, we have the boots you ordered.
Mario, do you know where we can get a coke?
In the afternoon after a long day of classes, Marie did not want to go to work.
Before skating on a lake, you should check the thickness of the ice.
For example, there is a type of ski wax for almost every kind of snow.

Separating Words in a Series

1. Use a comma to separate three or more items in a series.

Example
Leroy ate a whole pepperoni pizza, a dill pickle, a pint of rocky road ice cream, and a bag of marshmallows.

(Note: Some people leave out the comma before *and* if it doesn't create confusion.)

2. Use a semicolon to separate items in a series if the series also contains commas.

Examples
Leroy, the quarterback, went to the pizza place with John Garner, the fullback; Ray Browne, the wide receiver; Tony Lancetta, the field goal kicker; and Pete Wozniak, the center.

3. Use a comma to separate adjectives that describe the same noun *if* the order of the words can be changed or if *and* could be inserted between them.

Example
The police were looking for a clever, daring bank robber.
Note: The sentence could also read:
The police were looking for a clever and daring bank robber.

Also the adjectives could be reversed to read "daring and clever."

4. Use *no* comma if the adjectives can't be changed around or if they can't have *and* inserted between them.

Example
The surprising suspect turned out to be a little old lady who drove a red Porsche.

Setting Off Interrupters

Use a comma to set off words or phrases that come in the middle of a sentence and interrupt the flow of the sentence. These interrupters are often signaled by a pause if the sentence is read aloud, and they often can be left out without confusing the reader as to the meaning of the sentence.

Examples
Toby, my best friend, likes to explore new trails in the woods.
He is, on the other hand, somewhat accident-prone.
Mrs. Gray, the loan officer at the bank, approved my request for a loan.
Family vacations by car are, generally speaking, tests of everyone's patience.
Mr. Gillespie, who teaches physical education, also coaches the sixth-grade basketball team.

Major exception: If the word or phrase cannot be left out without creating confusion, then it is not an interrupter and does not need commas. Also, such words or phrases are generally read without pausing.

Examples
The gloves that were on the table have disappeared.
My friend Toby is always getting hurt.
The woman who asked for a bus transfer was angry when the driver said that he didn't have any.

A stormy sky that suddenly looks green means "watch for tornadoes" in some parts of the United States.

Note: As a general rule, don't put a comma before the word *that*.

Setting Off Places, Dates, and Quotations

1. Use a comma between a city and a state or between a date and a year. Also, in a sentence use a comma *after* the state and *after* the year.

   Examples
   Hopkins, Minnesota, is a suburb of Minneapolis.
   July 4, 1776, is celebrated today as Independence Day.

2. Use a comma to set off a quotation from other words in the sentence.

   Examples
   Fernando said, "The cause of the drought was the position of the jet stream."
   "Oh, that's interesting," replied Juanita. "I thought it was caused by the greenhouse effect."
   "Couldn't both causes," asked David, "be responsible?"

EXERCISES: *Joining Sentences*

When one complete sentence (that is, an independent clause having at least one subject and one verb) is joined to another complete sentence, the resulting compound sentence needs to be punctuated. (See A3 for a review of compound sentences.)

There are two options for joining two sentences:

		and	
		but	
		or	
		nor	
1.	Sentence,	for	sentence
		so	
		yet	
2. a.	Sentence	;	sentence
b.	Sentence	;	transition word, sentence

As mentioned, very short sentences joined by *and, but, or, nor, for, so,* or *yet* do not need the comma. Common transition words include *however, moreover, therefore, in addition, consequently, nevertheless,* and *in fact*.

EXERCISE 1

Join each pair of sentences in two ways: by inserting a comma and a conjunction (*and, but, or, nor, for, so, yet*) and by inserting a semicolon and a transition word followed by a comma. The first pair are done for you as an example.

Video games continue to rise in popularity. New games sell out as soon as they arrive.

   a. *Video games continue to rise in popularity, and new games sell out as soon as they arrive.*

   b. *Video games continue to rise in popularity; in fact, many new games sell out as soon as they arrive.*

1. Some consumers suspect that the companies create shortages of games deliberately. The companies say they can't get enough chips to meet the demand.

2. Some people question the value of video games. They think that the games are a waste of time, especially for students.

3. Doctors even warn game players about overuse of fingers and wrists during prolonged play. They recommend taking periodic breaks to rest the hands.

4. Video game fans say that the games develop eye-hand coordination. The games provide an escape from stress.

Working Collaboratively

Write at least six sentences on the subject of video games. Try to relate the sentences to each other so that you are writing a short paragraph. Join at least two sentences with a comma and a conjunction and two with a semicolon and a transition word.

EXERCISES: *Separating an Introduction from the Main Sentence*

Many times you will begin a sentence with an introductory idea before writing the main independent clause of the sentence. Any such introduction needs a comma after it, before the start of the main clause. There are several kinds of introductions:

Introductory clause or phrase beginning with a subordinating word such as *after, because, before, since, when,* or *while:*

> When it rained, we canceled the soccer game.
> Since he was new in town, he took the wrong freeway exit.
> Because she wanted to change her major, she made an appointment with her advisor.
> While waiting for her advisor, she overheard another student complaining about conflicts between her work and her class schedule.
> After working until 9:30, I don't have the energy to study until midnight.

Introductory prepositional phrases at least five words long:

> Under the street light on the corner, he could see the suspicious figure dressed in a trench coat.

Using yes or no or addressing a person by name at the beginning of a sentence:

> Yes, you may have your loan paid in three installments.
> No, I am sorry I can't help you.
> David, would you please close the door to the hall?

Using a transition at the beginning of a sentence:

> In fact, domed stadiums have become increasingly popular.
> However, cities find the cost of building a covered stadium much higher than the cost of one that is open.
> Furthermore, architects find domes harder to design.

EXERCISE 2

Add commas after any introductions to each main sentence in the following exercise. Some sentences do not have introductions and are already correctly punctuated.

1. When Jennifer was in high school she had many friends who went everywhere together.

2. In fact Jennifer and her friends even took jobs in different stores at the same mall so they could be together.

3. During the last half of their senior year Jennifer and her friends began planning what to do after graduation.

4. Some of them planned to go away to college; others were going to go to local schools or get full-time jobs.

5. However all of them vowed that their friendship would not change.

Working Collaboratively

Write at least five related sentences about a change in friendships that you have experienced. Try to use an introduction to the main sentence in at least two of the sentences. Punctuate properly.

EXERCISES: *Separating Words in a Series*

Commas and semicolons separate words, phrases, or clauses in a series so that a reader will be able to see the different elements and won't run them together. The most common example is a listing of three or more objects:

Mike picked up sandpaper, drop cloths, brushes, and paint at the hardware store.

Some writers omit the comma before *and* ("brushes and paint"). That's all right as long as there is no confusion. If you were writing about sandwiches being made in a deli and omitted a comma before the *and,* a reader could misunderstand your list:

The deli worker filled the order for bologna, salami, tuna fish, ham and cheese sandwiches.

(Were there ham sandwiches and cheese sandwiches or combination ham and cheese sandwiches?)

Another example of this use of the comma is a listing of three or more subjects or three or more actions: Inez, Nita, and Maria decided to meet after health class.

They needed time to choose a project for their term report, split up the task of researching the subject, and begin gathering information.

Note: When you write a series, each item in the series has to be the same form, that is, each must be parallel to the others. For example, in the previous sentence, you shouldn't say, "They needed time to choose a project for their term project, splitting up the task . . . , and gathering information." (For further information or keeping elements parallel, see A7.)

As explained earlier, semicolons are used in a series to mark the major divisions if the series also contains commas: The athletic department awarded most valuable player trophies to Joe Gunder, football; Tony Huong, soccer; Jerry Martinez, tennis; Ray Marshall, basketball; Mary Malone, swimming; and Kaya Dubcek, field hockey.

EXERCISE 3

Use commas and semicolons where needed to separate items in a series in the following sentences.

1. Animals in danger of extinction include elephants Bengal tigers spotted leopards black leopards and gray whales.

2. Tigers leopards and other fur-bearing animals are hunted for their valuable skins.

3. Measures to protect them include prohibiting the hunting of endangered species banning the sale of pelts and outlawing the sale of finished fur coats.

4. However, poor third-world economies a thriving black market and high demand for fashion furs render these protective measures useless.

5. Sometimes, changes in the environment, rather than hunting, threaten a species. Animals about to become extinct for this reason include the giant panda China the gorilla Africa the sea otter United States and the wild yak India.

Another need to separate items with a comma may occur when two adjectives modify a noun. You can join these adjectives with an *and* without a comma:

The quick and lanky basketball player got the rebound and stuffed the basket.

But many times the two modifiers appear without the *and:*

The quick, lanky basketball player got the rebound and stuffed the basket.

The comma here substitutes for the *and.* If you can't use an *and* between two adjectives or can't reverse them, then no comma is needed. For example, in the previous sentence, no comma is needed between *basketball* and *player.* Note the following:

The efficient executive secretary answered the telephone while preparing the vice president's daily schedule.

Since you wouldn't write "The efficient and executive secretary" or "The executive efficient secretary," no comma is needed.

EXERCISE 4

Determine whether you need to put a comma between adjectives in the following sentences. Use the test of inserting an *and* between them and reversing their order. If you can do either one, use a comma; if not, no punctuation is needed.

1. Besides animals, birds like the American peregrine falcon are endangered.

2. Exotic colorful birds like the macaw may be trapped for sale as pets, which prevents them from breeding in the wild.

3. Other birds have suffered from the effects of dangerous long-acting pesticides.

4. The beautiful bald eagle and the large whooping crane are two victims of pesticides in the environment.

5. Concerned informed citizens can ask for laws protecting these disappearing creatures.

Working Collaboratively

Write five related sentences about the environment, trying to use items in a series. Use commas and semicolons as needed.

EXERCISE: *Setting Off Interrupters*

As you write, you may include words in a sentence that interrupt the sentence's main idea. For example, you might write:

Bitterly cold "Bears" weather did not, as it turned out, help the home team.

The clause "as it turned out" interrupts the main idea that the weather did not help the home team. When you speak, such interruptions are indicated by pauses. In writing, commas are used before and after the interruption to show where the main idea stops and then starts again. Interruptions can be one word or several words and usually take one of the following forms.

Transitions

The same words that serve as introductions to sentences can be placed in the middle of or at the end of a sentence to serve as a transition or linking of ideas. Words and expressions such as *however, moreover, of course, in contrast, indeed, in fact,* and *on the other hand* should have commas placed before and after them in a sentence. (Obviously, if a transition comes at the end of a sentence, only a comma before the expression is necessary, since a period will come after it.)

Examples
Many people on diets will, in fact, give in to their urge for chocolate.
Diet food manufacturers make many products, therefore, in chocolate flavor.

Addressing by Name

Just as you put a comma after addressing a person by name at the beginning of a sentence, so do you set off the person's name with two commas when it appears in the middle of the sentence.

Example
Please, David, close the door to the hall.

Contrasts

Words expressing a contrasting idea are set off by commas.

Examples
Power, not money, was the reason for Smith's run for senator.
The student planned to take five years, instead of the usual four, to finish college.

Appositives and Nonrestrictive Modifiers

A group of words that restates or adds information to a word that it follows is set off by two commas.

Examples
Mrs. Schmidt, my first-grade teacher, thought I talked too much.
John's father, an immigrant from Scotland, tried to keep alive many Scottish traditions.
The bus driver, who appeared to be in a hurry, barked at the passenger requesting a transfer.
The baker, a small woman with flour-covered hands, braided the bread dough with expert speed.

Note: If the words are needed to identify who is being discussed or to make the meaning clear, then no commas are used. Compare:

Steve, my son's best friend, loves to play basketball.

But:

My son's friend Steve loves to play basketball.

(He could have more than one friend, and the name is necessary to identify the friend.)

Usually word groups beginning with *that* are necessary to the sentence and are not set off by commas. Word groups beginning with *which* and *who* can be set off or not, depending on the meaning of the sentence.

EXERCISE 5

Use commas in the following sentences to set off interruptions from the rest of the sentence. Some sentences have restrictive word groups that are not interruptions and so are correct as written.

1. People who diet have to be careful that they are not doing themselves harm.
2. Fad diets which frequently are the subjects of the latest best-selling paperbacks may cause a serious misbalance of body chemistry.
3. The water diet for example may cause too much potassium to wash out of the system.
4. The grapefruit diet which required the eating of grapefruit at nearly every meal upset many people's stomachs.
5. Most doctors and nutritionists agree that exercise not just diet alone is the key to effective weight control.

   Working Collaboratively
   Write at least five related sentences about diets or dieting. Follow all the punctuation guidelines discussed so far.

EXERCISE: *Setting Off Places, Dates, and Quotations*

Some special situations call for the use of commas. Most people put commas between the city and the state or between the date and the year, but they may neglect to put a comma *after* the state or the year when either of these is used in a sentence.

Examples
Orlando, Florida, is a vacation destination for many families.
George wondered why Katmandu, Nepal, was called the ceiling of the world.
Arbor Day was first observed on April 10, 1872, in Nebraska.

Use a comma to set off words directly quoted from other words in a sentence. Study the following examples:

Jane said, "I don't know how to study for biology."
"Neither do I," Tony replied.
"Perhaps what we should do," Anna said, "is form a study group."
"I have an idea," Anna said. "We could form a study group."

EXERCISE 6

Use commas to set off dates, places, and quotations in the following sentences.

1. Many Americans have a vivid memory of some dates in recent history, such as the attack on Pearl Harbor, December 7 1941 or the assassination of President Kennedy on November 22 1963.
2. In fact, anyone old enough to remember those two events can probably answer the question "Where were you when you heard the news?"

3. Younger people may recall January 28 1986 when the space shuttle *Challenger* exploded after being launched from Cape Canaveral Florida.

4. A history teacher once remarked "We seem to remember disasters or tragedies more clearly than victories or triumphs."

5. While that may be true for national events, I have a good memory for October 4 January 14 and May 27—my family's birthdays.

Working Collaboratively

Write five sentences about places and dates that mean something to you, and include a quotation or two about your feelings or the feelings of others about these dates.

Punctuating Sentences: Other Marks

Other marks of punctuation range from the most common, the period, to ones used more infrequently, such as the exclamation mark. Along with commas and semicolons, these marks help the reader understand the writer's ideas, substituting for the pauses and changes in tone used in speech.

End Marks

Period

A period, ., is like a stop sign on a street. It tells the reader that the sentence or idea has come to an end. A period also signals that the sentence is a statement and, if read aloud, should end with a falling tone of voice.

Example
I need to get my car washed.

Sometimes a sentence contains a word like *asks* or *wonders* that may make you think it is a question.

I wonder whether it will rain today.

Such sentences are not direct quotations, and therefore they use a period, not a question mark. Compare the following pairs:

Statement
George asked if Jill could meet him for lunch.

Question
Jill, can you meet me for lunch?

Statement
I wonder how I did on my biology exam.

Question
How did I do on my biology exam?

Periods are also used in abbreviations like *etc.*, A.M., and P.M., but not in the relatively new postal abbreviations for states, such as *PA, TX,* and *CA.* Other abbrevia-

Quick Reference Chart
Other Punctuation Marks

Guideline	Examples
Use a period . . .	
1. to end a statement	The hike up the mountain trail is difficult.
2. in an abbreviation.	Mt. McKinley has many popular trails.
Use a question mark to end a direct question.	Have you ever climbed above 7,000 feet?
Use an exclamation mark to show strong feeling in a sentence or in a phrase.	Help! My rope broke!
Use a colon. . .	
1. after a complete sentence to introduce a list or an explanation.	Every mountain hiker needs at least four things: sturdy boots, food, water, and a weatherproof jacket.
	The jacket is needed to protect the hiker from hypothermia: the dangerous drop in body temperature caused by sudden chilling.
2. after the salutation in a business letter.	Dear Ms. Kosloski:
3. in writing the time.	9:00 A.M.
4. in subtitles.	The Other Side of the Mountain: Part 2
Use a dash to show a break in thought.	I once hiked three miles in a snow— what's that sound?
Use parentheses to enclose extra information.	This lightweight poncho (cost $25.99) is ideal.
Use italics to indicate titles of long works like novels, plays, albums, films,and names of magazines.	*Life* magazine did a picture story on conquering Mt. Everest.
Use apostrophes . . .	
1. in contractions.	He couldn't move another step.
2. to show possession.	He needed the guide's help to crawl into the tent.
	He soon revived in the warmth created by the other hikers' bodies.
Use hyphens . . .	
1. to separate words at syllables at the end of a typed line.	His ascent of the mountain was postponed.
2. to join two or more words into one.	He made a trade-off: the ascent for his health.
Use quotations . . .	
1. to enclose the direct statements of a speaker or writer.	"I'll live to hike again," Bob said.
2. to set off titles of short works such as short stories, songs, essays, and poems.	"The Road Not Taken" by Robert Frost was one of Bob's favorite poems.
Use brackets to insert material into a quoted statement.	"Two roads diverged [split apart] in a yellow wood."
Use ellipses to leave out material from a quoted statement.	"I took the one less travelled . . . , and that has made all the difference."

tions such as *NASA* and *CIA*, don't use periods. Consult your dictionary when in doubt.

Question Mark

A question mark, ?, signals the reader or the listener that the sentence or idea is a question. If read aloud or spoken, a question ends with a rising tone of voice.

> **Examples**
> Are you going?
> Where should we meet?
> I know the area fairly well, but do you think I should call for directions?

Note that the last sentence starts as a statement but ends in a question and therefore takes a question mark.

Exclamation Mark

An exclamation mark, ! signals commands or strong feelings. If read aloud or spoken, such sentences or ideas usually keep the same tone throughout, neither falling nor rising. They are usually short.

> **Examples**
> Help!
> Open a window, quick!
> Stand back!

Use only one exclamation mark, and don't use them simply to add emphasis to statements. For example, a direction such as "Please put all towels in the bin" gets a period not an exclamation mark. Underline, use capital letters, or print your message in a different color for emphasis, but save exclamation marks for strong feelings.

Emphasis or Deemphasis Marks

Colon

The colon, :, is used at the end of a complete sentence to direct the reader's attention to a list, an example, or an explanation. It may also be used in the salutation of a business letter (*Dear Sir or Madam:*), to separate numbers (*9:30 A.M.*), to set off a title from a subtitle (*Friday the 13th: Part IV*), to separate the place of publication from the publisher of a book in a bibliography (*New York: Random House*), or to set off a heading, as in the following example.

> **Example—List**
> Janine had several things on her shopping list: books, notebook paper, pens, highlight markers, and instant coffee.

Note: A list following a verb such as *is* or *are* does not use a colon because the sentence has not been completed.

> **Example—No Colon**
> Bruce admits that he is lazy, disorganized, and easily distracted.

Note: A list following the expression *such as* also does not use a colon.

> **Example—No Colon**
> Bruce liked all the foods that were bad for him, such as red meat, butter, ice cream, and french fries.

Example—Illustration
Bruce found an activity that suited his diet and personality: eating buttered popcorn while watching his 100-channel remote control TV.

Example—Explanation
Janine knew of only one way to pass her biology exam: studying all night.

Dash

A dash, —, shows a bold change of idea, a contradiction, or an interruption in the flow of a sentence. If overused, dashes lose their emphasis.

Examples
Teresa walked out the door—and out of his life.
Sean pleaded—even begged—for her to return. His absences, his broken promises, his short temper—all were enough to make her resist his pleadings now.

Parentheses

Parentheses, ( ), deemphasize ideas. When a sentence with parentheses is read aloud, the reader's voice usually drops in tone to indicate that what is in parentheses is less important or is simply additional information.

Examples
To get there, follow Route 46 to County Road W (a scenic country road).
John Updike (born 1932) is a contemporary writer of novels and short stories whose book *The Witches of Eastwick* became a popular film.

Italics

Italics are the slanted letters you sometimes see in type that emphasize a word or phrase or indicate the title of a book, movie, play, or other long, full-length work. They are also used to set off foreign language expressions. In typing, italics are represented by underlining the words involved.

Examples
Les Miserables, a musical based on Victor Hugo's novel of the French Revolution, was popular worldwide.
I said *not* to call me after 10 P.M.
In Middle English the *k* in knife was pronounced.

Special Function Marks

Apostrophe

Apostrophes, ', are used in contractions to show that a letter is missing (*can't*) and to show possession (*the shoes of my father* = *my father's shoes*). Using the apostrophe to show possession follows these guidelines:

1. Use an apostrophe after all singular words:

    Mary's car
    Thomas's football
    one week's vacation
    an hour's pay

2. Use an apostrophe after all plural words that don't form the plural with an *s:*

    children's playground

women's work
men's shirts

3. Use an apostrophe after the *s* in plural words that form the plural with an *s*:

two weeks' vacation
families' yards
thieves' loot

Note: The words that often cause problems are those that sound alike.

who's = "who is"

whose = pronoun, already possessive, that means "belonging to whom"

it's = "it is"

its = pronoun, already possessive, that means "belonging to it"

Other pronouns that are already possessive include *my, mine, your, yours, his, her, hers, our, ours, their*, and *theirs*. Since they are already possessive, they don't need an apostrophe.

Hyphen

The hyphen, -, is used at the ends of typed lines to divide a word at a syllable. Hyphens are also used to join two words that may at one time have been separate words (*water-skier*), but you will probably have to check a dictionary because many similar words do not take a hyphen (*hitchhiker*, for example). Hyphens are used in numbers from *twenty-one* to *ninety-nine* and in certain modifiers and phrases, such as *well-known actor, eighteenth-century portrait, holier-than-thou, devil-may-care*.

Quotation Marks

Quotation marks, " ", enclose words written or spoken by another person. Typically, the quotation is introduced by a short statement (*he said, she explained*) followed by a comma or a colon, but the quote can come anywhere in a sentence.

Examples
The customer complained, "I should not be charged for something I did not get!"
"I'll see that it gets straightened out," said the credit manager. "I'm sorry that this happened."
"Well, I'm relieved to know that you agree with me, and I appreciate your help," replied the customer, calming down.

Note that most of the time other punctuation goes inside the quotation marks. An exception: Punctuating a question that is not part of the quotation.

Did the professor say, "Class ends in five minutes"?

Remember that indirect quotations do not use quotation marks.

The reporter said that she would not reveal the identity of her sources.

The direct version would read:

The reporter said, "I will not reveal the identity of my sources."

Quotation marks are also used to enclose titles of short works, such as poems, short stories, essays, and songs:

"Kubla Khan"
"The Pit and the Pendulum"
"Letter from the Birmingham Jail"

"Satisfaction"

Finally, quotation marks sometimes are used to enclose words being defined or being discussed as words:

Many people confuse the words "further" and "farther."

Brackets

Brackets, [   ], are used within a quotation to explain something not in the original quotation.

A comic book collector complained, "The character of The Joker [played in the movie version by Jack Nicholson] was originally a humorous practical joker, not a sadistic villain."

Ellipses

Ellipses (. . .) are used to show something left out of a quoted statement. They are helpful when a writer wants to shorten a lengthy quote but wants readers to know that something has been left out.

Example—Original Quotation (by John F. Kennedy)
"We stand today on the edge of a new frontier the frontier of the 1960s—a frontier of unknown opportunities and perils—a frontier of unfulfilled hopes and threats."

Example—Quotation with Ellipses
"We stand today on the edge of a new frontier . . . a frontier of unknown opportunities and perils. . . ."

EXERCISES: *Other Marks*

EXERCISE 1

Use the appropriate punctuation at the ends of the following sentences and quotations.

1. Some people can't wait to see the next movie blockbuster, while others don't care if they ever see another film

2. Most of the time it wouldn't matter that one person likes movies while another doesn't

3. However, if the two people are married to each other or are good friends, their difference in movie-going may create conflict

4. "I can't wait to see *Batman*" exclaims one partner

5. "How can you want to see such trash" questions the other

Working Collaboratively
Write five sentences with your classmates about your attitudes toward movies. Try to include all three end marks, and remember to use commas or other internal punctuation where needed.

EXERCISE 2

Punctuate the following sentences using colons, dashes, italics, and parentheses where necessary. Place the proper end punctuation as well.

1. Many communities have adopted an increasingly popular solution to their garbage problem recycling waste

2. Plastic bottles, glass jars and bottles, aluminum cans, newspapers are all becoming more economical to recycle.

3. Articles in publications like Scientific American explain new techniques for recycling materials

4. Instead of being a "throwaway society" as one sociologist put it we are becoming a "recycled society"

5. Some people object to sorting cans, bottles, and newspapers it does take more effort than throwing everything together in a Hefty bag

6. To overcome these objections, communities impose fines sometimes up to $500 to enforce their recycling programs

7. Usually though not always such fines convince even reluctant citizens of the need for their cooperation.

Working Collaboratively

Write five related sentences about your feelings about pollution, littering, recycling, or a similar subject. Punctuate correctly.

EXERCISE 3

Put apostrophes in their proper places in contractions or in possessives. Add hyphens to words used together to make one expression.

1. Many peoples study habits may be counter productive.

2. They may think theyre studying, but very little learning is going on because they are being constantly distracted.

3. For example, Jerrys TV is always tuned to a baseball, football, or basketball game, and when he thinks hes studying, hes really sneaking a look at almost every instant replay, especially in down to the wire games.

4. Teresas just as bad, but her distraction is MTV: she just cant keep her eyes off many rock groups videos.

5. Some people dont have a television set on but still get distracted by other family members conversations, the constant ringing of the telephone, or other interruptions.

EXERCISE 4

Use quotation marks to set off directly quoted statements and titles of short works such as speeches, essays, short stories, and songs. Indirect quotations do not need such marks. As indicated, insert brackets to add an explanation to the quote or ellipses to leave something out.

1. In Martin Luther King's speech I Have a Dream, he says, I have a dream that my four little children will one day live in a nation where they will not be judged by the color of their skin but by the content of their character.

2. He also quotes from the lyrics to the song America, ending with the line Let freedom ring.

3. The end of his speech builds on the last line of the song as Dr. King asks America to Let freedom ring from the mighty mountains of New York. Let freedom ring from the heightening Alleghenies of Pennsylvania!

4. Shorten the two sentences in the quote in number 3 by leaving out the first three words of the second sentence and inserting ellipses. Write the shortened version here:_____

5. Enclose in brackets the information *August 28, 1963,* after the word *today* in the following sentence. Dr. King says, I have a dream today.

A6

Being Consistent: Subject–Verb and Pronoun–Antecedent Agreement

Readers prefer to take it easy when they read. They like to glide their eyes over a page and understand what they are reading without having to reread a passage in order to understand the writer's ideas. One way writers help readers is by being consistent in the agreement of subjects and verbs and pronouns and antecedents. If a writer writes: "The coaches plans to meet with all his players soon after the term start." some readers may become confused: Is it one coach? Should it read *The coach's plan is to meet?* What is a *term start*? Not all of us follow standard usage in speech. But in writing, even more confusion may result from failure to be consistent because of the reader's inability to ask questions to clear up any misunderstanding.

Subject–Verb Agreement

Singular subjects have singular verbs, and plural subjects have plural verbs.

Examples
The students meet next week to plan the next campus rock concert.
The last concert was a great success.

Singular and Plural Verbs

Singular verbs end in *s* in the present tense:
She plans.
The train has already gone.
The monkey chatters.

Plural verbs do not end in *s* in the present tense:
They plan.
The trains have already gone.
The monkeys chatter.

Singular Subjects

1. Nouns not ending in *s,* in *es,* or in one of the other plural endings, such as *-ren (children), -en (men, women, oxen),* or that change to a plural form, such as *goose/geese.* Dictionaries list plural forms of each word.

2. Pronouns *I, he, she,* and *it;* forms of *-body* and *-one,* such as *everybody, anyone, nobody,* and *none;* and *each, either,* and *neither.*

3. Collective nouns such as *team* and *group* that act like one unit:
The football team practices each Tuesday afternoon.

Quick Reference Chart
Being Consistent: Subject-Verb Agreement and Pronoun-Antecedent Agreement

Guideline	Examples
Singular subjects have singular verbs.	One of the players has been named MVP.
Words ending in *-body* or *-one* are singular.	Everybody is happy that the MVP is the goalie.
Collective nouns are singular if the group acts as a unit.	The team lines up to congratulate the goalie.
Plural subjects take plural verbs.	The players cheer the goalie.
Subjects joined by *and* are plural.	The reporter and the coach smile at each other.
Collective nouns are plural if the group acts as many individuals.	The team take showers, dress, and walk to their cars.
If subjects are joined by *either-or* or *neither-nor*, the verb agrees with the closer subject.	Either the coach or the players leave the locker room first.
	Either the players or the coach leaves the locker room first.
Some words can be singular or plural, depending on the context.	All of the money for the goalie was worth it.
	All of the owners were happy.
Pronouns agree with the words they replace (their antecedents).	Everybody on the team did his best.
	All of the players did their best.
Pronouns must have clear antecedents.	The coach told the goalie that he had won MVP.

4. Singular subjects connected by *either-or* still remain singular:

   Either the rock band or the football team has scheduled the playing field for this Saturday.

5. Singular subjects followed by a prepositional phrase are still singular:

   George, along with his classmates, walks from the bus stop to the campus.

   Note: This usage sounds awkward to many people. You may want to change the sentence to:

   George and his classmates walk from the bus stop to the campus.

Plural Subjects

1. Nouns ending in *s*, in *es*, or in a plural ending such as *-ren*, *-en*, or that have changed form (*mouse/mice*).

2. Pronouns *we* and *they*, and the words *few*, *many*, and *several*.

3. Two subjects joined by *and* are plural:

   Maria and Kim are part of the field hockey team.

4. Collective nouns such as team and group that act as individuals—not as a unit:

The band play eight instruments among them.

Note: This usage sounds awkward to many people and, while correct, may be avoided by saying:

The members of the band play eight instruments among them.

5. Plural subjects connected by *either-or* remain plural:

Either the students or the teachers are wrong about the date for the game.

Special Situations

1. If a plural subject and a singular subject are connected by *either-or* or *neither-nor*, the verb agrees with the closer subject:

Neither the players nor the coach is aware of the penalty.
Either the crowd noise or the referees' unclear hand signals have caused the confusion.

2. Some pronouns (*all, any, more, most, none, some*) are either singular or plural, depending on the context:

All of the money was lost.
All of the members were late for the meeting.

3. If the subject comes after the verb, it still must agree with the verb. Be sure to find the true subject:

Here are the registration forms.
In the line stretching around the corner are students who still are trying to register.

Pronoun–Antecedent Agreement

Pronouns have to agree with the words they replace:

George eats his breakfast in a hurry.
Suzanna likes to linger over her coffee in the morning.
Both of them leave their houses at the same time each morning.

The word *antecedent* means something that comes before something else. For example, your parents and grandparents are your antecedents. In the case of pronouns, the nouns or pronouns they refer back to are their antecedents. In the preceding sentences, *George, Suzanna,* and *Both* are the antecedents for *his, her,* and *their,* respectively.

The same situations that cause problems for subject–verb agreement cause problems here.

1. Words such as *everybody, anyone,* and *none* are singular, and any other pronoun that replaces one of these words also has to be singular:

Everybody learns lessons in his or her own way.
Each student tries to find his or her own study method.

Note: If you find the use of *his* or *her* awkward, you can make the sentence plural:

All students learn lessons in their own ways.

Don't use only masculine pronouns to refer to words like *everybody* and *anybody*. Such use is sexist and offends many people.

2. Collective nouns used as a unit are singular and take singular pronouns:

The team played its heart out.

Collective nouns used to indicate individuals take plural pronouns:

The committee raised their hands to vote.

Note: Revising the sentence to read as follows may sound better to many people:

The committee members raised their hands to vote.

3. Just as the verb agrees with the closer subject in a sentence with *either-or* or *neither-nor*, so the pronoun agrees with the closer antecedent:

Either the coach or the players need an answer to their question before play can continue.

Clear Pronoun References

Make sure the pronoun has a clear antecedent. For example, don't write the following:

I like accounting, so I want to be one.

(One can't be *accounting*, but one can be *an accountant*.) Rather it should read:

I like the work of accountants, so I want to be one.

Or, don't write:

Students forgot to send in their housing forms, but it didn't matter.

(No word in the sentence is an antecedent of it.) Rather, write:

Students forgot to send in their housing forms, but they received room assignments anyway.

Don't write:

Maria told Kim that she would be late for practice.

(Which one will be late?) Instead, write:

Maria told Kim to hurry, or she would be late for practice.

Or write:

Maria said to Kim, "I will be late for practice."

Don't write:

Students' lives are busy, so they must organize their time wisely.

(*They* refers back to *students'*, but the possessive form is not a proper antecedent.) Rather, it should be:

Because the lives of students are busy, they must organize their time wisely.

EXERCISES: *Subject–Verb Agreement*

The key to being consistent in subject–verb agreement is knowing which words are singular and which words are plural. Several examples have already been mentioned above. The following examples may be even more helpful in completing the subsequent practice exercises.

Singular Subjects

child	goose	no one
someone	dish	everybody
ox	everyone	somebody
belief	the number	anybody
knife	anyone	woman
boy	each	amount of
mouse	none	

Collective nouns such as *team, squad,* and *committee* act as a unit and hence are treated as singular subjects.

Plural Subjects

children	mice	several
women	geese	a number
oxen	dishes	number of
beliefs	few	scissors
knives	many	
boys	both	

Subjects That Can Be Singular or Plural

all	more	sheep
any	most	deer
some	athletics	

EXERCISE 1

Change the following sentences to the plural form if they are singular and to the singular form if they are plural. Be sure to change both the subjects and the verbs.

1. The boy has a paper route.

1. _____

2. _____

2. The geese eat the corn in the field.

3. A dull knife makes a mess of a turkey.

3. _____

4. _____

4. Women have many career opportunities in the 1990s.

5. A child mimics adults' behavior.

5. _____.

Working Collaboratively

In groups, write at least five sentences in the present tense about extracurricular activities for students (plural) on your campus. Then change the sentences to singular form, keeping the verbs in the present tense. Try to use verbs besides *is* and *are*, *has* and *have*.

EXERCISE 2

Write the correct form of the verb in parentheses in the blank provided. Note that all pronouns used in the sentences are correct.

1. Many people simply _____ not realize the power of hurricanes. (do)

2. They _____ to take into account the very low pressure at the eye of the storm and the surges of water driven by hurricane-force winds. (fail)

3. As a result, when a hurricane _____, everyone _____ not left the coastal area, even though an emergency team _____ issued orders to leave. (hit, has)

4. Many of these people _____ to ride out the storm in the comfort of their own homes instead of going to a crowded shelter. (prefer) Some _____ also afraid of looters taking things after the storm _____. (is, pass) An emergency unit in a given area _____ the owners' concerns among themselves before deciding whether to force owners to leave or not. (debate)

5. Many emergency workers _____ that no reason _____ convincing if one's life _____ at stake. (decide, is)

Special Situations

As already noted, some special situations may cause difficulty in being consistent. The subsequent exercises will give you practice.

EXERCISE 3

Fill in the correct verb in each of the following sentences.

1. Herman and Georgio _____ been friends since childhood. (has)

2. Although each of them _____ different things, they _____ each other's preferences. (like, respect)

3. For example, on a fall Saturday that there _____ a baseball game and a college football game, the two friends _____ turns watching each other's favorite sport. (is, take)

4. If Herman _____ to see his favorite horror movie, Georgio will go along even though he _____ science fiction films. (want, favor)

5. There _____ other ways the two friends cooperate. (is)

6. If either Herman's mother or George's sisters _____ help with heavy shopping bags, both friends _____ in to carry the bags. (need, pitch)

7. All of their other friends _____ how well they get along. (admire)

8. No one ever _____ them argue for more than a few minutes. (hear)

9. However, there _____ a new situation that may test their friendship more than any other _____ to this day. (is, has)

10. Both friends _____ fallen in love with the same girl. (has)

Working Collaboratively

Write a story about a friendship between two people, with each member of your group contributing the next sentence as you go around the group. Sentences should be in the present tense, and group members should try to think of varied sentence structures. However, let your imaginations run freely to think of situations these two friends might encounter.

EXERCISES: *Pronoun–Antecedent Agreement*

As mentioned earlier, pronouns must agree with the words to which they refer, their antecedents. The same basic principle applies: singular pronouns agree with singular antecedents, and plural pronouns agree with plural antecedents. And remember:

1. If two words are joined by *and*, they will take a plural verb and hence a plural pronoun.
2. If two words are connected by *either/or*, the verb and the pronoun will agree with the closer subject.
3. Collective nouns may be used to indicate either a unit acting as one thing (singular), which will take a singular pronoun (*its*), or as many individuals (plural), which will take a plural pronoun (*their*).

EXERCISE 4

Fill in the blank with the appropriate form of the pronoun. Circle the antecedent with which the pronoun agrees. Note that the verbs used in the sentences are correct, which may help you choose the correct pronoun.

1. Everybody who has ever shared an office or a room with someone knows that people can be divided into two groups: _____ are either messy or neat.
2. A neat person always puts _____ clothes away in drawers or closets, while the messy person drops _____ clothes where _____ land.
3. The neat one cleans off _____ desk at the end of a day, while the messy one doesn't bother.
4. When a messy person and a neat person share the same space, _____ may get angry at each other.
5. "The Odd Couple," a movie and a television series, was based on this situation. Felix and Oscar are two divorced men who share an apartment. _____ habits are completely different.

Working Collaboratively

Write at least five sentences about someone you know who is either messy or neat. Keep sentences in the present tense. Make all subjects and verbs agree, and check to see that all pronouns agree with their antecedents.

Clear Pronoun References

As already mentioned, pronouns must have clear antecedents in order for the reader to understand what he or she is reading.

EXERCISE 5

In the following sentences, make sure pronouns clearly refer to a specific antecedent. You may need to rewrite sentences.

1. George told Barry that he had to declare a major by next week.
2. George said that he had chosen real estate but wasn't sure he wanted to be one.

3. Barry's choice was uncertain, but he was leaning toward marketing.

4. Many students are unprepared to choose majors because it comes so early in their college careers.

5. They shouldn't require students to choose majors until at least the end of their freshman year.

A7

Developing Clear Sentences: Placement of Modifiers and Parallel Structure

You may have seen or heard of the film *Throw Momma from the Train*, in which two characters actually try to throw one man's domineering mother from a moving train. Did you know, however, that the title may have been based on a Pennsylvania Dutch expression "Throw Momma from the train a kiss"? That expression sounds funny to speakers of Standard English because the word order puts kiss at the end of the sentence instead of closer to the word *throw*, as in "Throw a kiss to Momma from the train." In English, word order is very important; if words are changed around, meaning will change. Consider the following pair of sentences: Only I like Brad. [I am the one person who likes him.] I like only Brad. [Brad is the one person I like.] Changing the word order produces a change in the meaning of the sentence.

What this means for writers and readers is that if readers are going to understand a writer's ideas, the writer will have to make sure the word order clearly conveys the intended message.

Another aspect of keeping sentences clear can also be thought about in terms of an analogy with trains: A train runs on parallel tracks, and if one of the tracks is missing or twisted out of shape, the train may derail. A sentence may have parallel elements (for example, a list) that must be maintained in parallel form to be understood clearly. Consider the following example:

Maggie enjoys swimming in the summer, skiing in the winter, and to go to rock concerts all year around.

The last part of this sentence "derails," that is, it does not follow the reader's expectations that the list will be completed with another *-ing* phrase. If Maggie enjoys three things, then all three should appear as parallel items in a list:

Maggie enjoys swimming in the summer,

skiing in the winter.

and going to rock concerts all year around.

Placement of Modifiers

Put modifiers next to the words they modify.

Modifiers are words that give extra information about nouns and verbs. They may be adjectives (like *red, dull, shiny, large*) that modify nouns; adverbs (like *slowly, often, never, only*) that modify verbs; or prepositional phrases (like *in the treetops, on the hill, over the river and through the woods*) that modify either nouns or verbs; or verb phrases (like *singing in the shower* or *singed from head to foot*) that also modify nouns.

Quick Reference Chart

Developing Clear Sentences: Placement of Modifiers and Parallel Structure

Guideline	Examples
Put modifiers close to the words they modify.	He took only what he needed from the cash box.
Be especially careful with phrases at the beginning of the sentence.	Standing at the front of the room, Marvin broke out in a sweat.
Keep lists, pairs, and other patterns in the same grammatical structure.	Raking leaves, shoveling snow, and mowing grass were all new to the former city-dweller.
Be especially careful with constructions like *not only . . . but also, either . . . or,* and *neither . . . nor.* Remember that whatever structure follows the first term of the pair should also follow the second term of the pair.	Martha was not only an accomplished actress but also a skilled teacher. Either we have to raise taxes to pay for the new city buildings or the city will have to do without them.

Compare the following pairs of sentences.

He almost earned $100 parking cars last weekend.
He earned almost $100 parking cars last weekend.

Note that the first version sounds like he missed out on the money entirely!

Don't write:

The police officer in the parking lot searched for the car keys.

(unless you mean to indicate where the police officer was stationed). Rather, write:

The police officer searched in the parking lot for the car keys.

Don't write:

Although singed from head to foot, we saw our cat escape from the pile of burning leaves.

(Who is singed?) Write instead:

Although singed from head to foot, our cat escaped from the pile of burning leaves.

Parallel Structure

Use the same grammatical forms in lists, pairs, and other sentence patterns.

Example (three verbs all in past tense)
The burglar broke the window, reached in, and opened the door.

Example (two nouns as items)
The thief took not only the stereo but also the CDs.

Example (three prepositional phrases)
A government of the people, by the people, and for the people must not perish from the Earth.

Example (three verb phrases)
Paula wanted three things out of life: to have a worthwhile job, to have a warm family life, and to contribute to her community.

EXERCISES: *Placement of Modifiers*

As you have seen, words or phrases generally modify the parts of the sentence they are next to. We have to use the word *generally* because adverbs can sometimes be moved around in a sentence without confusion. For example, the sentence "The injured player moved slowly off the field" can also be written "Slowly, the injured player moved off the field" or even "The injured player moved off the field slowly." Where a writer puts the word *slowly* will depend on the emphasis he or she wants to give the word. However, many modifiers can't be moved so easily without creating confusion, or even humor.

EXERCISE 1

Read each of the following sentences and answer the questions and follow the instructions after each.

1. Opening the door, the rain-soaked carpet was ruined. Who opened the door? Put a person's name after the phrase "Opening the door" and revise the sentence: Opening the door, _____

2. He died almost ten times during the operation. Does this mean he died nine times? _____
   Place *almost* so the sentence means that he came close to dying ten times: _____

3. Frank bought a car from a used car salesman with a defective carburetor. Does the salesman have a defective carburetor? Revise the sentence: _____ _____

4. Swinging through the trees, the scientists admired the agile monkeys. Who was swinging through the trees? Reposition that phrase so as to modify those that probably were swinging: _____ _____

5. Having woven a rope made of bedsheets, the escape was going according to plan. Who made the rope out of bedsheets? After the word *bedsheets*, begin the main sentence with *the prisoners* and revise the sentence: Having woven a rope out of bedsheets, the prisoners _____

As you can see in Exercise 1, sometimes a modifier is misplaced and easily can be shifted to another position in the sentence to correct the sentence. At other times, however, a modifier may not have anything in the sentence to modify (as in #1 and #5) and the whole sentence must be revised. Such modifiers are called *dangling modifiers* because they are kind of left dangling without any word to modify. They frequently occur when a writer begins the sentence with a phrase that shows some human action (*opening a door, weaving a rope, strolling on a beach, climbing a hill*) and then doesn't supply the person doing the action as the subject of the sentence. Because people have more trouble with these constructions than with some others, the following exercise provides additional practice.

EXERCISE 2

Complete the following sentences, being careful to supply a subject that fits the action of the opening verb phrase.

1. Strolling on the beach,

2. Having studied carefully for my exams,

3. Arriving at the train station a bit late,

4. Confused and anxious,

5. After falling asleep while watching a movie,

Working Collaboratively

In a small group, write about an incident that uses the following modifiers. In making up sentences, you may use other modifiers as well.

in the dark alley

Hearing footsteps behind him (or her)

in the flash of a car's headlights

almost

only

Darting quickly from the sidewalk

a reddish-haired

EXERCISES: *Parallel Structure*

Most of the time, the key to using clear parallel structure is simply becoming aware of sentence patterns, such as lists, that readers expect to be parallel in form. When writers are writing a draft, sometimes they will begin a list in one pattern and end with a different pattern, as in the following example:

Pete couldn't decide whether to play soccer, to go out for cross country, or if he should join the swimming team. (Correction: or to join the swimming team.)

When writers revise, they may notice the pattern change and correct it. There are some patterns, however, that are easily overlooked when revising. See the following examples and the subsequent exercises.

Parallel Pairs

If you use any of the following pairs, whatever form follows the first word in the pair also must follow the second word:

not only	neither	or
both	but also	nor
either	and	

Examples

Steve needed not only the time to assemble the new bookcase but also the skill to put it together.
He looked at both the package diagram and the instruction manual, to no avail.
He either would have to admit defeat or pretend to know what he was doing.
Neither his ego nor his checkbook would let him pay the store for putting the bookcase together.

EXERCISE 3

Fill in the blanks of the following sentences, keeping forms parallel.

1. Mark asked his friend not only to _____ but also _____

   _____.

2. Kevin decided to accept either _____ or _____

   _____ but not both.

3. Leslie found neither _____ nor _____
_____ that she had been looking for.

4. The college offers not only _____ but also _____
_____ to needy students.

5. Bret discovered that he could neither _____ nor _____
_____ without feeling great pain.

EXERCISE 4

In each of the following word groups, one of the items is not parallel with the others. Correct the form of the item so that all are parallel.

1. short hours,
   high pay, and
   benefits that are generous

2. damming up streams, and
   siphoned water off to irrigate crops

3. both creative and having a sense of independence

4. singing,
   songwriter, and
   playing a guitar

5. pay any price,
   bear any burden, and
   fighting off foes that may exist

Working Collaboratively

In pairs or small groups, write about some choices you have had to make. Use such constructions as *either . . . or, neither . . . nor, both . . . and,* and *not only . . . but also.* Check your sentences for clear parallel structure.

A8

Revising for Economy, Emphasis, and Tone

Another way that writers can meet the needs of readers is to revise early drafts so as to improve the economy, emphasis, and tone of their sentences. You can think of economy in terms of using money wisely, but you can think of it also as using words wisely.

Put yourself in your reader's place, reading a ten-page term paper or business report. If the sentences are overly long and use too many words to get across the ideas, the reader will get tired of reading and may not pay as much attention to the content as you would like. For example, how much patience would you have with a paper in which all the sentences read like the following?

It is the belief and firm conviction of all mental health professionals that treatment of chronically ill male and female patients has declined due to lack of sufficient physical facilities and competent personnel.

Wouldn't you rather read this?

> Mental health professionals believe that treatment of chronically ill patients has declined due to lack of hospital beds and well-trained staff.

Writing your ideas with the right amount of emphasis also contributes to increased reader understanding. Many writers don't realize that putting important information at the beginning or end of a sentence draws more reader attention than if the idea is buried in the middle. Compare, for example, the following sentences:

> In my opinion, and I'm sure others agree, there are employees working more than twenty hours per week who should get a raise and increased benefits to be effective at the next pay period.
>
> Employees working more than twenty hours per week should immediately, in my opinion, get a raise and increased benefits.

As you can see, reorganizing ideas and reducing wordiness contribute to improving emphasis.

Finally, if anyone has ever said to you, "I don't like your tone of voice," you know that sometimes it's not what you say but the way you say it that is important. The words you choose may be formal (for example, "motor vehicles") or informal ("cars"), depending on your audience and purpose in writing. Actually, there are several levels of usage from formal to nonstandard that must be adjusted to fit the audience for a particular piece of writing.

Revising for Economy

1. Avoid redundancy (repeating what was just said in different words).

Not:	**But:**
each and everyone of you	each
final outcome	outcome
round in shape	round

2. Use active, not passive, voice—it saves words. Active sentences have the doer of the action as the subject of the sentence. Not:

> The man was hit by the red Ford Mustang. (nine words)

But

> The red Ford Mustang hit the man. (seven words—same idea)

3. Convert nouns ending in *-ing* or *-ion* or *-ment* or another suffix into the verb forms they came from. Not:

> The dean made a decision.

But

> The dean decided.

Not

> The student officers were in a meeting.

But

> The student officers met.

Note that the second version of these pairs is shorter and that the verbs *decided* and *met* do the work of both the noun and verb they replace—that's economy!

4. Begin with your main idea, not with a weak beginning such as *it is* or *there are*. Not:

> It is the faculty's decision to add a study day before exams.

Quick Reference Chart

Revising for Economy, Emphasis, and Tone

Guideline	Examples
Reduce wordiness by . . .	
1. Eliminating redundancies.	*Not:* It is each and every student's right
2. Using active not passive verbs.	to have received expert instruction.
3. Converting some nouns into verbs.	*But:* Students deserve expert teaching.
4. Eliminate weak beginnings.	
Give ideas proper emphasis by . . .	
1. Placing important thoughts at the beginning or end of a sentence.	*Not:* If you want to know what I think, we should hire professors who value teaching at least as high as something else.
	But: We should hire professors, in my opinion, who put teaching first.
2. Increasing grammatical rank of important ideas and decreasing grammatical rank of less important ideas.	
Use a level of usage appropriate to the writer's audience and purpose:	
Formal (academic and business writing)	I would like to borrow money for my college tuition.
Informal or colloquial (everyday use among strangers)	Could you lend me money for college?
Slang (among friends)	Can you spare some dough for the U?
Regional or dialectal (among groups that share the language)	I be needin' some 5's and 10's for bookin' it.
Nonstandard (use only when standard use is out of place)	Ain't you got money I can get off you for college?

But
The faculty decided to add a study day before exams.

Not
There are many reasons for why people vote.

But
People vote for many reasons.

Revising for Emphasis

1. Put an important idea at the end of the sentence (most important) or at the beginning of the sentence (next most important). The middle gets the least attention from a reader. Compare these versions. In which sentence does the drunk driving receive greater emphasis?

   The prominent businessman convicted of drunk driving lost his driver's license.
   Convicted of drunk driving, the prominent businessman lost his license.

Note too that besides reducing wordiness, beginning a sentence with the main idea instead of with *it is* or *there are* increases an idea's emphasis.

2. Give an important idea a high grammatical rank and a less important idea a lower grammatical rank.

Grammatical Rank from High to Low

Sentence:	We were happy to meet Pam Courtney at the airport. She is my cousin.
Independent clause:	We were happy to meet Pam Courtney at the airport, for she is my cousin.
Dependent clause:	We were happy to meet Pam Courtney, who is my cousin, at the airport.
Phrase:	We were happy to meet Pam Courtney, my cousin, at the airport.
Word:	We were happy to meet cousin Pam Courtney at the airport.

Notice that the information about Pam's being my cousin decreases in emphasis as the grammatical rank decreases. Notice also that the number of words needed to get across the information declines, thereby reducing wordiness.

Revising for Tone

1. Use the level of usage appropriate for your audience. A formal report, a letter to the editor of a newspaper, and a letter to a friend may each require different word choices.

2. Be sensitive to the connotations of words, that is, the shades of meaning or emotional response words create. Compare, for example, "Please be quiet" with "Shut your trap!"

3. Be aware that some usages may create a sexist tone. Avoid using the masculine forms when you mean all people, as in "Everyone should exercise his vote in this election" or "All men yearn for freedom from tyranny." Recast sentences to include women, or choose words that apply to both sexes: "Everyone should exercise his or her vote in this election," or "All people should be sure to exercise their right to vote in this election."

EXERCISES: *Revising for Economy*

EXERCISE 1

In the following exercise, substitute shorter expressions for the redundant or wordy ones.

1. in this day and age _____

2. at this point in time _____

3. each and every person _____

Guide to Levels of Usage

Level	Description	Example
Formal	Considered Standard English usage and required in some academic and business writing—formal usage means using no contractions (*won't* for *will not*) or informal or colloquial words or phrases. Jargon, or specialized words used by people in certain occupations or other special situations, may also appear in formal writing. Note that jargon may cause confusion for a reader who doesn't know the terms. Be certain your audience is familiar with any such words, or define them as you use them.	The police officers would not allow the alleged perpetrator to call his spouse, only his attorney.
Informal or colloquial	Also considered Standard English usage and employed in the media, in public conversation, and in much writing, this level of usage is marked by contractions and a mix of formal and informal words. Colloquial words include such expressions as "I don't get it" for "I do not understand." Dictionaries usually list "inf." or "colloq." next to a word if it is not formal.	The police wouldn't let the suspect call his wife, only his lawyer.
Slang	Words that are considered outside standard usage because they are used by a small group not empowered by a society—such as criminals, teenagers, minority groups, and working-class people. Many times, words begin as slang but eventually become considered merely informal if enough people in positions of influence use them. For example, *cop*, meaning "police officer," is still considered slang by most dictionaries, but some consider it informal and more may accept it as standard usage as time goes on. When in doubt, check a word's usage in a dictionary. Slang is generally unacceptable in academic or business writing.	The cop wouldn't let the wise guy call his old lady, only his ambu-lance-chaser.
Regional or dialectal	Regions in the United States have their own words and phrases that other regions may not understand. For example, in the Pittsburgh area someone might say that her house "needs cleaned." In Indiana, a woman might say she needs to "red up" her house (*to ready it* means "to clean it"). Using words or grammatical structures that are common only to a region is appropriate if the reader is from the region and the purpose of the writing is informal. However, regional expressions are generally not appropriate in academic and business writing. Dialects are common in the United States. Many times, we notice a dialect only in the way someone pronounces words, as in "pahk" for "park" in Boston. Pronunciation differences won't be evident in writing (unless they somehow produce misspellings). Sometimes, however, dialects use different grammatical forms that are evident in writing. If someone writes, "I became too soon hungry," readers outside a group of Pennsylvania Dutch speakers will notice the nonstandard use. Similarly, if someone writes, "I be hungry" instead of the standard "I am hungry," readers will notice the dialectal usage. Just as with region-alisms, dialectal expressions are appropriate in speech among members of the dialect group but are not appropriate in most academic or business writing.	
Nonstandard	This label is usually applied to an ungrammatical use of language, such as "ain't" or "He don't know nothin'." Writers should avoid using nonstandard words and structures.	

4. in the city of Chicago _____

5. pink in color _____

EXERCISE 2

Edit the following paragraph to eliminate redundant or wordy expressions.

First Job

If I think back in time to when I was in high school, I remember applying for my one and only job up to that time. I was nervous and anxious as I prepared for the interview, but since I had the basic and required credentials for the lifeguard job, my lifesaving certificate, I hoped and prayed that the pool director would hire me. I felt ready and able to handle any and all emergency situations at the pool. Trying to act more confident and assured than I really felt, I met the pool director, who asked me about my swimming and lifesaving experience. Once I began to answer questions, my nervousness and anxiety went away. I tried to give totally accurate and entirely complete answers. Soon the interview was over, and to my great relief and joy, I heard the pool director ask me when I could start to work.

Another way to streamline your sentences is to use active, rather than passive, verb forms. As was shown earlier, active sentences take fewer words, and the subject is doing the action of the verb, so the sentences seem more vigorous.

To make sentences active, make the subject of the sentence the doer of the action. Note that there are times when you don't know who did the action ("The store owner was held up at knife point") or when the doer of the action is not the point of the sentence ("The car was repainted after the accident"). At such times, passive verb forms are necessary. The following exercise will give you practice in noticing and changing passive verbs into active ones.

EXERCISE 3

Change each of the following sentences from passive to active forms. Look for the doer of the action in the phrase after the verb and move it to become the subject of the sentence.

1. The leaves were raked by the neighbors.

2. However, the leaves were soon blown by the wind back onto the neighbors' lawns.

3. Scenes of pine trees, or even cactus and palm trees, were pictured by the neighbors in their frustration.

4. These leaf-rakers were envied, however, by some city-dwellers who had few trees to enjoy.

5. On the other hand, freedom from lawn chores was appreciated by others who live in treeless areas.

A second way to let verbs help you streamline your sentences is to convert some nouns into verbs. Notice that certain nouns, like *development, argument, interference,* and *reliance,* are really verb forms with a suffix added to make them nouns. Notice, too, that when you use such words, you may be adding words to your sentences. Compare the following two sentences:

The lawyer and his client got into a heated argument.
The lawyer and his client argued heatedly.

If your writing seems wordy, check sentences for nouns ending in *-ment, -ance, -ence, -ion*, or *-tion*. Try to convert them to their verb forms, and rewrite the sentence. The following exercise will give you practice.

EXERCISE 4

Streamline the following sentences by converting nouns ending in *-ment, -tion, -ance*, and the like into verbs and revising the sentence.

1. The city engineer made an argument for a new water treatment plant.
2. The city could no longer maintain its reliance on the present plant.
3. The old plant makes treatment of water inefficient, resulting in shortages.
4. Furthermore, the present plant makes the distribution of water uneven throughout the city, which could be the causation of low-pressure areas and fire safety problems.
5. The development of a new plant will be the solution for these problems.

Finally, you can reduce wordiness by eliminating weak beginnings from sentences. Starting a sentence with "It is" or "There are" adds two extra words and delays the main idea to the middle of the sentence (a weak position). Writers often start sentences in this way in a draft because they don't yet know what to say, so they begin weakly just to begin. During the revision process, you can spot such sentences and make them less wordy and more emphatic.

EXERCISE 5

Revise the following sentences by omitting the "It is" and "There are" beginnings. You will need to supply another main verb for the sentence.

1. There are many reasons why people commute to colleges near their homes.
2. It is reasonable to say that they save money by living at home.
3. There are also those that work full-time and go to school at night.
4. It is possible that some may like the privacy of their own homes, and don't wish to share a dorm room with a stranger.
5. For whatever reasons, there are increasing numbers of student commuters.

EXERCISES: *Revising for Emphasis*

An idea receives the greatest emphasis at the end or beginning of a sentence, so writers don't want to clutter up those positions with extra words. As you have seen, eliminating weak beginnings helps. Be aware, too, of too many prepositional phrases or transitional expressions that can clutter up the end or beginning of a sentence. Revise sentences so the main content receives the emphasis.

EXERCISE 6

Revise the following sentences by changing the position of the italicized words to either the beginning or the end of the sentence. Eliminate weak beginnings and extra phrases.

1. There is no doubt in anyone's mind that *a major earthquake will occur in California* in the next 30 years.

2. Although new buildings have been successfully "quake-proofed," *many older buildings and highways may collapse in a quake that registers above 7 on the Richter scale* according to geologists who have studied matters of this kind.

3. There is another problem with building construction, which is the fact that *some houses and office buildings have been built on landfill* near the ocean or on the sides of mountains instead of solid rock, which can better withstand a quake.

4. For example, during the 1989 San Francisco earthquake, *the Marina district suffered more damage than other residential areas* because houses there were built on unstable landfill.

5. In contrast to the Marina district situation, *other buildings in the city built on solid rock foundations had much less damage* as a rule, which, of course, is subject to occasional exceptions.

Working Collaboratively

In pairs or small groups, combine the following sentences into a paragraph that emphasizes the main points and deemphasizes or eliminates lesser ideas.

Earthquake Preparation

1. There was an earthquake in San Francisco.

2. It was in 1989.

3. It taught many lessons.

4. One lesson was to have bottled water, canned food, and batteries.

5. Every citizen learned this lesson.

6. City officials learned another lesson.

7. This lesson was to have more fire and rescue equipment.

8. Some of the equipment should be cranes and high ladders.

9. This equipment could rescue people from highways and tall buildings.

10. Engineers learned other lessons.

11. One was building shock absorbers into buildings and highways.

12. Some buildings with rollers or flexible hinges swayed.

13. But they did not break.

14. Another lesson was to seek solid foundations for buildings.

15. Nothing can prevent an earthquake.

16. Preparation can lessen its effects.

17. Preparation may be expensive.

18. Loss of lives and property is expensive too.

EXERCISES: *Revising for Tone*

As you have learned, there are five levels of usage: formal, informal or colloquial, slang, regional or dialectal, and nonstandard. Effective writers use the level of usage suited to their audience and their purpose. The football coach doesn't write a recruiting letter to a prospect in the same language that he or she would use in a request for funds from the president of the college. Being able to adapt your language to different situations will enable you to communicate with a wide variety of people in many different circumstances. In contrast, if you can use only nonstandard, dialectal or regional expressions, or slang, you will be at a disadvantage in more formal writing situations.

EXERCISE 7

Change the following expressions into formal usage. Check your dictionary if needed.

1. The cops busted the crack dealer.
2. The movie was awesome.
3. George tried to get money off his brother.
4. Margie should of went home, instead of hangin' on the corner.
5. The people be clappin' their hands while the band be playin'.

A9

Using Standard English Forms

In A8 you learned about levels of usage and the need to adjust your level of usage to your audience. As explained, formal usage is required most frequently in academic and business writing situations. Knowledge of Standard English forms will enable you to write at the appropriate level of usage. Many of these forms may be familiar to you, but there may be some forms not common in speech that you have to learn to use in writing. For example, the distinction between *who* and *whom* is one almost everybody needs to practice because it is still required in formal writing situations but is almost universally ignored in speech. Since language use is dynamic and ever-changing, at some point the *who-whom* distinction may disappear. But until it does, people needing to communicate informal situations still must know it.

While learning Standard English forms depends more on memory of those forms than on learning rules, there are some basic principles. Lists of the most troublesome forms of Standard English verbs, adjectives, adverbs, and pronoun cases follow.

Standard Verb Forms

All verb forms are derived from the three principal parts of the verb: the present tense, the past tense, and the past participle. The *present* tense is the base form of the verb, often written as an infinitive (*to* + verb, as in *to go, to walk, to swim*). The *past* tense shows action or state of being that has already happened; it frequently ends in *-ed* (for example, *walked*). However, there are many verbs, called *irregular* verbs, that do not end in *-ed*, and their forms must be memorized or checked in a dictionary. The past participle is the form used to make other, more complicated tenses (for example, *has walked, will have walked, had walked*) and always uses a helping verb (auxiliary) with it.

Quick Reference Chart
Using Standard English Forms

1. Learn the principal parts of irregular verbs, paying particular attention to commonly confused verbs like *lie/lay*, *sit/set*, and *rise/raise*, and the forms of the verb *to be*.

2. Use adjective forms to describe nouns:

    The quiet man ate his small meal.

    Use adverb forms to describe verbs, adjectives, and other adverbs. Many adverbs end in *-ly*:

    He is really tired.

3. Since linking verbs and sense verbs act as equal signs, connecting the subject of the sentence to the adjective that follows the verb, use the adjective form:

    Marvin was cold.

    She felt guilty.

4. Use a subject pronoun as the subject of a sentence or following a linking verb:

    She is the doctor.

    It is he who called.

5. Use an object pronoun to receive the action of the verb:

    The car hit him.

    Whom did the car hit?

6. When two pronouns or a noun and pronoun are used together, test the pronoun use by using each word separately:

    Mary and she are going to the play on Friday.

    It occurred to us students that the term was nearing the end.

7. When a pronoun is used at the end of a comparison, finish the comparison to determine the form:

    Linda swims faster than she (does).

Example (present)
I take my car for regular oil changes.

Example (past)
I took my car to the service station yesterday.

Example (present perfect—action that happened more than once in the past)
I have taken my car to have the oil changed every six months.

Example (past perfect—action that happened before some other past action)
I had taken my car to be serviced just before it broke down.

There are many other verb tenses, but all are formed from the three principal parts just illustrated.

Standard Adjective and Adverb Forms

Adjectives are used to describe nouns and pronouns, as in:

the red pony   the quiet room   silly me

Adverbs describe verbs; they also describe adjectives and other adverbs:

Describing Verbs	Describing Adjectives	Describing Other Adverbs
ran *quickly*	*really* quiet room	ran *quite* quickly
went *soon*	*spotlessly* clean window	went *very* soon

Problems with standard adjective and adverb forms usually occur in two situations:

1. People may use the adjective form when they should use the adverb form:

Not:	But:
He ran quick.	He ran quickly.
The construction job paid good.	The construction job paid well.
The child asked a question in a real quiet voice.	The child asked a question in a really quiet voice.

2. After a linking verb, an adjective form is usually needed to describe the subject:

The car's paint job was bad.

Some verbs referring to the senses (*feel, look, hear, taste*) and certain others (*grow, become, seem*) may act as linking verbs and need adjective forms after them:

The patient looked bad to me.

(*Bad* describes *patient*.)

The marathon runner grew faint.

(*Faint* describes *runner*.)

The banquet food tasted good to me.

(*Good* describes *food*.)

The athlete felt good about the performance.

(*Good* describes *athlete*.)

Exception: When *well* refers to *health*, it may be used after a linking verb:

How is your father feeling? He is well, thank you.
After a few days' rest, the students felt well again.

Standard Pronoun Cases

In English, a noun keeps the same form whether it is a subject or an object:

The train was on time.
Don't miss the train.

Pronouns, however, have three distinct forms, called *cases*:

Subject case	I	you	he	she	it	we	they	who
Possessive case	my	your	his	her	its	our	their	whose
	mine	yours		hers		ours	theirs	
Object case	me	you	him	her	it	us	them	whom

So, for example, in Standard English you would use the following forms:

They were late. (subject)
Did you miss *them*? (object)
Who saw the accident? (subject)
To *whom* did you report the accident? (object)
This is *she*. (predicate noun—same case as subject)

Note that *whom* has the same ending as *him* and *them*. This similarity may help you choose the correct case—try substituting *him* or *them* in normal sentence order to see whether *who* or *whom* is the correct form.

Did you report the accident to them?

EXERCISES: *Standard Verb Forms of Troublesome Verbs*

If you have been around young children, you may have heard them say, "She throwed the ball." They were applying to irregular verbs what they had learned about *-ed* endings from listening to others speak. Of course, you know that *throw* doesn't behave like the regular verbs and the the Standard form is *threw*. Children learn the difference if the people around them speak Standard English. However, if they are not exposed to Standard English, they may continue to use other verb forms.

The following table gives you the three principal parts of many troublesome verbs. It may help you to think of the three as used in a sentence with a subject such as *I*. In some cases, there may be more than one accepted form. Check your dictionary for verbs not in this table.

Principal Parts of Some Troublesome Verbs

Present ("I . . .")	Past ("I . . .")	Past Participle ("I have . . .")
agree	agreed	agreed
am (he is, we are)	was (we were)	been (he has been)
arise	arose	arisen
become	became	become
begin	began	begun
bite	bit	bitten, bit
blow	blew	blown
break	broke	broken
bring	brought	brought
burst	burst	burst
buy	bought	bought
catch	caught	caught
choose	chose	chosen
come	came	come
dive	dived, dove	dived, dove
do	did	done
draw	drew	drawn
dream	dreamed, dreamt	dreamed, dreamt

Present	Past	Past Participle
drink	drank	drunk
drive	drove	driven
eat	ate	eaten
fall	fell	fallen
find	found	found
fly	flew	flown
forget	forgot	forgotten
freeze	froze	frozen
get	got	got, gotten
give	gave	given
go	went	gone
grow	grew	grown
hang (people)	hanged	hanged
hang (objects)	hung	hung
know	knew	known
lay (to place)	laid	laid
lie (to recline)	lay	lain
pay	paid	paid
prove	proved	proved, proven
ring	rang, rung	rung
rise (to go up)*	rose	risen
run	ran	run
say	said	said
see	saw	seen
set (to place)	set	set
shake	shook	shaken
shrink	shrank, shrunk	shrunk, shrunken
sing	sang, sung	sung
sit (in a chair)	sat	sat
speak	spoke	spoken
steal	stole	stolen
sting	stung	stung
swear	swore	sworn
swim	swam	swum
take	took	taken
tear	tore	tore
throw	threw	thrown
wear	wore	worn

Present	Past	Past Participle
write	wrote	written

*Note that *raise* (to lift up) is a regular verb.

EXERCISE 1

The following groups of sentences will give you practice with *lie/lay*, *sit/set*, *rise/raise*, and forms of the verb *to be*.

1. lie/lay

   a. The hens at Farmer Brown's _____ more eggs after Mr. Brown piped in music to the hen house.

   b. Jeremy couldn't remember where he _____ down his car keys.

   c. The new mother wearily _____ down for a nap after feeding her newborn daughter.

   d. Before being arrested, the protesters had _____ on the sidewalk of the government building.

2. *sit/set*

   a. Please _____ the tables for a party of fifty guests.

   b. _____ at the head table will be the mayor and the governor.

   c. If you can _____ still long enough, you will be rewarded with dessert.

   d. Last evening, the badly injured man _____ patiently waiting for treatment in the emergency room.

3. *rise/raise*

   a. The caretaker _____ the flag at school each morning.

   b. The people had to be evacuated when the flood waters _____.

   c. The professor has _____ to a position of national importance.

   d. Some people are said to _____ themselves by their own bootstraps.

4. *am, is, are, was, were, has been, have been*

   a. Monsters _____ commonly feared by children.

   b. One such monster _____ the one hiding in the closet or under the bed.

   c. If we would admit it, most of us _____ have been _____ frightened by thoughts of such creatures.

   d. However, after being reassured that there _____ no monsters in the room, we _____ able to go to sleep.

EXERCISES: *Standard Adjective and Adverb Forms*

As explained, adjectives describe only nouns and pronouns, whereas adverbs describe verbs, adjectives, and other adverbs. It may help to think of these words as occupying a particular place in a sentence. Look at the following sentences to see the usual places that adjectives and adverbs appear.

       (adj.)   *(adv.)*

1. The _____ car crashed _____ into the wall.

2. The driver was taken ___*(adv.)*___ to the hospital with

___*(adv.)*___ ___*(adj.)*___ injuries.

3. The car was a ___*(adj.)*___ wreck.

4. ; ___*(adv.)*___ the driver survived.

To test these places, try substituting single words in the blanks. You will most likely recognize the words as adjectives or adverbs.

When a word has both an adjective and an adverb form, such as *real* and *really, frequent* and *frequently,* and *serious* and *seriously,* then the *-ly* ending indicates the adverb form. Sometimes the forms change completely, as in the case of *good* (adjective) and *well* (adverb).

Remember that after a linking verb (*is, am, are, was, were, has been, have been*) and after sense verbs, such as *see, look, smell, taste, feel,* the adjective form is probably needed to describe the subject. You may want to think of a linking verb as an equal sign with one side equal to the other.

Joan is small.   Joan = small

The perfume smells strong.   perfume = strong

This sandwich tastes good.   sandwich = good

The major exception to this rule (as previously mentioned) when the word *well* means "in good health," and it may be used after a linking verb.

Example
I was sick, but I feel well now.

Sometimes you will have to use your judgment to decide which form is correct:

Dressed in a suit for his interview, George looked good.

(*Good* is an adjective describing *George.*)

Before he left, George looked carefully for his notebook.

(*Carefully* is an adverb describing *looked.*)

After other kinds of verbs, use the adverb form to describe how something was done (*well, completely*), when it was done (*soon, immediately*), or how much (*very, really*).

EXERCISE 2

Fill in the blank with the correct word of the pair of words in parentheses.

1. Tina _____ (real, really) did _____ (good, well) on her first day in the job.
2. She dressed _____ (conservative, conservatively) in a navy blue suit, which she thought would show that she wanted to be taken _____ (serious, seriously).
3. Her boss greeted her _____ (warm, warmly) and told her that he _____ (sure, surely) needed her help.

4. Even before lunch, Tina had analyzed a problem _____ (correct, correctly) that had stumped others for a _____ (real, really) long time.

5. She felt _____ (good, well) about her ability to do the job.

EXERCISES: *Standard Pronoun Cases*

The forms of the personal pronouns as shown at the beginning of the chapter are divided into subject, object, and possessive forms. There are really just a few situations that confuse many people.

1. Sometimes when two pronouns or a noun and pronoun are together, people have trouble with the correct form:

   Joe and (*I, me*) left for school early.
   We met Marty and (*she, her*) on the way.
   Joe gave Marty and (*she, her*) a smile and said, "(*We, Us*) early birds may not get the worm, but we will get seats on the bus!"

Although you could analyze the sentence to determine whether the word needed is a subject or an object, an easier way is to try the word alone. The correct form is often then apparent:

Correct	Incorrect
I left for school early.	Me left for school early.
We met her on the way.	We met she on the way.
Joe gave her a smile.	Joe gave she a smile.
We may not get the worm.	Us may not get the worm.

2. If a sentence expresses a comparison, it may end with a pronoun, as in:

   She is shorter than (*I, me*).

   To help decide what the correct form of the pronoun should be, finish the comparison:

   She is shorter than I am.

3. Linking verbs act as equal signs, as was explained earlier. That means that a pronoun after a linking verb should be in the subject form, since it equals the subject:

   This is she.   It is I.

   Since many people do not use this construction when they talk, they need to pay attention to the need for this form in formal writing situations.

4. The use of *who* and *whom* is another example of a distinction being made in formal writing that is not frequently made in speech. To repeat: *Who* is a subject form, and *whom* (like *him* and *them*) is an object form. Because sentences using these words frequently either are questions or contain dependent clauses, some special techniques help choose the correct form:

   a. Put reverse-order sentences in normal order:

   (*Who, Whom*) do you trust?   becomes   You do trust (*who, whom*)?

   You should choose *whom* because it is an object, like *them.*

b. If the *who/whom* choice is in a dependent clause, look at the usage in that clause only:

Give the ball to (*whoever, whomever* can make the first down).

Here, the choice is *whoever,* because it is the subject of *can make.*

EXERCISE 3

Circle the correct form of the pronoun.

1. Felicia and (she, her) have the same math instructor.
2. My father gave my sisters and (I, me) our allowance on Saturday. They were older and got more money than (I, me).
3. Do you know anyone (who, whom) collects baseball cards?
4. You should write to (whoever, whomever) is in charge of billing for the insurance company to straighten out your bill.
5. To (who, whom) should I speak?
6. My friends bought lunch for (she, her) and (I, me) when we were broke. They were nice to save (we, us) students from starving to death before our paychecks came.
7. May I speak to Jerry, please? This is (he, him).
8. The prosecutor turned to the jury and asked, "Do you wonder about (who, whom) I am speaking? I am talking about the defendant."

A10

Using Correct Spelling

Some people think that being a good or bad speller is the essence of being a good or bad writer. I have heard people say, "I am a terrible writer; I can't spell." By now, you should be aware that writing involves putting ideas into words in ways meaningful to a reader and that spelling is only a small part of editing a written manuscript. In fact, with today's spelling checkers on word processing programs, bad spellers are getting more help than ever before.

It may interest you to know that one's ability to spell may be innate—experts believe that a person's ability to spell ranges from perfect recall of the printed word (the people with so-called photographic memories) to almost no recall of what a word looks like in print (people who are severely dyslexic). Most of us fall somewhere along this continuum, with good, mediocre, and bad spellers sprinkled among us.

Even if spelling is related to visual recall ability, you can do some things to help you spell better. One suggestion is to keep a list of the *correct* spelling of words you have misspelled and to look at it frequently to help your visual-recall memory. Add to the list every time you get a paper returned. Sometimes say and spell the words on your list out loud so that your brain pathways receive the sound of the spelling of the words. This process also helps your memory. Another suggestion is to learn some of the rules that govern English spelling that will help with some of the most frequent errors. Finally, learn the words that sound the same or nearly the same but are spelled differently, so that they are not a frequent source of error.

Quick Reference Chart
Selected Rules of English Spelling

1. *i* before *e* except after *c* or when sounded like *a* as in *neighbor* and *weigh:* believe, ceiling, neighbor, piece, perceive, weigh, relief, deceive, sleigh.

   Exceptions: their, either, neither, leisure, seize, weird, financier, species

2. If a word ends in silent *e* and you add a suffix beginning with a vowel (*a, e, i, o, u, y*), then drop the *e:* care + ing = caring, fame + ous = famous, noise + y = noisy. If a word ends in silent *e* and you add a suffix beginning with a consonant (anything but *a, e, i, o, u, y*), then keep the *e:* hope + less = hopeless, lone + ly = lonely, force + ful = forceful, state + ment = statement.

   Exceptions: Words ending in *-ce* or *-ge* keep the *e* if you add *-able* or *-ous:* noticeable, courageous, advantageous. *Also,* truly, awful, dyeing, ninth.

3. Double the last letter of a word ending in a vowel-consonant combination (*vc*) when you add a suffix that starts with a vowel:

   drag + ed = dragged   equip + ing = equipping

   But

   equip + ment = equipment

   (suffix begins with consonant)

   Exceptions: If the word is accented on the first syllable, don't double the final letter:

   differ + ent = different   open + ed = opened

4. If a word ends in *y* with a consonant before it, change the *y* to *i* when adding a suffix not beginning with *i:*

   busy + ly = busily   icy + er = icier

   try + ed =tried   study + es = studies

   But

   buy + er = buyer   monkey + s = monkeys.

   And when the suffix starts with *i:* enjoy + ing = enjoying

5. Adding a prefix to a word does not change the spelling of the root word:

   mis + spell = misspell   un + necessary = unnecessary

6. Most nouns add *s* to form the plural, but some nouns add *es* or change form or stay the same.

   Add *es* to nouns ending in *s, sh, ch, x,* or *z:*

   boxes   kisses   catches   bushes   buzzes

Add *es* to nouns ending in a consonant and *o*:

heroes   tomatoes   potatoes

Exceptions

pianos   banjos   photos   autos

Change the form of certain words:

knife-knives   wolf-wolves   thief-thieves

child-children   man-men   mouse-mice

fungus-fungi

Keep the same form:

sheep   deer   moose

Similar Sounding Words

Word: Meaning	Examples
accept: to agree	I accept the invitation.
except: excluding	He lost everything in the fire except his dog.
advice: counseling, recommendation (noun)	Marv took the professor's advice.
advise: to suggest, to make a recommen-dation (verb)	The teacher advised him to study.
affect: to influence (verb)	Being called names doesn't affect me.
effect: result (noun)	The terrible effects of the wind were apparent.
all ready: prepared	They were all ready for the party.
already: indicating before some other time	He had already left the house before I could remind him of the appointment.
all together: in a group	The club worked all together on the marathon.
altogether: entirely	He was altogether exhausted after running.
altar: place of worship (noun)	The altar was covered with flowers.
alter: to change (verb)	The driver needed to alter his direction when he saw the tree in the road.
aloud: to speak or make a noise that can be heard	She read aloud from the script.
allowed: to be given permission	Students were allowed to leave the room after they finished the exam.

Word: Meaning	Examples
angel: a spirit	Angel food cake is so light that even an angel could eat it.
angle: two lines or directions coming together; a point of view	The airplane had a sharp angle of descent.
	The senator took a new angle in the debate.
berth: a place to rest	She took a berth on the train.
birth: a new life, or beginning	The birth of a child is often a joyous occasion.
brake: to stop, or something that stops	He put on the brakes.
break: to cause destruction, or something that is disrupted	The gas company reported a break in service.
capital: the city where a government meets; money for a business; or a descriptive word meaning "execution for a serious crime"	Legislators met today in the capital to discuss raising more capital for state businesses and to vote on whether to allow capital punishment.
capitol: the building where a legislature meets	The architect met with legislators to discuss renovating the capitol.
cite: to quote	The speaker cited the new law.
sight: ability to see	He sighted the ship's mast.
site: a location	What will be built on this site?
close: to shut or end (verb)	Please close the door.
clothes: things to wear (noun)	Do clothes make the man or woman?
coarse: rough	The coarse beach sand hurt our feet.
course: path; or school subject	The course of life never is smooth.
	Mike was having trouble with his chemistry course.
conscience: one's moral sense	The thief's conscience began to bother him.
conscious: aware	She became conscious of people staring at her.
	The patient soon became conscious after surgery.
desert: sandy, dry place (noun)	Some people love the desert landscape.
desert: to leave (verb)	The soldier tried to desert but was caught.
dessert: a treat at the end of a meal	The chef made a wonderful chocolate dessert.
dining: eating	The dining room was empty.
dinning: making noise	The engine whine was a dinning in her ears.
dying: to stop living	The old man was dying.
dyeing: adding or changing the color of something	People try to look younger by dyeing their hair.

Word: Meaning	Examples
emigrate: to leave a country	His relatives emigrated from Puerto Rico.
immigrate: to enter a country	He immigrated to America to start a new life.
fair: a festival (noun)	We loved the county fair.
fair: reasonable (adjective)	The teacher was a fair grader.
fare: fee for transportation	City council raised the bus fare.
forth: forward	The hero went forth to seek his fortune.
fourth: after *third*	The child was fourth in line to the throne.
hear: to receive sound	Do you hear me clearly?
here: in this place	I will stand over here.
hole: an opening	The squirrel dug a hole in the ground.
whole: entire, complete	Mark ate a whole pizza.
its: pronoun showing ownership	The cat licked its fur.
it's: contraction meaning "it is"	It's a lovely day.
know: to understand, or recognize	Do you know the author?
no: negative	I have no money.
loose: not tight	She likes loose jackets.
lose: to abandon an object; or to not win a contest	Losing your ticket will mean losing the lottery, even if you choose the right numbers.
passed: completing a course; overtaking someone; or approving a law (verb)	Joan passed the course by answering a question about a law that had just been passed. When she passed her friend in the hall, she gave her a thumbs-up sign.
past: a time gone by (noun or adjective)	That is in the past. She is the past president of the association.
past: a direction (preposition)	He drove past her house.
peace: quiet; not war	The country longed for peace.
piece: a portion	I would like a piece of pie.
personal: individual	I have personal business.
personnel: people who work for a company (noun or adjective)	All personnel should fill out benefit forms. A personnel officer will answer your questions.
principal: head of a school (noun)	The principal is your pal.
principal: amount of money (noun)	The loan includes principal and interest.
principal: main or chief (adjective)	My principal reason for quitting the team was my grades.
principle: a belief or value	She is a woman of strong principles.

Word: Meaning	Examples
precede: to go before	The queen preceded her husband.
proceed: to continue	The meeting will not proceed without more members being present.
quiet: not noisy	Susan was a quiet person.
quite: completely or very	Aaron was quite tired.
stationary: not moving	The statue looked alive but remained stationary.
stationery: paper used to write on	He ordered new stationery for the office.
than: a word used to show comparisons	My sister is taller than I.
then: indicates time	Then the pitcher made a motion to first base.
there: a place	Put the box there, please.
their: ownership	Those are their books.
they're: contraction meaning "they are"	They're going to the concert.
to: toward	The mayor walked to his office from the rally.
too: also	The city council president went too.
two: the number after *one*	The two of them talked as they walked.
weather: the climate	The weather is cold and windy.
whether: indicates a choice	He could not decide whether to wear his coat or not.
were: past tense of *are*	Were you at the meeting?
where: a question of place	Where is my key?
who's: contraction meaning "who is"	Who's going to claim this coat?
whose: shows ownership	Whose car is blocking my driveway?
your: shows ownership	Your letter arrived yesterday.
you're: contraction meaning "you are"	You're scheduled to work on Saturday night.

CREDITS

Photo Credits

INDEX